FLUSH BIDEN

ANTHONY STARNES

ISBN: 979-8-88640-241-4 (sc)
ISBN: 979-8-88640-242-1 (hc)
ISBN: 979-8-88640-243-8 (e)

One Galleria Blvd., Suite 1900, Metairie, LA 70001
1-888-421-2397

CONTENTS

After writing my numerous prophetic books about the end times and warning Christians and others to unlearn the stupid American dispensational false doctrines like the Pre-tribulation rapture known as Rapture Rip-off that they have been taught since Sunday school, the Lord Jesus told me to write the truth about Christianity being a Person (THE LORD JESUS CHRIST) and not just another teaching about the end times: ('HE THAT HAS THE SON HAS LIFE AND HE THAT HAS NOT THE SON OF GOD DOES NOT HAVE LIFE', 1 John 5:12).

Christianity is not just another teaching to stimulate one intellectually. Some Christians and others also boast that they go to a real Bible believing church where they learn to say scriptures by heart. But real Christianity is a Person that you can marry, 'THAT YOU SHOULD BE MARRIED TO ANOTHER, EVEN TO HIM THAT IS RAISED FROM THE DEAD, THAT YOU SHOULD BRING FORTH FRUIT UNTO GOD', (Romans 7:4) as in the Bride of Christ and not just a book like the Bible full of a bunch of love letters from God to man.

It appears to me, that only 5% of the people attending any church are truly born again by the Spirit of God. That is why it was just on the nightly news that the Southern Baptist Convention (a dispensational church of the deceived by the false doctrines of The Pre-Tribulation Rapture and Eternal Security) has lost over a million members last year. Thanks to this COVID 19 plague which was not supposed to happen to them as they would be gone to heaven because of this false doctrine known as The Pre Tribulation Rapture before any plagues or tribulation begins to happen.

Therefore, I am including in this prophetic book my two prophetic chapters about COVID 19 entitled: **COVID 19, FIRST ENDTIME PLAGUE** and **COVID 19 VACCINE OR REPENTANCE**.

Actually these vaccines are a 'portal' for COVID 19 as evidence of the thousands of people that have died as a result of being forced to take them.

This cataclysmic revelation went on to say that: 'BY THE YEAR 2025 THE DEATHS FROM THESE COVID 19 VACCINATIONS TO SUPPOSEDLY PREVENT DEATH WILL NO LONGER BE MEASURED JUST IN THE THOUSANDS BUT IN THE MILLIONS AS THESE COVID 19 VACCINATED CHILDREN (NOW TEENAGERS) WHO HAVE HAD A SEX CHANGE OPERATION TOO INTERACT WITH THE SEX HORMONES OF NORMAL TEENAGERS HAVING PUBERITY.

Before this date (October 18, 2021) few people believed that these COVID 19 vaccinations actually caused anyone's death. But later that same day it was revealed on the news by mistake that a fully vaccinated man, Colon Powell had died from 'complications' of COVID 19. So it appears that President Biden's COVID 19 vaccination mandates are 'bull spit'. Too bad some 'born losers' can't seem to win even at their best laid plans. **Biden the deceitful was hoping to use these COVID 19 vaccinations to replace America's White population of conservatives and even some liberals with these illegal aliens who will vote Democratic as their overrunning of the Border and disregard for our laws demonstrates.**

So to make my revelation above clearer for you, let me say that this is a pure prophecy which no one has dared to say before and at this time has no confirming basis in reality. Although in its time it will become real. That's how God works especially with His judgments that have been ignored by all these Progressive Democrats.

In the Old Testament it was also seen how that 'JUDGMENT FOR SIN IS VISITED UPON THE CHILDREN TO THE THIRD AND FOURTH GENERATION OF THEM THAT HATE ME', (Exodus 20:5).

However many adults too have been killed by these vaccinations including my niece's mother in law. They even call that the new adult death syndrome, but fail to mention that it comes from COVID 19.

So I am also including my prophetic chapters entitled: **RAPTURE RIPOFF I** and **RAPTURE RIPOFF II** which should be self-explanatory.

After that I hope to include my prophetic chapter on **FAKE NEWS** as many have been deceived not only by these false doctrines but also by stupid secular ideals over the first few months of President Biden's term.

By an open vision revelation on October 15, 2021 God told me that the government claim that these COVID 19 vaccinations were safe for children was just another falsehood of the Progressive Democrats or **FAKE NEWS.**

Another conflict besides Ukraine shows that war is open conflict resulting from hostility. The participants in any war are usually nation states whereas any disagreement resulting in battle between two individuals is just a fight, even if it results from bullying and involves the school board, the authorities like the police, other family members or your neighborhood too. This conflict reminds me of **The American Civil War**, so I am including my prophetic chapter about that in this prophetic book too.

However, when a conflict escalates to the point of bombing innocent people as in 'The MARATHON Bombing in Boston then that attack constitutes 'AN ACT OF WAR' upon our society. Especially if the bomber admits that the reason why this was done was because of America's war in Iraq that's killing Muslims.

In such case the Boston bombing is just an extension of the Iraq War and the bomber or perpetrator is an enemy combatant not just a criminal bomber and another evil Muslim to boot.

When I heard the word 'Marathon' of the Boston Marathon bombing it sparked my memory of that word in the history book: Lessons From Fallen Civilizations, Can a Bankrupt America Survive the Current Islamic Threat? By Larry Kelly.

This book goes on to point out that the Greeks defeated the Persians at Marathon which was the first resolution by war of their threats against Western Civilization. The Greeks won because they were more highly skilled, Olympic and athletic runner warriors armed with long iron tipped pikes. Who as free men both decided and determined to fight to the death if need be to resist the Persians even against overwhelming odds, (there were only about 11,000 Greeks against 26,000 Persians).

To show more about this type of war I am including in this prophetic book my two prophetic chapters about Muslim deceit which hides their real evil intentions, entitled: **MUSLIM OBAMA'S MUSLIM DECEPTION** and **MUSLIM JESUS vs JESUS CHRIST.**

Muslims like Obama are allowed by their lies thanks to Muslim false doctrine to conceal, disguise and hide their personal beliefs, ideas, feelings and opinions about anything and everything in order to achieve personal success for the Muslim cause. Like ruling over Christians or even hiring other Muslims like Valerie Jarrett as public employees to abuse Christians and promote Iran's nuclear arms as well. To make my disclosure about Muslim lying clearer, it must be reiterated that as long as a Muslim is in a country where Islam is a minority, then the Muslim (in this case, Obama's) deceptiveness about anything and everything is officially expected and sanctioned by the 'evil religion of Islam' (the Muslim faith). That's why we should throw all the Muslims out!

What judgment now awaits Obama and his many czars for telling thousands of lies about 'everything under the sun' to the American people in two terms of office? With President Biden now serving out Obama's third term to do the same evil that former President Obama did resulting in the same entitlements for deserved plagues and **joining former President Obama to dump Christianity has bequeathed America and the entire world to deceptions, wars, delusions, deficits, disasters and many more plagues, Watch out!**

. Other Teachings even if they sound good and are backed up with historical truth and letters of the love of God from the Bible cannot save anyone from the bad consequences of their sins.

I suppose if I used the word sacrifice it would become more clear to you that the Person of Christ purchased our redemption from our sins on the Cross of Christ by His Own sacrifice of His Own blood: (WITHOUT THE SHEDDING OF BLOOD THERE IS NO FORGIVENESS OF SIN, (Hebrews 9:22) and so the Lord Jesus Christ opened Christianity for us all.

No teaching accomplished this for those of us who are saved. Church attendance did not bring this about nor cause us to become Christians. No amount of Bible reading, reciting of Bible verses from memorization nor the repeated saying of numerous prayers 'FOR WHEN YOU PRAY USE NOT VAIN REPETITIONS LIKE THE HEATHEN DO, FOR THEY FEEL THAT THEY SHOULD BE HEARD FOR THEIR MUCH SPEAKING', (Matthew 6:7), nor even infant baptisms have any real effect on reconciling us to God.

Saint John 'THE APOSTLE WHOM JESUS LOVED', (John 13:23) wrote the book of Revelation which revealed among many truths that Jesus, the Son of God will be seen by everyone when He comes again. This means every eye shall see Him. He is not coming in some secret rapture but openly and as lightning. 'FOR JUST AS LIGHTNING COMES FROM THE EAST AND FLASHES EVEN UNTO THE WEST, SO SHALL THE COMING OF THE SON OF MAN BE', (Matthew 24:21).

Now this is a revelation you have never heard before in any church but its validity rings true. Some have wondered what all the Lord Jesus Christ will be doing during the Millennium. Some even feel that He will be taking on the duties of upper class judges determining issues like bankruptcy, embezzlement or robbery and other felonious crimes. Yes, people will be doing naughty and bad things even in front of the Lord Jesus Christ.

Nevertheless, you and I will be doing judgment for these high-class crimes and for low class small claims crimes too. Some of we Christians will even be judging angels, (I Corinthians 6:3) and the world as well.

This leaves the Lord Jesus free to judge all those who refused to accept Him as their savior. 'SINCE THE FATHER HAS GIVEN ALL JUDGEMENT TO THE SON' (John 5:22).

To know this may upset some people to learn that the Lord Jesus Christ is not like a dictator but intends to give each person who has ever lived adequate time in a personal audience with the King to explain just why they neglected His offer of salvation. Obviously, this alone will consume the one thousand year reign of THE LORD JESUS CHRIST in the Millennium.

St. John 'THE APOSTLE WHO JESUS LOVED', (John 13:23) wrote the book of Revelation which revealed among many truths that the Lord Jesus, the Son of God will be seen by everyone when He comes again. This means that every eye shall see Him of all races, colors, nationalities and creeds both the young and the old, the male and the female and the rich and the poor. He is not coming in some secret rapture but openly 'JUST AS LIGHTNING SHINES OUT OF THE EAST AND GOES EVEN TO THE WEST SO SHALL THE COMING OF THE SON OF MAN BE, (Mathew 24:27).

After the Lord Jesus comes again in His second coming He needs to start judging as 'IT IS APOINTED UNTO MAN ONCE TO DIE AND AFTER THAT THE JUDGEMENT', (Hebrews 9:27) AND 'GOD THE FATHER JUDGES NO MAN BUT HAS GIVEN ALL JUDGEMENT TO THE SON, (John 5:22).

As we now see from the situation above the Lord Jesus Christ is both loving, kind and practical. In Armageddon he acts as a soldier fighting the enemies of God. He does not show love to the enemies of God, nor should you. But in the Millennium He acts as a kind judge. So then the Lord Jesus shows the whole range of human emotions.

Since human emotions reveal one's psychological problems and mental health, it seemed necessary for me to study such as I wanted to become a professional counselor. This is probably why I went to Fuller Seminary from a mental standpoint since at that time it was the only seminary in the country that also had a graduate school of psychology approved by the American Psychological Association. There I also got to take a few advanced psychology classes (since I already had a college degree in psychology) which I would need in order to become a professional counselor.

But the real reason I went to Fuller Seminary was because of a spiritual sign given to me. The morning I went to take the graduate record exam some student on campus had left his stereo on and it was playing an old surfer tune called 'The Little Old Lady from Pasadena'. Of course since I grew up in Daytona Beach, Florida and used to surf there as a kid, I knew that song by the Beach Boys pretty well. When I remembered that Fuller Theological Seminary was also located in downtown Pasadena, California I took that song as my spiritual sign to go to Fuller Seminary and I'm now glad that I did so.

Today many Pentecostal and Evangelical Pastors don't care much for psychology because it was discovered by the ungodly. Nevertheless here is one mental point of interest: a successful pastor in Las Vegas was offered a new big house because a wealthy stranger wanted to bless him. But at first the pastor refused because he felt that the water bill would be too high. (This pastor had what the psychologists called a poor self image). Which may have been true under the circumstances. However, the severe drought in the West, where Las Vegas is adds credence to the pastor's objection. So you need to be careful about accepting what professionals say to you. As a Christian Minister you should always follow your heart not your head even if it sounds good and makes good sense.

I understand that some of you still don't want to become Christians but for ours and the country's good let's not neglect to realize what President Biden is up to in order to gain his reelection. President Biden still hopes to win reelection due to distraction from his evil policies. Unfortunately, for the Progressive Democrats the January 6th supposed insurrection does not seem to be working much at all. So now the false claim of Russia using space weapons against Ukraine has also fallen short. And America has had to supply Ukraine with $billions in weapons and food and oil that we need for our own people.

There is another trick that President Biden can use to stay in office to destroy America's capitalist economy. That is he can conspire with the deep state to release information about extra terrestrials being a real threat to our society that only President Biden can protect us from.

But real Christians should remember that verse that says that: THAT THE WORLDS WERE MADE BY THE WORD OF GOD', (Hebrews 11:3). so Jesus not Biden is over these extra terrestrials, moreover He has given dominion over the earth to we the people not to any extra terrestrials.

As you know Joe Biden is a 'pathological liar' just like that other reprobate of COVID 19 fame, Dr. Anthony Fauci. And President Joe Biden has told many lies including: On immigration, 'We are sending back the vast majority of the families that are coming'. On civil rights: 'As a youth, I got arrested protesting for civil rights'. On that war in Afghanistan: 'I've been against that war in Afghanistan from the very beginning'. On the economy: 'The number of small businesses is up to 30% compared to before the pandemic'. On elections: 'No Governor in Virginia has ever won when he or she is the same party as the sitting President'. On no price increases: 'The cost of an automobile, it's kind of back to where it was before the pandemic'. On the second amendment: 'The second amendment, from the day it was passed, limited the type of people who could own a gun and what type of weapon you could own'. On the minimum wage: 'If we had kept the minimum wage indexed to inflation, people would be making twenty dollars an hour right now'. On crime: 'In the 1990's the Biden crime bill added 100,000 cops to America's streets. As a result, murder and violent crime rates went down eight years in a row'. On bombing: Joe Biden said that 'Donald Trump is going out and carpet bomb the Middle East'. On clemency: 'During the Obama/ Biden administration 18,000 people got clemency'. And Biden also said that 'Barack Obama hasn't passed any bills'.

After closing down the Keystone Pipeline, and forbidding the drilling for oil on federal lands Biden said: *'It's simply not true that my administration or policies are holding back domestic energy production'.* **When the truth is that Biden has done nothing but sabotage the US oil and gas industry with his pathological green energy policy that has wrecked domestic production of oil and gas with painful prices that are ever increasing due to Biden's inflation.** This all began before the war in Ukraine. So, this inflation is not due to Putin but Biden.

You can also rescue yourself from this abuse by giving President Joe Biden's bad policies and bad people their walking papers this November. Please do not fail to do so, as your children and grandchildren are depending on you to at least make America decent and livable for them once again.

President Biden still refuses to repent of his abortion and same sex marriage evil policies for the American people. So I am including my three prophetic chapters about President Biden called: **BIDEN'S SORROWS 1, BIDEN'S SORROWS II** and **BIDEN'S SORROWS III.**

I hope that my Prophetic and Revelatory truths about President Biden will get you out to vote against him thus flushing this Biden crap of the COVID 19 vaccination mandates and these Green New Deal tirds mixed with the building back better toilet paper down the toilet.

DEDICATION

The three kings of Israel, Judah and Edom sought counsel from the Lord regarding a war with Moab in (II Kings 3: 11, 12). So, they called for the prophet Elisha. Who said 'bring me a minstrel' (II Kings 3:15e could get a word from God. Over the years these minstrels have helped me get this word from God for you.

Vestal Goodman of 'The Happy Goodman's'

The Original Jesus Movement singers

The Original Maranatha Singers

The Bill Gaither Singers

The original singers of John Wimber's Vineyard in Anaheim, California

My distant relative; the anointed singer John Starnes

Jimmy Swaggart's Family Worship Center Singers

And the anointed singer Nancy Harman.

Since Wars are coming then Famines, Pestilences and Earthquakes composing 'The Beginnings of Sorrows' according to the prophecy of the Lord Jesus (Matthew 24:6-8) I got inspired by these minstrels in this exact Biblical method to receive this word from God for you, your safety and your well-being.

DEDICATION

ACKNOWLEDGMENTS

I want to express my Appreciation first to my speller, typist and all around accomplished assistant in this grueling task: Patrick Mc Clenahen. And the staff of the Dickerson Heritage library Center on Keech street and the Volusia County Library Center at City Island in Daytona Beach, Florida who kept their old public computers up and running like new to keep my manuscript legible enough for publication.

MY AUTOBIOGRAPHY

Once my dad went to retrieve his family Victrola in Virginia. Some of these old records were gospel songs of famous quartets like 'The Carter family', 'The Chuck Wagon Gang' and 'The Smokey Mountain Boys'. Of course, that type of music was different from what we heard over the radio back then and now. I grew up in a typical middleclass neighborhood on Mulberry Street in Daytona Beach, Florida. Mulberry Street is on the mainland side of town, east of US 1, west of Beach Street and the part we lived on was south of Madison Ave.

My family never went to church so neither did I. Therefore, I grew up American pagan. But one day I stopped by a church in our neighborhood. These church people were singing old fashioned gospel songs just like I heard from that old Victrola my dad gave me. This church was of a holiness denomination called the First Church of the Nazarene. They had a song leader who was a very big man. He was both very tall and very heavy, and he had a booming voice.

Sometimes I would stop by that church when they were singing. The song leader, that big man, would tell them the page number of the song and hum the key so that the congregation could start to sing. But once he started singing too, no one could hear anyone else but him. His voice carried up and down the street and even across the street. **His singing somehow made me shake;** I liked the feeling even though I did not fully understand it back then. Folks in the neighborhood said that he was an anointed singer set apart by God with the gift of praise. Others said that he was the only truly sanctified man that they had ever seen. In any case this was the first time I ever felt God. No one had ever told me that it was even possible to feel God. So, I must have had that old 'hard shell, hog and hominy' Baptist belief drilled into me; that any religious experience or relationship with God was based on rules, regulations and laws of scripture or faith that one just accepted as true instead of any feelings at all.

Around the same time a TV Program came on the air each week called: 'The Happy Goodman's'. They sang the same old gospel tunes that that church sang. So, I thought that that same feeling like exhilaration with shaking might happen again as the wife of the evangelist, Vestal Goodman also sang with an anointed voice. **By this time I had learned by experience that the anointing on others somehow made me shake.**

One day they described how this anointing had come on Vestal. Vestal Goodman and her husband Howard were holding revivals in a small town in Louisiana. A bad hurricane had come through, torn the tent and things up and rained all over the electrical equipment so that they had no working microphone. Vestal got up to sing anyway by faith with her soft soprano voice. Just then the Holy Spirit came upon her and her voice boomed throughout that tattered tent, everyone heard her. Her shocked family was astonished and asked what had happened. An old woman replied that the Spirit of God had just anointed her with power to do God's will.

Since that day the fame of this woman and her voice has gone throughout the land and even onto television, which was just black and white back in those days. Although I was still not yet a born-again Christian, nevertheless I watched that show religiously every week because it made me feel good and I got to shake just like a 'holy roller' even though I was just an unsaved street kid.

About that same time, a Baptist evangelist who drove a new Cadillac car (and was secretly into prosperity) put up a big tent to hold revival in Holly Hill, Florida, the town next door. I remember that his tent was put up in a swampy area which is now filled in with luxury homes. I guess those people living in those luxury homes would be horrified to know that their expensive homes were built on filled in swamp.

These Baptist people sang those same gospel tunes, but without any feeling in them. Never the less I went forward to get saved anyway since I wanted to get closer to God in order to shake. But since there was no feeling in that experience and I never shook there, it did not seem to last.

It lasted a little while though and I even got adopted by a well to do childless couple named O'Brien who took me to every Sunday service at White Chapel Church of God where I was baptized in water in 1961. But since there was no feeling there in time I fell away into naughtiness, common to the street life I grew up in. Gradually my bad behavior sank into open sin.

In time I was convicted of forgery and sent away to serve a couple of years in the Florida State Prison. But then my second chance to experience God and shake 'big-time' began right in that prison.

This was really weird but before I share it, let me describe my prison experience first. At first, I was somewhat apprehensive because I was a good looking former surfer with blonde hair. Back then I was already a high school graduate with some college and could type, therefore the classification supervisor of the Florida prison system had me become his new clerk. This was a trustee position complete with a white uniform and a special pass to go anywhere in the prison without having to be guarded.

My prison job involved my assembling of all-important papers on each new inmate for the classification committee. Only free people, employees of the State of Florida get to do that same kind of work now. But back in those days I got to do it. These papers I had to acquire and assemble included official court commitment papers with any pre-sentence investigation reports or probation and parole papers, psychological reports made by the prison psychologist including IQ tests, social reports of the classification officer, chaplain's report and custody recommendation of the prison guards and whatever else was pertinent to that particular case including ID pictures and all demographic data.

Working with these papers required personal trust. I was not allowed to disclose whatever I saw. I remember one strange case that appalled me back then and still troubles me some as I wonder how a person created in the image of God could possibly do such an evil act. I'm talking about a young Black man who told everyone that he got twenty years for robbery when the court commitment papers showed that he actually got the twenty years for sexually assaulting an infant by sticking his finger into her. If I had ventured to set the record straight, that guy's life would have been forfeit and I did not want his blood on my hands so I kept my mouth shut.

Otherwise this prison job was just like any other nine to five office job. Only we also had to work sometimes on weekends like Saturday or Sunday because the classification committee which met every week had to have their papers ready for them so they could decide which rehabilitation program to put each new inmate in, which correctional center to send them to and what custody was most appropriate for their rehabilitation.

A few months after I arrived it was already time for Easter. Since I had been a surfer on the outside, I was used to getting up early. So I went to Easter Sunrise Service which was one of my trusty privileges. Since this was the only day of the year when we could get out of our cells early in the morning many trustees came from all over the prison not only for the Easter service but also to remember what early mornings with sunrise was like.

Once we filled up the bleachers set up in the prison yard the Chaplain prayed. Down in front was a visiting prison chain gang dressed in prison blues. I thought that they had come to worship with us too. Instead one of their guards set down his rifle and introduced one of them to sing for us. This singer was a young Black man who started to sing the old Negro Spiritual about 'Sometimes It Causes Me to Tremble'. At once I recognized that this man had a professional voice, since I had studied voice in college and knew that his voice had a three-octave range. In other words, he could hit any note in music both low notes and high ones too. So I wondered why a guy with such a fabulous voice, better than anyone I had ever heard was in prison with the rest of us.

Then my mind moved from being centered on his voice to the words of the song he sang for us. As he finished singing the first verse he went on to sing the chorus about 'Sometimes It Causes Me to Tremble' and **I started to shake uncontrollably again just as I had done before as a kid.**

This time my shaking was 'big time'. As it would not stop. One of my friends gave me my prison jacket but I still shook since I really wasn't cold. **I had learned by experience that my shaking accompanied someone's anointing and when their anointing was over, my shaking ended too**.

But this time I shook after that Black man finished singing and for the rest of that Easter Sunrise service. I shook on the way back to our cells too. Once we arrived I still shook. I even shook for count time that morning. When I went to eat breakfast I still shook. It's hard to eat when you're shaking but somehow I managed to eat my oatmeal.

Afterward, since it was a holiday and I did not have to work, I returned to my housing area and laid down to take a nap. But I could not go to sleep as I still shook. By this time my shaking had gone from just my usual feeling to concern and even alarm for my well-being.

Then it came lunch time. We all lined up to go to lunch. I still shook but I was determined to eat this good holiday meal anyway. The lunchroom people had prepared Black Angus steaks from the prison farm for us. These steaks were big, juicy and filled the whole plate. So big that our vegetables had to be put on top of our steaks. Actually, all this food was both very fresh and very good back in those days. Eating good was seen to be a basic human right even for prison inmates back then. So, the steaks were real, without soy fillers. The State of Florida had a huge Division of Corrections farm and ranch in Belle Glade, Florida from whence our food came.

As we sat down to eat people avoided sitting by me as if I were contaminated with some sickness that they were afraid to catch, since I still shook but I managed to eat my steak anyway.

After eating our group of inmates returned to our dorm to watch TV sports. But I laid down to take an afternoon nap. Since I was still shaking I could not go to sleep. So, after a few hours of self-imposed semi-rest I got up to get ready for supper.

At supper I sat at a corner table by myself since I was still shaking. As the other guys came in they sat together at the main tables in the center. I don't remember what we ate for that meal but I'm sure it must have been good. After we ate we returned to the dorm where most of us watched the TV news. I saw the TV news too then some wrestling program.

Suddenly count time crept up on us. We all stood by our beds as the prison guard would call out our last names and we responded with our prison number. When he got to me, He called my last name; Starnes and I responded; 020,563. You never forget your prison number.

Then before moving on to the next bed, he asked me if I was still shaking. I said; 'Yes Sir'. You can't hide your personal problems from the guards since it's their job to stay fully informed about those they're guarding. Then he took out a pad of colored papers and wrote me out a sick pass and told me; 'If you're still shaking in the morning be sure you make sick call. There's a bad flu going around that's killing people' (like Corona Virus) 'and we don't want you to cheat the State of Florida out of its time'. I said; 'Yes Sir' then he moved on.

I thought later that his statement to me was rather cold. But I had learned by this time to always treat prison guards with respect and common courtesy.

After count time was over we all got into our beds. Then the guard turned off our light. I tried to go to sleep but my shaking wouldn't quit. Eventually my shaking seemed to subside enough for me to go to sleep. So I slept well that night. The next morning as I woke up I noticed that my shaking was gone. Of course this all was a mystery to me back then. So I just put it out of my mind and went on doing what I had to face that day.

I did wonder a few times about the gospel singer at that Easter Sunrise Service if I'd ever hear his voice again. It's now been over 60 years.

Once I had to go over to the photographer to retrieve some ID pictures for the Classification Committee. While there I saw the prison photographer taking ID photos of a death row inmate. Because this guy was about my same age back then and I saw on his court commitment papers under the word: sentence the word: DEATH in capital letters. So I could not look at the guy as a cold feeling would come over me. Just then the devil seemed to say that this is what happened to that singer. But I knew better as death row inmates stay on death row in maximum security, they do not work on chain gangs nor go out to sing.

My life was rather uneventful and went on normally from that day. A few months later I received an official letter from the Florida Probation and Parole Commission in Tallahassee, Florida. They told me what they were going to do and what would be happening to me. They also ordered my classification boss to have me transferred to minimum security at the Avon Park Correctional Institution in Avon Park, Florida in preparation for my release.

They said that my family had moved to California and had even found me a job out there. So they were going to give me an interstate parole, which was rare back in those days. First they would send me to Avon Park Correctional Institution for a few months of minimum custody. Then I would be released on parole to California. I was to be given bus fair to Tampa, Florida. Then fly nonstop to LA. There I would meet my folks and go to work that week. The next week I was to report to my California parole officer who would meet me at home so he could check out my living arrangements, meet my folks and interview me there in person.

When I left the Florida State Prison and arrived at Avon Park Correctional Institution the first thing I noticed was the quality of the food. It seemed to me that good food was used to pacify those hoodlums, thugs and lowlifes at the main prison but not wasted on the older career criminals and white collar criminals of Avon Park Correctional Institution.

I thought that my job skills at the main prison would ease me into some type of office job. But in prison you don't get to choose what you want. You do what they need done. Back then they needed another tailor to work with the sewing machine. Of course I knew nothing about sewing but I learned quickly.

This correctional institution was much different from what I had become used to. There were less Black inmates there and much older inmates. This correctional institution also included the prison hospital, so there were some amputees and some in wheelchairs too.

Usually I keep to myself but there a middle-aged Jewish inmate from South Florida became my friend. He was a very sarcastic New York Jew and conman with an unusual ability to read people like books. One day I showed him my letter from the Parole Board. After he read it, he unexpectedly broke down and told me that these people were giving me a second chance and I should feel very blessed to be given a brand-new life.

After serving a few months there it was time for my release, everything happened just as the parole board had authorized. First I was dismissed from my prison job. Then sent back to my dorm to put my few personal things and papers into a plastic bag. There ordered to strip my bed and take my sheets and blanket to the laundry room. After I turned in my bedding there I was ordered to take off my prison clothes. I was then given street clothes including a new suit complete with black shoes.

After I changed into the new street clothes and returned my old prison clothes I boarded their prison bus bond for the local Greyhound bus station. There I gave them my ticket to Tampa, Florida. Once I arrived in Tampa I went to their airport there and gave them my direct non-stop ticket for flight to LA. (Even though I was an ex-offender on parole there was no TSA in those days with all their bureaucratic searching of you and your baggage to prevent terrorism. See how much freedom we have lost.) After I boarded the plane I strapped myself in. The plane trip only took a few hours and since we crossed several time zones it was still morning when I got to LA.

After the plane landed I headed for the noisy terminal to meet my folks. When I stepped into that big terminal in LA, California it was like a whole new world. I had landed right into The Jesus Movement Revival complete with deliverances, healings and other Pentecostal manifestations of God's grace. Of course, I was very surprised to see with my own eyes the book of Acts coming back to life right in a public place, not a church. All sorts of ministry and other things were happening there. People there were praying, crying, hollering, shouting, talking and even singing. Deliverances were happening and hands were being laid on some with miracle manifestations. Anyway, there was just pandemonium there. My folks saw me and my mother got me out of there with my bag of stuff. But before we left I saw one of those Jesus people by the door handing out cards to their church, so I grabbed one and put it in my pocket.

Once I got home and unwound some and went through some debriefing I asked about these Jesus people. I was told that these people were very famous and were even on the TV news because of all the genuine stuff that they were doing and the truth that they lived as a major contrast to all the political lies about the Vietnam War. These people were mainly ex-dopers who God had forgiven and anointed to speak and do what politicians should be saying and doing. Anyway, it was an 'out of sight' scene. That night I was glad to take my first bath at home. Then I got up early to get ready to go to my new job.

My work site was a small machine shop in another town that I had to drive to. (My mother let me use her new car). I was very careful driving but it was hard after a couple of years of not driving at all.

Once I got there and met my new boss he told me that my new job involved me having to stand all day drilling parts for airplanes that had to be exact. I was used to office work, then sewing. I had never worked in a machine shop before. I was required to stand all day in front of a drill press and pull it down to make my little metal hole that this part needed. This was very exacting work and required occasional inspection by the owner.

The owner of the shop stayed with me that first day to insure that I did things right. His son also worked in the shop with several other men. The job was a good job and paid well. After working there that first day I drove home to eat my spaghetti dinner. (My mother is Italian and a good cook).

After we ate we watched some TV news, where we saw the Jesus people again at the airport. Then I helped my sister do her homework and went to bed. The next day I went to work again and settled into a daily routine.

THE ORIGINAL JESUS MOVEMENT

In time my parole ended and I got a better job that paid more where my mother worked. Since I now had the weekend free, I decided to check out that Jesus Movement Church. I had to drive there as it was in another town. As I pulled in their parking lot, I heard them singing those same old gospel songs that I first heard on the old family Victrola that my dad had given me when I first became a teenager. I felt comfortable so I went in and found a seat although it was crowded. After the singing ended and their evangelist gave his sermon it was time to pray. Since I was already a nominal Christian and knew more Bible than they did since I came from the Bible belt, I didn't think that I needed much prayer since God was already blessing me big time. Why ask for more, if you have much?

But I went down to the altar to pray anyway even though I felt that I didn't have any real needs since God was already blessing me and I felt thankful. So while I was thanking God in English, suddenly I began to thank God in other tongues too. (Now at this time there had been no mention of the baptism in the Holy Ghost). So at first I didn't really understand what had just happened. Until a few minutes later when **I started to shake again just as I had done as a teenager.**

Then things came together as I figured out that my shaking had something to do with God. The Pastor of their fellowship also seemed to recognize that God was all over me and motioned me to pray for another young man nearby. Which I moved over to do and that guy began to speak in tongues too. Then I moved over to another and then another with the same results. **No one realized nor mentioned back then that I was apparently operating in the spiritual gift of laying on of hands by which the Holy Ghost baptism was being imparted.** Well it was all wonderful and I drove home thanking God. But I still did not fully understand it all.

I first learned on subsequent visits to their church that these Jesus people were mainly of two different types. Most, especially the regular worshippers were native Californians. Other Jesus people were transients from everywhere and anywhere. The native Californians were more educated and more middle class than most Americans. They were the all-white children of California aerospace workers. They were not racially diverse, no Blacks, Hispanics, nor disabled but they still had revival anyway. So diversity is just another Democratic heresy.

The next Sunday I visited that church again. After service and praying some it was time to go to Katherine Khulman's miracle crusade that afternoon in downtown LA. I went because I liked to see God doing stuff. I guess I went several times. Her meeting was held in the Shrine auditorium in downtown LA, once each month back in the late 1960's and early 1970's.

Once I happened to arrive late at one of her meeting. So I was at the entrance, way down in back trying to find a seat like everyone else. Katharine Khulman was far away up on the stage. The service had just started and they had sung her theme songs about 'Believing in Miracles' and 'He Touched Me'. As the songs ended, she stopped the service and pointed to where I was standing and said that the Holy Ghost was doing something back there where I was.

Some of the women by me started shrieking. We all looked to see what was happening. We saw a young woman with a red dot on her forehead (apparently a Hindu) carrying a baby that had water on the brain with a head as big as a watermelon. As we looked at the baby's head I guess our vision became like what the dopers call 'trails' or intermittent vision. Anyway, we saw the baby's head shrink in stages from watermelon size down to the size of a football right in front of our eyes. This was the most 'out of sight' miracle that I ever personally saw. It caused some of us, including me who realized that we were now in the presence of the living God to fall on our faces.

The next Sunday I went to that Jesus people church again and found out that it was called Bethel Tabernacle, founded by the pastor Lyle Steenis of the California Evangelical Association. It was full gospel but not part of any Pentecostal Denomination. It was not a teaching church. Instead it was a Spirit filled independent deliverance church that took most scriptures literally.

It seemed that their main concern was to get new converts baptized in the Holy Spirit. Since the ex-dopers there believed in feeling and had taken dope for that purpose, they insisted that one's conversion and salvation was not complete without feeling God in Holy Spirit baptism.

And once one was baptized in the Holy Spirit they did not need any man to teach them **(1 John 2:27).** This seemed to work out well as I never saw any of them arguing about anything. No one ever seemed to raise their voice and I never saw any fights there.

Although I was neither a native Californian nor an ex-doper these Jesus people wanted me to move in with them and become part of their ministry of evangelism and miracles. They seemed to recognize that I knew more Bible than they did. But this was because I was from the Bible belt of the South. Where almost all of us know a whole lot more Bible than what we really live out in our daily lives. Since I had also always been a loner to some degree I was reluctant to move in and told them I'd pray about it.

I knew that these people also prayed about things first before they did them, so I figured that this must be God and I moved in and went where they went all over Southern California ministering.

Looking back on it all now, I spent the best three years of my life there and I thank God that I was given the privilege and the high honor to give to the Lord Jesus the best three years of my life, from age 21 to 24. And I was not yet wheelchair disabled back then. Thank You Jesus.

I moved into one of their apartments. (That church owned several apartments). I had my own room in one of them. My days were very busy. We did not read devotions, we lived them. Sometimes we'd get to pray before we ate. Sometimes we didn't even have enough time to eat. Each day began with me going with big AL on his flatbed truck to obtain groceries for the beloved. We got that food by 'dumpster diving', eating for free what the supermarkets had thrown away. Our job was to keep five separate rehabilitation homes supplied with good food. We always had enough and sometimes we gave good food away at the church or on the street or at the beach or at the airport.

Every Sunday Pastor Steenis, the old dirt farmer from Kansas would give us our 'Marching orders' via his sermon for that week. One Sunday he told us that he had heard about a new book about the end times that some of us were reading. This book was entitled: The Late Great Planet Earth by Hal Lindsey.

He went on to tell us that Hal Lindsey had been a student at Dallas Theological Seminary, a Baptist school in Texas and had just published information taken from his class notes in his eschatology class. The pre-tribulation rapture was a common heretical Baptist Viewpoint which Hal Lindsey had presented as his own. **Such plagiarism and calling it revelation is theft. And theft does not authenticate any theology especially Revelation.** Moreover, no Baptist who doesn't even believe that the gifts of the Holy Spirit are for today could possibly receive the Gift of Revelation required to write a True Prophetic Book.

Now we're gonna sing a song for a few moments while you all can get some pencils and pens and notepads to take notes to write down these Three Words of Wisdom that will blow away this Pre-Tribulation Rapture heresy.

The Pre-Tribulation Rapture heresy began with notes from the old Scofield Reference Bible some of us used in Kansas when I was a kid. Remember as our preacher told us back then: 'the Bible is inspired, but Scofield's notes are not'. The Bible says in Ecclesiastes 4:12 'THAT A THREEFOLD CORD IS NOT EASILY BROKEN'. So here are your Three Words of Wisdom: 1. At Revelation 4:1 the deceived say that the whole church is called to come up. (As in the Pre-Tribulation Rapture heresy). But the scripture only calls the Prophet John up to be shown or given a road map about the future. This type of impartation is typical of prophets in receiving revelatory words from God that Baptists know nothing about. 2. The 'trumpet' in Revelation 4:1 is not the same as the last trumpet of first Corinthians 15:51, 52. Let's read Revelation 4:1 'AFTER THIS I LOOKED, AND, BEHOLD A DOOR WAS OPENED IN HEAVEN: AND THE FIRST VOICE WHICH I HEARD WAS AS IT WERE A TRUMPET TALKING WITH ME; WHICH SAID, COME UP HITHER AND I WILL SHOW THEE THINGS, WHICH MUST BE HEREAFTER'. In addition, 1 Corinthians 15:52 'IN A MOMENT, IN THE TWINKLING OF AN EYE AT THE LAST TRUMP: FOR THE TRUMPET SHALL SOUND, AND THE DEAD SHALL BE RAISED INCORRUPTIBLE, AND WE SHALL BE CHANGED'.

In the first trumpet John is shown the future but in the last trump we meet Jesus. Then we realized that Pastor Steenis was somewhat prophetic too. But the whole truth about this Pre-trib. false doctrine would not become crystal clear until years later when the messianic Jewish Rabbi Kirt Schneider of the Jewish Jesus TV program wrote a book called: Revelation Decoded. In which he compared the Jews being delivered from Egypt to Christians being delivered from tribulation at the last trump before the judgment of the bowls of wrath, since Christians are not appointed unto wrath. **God's wrath does not happen in the first part of the tribulation while the Christians are still here.**

Rabbi Schneider's revelation was about trumpets then I received a revelation about blood. The first part of this revelation was about a song about the Jewish Passover called: 'When I see the blood, I'll pass over you'. This signified the time of the Jews deliverance from Egyptian bondage. The other time, universal blood is mentioned is in Revelation's battle of Armageddon. Every Bible student knows that that's when Jesus comes, so now the prophetic word is crystal clear – **there will be no pre-trib. rapture. Get over it and get prepared for tribulation.** And three, There is no mention of saints but only angels around the thrown of God in the rest of Revelation Chapter four, If the saints had been raptured either they or their churches would have been mentioned as being somewhere up there, as you can read and see for yourself.

'I think that I have made my point, I could go on by saying that this false doctrine (from years ago) was also the pet of the Christian elite just like the common capitalist practice of exploitation which says; 'get what you can get while the getting is good then get out'. Only to Christians that are into prosperity say: 'get what you can get while the getting is good and then God will get us out before any trouble or tribulation by the Rapture'.

'Many capitalist investors and farmers once believed this same foolish theory but they saw their money lose value, their stocks fall and the depression still come anyway. Farmland became dust and blew away. We lived in Kansas and saw part of Oklahoma blow our way in the dust bowl right before our eyes'.

'Someone once said that the Bible is a road map from here to heaven. If so, no map has ever described in detail an eventful trip that no one really needs to know about since they won't ever be around to take it anyway, since they'll already be gone. **Revelation is included in the Bible roadmap because it's part of the trip that we're all gonna take someday**. And taking any trip instantly, secretly and on impulse without proper preparation and following its prescribed order is folly. **The prescribed order is in Matthew 24** which you can read yourself after we pray. Are there any questions? If not it's time to pray'. After we prayed for some to get saved and to receive the baptism in the Holy Spirit, some of us discussed what the pastor had shared.

Two wealthy Jewish girls who lived up the hill from the church in Palos Verdes said that Hal Lindsey also lived up there with the rich. Apparently, he had written that book to help fund his lavish lifestyle up there. In other words, his book from his college notes was seen as a wise entrepreneurial play by some, especially Jewish investors. But that same book composed of false prophecy was being used as a scam on the Christian community.

But Hal Lindsey had one good thing going for him. Some of his opponents, critics and others called him a Christian Zionist. If so that probably aided his prosperity so much so that he really didn't need this book to raise funds.

When considering nourishment and insight from his ministry, I believe that Christians should eat the fish but spit out the bones. His pre-tribulation rapture heresy should thus be spit out. But Hal Lindsey has made a few good points of insightful knowledge especially in his TV program to benefit both the Christian community and informed voters by publically rebuking anti-Semitic acts of these foolish politicians that bring God's judgment upon America. I'll just list a few: On October 30, 1991 the then Republican President George H. W. Bush, (Bush 41), opened the Madrid conference about the land of Israel for Middle East Peace. A rebuke from the God of Israel in the form of a storm sent 35 ft. waves to cause much damage to President Bush's Kennebunkport, Maine home.

On January 16, 1994 the then Democratic President Bill Clinton met with the Syrian President to discuss land for peace, about Israel surrendering the Golan Heights. Within 24 hours the powerful 6.9 Northridge earthquake rocked Southern California.

Especially for you environmentalists: on April 19, 2010 the Democratic President Obama told the UN that the US no longer would automatically side with Israel at the UN. Within 24 hours of Muslim sympathizer President Obama's statement an explosion causing British Petroleum's oil rig disaster in the Gulf of Mexico resulting in the multibillion-dollar Gulf of Mexico oil environmental catastrophe happened.

After showing us so much truth that the liberal press fails to report, Hal Lindsey manages to still show us support for his pre-tribulation rapture heresy. Some may feel that the word: 'heresy' is too strong a word to describe the pre-tribulation rapture.

But when someone's belief directly opposes the clear teaching of the Lord Jesus Christ, it ceases to be just a matter of opinion but has now become heresy. For the Lord Jesus Christ in describing his revelation or coming again says in Matthew 24:29 'IMMEDIATELY **AFTER** THE TRIBULATION OF THOSE DAYS' to say that: 'before the tribulation, Jesus comes again' instead of 'AFTER' like the Lord Jesus really said is not just twisting the truth but 'bearing false witness' worse than heresy . All heresy does contain a small measure of truth however so that it will be easily accepted as being so. For example: The Bible says in 1 John 1:1 'In the beginning was the Word, and the Word was with God, and the Word was God'. But to the Jehovah's Witness; Jesus the Word was just 'a' god and nothing more.

Having studied Greek at Fuller Theological Seminary, the original language in which the New Testament was written, it is clearly shown that the definite article in Greek is usually translated 'the' as you can see from the word: 'the' in this phrase. But the definite article is also used in Greek to also determine which part of the phrase is subject and which part is predicate. Since the definite article has already been used to signify that 'Word' is subject, the predicate: 'God' can now have no definite article, thus no 'a' before God. So the Jehovah's Witnesses are wrong.

Back at Bethel Tabernacle we went on to read Matthew 24 and found our own few words of wisdom. At the start of this chapter the Lord Jesus disciples said in Verse 3: 'TELL US WHEN SHALL THESE THINGS BE? AND WHAT WILL BE THE SIGN OF YOUR COMING AND OF THE END OF THE AGE?' The Lord Jesus answered by saying: Matthew 24:5-30: Verse 5: 'FOR MANY SHALL COME IN MY NAME, SAYING, I AM CHRIST; AND SHALL DECIEVE MANY. (among these many will be the false gods of old like Lord Krishna and various avatars, Buddha, Maharishi Yogonanda, Odin, and other false and pagan gods of old plus the new artificial intelligence or technological ones like the False Prophet, the Beast and the Antichrist. Most of these will be able to do impersonal supernatural acts (like causing a statue to another false god to have life and to talk; Revelation 13:15, but none of these will be able to save anyone from the consequences of their sins like Jesus does and be reconciled to God thereby). Verse 6: AND YE SHALL HEAR OF WARS AND RUMORS OF WARS: SEE THAT YE BE NOT TROUBLED: FOR ALL THESE THINGS MUST COME TO PASS, BUT THE END IS NOT YET. Verse 7: FOR NATION SHALL RISE AGAINST NATION AND KINGDOM AGAINST KINGDOM: AND THERE SHALL BE FAMINES, AND PESTILENCES, (like Corona Virus), AND EARTHQUAKES, IN DIVERSE PLACES. Verse 8: ALL THESE ARE THE BEGINNINGS OF SORROWS. Verse 9 (this contradicts the dispensational delusion): THEN SHALL THEY DELIVER YOU UP TO BE AFLICTED AND SHALL KILL YOU: AND YE SHALL BE HATED OF ALL NATIONS FOR MY NAME'S SAKE. Verse 10: AND THEN SHALL MANY BE OFFENDED, AND SHALL BETRAY ONE ANOTHER, AND SHALL HATE ONE ANOTHER. Verse 11: AND MANY FALSE PROPHETS SHALL RISE, AND SHALL DECIEVE MANY (real prophecy is a gift from God, false prophecy comes from the false doctrines of denominational Bible schools and as such it is intentionally and deliberately taught with malice). Verse 12: AND BECAUSE INIQUITY SHALL ABOUND, THE LOVE OF MANY SHALL WAX COLD. Verse 13: BUT HE THAT SHALL ENDURE UNTO THE END, THE SAME SHALL BE SAVED. Verse 14: AND THIS GOSPEL OF THE KINGDOM SHALL BE PREACHED IN ALL

THE WORLD FOR A WITNESS UNTO ALL NATIONS; AND THEN SHALL THE END COME. Verse 15: WHEN YE THEREFORE SHALL SEE (how can you see it if you're not here) THE ABOMINATION OF DESOLATION, SPOKEN OF BY DANIEL THE PROPHET, STAND IN THE HOLY PLACE (WHO SO READITH, LET HIM UNDERSTAND). Verse 16: THEN LET THEM WHICH BE IN JUDEA FLEE INTO THE MOUNTAINS. Verse 17: LET HIM WHICH IS ON THE HOUSETOP NOT COME DOWN TO TAKE ANYTHING OUT OF HIS HOUSE: Verse 18: NEITHER LET HIM WHICH IS IN THE FIELD RETURN BACK TO TAKE HIS CLOTHES. Verse 19: AND WOE UNTO THEM THAT ARE WITH CHILD, AND TO THEM THAT GIVE SUCK IN THOSE DAYS! Verse 20: BUT PRAY YE THAT YOU'RE FLIGHT BE NOT IN WINTER, NEITHER ON THE SABBATH DAY. Verse 21: FOR THEN SHALL BE GREAT TRIBULATION, SUCH AS WAS NOT SINCE THE BEGINNING OF THE WORLD TO THIS TIME, NO, NOR EVER SHALL BE. Verse 22: AND EXCEPT THOSE DAYS SHOULD BE SHORTENED THERE SHOULD NO FLESH BE SAVED: BUT FOR THE ELECT'S SAKE THOSE DAYS SHALL BE SHORTENED. Verse 23: THEN IF ANY MAN SHALL SAY UNTO YOU, LO, HERE IS CHRIST, OR THERE: BELIEVE IT NOT. Verse 24: FOR THERE SHALL ARISE FALSE CHRISTS, AND FALSE PROPHETS, AND SHALL SHOW GREAT SIGNS AND WONDERS (the devil and his followers can do miracles too, but only God's miracles are confirmed with the message of salvation from sin and reconciliation to God as Jesus taught), INSOMUCH THAT, IF IT WERE POSSIBLE, THEY SHALL DECIEVE THE VERY ELECT. Verse 25: BEHOLD, I HAVE TOLD YOU BEFORE. Verse 26: WHEREFORE IF THEY SHALL SAY UNTO YOU, BEHOLD, HE IS IN THE DESERT; GO NOT FORTH: BEHOLD, HE IS IN THE SECRET CHAMBERS; BELIEVE IT NOT. Verse 27: FOR AS THE LIGHTNING COMETH OUT OF THE EAST AND SHINETH EVEN UNTO THE WEST; SO, SHALL ALSO THE COMING OF THE SON OF MAN BE. Verse 28: FOR WHERESOEVER THE CARCUSES IS, THERE WILL THE EAGLES BE GATHERED TOGETHER. Verse 29: IMMEDIATELY **AFTER** THE TRIBULATION OF THOSE DAYS SHALL THE SUN BE DARKENED, AND THE MOON SHALL NOT GIVE HER LIGHT, AND THE STARS SHALL FALL FROM HEAVEN, AND THE POWERS OF THE HEAVENS SHALL BE SHAKEN. Verse 30: AND THEN SHALL APPEAR THE SIGN OF THE SON OF MAN

IN HEAVEN: AND THEN SHALL ALL THE TRIBES OF THE EARTH MORN, AND THEY SHALL SEE THE SON OF MAN COMING IN THE CLOUDS OF HEAVEN WITH POWER AND GREAT GLORY'.

Please note that while the Lord Jesus runs down these unpleasant future events, He never once said to his disciples: Do not fear these things for while they are happening on earth, you'll be safe in heaven with Me. Or, you'll only see these things from afar, but they will not happen to you. Nor, 'Thousands shall fall on your right hand and tens of thousands on your left, but it shall not come nigh thee'.

Back when you were a child going to Sunday school they used to sing a song about the Bible that said: 'Every promise in the book is mine, every chapter, every verse, every line'. But today's theologians now say that Matthew is only for the Jews or Israel as all Christians will be gone from tribulation thanks to the pre-tribulation rapture. Just like over a hundred years ago they used to say that certain verses applied to the slaves, while others applied to Whites only. But the Bible says that: 'ALL SCRIPTURE (including Matthew) IS GIVEN BY THE INSPIRATION OF GOD AND IS PROFITABLE FOR DOCTRINE, FOR REPROOF, FOR CORRECTION, FOR INSTRUCTION IN RIGHTEOUSNESS', (II Timothy 3:16). Moreover: 'THERE IS NEITHER JEW NOR GREEK, BOND NOR FREE, MALE NOR FEMALE IN CHRIST JESUS', (Galatians 3:28). And as far as tribulation is concerned: 'SHALL WE RECEIVE GOOD FROM THE HAND OF THE LORD AND NOT EVIL ALSO?', (Job 2:10).

ARTICLES FROM THE ORIGINAL JESUS MOVEMENT

I consider myself blessed to still have the notes I took of the Jesus Movement many years ago. Since I lived both in California and Florida where everything from earthquakes to hurricanes could have destroyed my historical papers about the Original Jesus Movement I feel blessed indeed that all has survived.

I said at one time that I would share what these historical records contained. And that is my purpose here. I am NOT sharing these records about The Jesus Movement to say that this is the way that God sends and maintains His awakenings. But only to say that this is the way God acted once. Today both God and you may emphasize or do something different since God is sovereign.

But certain spiritual things are needed for every revival and/or awakening. These spiritual things include prolonged praying in the spirit, not just short prayers of no consequence in your own language. Deliberate witnessing to strangers, not just friends and family. Consistent church attendance at a full gospel church where they pray in tongues. Proper Biblical knowledge about who Jesus is and who you are meant to be for God's glory. And a desire to overcome evil by taking dominion by voting Jesus words into law.

In fact, the difference is already quite clear. As few have ever witnessed God beginning a spiritual awakening with a political reformation like the Trump election.

I also said that I would review my historical notes on the Jesus Movement and to tell you what they meant to me. The first article I pulled out of my folder was a newspaper clipping about the funeral of Pastor Lyle Steenis from the Daily Breeze of Saturday February 5th, 1972. This article states how that

Reverend Lyle Steenis the founder of Bethel Tabernacle and spiritual father of thousands of rejected young people had died in an airplane crash. And this funeral service was a time for those young people to honor him and accept the end of the Jesus Movement that he led. This newspaper clipping is ***My 1st article.***

It was a 'lively' service complete with camp meeting songs and hand clapping unlike most quiet funeral home services. There were even Pentecostal tongues and interpretation. From being there I remember that those instances were four. The tongues messages were given by Sister Word, our 84 year old prophetess. The interpretations, all four of them, were given by me as I had a clear loud voice back then and was not yet wheelchair disabled. I do not remember all that was said only that **the last word mentioned another future revival which would be coming in power to deliver from sin and to awaken many to God.** Mainly I remember the strong anointing on that service. In my case, my skin tingled like an electric shock and I shook as if a cold wind was blowing on me. This heavenly feeling helped me to realize that **'I'd rather have Jesus than anything this world affords today'.** Since I had gone to college I was used to taking notes and took some automatically during the Original Jesus Movement. I did not have any note pads so I wrote on the back of offering envelopes since I had no money to give back then.

My first offering envelope says on ***My 2nd article*** something very important about sowing which many prosperity preachers have never heard. In fact, this sort of statement you just don't here today. This is the statement in Mathew 13:25 which says that while Christians slept the enemy sowed tares. So, the enemy was growing obstacles for our ministry. Whereas today we hear about our need to sow money to help ministries succeed. *What about praying against tares sowed by the enemy to keep ministries from flourishing?*

The pastor also discussed Elijah calling down fire from heaven and said a revelation you don't hear any more in church is Romans 1:20. **The people recognize God when they see Him in operation.** We must justify our faith by doing deeds just as we believe, God will do it. God tested Gideon with the number of his men. Back then God tested the church with thousands of stinking hippies. Every person is important to the body of Christ. So never try to put on another person's armor or exercise another person's gift. 'All Christians are not like hotdogs, all the same size, color, weight and boiling point and all boiling at the same temperature.' Devils have given many of these young people addictions to dope, depression, phobias, and mind games which need to be cast out not argued with and talked away as in counseling.

This is one of the main deliverance skills that the Lord Jesus gave His disciples when he sent them out. He said: 'CAST OUT DEVILS'.

'Do not sleep in any prayer meeting because every real saint is made between the prayer meeting and the answer that God gives'. 'One with God is always a majority'. 'In the later times God will send latter day rain'.

While I was writing this I thought of a testimony that I should share: we can't afford our own computer so we usually use the public one at the library. But our financial situation may be getting ready to change for the better. This morning I was able to use our broken toilet as if it had been fixed. Last night the kid was able to flush it as well. But it had been stuffed up with a pair of underwear that worked its way loose. Last week I also gave an offering for Israel's 70th anniversary and to reach out evangelically to Jews there and then this toilet got fixed.

This is very strange for me since I have limited funds as I'm a Social Security retiree. Nevertheless, once I gave to that evangelical outreach this toilet got fixed supernaturally without any plumbing bill. This new revelation came to me which said if you have something that needs to be fixed or repaired, give a significant gift to a Christian ministry that's serving God by spreading the gospel. In that light I have now given another offering to Ted Shuttlesworth for his gospel outreach. I have many needs and we'll soon see what happens.

I have too much fear of God to tell Him what kind of blessing I want, so I won't be naming it and claiming it for now. But in time I may progress to that since I'm already part of God's family. You know we tell our parents what we want but I still feel presumptuous and uncomfortable about 'blabbing it and grabbing it'. I don't want to tell God how it needs to be. To me that looks too much like trying to boss God around.

Next in ***My 3rd article*** I found a survival plan from Christians in Action of Long Beach, California. This was a missionary training school I attended while serving the Original Jesus Movement some too. I remember praying for gas money to attend that school which was 15 miles away. The next day there was a gas war in Long Beach and I filled up for 23.9 cents per gallon. I expected to pay about $10.00 for gas but it only came to about $5.00.

That school gave me opportunity to go on the radio and share my Jesus Movement experience with that whole area of Southern California. It was a very good school, even somewhat strict. They had a young man who once confessed to masturbation as if such was a grave sin. I didn't care for that as we had no such problems in the Original Jesus Movement. That young man had served in the Navy and I guess his problem came from being confined to ship for so long. In any case he took me to the Navy base in San Diego to see the moth ball fleet. There I went on battleships from World War 1 and II plus other warships but no aircraft carriers.

Even though this school was strict they had made an agreement with their local Mormon Youth Center not to witness to Mormons so that Mormons would not approach Christians. I did not like this youth policy of appeasement. So I kept witnessing with the Jesus Movement instead of with Christians in Action. This was good for me since I was more of a confrontive person back then.

Christians in Action survival plan consisted of a five-point plan of salvation. One was a need to believe in the divinity of Christ. 'BUT THESE ARE WRITTEN THAT YOU MIGHT BELIEVE THAT JESUS IS THE CHRIST, THE SON OF GOD, AND THAT BELIEVING YOU MIGHT HAVE LIFE THROUGH HIS NAME', (John 20:31). And 2 that 'ALL HAVE SINNED, even you (Romans 3:23). And 3, that 'THE WAGES OF SIN IS DEATH', (Romans 6:23). And 4 FOR GOD SO LOVED THE WORLD THAT HE GAVE JESUS FOR YOU, (John 3:16). Finally 5, JESUS KNOCKS ON THE DOOR TO YOUR SOUL, OPEN THE DOOR AND LET HIM IN TO BECOME YOUR PERSONAL SAVIOR, (Revelation 3:20).

My 4th article is from a tract by Jean Isabell one of my fellow missionaries on the foreign field. This big woman was unusually gifted and her people were good givers too. She must have weighed over 300 pounds and no doubt had put up with much discrimination from many American mission agencies. Some American mission agencies do not realize that **in some foreign cultures bigness is a sign of abundance not obesity**. (Oh Yes, before I forget no one has ever mentioned that obesity is a leading cause of COVID 19 infection. So make it your goal to lose weight and get healthy by taking multivitamins with C and D and zinc each day). In any case she got placed with Gerald Derstine's ministry out of Bradenton, Florida who saw that her gifts outweighed her pounds.

Speaking of her gifts this woman had the ability to get people connected with God in such a way as to get their needs met too. Her people would confide in her about their problems and needs and she would pray for them out loud in tongues while walking on the beach early in the morning. The next day or later that week the answer would come directly to them. She did not tell them what God would do. She let God be God and reveal Himself as He saw fit in answering their prayer.

Her tract was mainly about end time truth and our need to know the scriptures. She began by quoting from Matthew 22:29 'YE DO ERR, NOT KNOWING THE SCRIPTURES'. Then she said how that Jesus said that all this end time anti-Christ doctrine 'WOULD DECIEVE THE VERY ELECT IF IT WERE POSSIBLE'.

Then He said, 'WHOSOEVER BELIEVETH THAT JESUS IS THE CHRIST IS BORN OF GOD: AND EVERYONE THAT LOVETH HIM THAT BEGAT LOVETH HIM ALSO THAT IS BEGOTTEN OF HIM'. (1 John 5:1).

She was very strong about getting back to the basics of the Christian faith. She said**;** 'MIND NOT HIGH THINGS, BUT CONDESCEND (COME DOWN) TO MEN OF LOW ESTATE. BE NOT WISE IN YOUR OWN CONCEITS', (Romans 12:16).

She spoke against so called depth ministries that were preaching unscriptural, Antichrist heresies. She particularly liked John 20:31 'BUT THESE ARE WRITTEN THAT YE MIGHT BELIEVE THAT JESUS IS THE CHRIST, THE SON OF GOD, AND THAT BELIEVING YE MIGHT HAVE LIFE THROUGH HIS NAME'. And for end time teachers of error she liked Matthew 24:23-27 which said 'THEN IF ANY MAN SHALL SAY UNTO YOU LO. HERE IS THE CHRIST, OR THERE, BELIEVE IT NOT. FOR THERE SHALL ARISE FALSE CHRISTS AND FALSE PROPHETS, AND SHALL SHOW GREAT SIGNS AND WONDERS; IN SO MUCH THAT IF IT WERE POSSIBLE, THEY SHALL DECIEVE THE VERY ELECT. BEHOLD I HAVE TOLD YOU BEFORE. WHEREFORE IF THEY SHALL SAY UNTO YOU, BEHOLD, HE IS IN THE DESERT; GO NOT FORTH; BEHOLD, HE IS IN THE SECRET CHAMBERS; BELIEVE IT NOT. **FOR AS THE LIGHTNING COMES OUT OF THE EAST AND SHINES EVEN UNTO THE WEST, SO SHALL ALSO THE COMING OF THE SON OF MAN BE'.**

Then she went on to say: 'don't let anyone deceive you, Jesus Christ is coming in the clouds of glory. In fact, the scriptures say this same Jesus will come back the same way he went away. King James says: In like manner. The Greek says; the very same manner.

Her objection was when many of these false teachers tried to lift us up to take Christ's place. We are to be joint heirs not replacements for. We are ambassadors for Christ. We are adopted, not begotten. Back in her day there was a false theology called 'manifested sons' composed of those who felt they had ascended into divinity themselves and just used Jesus as an example and no longer served Him as Lord.

My 5th article, also from an offering envelope is a message about forgiveness too. It starts in Luke 23:34 where Jesus says 'FATHER FORGIVE THEM, FOR THEY KNOW NOT WHAT THEY DO'. Once you think about this statement it seems to be illogical in relating to competent adults. It therefore seems to be designed for children that don't know any better. In fact, I perceive that I might be on the cusp of another revelation. To me it seems that those who sinned against Jesus and Steven are considered naughty children that don't know any better. Not hardened evil sinners that hate both God and you or me.

My notes say that we have never been wronged like Jesus was. We must not hold grudges, we must also forgive one another. In fact we should not have disputations with our brothers. **But no Bible verse tells us to forgive the enemies of God.**

Of two servants one was forgiven by his master but then would not forgive his fellow servant who also owed him so the master of the first servant delivered him to the tormenters. Yes, lack of forgiveness or failing to forgive costs. Hopefully all can see that clearly.

Then he concluded his sermon on forgiveness with first Corinthians 8:12 which says that 'WHEN YOU SIN SO AGAINST THE BRETHREN AND WOUND THEIR WEAK CONSCIENCE, YOU SIN AGAINST CHRIST'. Although this is a Bible verse it nevertheless shows once again where Paul's use of personal relationships determines our standing with God. As an evangelical Christian who believes that only 'THE BLOOD OF JESUS CLEANSES US FROM ALL SIN', (1 John 1:7), I cannot accept whatever you or I do or don't do can determine our standing with God and I also have the Holy Ghost and the Holy Ghost has me.

I've heard so much about this forgiveness junk that it infuriates me. Thanks to this false doctrine our society today is so full of incorrigible, insulant and indecent reprobates that it's hard for the decent or godly among us to continue to function here.

All students are already given many tests in school. So, when are we going to take advantage of those tests and eliminate the insane, the emotionally disturbed, the drug addicted, the violent and the anti-social from having to interact with the rest of us because of some stupid anti-discrimination law which considers equality more important than our peace and safety?

Look a trained dog is not equal to a dog that has rabbis. Neither is a sane and teachable person equal to a hardened criminal. The special education of reprobates should not include their inclusion into descent society.

TO EVERY THING THERE IS A SEASON, AND A TIME FOR EVERY PURPOSE UNDER THE SUN', (Ecclesiastes 3:1). Therefore, I submit to you that it is no longer time to just forgive everyone for everything like some passive Christian nerd. **But it is now time to stand up and fight in this spiritual warfare against evil**. Those who have wronged us are not just other people that we need to forgive but employers and businesses who will not pay us a fair wage because of our sex or some other stupid and unlawful discriminatory practice. So, let's go to court and fight for our rights. Yes, I'd probably like to be more like Jesus even in this but my blood won't save anyone and God has never called me to be a martyr. Moreover, I have no problem in relating to other people. Just like I was toilet trained as a child, I also learned manners: such as: do not interrupt another person when they are talking and do not provoke them or agitate them. Do not bully them, or make fun of them, their actions or their clothes. Always forgive first and never hold a grudge. I learned all of this before I started school and before I became a Christian.

Today we have many problems the lack of forgiveness as teenagers and adults because we never learned manners and proper conduct as children. As a result most Christians feel that salvation will remedy this. But I submit to you that the remedy needed for this is deliverance (casting out demons). Dogs that run free pick up fleas and ticks. Likewise, children that run free without supervision pickup stolen property, drugs and demons.

Liberal mainline Christians maintain that even the Lord's Prayer says: 'TO FORGIVE US OUR DEBTS AS WE FORGIVE OUR DEBTORS', (Matthew 6:12). And this was said by Jesus Himself. True this was said by Jesus but before the cross. After the cross the scripture says that 'THE BLOOD OF JESUS CLEANSES US FROM ALL SIN, AND NOT JUST OURS ONLY BUT THE SINS OF THE WORLD' (1 John 1:7 & 1 John 2:2).

My 6th article was another track by the missionary Jean Isbell about being ready to meet Christ. She said that she really doesn't care how she escapes the wrath to come whether it be by a catching away or being hid somewhere**. Jesus did not tell us how this is to take place**. So then it's His business not mine.

In the meantime, much teaching is occurring which goes into deep theological discussions about many issues that we don't need to know about since these are not about salvation the intention of Christ. More teaching of the knowledge of Christ is needed so that whenever 'HE SHALL APPEAR WE SHALL BE LIKE HIM', (1 John 3:2).

We should be teaching salvation from sin through Christ and preparing people to meet God in the evangelical method. Then we should move on to perfection by the ministry gifts 'FOR THE PERFECTING OF THE SAINTS, FOR THE WORK OF THE MINISTRY, FOR THE EDIFYING OF THE BODY OF CHRIST UNTIL WE ALL COME IN THE UNITY OF THE FAITH AND KNOWLEDGE OF THE SON OF GOD UNTO A PERFECT MAN, UNTO THE MEASURE OF THE STATUE OF THE FULNESS OF CHRIST', (Ephesians 4:11 & 12).

My 7th article is from a long envelope of scripture references. None of which are spelled out reflecting exactly what the verse meant. I guess that apparently I remembered these verses very well back then. So, I'll record them and for your benefit I'll look them up to see exactly what they say. Our first verse is Romans 3:23 which says that 'ALL HAVE SINNED AND FALLEN SHORT OF THE GLORY OF GOD'.

Our second verse is Acts 17:30 which says: 'BUT NOW COMMANDETH ALL MEN EVERYWHERE TO REPENT'.

Acts 9:6 says: 'LORD WHAT WILL THOU HAVE ME TO DO? And the 'LORD SAID UNTO HIM, ARISE AND GO INTO THE CITY, AND IT SHALL BE TOLD THEE WHAT THOU MUST DO'.

Acts 26:13 then goes on to say: 'AT MIDDAY, OH KING, I SAW IN THE WAY A LIGHT FROM HEAVEN, ABOVE, THE BRIGHTNESS OF THE SUN, SHINING ROUND ABOUT ME AND THEM WHICH JOURNEYED WITH ME. AND WHEN WE ALL FELL TO THE EARTH, I HEARD A VOICE SAYING TO ME IN THE HEBREW TONGUE: SAUL, SAUL, WHY PERSECUTEST THOU ME? IT IS HARD FOR THEE TO KICK AGAINST THE PRICKS. And I said, who art thou Lord? And he said, 'I AM JESUS WHOM THOU PERSECUTES. BUT RISE, AND STAND UPON THY FEET: FOR I HAVE APPEARED UNTO THEE FOR THIS PURPOSE. TO MAKE THEE A MINISTER AND A WITNESS BOTH OF THESE THINGS WHICH YOU HAVE SEEN AND OF THOSE THINGS WHICH I WILL APPEAR UNTO YOU. DELIVERING THEE FROM THE PEOPLE, AND FROM THE GENTILES UNTO WHOM NOW I SEND YOU TO OPEN THEIR EYES, TO TURN THEM FROM DARKNESS TO LIGHT AND FROM THE POWER OF SATAN UNTO GOD, SO THEY MIGHT RECEIVE FORGIVENESS OF SINS AND INHERITANCE AMOUNG THEM WHICH ARE SANCTIFIED BY FAITH THAT IS IN ME'.

WHEREFORE OH KING AGRIPPA I WAS NOT DISOBEDIENT UNTO THE HEAVENLY VISION. BUT SHOWED FIRST UNTO THEM OF DAMASCUS AND AT JERUSALEM AND THROUGHOUT

ALL THE COASTS OF JUDEA AND THEN TO THE GENTILES, THAT THEY SHOULD REPENT AND RETURN TO GOD AND DO WORKS MEET FOR REPENTANCE', Acts 3:19 confirms the word repent by saying: 'REPENT YE THEREFORE, AND BE CONVERTED, THAT YOUR SINS MAY BE BLOTTED OUT, SO THAT THE TIMES OF REFRESHING MAY COME FROM THE PRESENCE OF THE LORD'.

Then Mark 1:15 says: 'THE TIME IS FULFILLED, AND THE KINGDOM OF GOD IS AT HAND: REPENT YE, AND BELIEVE THE GOSPEL'.

We get from these few Bible verses the basic creed of the Christian faith that is: **'All have sinned, so all need to repent'**. You don't get reconciled to God by being good and doing good works from now on. But first you must obtain forgiveness for your past misdeeds. Then you must bring forth fruits meet for repentance. That is to demonstrate that you have really changed for the better after you get rid of all the naughtiness that has made you sinful, start by keeping the commandments.

Begin with John 14:15 which says: 'IF YOU LOVE ME, YOU WILL KEEP MY COMMANDMENTS'.

Then John 14:21 says: 'HE THAT HATH MY COMMANDMENTS AND KEPT THEM, HE IT IS THAT LOVETH ME: AND HE THAT LOVETH ME SHALL BE LOVED OF MY FATHER, AND I WILL LOVE HIM. AND I WILL MANIFEST MYSELF TO HIM'.

These additional verses also confirm other basic beliefs of the Christian faith. They are: Luke 24:47: 'AND THAT REPENTANCE, AND THAT FORGIVENESS OF SINS SHOULD BE PREACHED IN HIS NAME TO ALL NATIONS, BEGINNING FROM JERUSALEM'.

Then Mark 1:15 which says: 'THE TIME IS FULFILLED AND THE KINGDOM OF GOD IS AT HAND, REPENT YE AND BELIEVE THE GOSPEL'.

And John 14:23 which says: 'IF A MAN LOVE ME, HE WILL KEEP MY WORDS: AND MY FATHER WILL LOVE HIM AND WE WILL COME UNTO HIM, AND MAKE OUR ABODE WITH HIM'.

THEN John 15:10 goes on to say: 'IF YOU KEEP MY COMMANDMENTS, YOU SHALL ABIDE IN MY LOVE, EVEN AS I KEEP MY FATHERS COMMANDMENTS AND ABIDE IN HIS LOVE'.

Then II John 6 says 'AND THIS IS LOVE, THAT WE WALK AFTER HIS COMMANDMENTS. THIS IS THE COMMANDMENT, THAT AS YOU HAVE HEARD FROM THE BEGINNING, YOU SHOULD WALK IN IT'.

Then Jesus sums this up by saying in Luke 6:46 'AND WHY CALL YE ME, LORD, LORD, AND DO NOT THE THINGS WHICH I SAY'? Repenting and keeping God's commandments has good results as we see in 1 Corinthians 2:9 'BUT AS IT IS WRITTEN, EYE HAS NOT SEEN, NOR EAR HEARD, NOR HAS IT ENTERED INTO THE HEART OF MAN THE THINGS WHICH GOD HAS PREPARED FOR THEM THAT LOVE HIM'.

And in James 2:5 'HARKEN, MY BELOVED BRETHREN, HATH NOT GOD CHOSEN THE POOR OF THIS WORLD RICH IN FAITH, AND HEIRS OF THE KINGDOM WHICH HE HAD PROMISED TO THEM THAT LOVE HIM'.

The Lord Jesus is coming back but not as an innocent baby this time, but 'IN FLAMING FIRE TAKING VENGEANCE ON THEM THAT KNOW NOT GOD, AND THAT OBEY NOT THE GOSPEL OF OUR LORD JESUS CHRIST', (II Thessalonians 1:8). 'WHO SHALL BE PUNISHED WITH EVERLASTING DESTRUCTION FROM THE PRESENCE OF THE LORD, AND FROM THE GLORY OF HIS POWER', (II Thessalonians 1:9).

In order to avoid this judgment only two commandments need to be obeyed according to the gospel of Mark: 'AND ONE OF THE SCRIBES CAME AND HAVING HEARD THEM REASONING TOGETHER AND PERCIEVING THAT HE HAD ANSWERED THEM WELL, ASKED HIM, WHICH IS THE FIRST COMMANDMENT OF ALL? AND JESUS ANSWERED HIM, THE FIRST OF ALL THE COMMANDMENTS IS, HEAR O ISRAEL: THE LORD OUR GOD IS ONE LORD. AND THOU SHALT LOVE THE LORD THY GOD WITH ALL THY HEART, AND WITH ALL THY SOUL, AND WITH ALL THY MIND, AND WITH ALL THY STRENGTH, THIS IS THE FIRST COMMANDMENT. AND THE SECOND IS LIKE NAMELY THIS: THOU SHALT LOVE THY NEIGHBOR AS THYSELF. THERE IS NONE OTHER COMMANDMENT GREATER THAN THESE', (Mark 12:28-31).

Then the Lord Jesus applies this to our daily lives by answering in the gospel of Luke who our neighbor is: 'AND JESUS ANSWERING SAID, A CERTAIN MAN WENT DOWN FROM JERUSALEM TO JERICHO AND FELL AMOUNG THEIVES WHICH STRIPPED HIM OF HIS RAIMENT AND WOUNDED HIM AND DEPARTED LEAVING HIM HALF DEAD. AND BY CHANCE THERE CAME DOWN A CERTAIN

PREIST THAT WAY: AND WHEN HE SAW HIM, PASSED BY ON THE OTHER SIDE. AND LIKEWISE A LEVITE WHEN HE WAS AT THE PLACE, CAME AND LOOKED AT HIM AND PASSED BY ON THE OTHERSIDE. BUT A CERTAIN SAMARITAN AS HE JOURNEYED CAME WHERE HE WAS AND WHEN HE SAW HIM, HE HAD COMPASSION ON HIM. AND WENT TO HIM, AND BOUND UP HIS WOUNDS, POURING IN OIL AND WINE, AND SAT HIM ON HIS OWN BEAST AND BROUGHT HIM TO AN INN TO CARE FOR HIM. AND ON THE MORROW WHEN HE DEPARTED HE TOOK OUT TWO PENCE AND GAVE THEM TO THE HOST AND SAID UNTO HIM: TAKE CARE OF HIM AND WHATSOEVER THOU SPENDEST MORE, WHEN I COME AGAIN, I WILL REPAY YOU. WHICH NOW OF THESE THREE, THINKEST THOU WAS NEIGHBOR TO HIM THAT FELL AMOUNG THEIVES? AND HE SAID, HE THAT SHOWED MERCY ON HIM. THEN JESUS SAID: GO AND DO THOU LIKEWISE', (Luke 10:30-37).

After that Jesus words and thoughts had been well received: 'ONE SCRIBE SAID UNTO HIM: WELL, MASTER, THOU HAST SAID THE TRUTH: FOR THERE IS ONE GOD; AND THERE IS NONE BUT HE. TO LOVE HIM WITH ALL THY HEART AND WITH ALL THY UNDERSTANDING, AND WITH ALL THY SOUL, AND WITH ALL THY STRENGTH, AND TO LOVE HIS NEIGHBOR AS HIMSELF, IS MORE THAN ALL WHOLE BURNT OFFERINGS AND SACRIFICES. AND WHEN JESUS SAW THAT HE ANSWERED DISCREETLY, HE SAID UNTO HIM: THOU ART NOT FAR FROM THE KINGDOM OF GOD. AND NO MAN AFTER THAT DURST ASK HIM ANY QUESTION', (Mark 12:32-34).

James sums this up by telling us clearly that: 'PURE RELIGION AND UNDEFILED BEFORE GOD AND THE FATHER IS THIS, TO VISIT THE FATHERLESS AND WIDOWS IN THEIR AFFLICTION, AND TO KEEP HIMSELF UNSPOTTED FROM THE WORLD', (James 1:27). 'IF YOU FULFILL THE ROYAL LAW ACCORDING TO THE SCRIPTURE, THOU SHALT LOVE THY NEIGHBOR AS THYSELF, YE DO WELL', (James 2:8). In John 13:34 Jesus says: 'A NEW COMMANDMENT I GIVE UNTO YOU. THAT YOU LOVE ONE ANOTHER AS I LOVED YOU, THAT YOU LOVE ONE ANOTHER'.

Of course, all this emphasis on love did not sit too good with some people because love is evil spelled backwards and some people, while they wanted to love God did not want to have to love everyone. So John records in John 6:66 that 'FROM THAT TIME MANY OF HIS DISCIPLES WENT BACK AND WALKED NO MORE WITH HIM'.

Then in Luke 9:59-62 another issue comes up, let's look at it: 'AND HE SAID UNTO ANOTHER: FOLLOW ME. BUT HE SAID, LORD, SUFFER ME FIRST TO GO BURY MY FATHER. AND JESUS SAID UNTO HIM, LET THE DEAD BURY THEIR DEAD: BUT GO THOU AND PREACH THE KINGDOM OF GOD. AND ANOTHER ALSO SAID, LORD, I WILL FOLLOW THEE: BUT LET ME FIRST GO BID FAREWELL, WHICH ARE AT HOME AT MY HOUSE. AND JESUS SAID UNTO HIM: NO MAN HAVING PUT HIS HAND TO THE PLOW, AND LOOKING BACK, IS FIT FOR THE KINGDOM OF GOD'. In this we see clearly that the issue of preeminence is raised. Preaching the kingdom of God obviously supersedes common folkways and moral entitlements of manners and the lack of faith demonstrated by desertion. This also results in the same objections previously encountered in John 6:66-68 namely: 'FROM THAT TIME MANY OF HIS DISCIPLES WENT BACK, AND WALKED NO MORE WITH HIM. THEN SAID JESUS TO THE TWELVE, WILL YE ALSO GO AWAY? THEN PETER ANSWERED HIM, LORD, TO WHOM SHALL WE GO? THOU HAST THE WORDS OF ETERNAL LIFE. AND WE BELIEVE AND ARE SURE THAT THOU ART THE CHRIST, THE SON OF THE LIVING GOD'.

Then the question arises what you are willing to do if you truly believe that Jesus is the Christ, the Son of God.

I John 5:12 says that 'HE THAT HAS THE SON, HAS LIFE: AND HE THAT DOES NOT HAVE THE SON OF GOD DOES NOT HAVE LIFE'.

So then apparently this kingdom of God stuff is not just an ideology, theory or theology but a Person, The Son of God. Moreover, your success in expanding that kingdom depends upon your personal relationship with the King. John 15:1-8 confirms this: 'I AM THE TRUE VINE, AND MY FATHER IS THE HUSBANDMAN EVERY BRANCH IN ME THAT BEARS NOT FRUIT HE TAKES AWAY; AND EVERY BRANCH THAT BEARETH FRUIT HE PURGES IT THAT IT MIGHT BRING FORTH MORE FRUIT. NOW ARE YOU CLEAN THROUGH THE WORD WHICH I HAVE SPOKEN UNTO YOU. ABIDE IN ME, AND I IN YOU. AS THE BRANCH CANNOT BEAR FRUIT OF ITSELF, EXCEPT

IT ABIDE IN THE VINE; NO MORE CAN YE, EXCEPT YE ABIDE IN ME. I AM THE VINE, AND YOU ARE THE BRANCHES, HE THAT ABIDETH IN ME, AND I IN HIM, THE SAME BRINGETH FORTH MUCH FRUIT: FOR WITHOUT ME YE CAN DO NOTHING. IF A MAN ABIDE NOT IN ME HE IS CAST FORTH AS A BRANCH, AND IS WITHERED, AND MEN GATHER THEM, AND CAST THEM INTO THE FIRE, AND THEY ARE BURNED. IF YE ABIDE IN ME, AND MY WORDS ABIDE IN YOU, YOU SHALL ASK WHAT YOU WILL, AND IT SHALL BE DONE UNTO YOU. HEREIN IS MY FATHER GLORIFIED, THAT YE BEAR MUCH FRUIT, SO SHALL YOU BE MY DISCIPLES'.

Then the Lord Jesus concludes with a rather harsh statement in Matthew 21:43, 'I TELL YOU, FOR THIS REASON THE KINGDOM OF GOD WILL BE TAKEN AWAY FROM YOU AND GIVEN TO A PEOPLE WHO WILL PRODUCE THE FRUITS OF IT'.

This is also confirmed by the preaching of John the Baptist: 'IN THOSE DAYS CAME JOHN THE BAPTIST PREACHING IN THE WILDERNESS OF JUDEA, AND SAYING, REPENT YE: FOR THE KINGDOM OF HEAVEN IS AT HAND: FOR THIS IS HE THAT WAS SPOKEN OF BY THE PROPHET ESAIAS SAYING, THE VOICE OF ONE CRYING IN THE WILDERNESS, PREPARE YE THE WAY OF THE LORD, MAKE HIS PATHS STRAIGHT, AND THE SAME JOHN HAS HIS RAIMENT OF CAMEL'S HAIR, AND A LEATHER GIRDLE ABOUT HIS LOINS, AND HIS MEAT WAS LOCUSTS AND WILD HONEY. THEN WENT OUT TO HIM JERUSALEM, AND ALL JUDEA, AND ALL THE REGION ROUND ABOUT JORDAN, AND WERE BAPTIZED OF HIM IN JORDAN, CONFESSING THEIR SINS. BUT WHEN HE SAW MANY OF THE PHARISEES AND SADDUCEES COME TO HIS BAPTISM, HE SAID UNTO THEM. O YE GENERATION OF VIPERS, WHO HATH WARNED YOU TO FLEE FROM THE WRATH TO COME? BRING FORTH THEREFORE FRUITS MEET FOR REPENTANCE, AND THINK NOT TO SAY WITHIN YOURSELVES, WE HAVE ABRAHAM TO OUR FATHER: FOR I SAY UNTO YOU, THAT GOD IS ABLE OF THESE STONES TO RAISE UP CHILDREN UNTO ABRAHAM. AND NOW ALSO THE AXE IS LAID UNTO THE ROOT OF THE TREES: THEREFORE, EVERY TREE WHICH BRINGS NOT FORTH GOOD FRUIT IS HEWN DOWN, AND CAST INTO THE FIRE', (John 3:1-10).

Then Luke brings this into sharper focus by saying: 'AND HE CAME INTO ALL THE COUNTRY ABOUT JORDAN, PREACHING THE BAPTISM OF REPENTANCE FOR THE REMISSION OF SINS; AS IT IS WRITTEN IN THE BOOK OF THE WORDS OF ESAIAS THE PROPHET SAYING; THE VOICE OF ONE CRYING IN THE WILDERNESS, PREPARE YE THE WAY OF THE LORD, MAKE HIS PATHS STRAIGHT. EVERY VALLEY SHALL BE FILLED, AND EVERY MOUNTAIN AND HILL SHALL BE BROUGHT LOW, AND THE CROOKED SHALL BE MADE STRAIGHT, AND THE ROUGH WAYS SHALL BE MADE SMOOTH. AND ALL FLESH SHALL SEE THE SALVATION OF GOD, THEN SAID HE TO THE MULTITUDE THAT CAME FORTH TO BE BAPTIZED WITH HIM, O GENERATION OF VIPERS, WHO HAS WARNED YOU TO FLEE FROM THE WRATH TO COME? BRING FORTH THEREFORE FRUITS WORTHY OF REPENTANCE, AND BEGIN NOT TO SAY WITHIN YOURSELVES WE HAVE ABRAHAM TO OUR FATHER: FOR I SAY UNTO YOU. THAT GOD IS ABLE OF THESE STONES TO RAISE UP CHILDREN UNTO ABRAHAM. AND NOW ALSO THE AXE IS LAID UNTO ROOT OF THE TREES, EVERY TREE THEREFORE WHICH BRINGETH NOT FORTH GOOD FRUIT IS HEWN DOWN AND CAST INTO THE FIRE. AND THE PEOPLE ASKED HIM, SAYING, WHAT SHALL WE DO THEN? AND HE ANSWERED AND SAID UNTO THEM. HE THAT HAS TWO COATS, LET HIM IMPART TO HIM THAT HAS NONE, AND HE THAT HAS MEAT LET HIM DO LIKEWISE. THEN CAME ALSO PUBLICANS TO BE BAPTIZED, AND SAID UNTO HIM, MASTER, WHAT SHALL WE DO? AND HE SAID UNTO THEM, EXACT NO MORE THAN THAT WHICH IS APPOINTED YOU. AND THE SOLDIERS LIKEWISE DEMANDED OF HIM SAYING, AND WHAT SHALL WE DO? AND HE SAID UNTO THEM, DO VIOLENCE TO NO MAN, NEITHER ACCUSE ANY FALSELY AND BE CONTENT WITH YOUR WAGES', (Luke 3:3-14).

This theme that all must repent and come to repentance is summed up in II Peter 3:9 which says: 'THE LORD IS NOT SLACK CONCERNING HIS PROMISE, AS SOME MEN COUNT SLACKNESS; BUT IS LONGSUFFERING TO US-WARD, NOT WILLING THAT ANY SHOULD PERISH, BUT THAT ALL SHOULD COME TO REPENTANCE'.

Now we see that this question became common throughout Israel and wherever the gospel was preached: 'SIRS, WHAT MUST I DO TO BE SAVED'? (Acts 16:30).

My 8th article begins by saying that salvation and most gifts of God are not just an individual occurrence but usually involves one's whole house. Doubting Thomas was one significant example. Since he was not with the other disciples who saw Jesus alive after the resurrection he could not believe. Being in one accord, in one place aids belief and especially blessings.

Jesus appeared to over 500 people once he rose from the dead according to I Corinthians 15:6: 'AFTER THAT, HE WAS SEEN UP ABOVE FIVE HUNDRED BRETHREN AT ONCE, OF WHOM THE GREATER PART REMAIN UNTO THIS PRESENT, BUT SOME ARE FALLEN ASLEEP'. Yet only 120 persons waited 10 days for Pentecost according to Acts 1:15: 'AND IN THOSE DAYS PETER STOOD UP IN THE MIDST OF HIS DISCIPLES, AND SAID, (THE NUMBER OF NAMES TOGETHER WERE ABOUT A HUNDRED AND TWENTY).

Nevertheless he told all five hundred of them to 'TARRY YE IN JERUSALEM, UNTIL YE BE ENDUED WITH POWER FROM ON HIGH', (Luke 24:49).

This commandment was given by the resurrected Jesus. And his resurrection confirms this: Mathew 27:52, 53 says: 'AND THE GRAVES WERE OPENED AND MANY OF THE BODIES OF THE SAINTS WHICH SLEPT AROSE. AND CAME OUT OF THE GRAVES AFTER HIS RESURRECTION, AND WENT INTO THE HOLY CITY, AND APPEARED TO MANY'. (This is one of the few places in the Bible that mentions dead saints. Please note that no Bible verse ever encourages the praying to dead saints for any reason and there is no indication that any dead saint ever appeared to help anyone in bearing their burdens or to help solve anyone's problems or issues of concern).

After this Galatians declares what state we are now in by saying: 'I AM CRUCIFIED WITH CHRIST: NEVERTHELESS I LIVE: YET NOT I, BUT CHRIST LIVETH IN ME: AND THE LIFE WHICH I NOW LIVE IN THE FLESH I LIVE BY THE FAITH OF THE SON OF GOD, WHO LOVED ME, AND GAVE HIMSELF FOR ME', (Galatians 2:20). This works out well until we are drawn the way of our own lust and enticed. But 'IF WE WALK IN THE LIGHT AS HE IS IN THE LIGHT WE HAVE FELLOWSHIP ONE WITH ANOTHER AND THE BLOOD OF JESUS CLEANSES US FROM ALL SIN', (I John 1:7).

My 9th article consists of some truths written on the back cover of a radio Bible class booklet. The notes begin by saying: Some Christians have spoken unwisely against God by saying that it is in vain to serve God.

Here we see this in Malachi 3:14-4:1: 'YE HAVE SAID, IT IS VAIN TO SERVE GOD: AND WHAT PROFIT IS IT THAT WE KEEP HIS ORDINANCES AND THAT WE HAVE WALKED MOURNFULLY BEFORE THE LORD OF HOSTS? AND NOW WE CALL THE PROUD HAPPY; YEA, THEY THAT WORK: YEA THEY THAT TEMPT GOD ARE EVEN DELIVERED. THEN THEY THAT FEARED THE LORD SPOKE OFTEN ONE TO ANOTHER: AND THE LORD HARKENED AND HEARD IT, AND A BOOK OF REMEMBERANCE WAS WRITTEN BEFORE HIM FOR THEM THAT FEARED THE LORD, AND THAT THOUGHT UPON HIS NAME. AND THEY SHALL BE MINE, SAITH THE LORD OF HOSTS, IN THAT DAY WHEN I MAKE UP MY JEWELS. AND I WILL SPARE THEM, AS A MAN SPARES HIS OWN SON THAT SERVES HIM. THEN SHALL YOU RETURN, AND DISCERN BETWEEN THE RIGHTEOUS AND BETWEEN THE WICKED, BETWEEN HIM THAT SERVES GOD AND HIM THAT SERVES HIM NOT. FOR BEHOLD, THE DAY COMES, THAT SHALL BURN AS AN OVEN: AND ALL THE PROUD, YEA, AND ALL THAT DO WICKEDLY, SHALL BE AS STUBBLE: AND THE DAY THAT COMETH SHALL BURN THEM UP, SAITH THE LORD OF HOSTS, THAT IT SHALL LEAVE THEM NEITHER ROOT NOR BRANCH'.

And in another scripture, we see this where Jesus was led by the Holy Spirit of God not to blessing but to be tempted of the devil. 'THEN COMETH JESUS FROM GALILEE TO JORDAN UNTO JOHN, TO BE BAPTIZED OF HIM. BUT JOHN FORBADE HIM, SAYING, I HAVE NEED TO BE BAPTIZED OF THEE, AND COMEST THOU TO ME? AND JESUS ANSWERING SAID UNTO HIM, SUFFER IT TO BE NOW: FOR THUS IT BECOMETH US TO FULFILL ALL RIGHTEOUSNESS. THEN HE SUFFERED HIM. AND JESUS WHEN HE WAS BAPTIZED, WENT UP STRAIGHT WAY OUT OF THE WATER: AND LO, THE HEAVENS WERE OPENED UNTO HIM, AND HE SAW THE SPIRIT OF GOD DESCENDING LIKE A DOVE, AND LIGHTING UPON HIM. AND LO, A VOICE FROM HEAVEN CAME SAYING, THIS IS MY BELOVED SON, IN WHOM I AM WELL PLEASED'.

'THEN WAS JESUS LED UP OF THE SPIRIT INTO THE WILDERNESS TO BE TEMPTED OF THE DEVIL', (Matthew 3:13-4:1).

Some Christians don't think that they need the Holy Ghost power in their mediocre and dull lives. But in these trying days we need all of God that we can get. It is sad to see how few Christians have the resolve Simon the sorcerer had who said in Acts 8:19: Lets stand and read together 'GIVE ME ALSO THIS POWER'.

In these last days there is a sound of abundance of rain. For now we must pray in faith believing. Soon a small cloud will appear and there will be a great rain. This happened in Elijah's day and it can happen today for God has not changed, it is we who have lost faith. While we wait for the clouds to gather let us go on to perfection. Some good advice for us is found in II Peter 1:5-10, 'ADD TO YOUR FAITH VIRTUE; AND TO VIRTUE KNOWLEDGE. AND TO KNOWLEDGE TEMPERANCE; AND TO TEMPERANCE PATIENCE; AND TO PATIENCE GODLINESS. AND TO GODLINESS BROTHERLY KINDNESS; AND TO BROTHERLY KINDNESS CHARITY. FOR IF THESE THINGS BE IN YOU, AND ABOUND, THEY MAKE YOU THAT YE SHALL NEITHER BE BARREN NOR UNFRUITFUL IN THE KNOWLEDGE OF OUR LORD JESUS CHRIST. BUT HE THAT LACKETH THESE THINGS IS BLIND, AND CANNOT SEE FAR OFF, AND HATH FORGOTTEN THAT HE WAS PURGED FROM HIS OLD SINS. WHEREFORE THE RATHER, BRETHREN, GIVE DILIGENCE TO MAKE YOUR CALLING AND ELECTION SURE: FOR IF YE DO THESE THINGS, YE SHALL NEVER FALL'. (II Peter 1:5-10).

Opps, I feel the Holy Ghost wanting me to say that our pastor, Lyle Steenis, had the congregation especially the Jesus people who had no religious training nor faith speak the scriptures out loud as he and dad Hagin both knew that 'FAITH COMES BY HEARING AND HEARING BY THE WORD OF GOD', (Romans 10:17). And they knew and practiced this before the advent of today's faith teachers.

Yes reading the Bible out loud and in unison with other believers was a common practice in our part of the Jesus Movement. Not all churches did this back then and few if any do it today. Perhaps that's why there is such a lack of real faith for anything that matters today. Resulting in chronic unbelief for salvation, for healing, for successful marriage, for saved and happy children, for saved and happy extended family and neighborhoods, for prosperity including jobs, businesses, inventions and risk-taking faith that results in increase and abundance. 'SINCE JESUS CAME THAT WE MIGHT HAVE LIFE, AND HAVE IT MORE ABUNDANTLY', (John 10:10).

In this instance we also notice several fruits of the Holy Spirit mentioned. Let me be clear about this: fruits of the Spirit do not come by study in some church of unbelief, we must have the Holy Spirit via Spirit baptism in order to have the fruits. So, we always need to be baptized into the Holy Spirit and be filled with Him time and again and be yielded to Him in order to exercise His power and His gifts.

Moreover, if we withdraw or stumble we can be drawn the way of our own lusts and enticed but 'IF WE WALK IN THE LIGHT AS HE IS IN THE LIGHT WE HAVE FELLOWSHIP (NOT GRUDGES) ONE WITH ANOTHER AND THE BLOOD OF JESUS CHRIST HIS SON CLEANSES US FROM ALL SIN', (I John 1:7).

While you are growing spiritually remember you must always be patient and not get frustrated to see God's will manifested: 'BE PATIENT THEREFORE BRETHREN, UNTO THE COMING OF THE LORD. BEHOLD THE HUSBANDMAN WAITETH FOR THE PRECIOUS FRUIT OF THE EARTH AND HAS LONG PATIENCE FOR IT, UNTIL HE RECIEVES THE EARLIER AND LATER RAIN', (James 5:7).

And always remember that: 'I AM CRUCIFIED WITH CHRIST NEVERTHELESS I LIVE, YET NOT I, BUT CHRIST LIVES IN ME AND THE LIFE WHICH I NOW LIVE IN THE FLESH, I LIVE BY THE FAITH OF THE SON OF GOD WHO LOVED ME AND GAVE HIMSELF FOR ME', (Galatians 2:20).

OPPS, I FEEL THE HOLY GHOST NOW WANTING ME TO SAY FROM MEMORY THAT THESE JESUS PEOPLE FELT THAT FEELING GOD IN HOLY SPIRIT BAPTIZM WAS FAR MORE IMPORTANT THAN SUNDAY SCHOOL, READING THE BIBLE OR DOING ANY KIND OF CHRISTIAN CALISTHENICS LIKE PRAYER MEETINGS AND STUFF.

Before these street people became Jesus people they used to take dope in order to feel good. And once they became Christians or Jesus people it was also to feel good by feeling God.

As the Pastor was serving communion one Sunday he happened to mention that as a protestant church we did not believe in the Catholic doctrine of transubstantiation. He said this mainly because some of the girls of our Jesus movement worked as nurses for Little Company of Mary Catholic Hospital in Santa Monica. Moreover, he did not believe that the wine became blood in the Catholic Mass since the Catholics had a rehabilitation center for alcoholic priests.

My 10th article was a few Bible verses written on a church ID card. One of the verses is II Corinthians 8:17 which says: 'FOR INDEED HE ACCEPTED THE EXHORTATION; BUT BEING MORE FORWARD, OF HIS OWN ACCORD HE WENT UNTO YOU'.

Here we see that not only did Titus 'NATURALLY CARE FOR YOUR ESTATE', (Philippians 2:20). But also demonstrated some unction from the Holy Ghost by being forward. Our next Bible verse is Acts 16:4, which says: 'AND AS THEY WENT THROUGH THE CITIES, THEY DELIVERED THEM THE DECREES FOR TO KEEP, ORDAINED OF THE APOSTLES AND ELDERS WHICH WERE AT JERUSALEM'.

To understand this verse more clearly it would be wise to consider its context. The next verse right after it gives its result. Mainly churches were established in the faith and increased in numbers daily. Here we also see that Paul did not just deliver his personal testimony or knowledge of the scriptures from personal experience and study but **he delivered the ordained decrees of the apostles and the elders at Jerusalem.**

From this main verse we also see how they went. They is plural. So you don't do evangelism alone. You always come up with someone of like precious faith to help you spread the gospel. They also went through cities. Not beaches or parks or wilderness areas where there were no people. Important things like decrees are ordained by the apostles and elders which were at Jerusalem, the main city of God's people, from which Christ will reign. Any decrees without scriptural support were not meant for us or them to keep.

At the end of this our pastor also said that the modern church with its whimpering, crying and complaining needs a pacifier. But a victorious Christian and Christian church has the satisfier-Jesus.

After using the public computer at that public library to write some more of this book I got home in time to watch some Christian TV. A certain end time prophet who I will not name appeared as a guest on a TV program encouraging Christians to buy food for others including not just their extended families but also neighbors (saved or unsaved) and even strangers and homeless bums.

His supposed exhortation aroused my righteous indignation as no Bible verse tells us to feed the enemies of God whether they are family, neighbors or bums.

I do believe in the end time harvest but as a Social Security recipient my next preparation may be to acquire a generator since I live in a hurricane zone. It is not my duty to feed bums who have come down from up North to squat on the Christians here. But some local churches have feeding programs for the homeless.

But since I was homeless once myself, I know something about homeless operators taking advantage of Christians with no real intentions of ever serving God and just using the Christian food as a way of saving their own money to buy booze and drugs. So, tell that false prophet that I refuse to be part of any such scam. Moreover, there are Bible verses that confirm my position. Let's look at them in Matthew 25:1-13: 'THEN SHALL THE KINGDOM OF HEAVEN BE LIKENED UNTO TEN VIRGINS, WHICH TOOK THEIR LAMPS, AND WENT FORTH TO MEET THE BRIDEGROOM. AND FIVE OF THEM WERE WISE, AND FIVE WERE FOOLISH. THEY THAT WERE FOOLISH TOOK THEIR LAMPS, AND TOOK NO OIL WITH THEM: BUT THE WISE TOOK OIL IN THEIR VESSELS WITH THEIR LAMPS. WHILE THE BRIDEGROOM TARRIED, THEY ALL SLUMBERED AND SLEPT. AND AT MIDNIGHT THERE WAS A CRY MADE, BEHOLD THE BRIDEGROOM COMETH; GO YE OUT TO MEET HIM. THEN ALL THOSE VIRGINS AROSE, AND TRIMMED THEIR LAMPS. AND THE FOOLISH SAID UNTO THE WISE, GIVE US OF YOUR OIL; FOR OUR LAMPS ARE GONE OUT. BUT THE WISE ANSWERED, SAYING, NOT SO; LEST THERE BE NOT ENOUGH FOR US AND YOU: BUT GO YE RATHER TO THEM THAT SELL, AND BUY FOR YOURSELVES. AND WHILE THEY WENT TO BUY, THE BRIDEGROOM CAME; AND THEY THAT WERE READY WENT IN WITH HIM TO THE MARRIAGE: AND THE DOOR WAS SHUT. AFTERWARD CAME ALSO THE OTHER VIRGINS, SAYING, LORD, LORD OPEN TO US. BUT HE ANSWERED AND SAID, VERILY I SAY UNTO YOU, I KNOW YOU NOT. WATCH THEREFORE, FOR YE KNOW NOT NEITHER THE DAY NOR THE HOUR WHEREIN THE SON OF MAN, COME'.

In Mathew 25:9 we see where the wise virgins (apparently Spirit filled Christians) refused to share their oil with the foolish denominational virgins. This common folkway seems to go against what most morale parents teach their children about sharing and proper behavior and manors. Nevertheless when it comes to the bottom line of survival one must always obey the bridegroom. That's one part of marriage that many who get involved in domestic disputes fail to grasp.

There is another point which needs to be made here. Some wonder why the bridegroom comes at midnight, especially since almost all marriages occur in the day light. Well 'God is light' and the best time for light to get noticed is when it is surrounded by darkness.

I saw the evangelist Perry Stone saying some things on the Jim Bakker show on Thursday, May 31 that need to be said again. Jim Bakker asked Perry Stone about the prophecy in Joel chapter two, about God pouring out His Spirit upon all flesh. Perry answered with the typical Bible school interpretation that all flesh means all ethnic groups of people. But when the Bible talks of flesh other than sins of the flesh it also mentions the flesh of beasts, birds and fish not just the flesh of men. In fact, there's a verse about this that says: 'ALL FLESH IS NOT THE SAME FLESH, BUT THERE IS ONE KIND OF FLESH OF MEN, ANOTHER FLESH OF BEASTS, ANOTHER OF FISHES AND ANOTHER OF BIRDS', (I Corinthians 15:39).

Anyway, it may be that different creatures besides just man are also destined to live in heaven with God. Or else why does the scripture say to: 'PREACH THE GOSPEL TO EVERY CREATURE', (Mark 16:15)?

This concept may be too controversial so I'll just leave it for some of you egotistical theologians to discuss. Some people are so proud and elitist that they think only people like them are worthy of salvation. What about the crumbs that fall from the master's table that dogs lick up?

I had thought that perhaps this might have been another revelation, but you may not think so. Therefore, I'll give you this one that I'm certain you will accept as the revelation it is:

I received a very unusual revelation about abortion on the afternoon of May 29, 2018. Since I am a man, I had always though that abortion was mainly a woman's issue. But I remembered from prison those few men who had been convicted of manslaughter for shaking babies that would not stop crying. Today, those few men have now become many and that manslaughter is now called 'shaking baby syndrome'.

Some of you who may have once gone to Sunday school as children and remember from Bible stories how that Cane slew Able his brother. 'AND THEN GOD ASKS CANE WHERE ABLE WAS. AND CANE SAID; I DON'T KNOW, AM I MY BROTHER'S KEEPER? AND GOD REPLIED; THE BLOOD OF YOU BROTHER ABLE CRIES TO ME FROM THE GROUND', (Genesis 4:10).

For you hard shell hog and hominy Baptists, lukewarm and unbelieving here is the revelation that God has sent me. The crying, no the constant wailing of sixty million aborted babies has infuriated God and he is about to shake America. Instead of a shaking baby syndrome, God will soon shake the land of the abortionist.

I learned from childhood that **when God speaks you move at once to obey.** Therefore, from this day forth I will not be voting for any abortionist Democrat for any office. Some democratic candidates are Roman Catholic which has an anti-abortion church policy therefore such candidates should be excommunicated and voted against.

My 11th article is from a very old devotional about wasted prayers. It seems that a lot of praying is just so much oral masturbation. I know that this expression does offend many of you. You know Paul called himself in the Bible; 'A WISE MASTER BUILDER', (I Corinthians 3:10). But some mischievous Christian teenagers say that actually the expression means in the original Greek; a wise masturbator. Not so, but even if true be that as it may, the ancient Greeks did have sexual problems and their language reflects such but that's not my concern now. And there are other problems with Christian prayer like 'if it be thy will'. Not one verse in the Bible ever records that being used with prayer except when the Lord Jesus asked the Father to take away the cup he was given in the garden for his sacrifice.

In this prayer issue things which the Lord has already promised to give us are harped on too much by the unbelieving unfaithful. If God said it, that settles it, but only if I believe it. Instead of thanking him for what he has promised you, we keep asking as if we really don't believe his word. The Bible is a book full of thousands of promises, not all are conditional. Some will happen whether we like it or not. Each blank check promise is signed by the Savior himself. You do not need to keep asking as though he were unwilling and must be pressed into action by your prayers. Instead fill in the blank by your faith as you believe and then thank him for the answer to your request. You don't have to ask God to keep his promises. This way your prayers will have more adoration and less petition.

When I got home from the library I began watching our brother Dr. Bill Winston talk on the same subject on Christian TV. He mentioned how that the king of Israel got a threatening letter from the king of Assyria in II Kings 19. The king of Israel took the letter up to the temple and laid it down before the Lord and prayed against it and for the Lord to intercede and help Israel. The Lord heard his prayer and that night the angel of the Lord slew one hundred and eighty thousand Assyrian soldiers.

This quickened my memory of my experience with this exact type of prayer I had when I had just graduated from Fuller Seminary in 1985. And I began sleeping with the homeless since I could not afford the high rents out there and could get no ministerial job to pay rent anyway since 'wheelchairs do not inspire faith'.

One night as I was sleeping outside, a local police officer kicked me awake and wrote me a ticket for trespassing. But I knew the Bible well and that I was on public land. So once that policeman left, I laid that ticket down before the Lord to pray over it just like the king of Israel had done. But since I was too tired to think up a long religious prayer, I simply quoted the part of the twenty fourth Psalm which says that: 'THE EARTH IS THE LORDS'. And asked God to judge between his word and trespassing and do whatsoever to Him seemed best and rolled over and went back to sleep.

Now I see where I was wrong there. God has magnified his word even above his own name. So anything compared to the supremacy of God's word, like some dumb human law over trespassing on God's land does not hold up well. And in fact, it is automatically put down.

That morning I caught the bus to go to the mission to eat my oatmeal. The bus passed the police station with its flag at half-staff. So I asked the mission director what had happened. He said that a local police officer had had a fire arms accident and had shot and killed himself. It was written up in the paper that he gave to me. Afterward for some reason I looked to see the name of that officer if it matched the name on my ticket. It matched. Of course, I was horrified. And I thought that it was an overreaction by God to put someone to death just for a mistake over trespassing, but I said nothing and held my peace. For I had learned in that seminary never to question or criticize our Sovereign Lord especially about things I didn't fully understand.

Then I remembered how strongly God feels about his word. And that as the Sovereign Lord his acts are not for me to evaluate, judge, or correct. So I just thanked him and forgot about it all until now.

Before I leave this however I must make one more point that is: If the loving Jesus would have something like this be done just for a simple mistake over trespassing, what do you think is getting ready to happen over the deliberate and court mandated killing by abortion of over sixty million babies? Or what about those candidates who support this evil?

My 12th article is from a church offering envelope whose note quotes John 10:27 which says; 'MY SHEEP KNOW MY VOICE, AND I KNOW THEM AND THEY FOLLOW ME'. At first Moses heard God speaking through the burning bush. Then Elijah heard the Lord speaking from Mount Carmel. Isaiah heard God, and said here am I, send me. Saul heard in Acts 9. Peter heard in Acts 10.

We can hear God in two ways, both by his published word and by his answer to our prayers.

My note says also that we need to be aware of confusing sounds and of undegenerated advice from the devil.

The person who makes preparation hears God's voice, while those who are indifferent in reading the Bible don't.

Nehemiah obeyed God and God works through those that obey him.

Find a good church to go to. For in a place of vision you can hear God's voice.

If you are going to have a vision of the harvest field you will need one of Jesus too.

The prodigal church of Luke 15:11 is just eating husks when God has blessings for them through answers to prayer.

Bend the church to save the people since the last love of the Father is the desire to save souls.

Lost revival fire because older brother complains against babies as older selfish saints are critical.

This forced the prodigal to go out from his father to take things into his own hands.

As I read these notes, tears come to my eyes, as I remember the man of God, Reverend Lyle Steenis saying this to us so many years ago. He and 'Dad' Hagin gave very similar exhortations since the Pentecostal movement they came from (Topeka, Kansas) emphasized Christian values and the right way to do stuff. Whereas the Pentecostal movement from Dallas, Texas emphasized old line dominion over the earth. Especially for getting water and later for finding oil and now using faith for money.

I had to say this because some critics accused our brother Kenneth Hagin of plagiarizing from the philosopher Kenyon. This couldn't be so, for both he and Reverend Steenis naturally said mostly the same things as they came from the same Pentecostal background. Only Dad Hagin was also a renowned prophet as well as a pastor.

My 13th article is from a piece of scrap paper. It starts by talking about the Holy Ghost in John 16:9-11. Let's look at that.

In the first part of this chapter, Jesus talks about the Holy Ghost as the comforter and that he will aid your memory. 'WHEN HE COMES HE WILL REPROVE THE WORLD OF SIN, AND OF RIGHTEOUSNESS AND OF JUDGEMENT. OF SIN, BECAUSE THEY BELIEVE NOT ON ME. OF RIGHTEOUSNESS BECAUSE I GO TO THE FATHER, AND

YE SEE ME NO MORE. OF JUDGEMENT, BECAUSE THE PRINCE OF THIS WORLD IS JUDGED'.

As from here we see that the Holy Ghost's job is to convict of sin. And 'WHATSOEVER IS NOT OF FAITH IS SIN', (Romans 14:23). Receive the weak in the faith, but don't let anyone tell you that what you have is not real. Those like Job's comforters will come bringing with them false accusations. Don't listen to them, but be faithful in little things.

Sometimes it was necessary to have a second touch of Jesus. This way you see men as human beings not as trees walking. But a second hand experience is insufficient, example: we adjure you in the name of Jesus who Paul preaches to come out of him. (We can't cast out devils unless we are believers and receivers). Mark says that: 'THESE SIGNS SHALL FOLLOW THOSE THAT BELIEVE: IN MY NAME SHALL THEY CAST OUT DEVILS (the idea that Christians can be possessed by demons is false doctrine) For Christians have the authority and means to act. Demons are defeated when we recognize and then reject their lies THEY SHALL SPEAK WITH NEW TONGUES; THEY SHALL TAKE UP SERPENTS; AND IF THEY DRINK ANY DEADLY THING, IT SHALL NOT HURT THEM: THEY SHALL LAY HANDS ON THE SICK, AND THEY SHALL RECOVER', (MARK 16:17 & 18).

Since our God is a speaking God, we are also supposed to speak to demons and command them to leave, then they will listen and obey us.

Most Jesus people were never sick because they practice this scripture that's in the Bible and have been delivered from drugs without having any withdrawals.

Many need to be careful for they have built up a tolerance to the blessings of God and wonder why they can't feel and experience the blessing. *Work on getting rid of the junk first then more of God will come by praising and praying more.* Instead of analyzing the junk just cast it out. And if we do nothing the devil will win.

Your personal junk does not include generational curses or the bad experiences of other people's bad trips but from family familiar spirits. You don't get rid of these things by doing penance, praying to some dead saint or asking everyone for forgiveness like some religious nerd. These acts of religion have not saved nor delivered you. Religious spirits are not of God. They're just like worthless Hindu meditations that wastes time and helps no one. So just cast it out.

Always remember whenever you're sharing the word, preaching or witnessing; the dog who yelps the loudest is the one that God's word hit.

Some Christians are too giving, like the lighthouse keeper who gave away all his oil for lamps and heaters for the locals and the ship sank because there was no oil for the lighthouse left. Just like today bums kept Christians from doing their job. Don't let this happen to you.

The 14th article concerns the New Testament Church. 'AND THEY, CONTINUING DAILY WITH ONE ACCORD IN THE TEMPLE, AND BREAKING BREAD FROM HOUSE TO HOUSE, DID EAT THEIR MEAT WITH GLADNESS AND SINGLENESS OF HEART. PRAISING GOD, AND HAVING FAVOR WITH ALL THE PEOPLE. AND THE LORD ADDED TO THE CHURCH DAILY SUCH AS SHOULD BE SAVED', (Acts 2:46 and 47). Here we see that Jesus loves the church and we should too. He established the church. We are part of the body. The church must be glorious for Jesus is an intical part of it. So then it must be without spot or blemish according to I Corinthians 14. The church is built by sacrificial love 'labor of love' therefore those that endured established churches.

The Lord added to the church daily such as should be saved. So God adds to the church. Many churches however won't let young people into their church but keep them in coffee houses instead. The way to add to the church is to get young people saved. But high-powered evangelism has hung up the church. Because everyone not just some evangelist needs to preach. It's the personal individual responsibility of every Christian. So, don't let sin hinder moves of the Holy Spirit through you. God wants to work through you. Let Him, for the good of you all.

Bad circumstances can happen in nature that shows what happens to Christians that fall for a lot of noise but never get fed. Woodpeckers can bang on a hog's trough like it's time to eat. But the hog stays lean from running for an empty trough.

John Westley once said that a minister should pray 6 hours a day. I just thought I'd add that for those who feel we are becoming too religious.

Once a chicken and a pig were looking at a sign of bacon and eggs for breakfast at a restaurant. The pig said to the chicken: 'for you it's just a commitment, but for me it's a total dedication'.

'AND BEING IN BETHANY IN THE HOUSE OF SIMON THE LEPER, AS HE SAT AT MEAT, THERE CAME A WOMAN HAVING AN ALABASTER BOX OF OINTMENT OF SPIKENARD VERY PRECIOUS; AND SHE BRAKE THE BOX, AND POURED IT ON HIS HEAD. AND THERE WERE SOME THAT HAD INDIGNATION

WITHIN THEMSELVES AND SAID, WHY WAS THIS WASTE OF THE OINTMENT MADE? FOR IT MIGHT HAVE BEEN SOLD FOR MORE THAN THREE HUNDRED PENCE, AND HAVE BEEN GIVEN TO THE POOR. AND THEY MURMURED AGAINST HER. AND JESUS SAID, LET HER ALONE, WHY TROUBLE YE HER? SHE HAS WROUGH A GOOD WORK ON ME. FOR YE HAVE THE POOR WITH YOU ALWAYS, AND WHATSOEVER YOU WILL YOU MAY DO THEM GOOD: BUT ME YE HAVE NOT ALWAYS. SHE HAD DONE WHAT SHE COULD: SHE HAS COME AFOREHAND TO ANOINT MY BODY TO THE BURYING. VERILY I SAY UNTO YOU, WHERESOEVER THIS GOSPEL SHALL BE PREACHED THROUGHOUT THE WHOLE WORLD THIS ALSO THAT SHE HAS DONE SHALL BE SPOKEN OF FOR A MEMORIAL OF HER', (Mark 14:3-8).

There are several words in this that stand out. The first word I'll center on is 'waste' as in why was this waste? Excuse me, **but whatever is done for Christ is not waste.**

The second word is 'poor.' There is no set percentage of anything to be given to the poor. There is not any distinction made as to what type of assistance should be offered: food, money, or some other type of physical or spiritual gifts. But the word poor only includes those that are deprived of the basic necessities of life. Not addicts many of whom are thieves and are poor because they waste all their value on drugs. Bums are also poor not because of fate but because they refuse to work and expect you to support them. I remember helping out at the Los Angeles Mission where one bum had another get a few cents out of his pants pocket because he was too lazy to get it himself. Feeding programs in churches do not result in saved Christians that are full of the Holy Ghost. Their stomachs may be full, but their hearts are still empty.

The above scripture points out what love motivates one to do for Jesus. Whereas in a non-church revival there is no commitment to serve Christ but only to prepare people to die. But we must prepare people to live and serve Christ.

There is a problem with restlessness in a non-church setting as people need to be rooted and grounded in order to be settled. Colossians 1:23 mentions that to continue in the faith grounded and settled you must not be moved away from the hope of the gospel.

Jesus in Luke 9:51 set his face steadfastly to go up to Jerusalem to fulfill his purpose. Many on the other hand are restless and need to be grounded and settled instead of running to and fro. It's alright to go where God leads, into all the world. But first we must become grounded and settled in the faith or else we will lack direction and not become perfected by pastors or teachers. Therefore, you may be saved, but if you're not amounting to much this leads to laziness and indifference as such a person has not surrendered all to Jesus.

As a wise man you should get all you can get from God before going back out into the world. A battery with some corrosion on it from the world won't ground out right, it might turn on the lights and even honk the horn but it won't start the car. If you do not work on yourself to fulfill God's will, you will become busy bodies talking about everyone else's problems instead of solving your own. Always remember that there is no commandment that says confess other people's sins. In fact, there is a Bible verse that says: 'LOVE COVERS A MULTITUDE OF SINS', (I Peter 4:8).

Thank God, that at this church no such problem has arisen yet. I noticed from your testimonies that you always talk about what God is doing in your life. You never use your testimony time to 'rat' on other people and blame them for stuff. No one ever seems to hold any grudges and there are never any bad feelings about anyone expressed. So, you people are growing in God, praise the Lord! In Luke 9:51 we see where Jesus went on ahead to do God's will, and we need to serve Jesus all the time the way he faced Calvary.

The Church today needs courage and direction just like in Moses' day, if they looked at the serpent, they lived, but if not, they died, so is everyone who will or won't look to Christ.

I said before that you Jesus people were growing in God. That means you are becoming more Christ like. It does not mean that you are becoming more conformed to typical middleclass standards by dating and obtaining husbands or wives, securing better paying jobs to evidence financial blessing and growing and financial independence by secular pursuits.

But now that you have become a Christian, you have the mind of Christ. And as such could go on to college as your vocation requires. Who knows **you could lead someone to Christ there that could bless this nation.** That's right, Christ in you could be the intervening variable that changes this nation from darkness to light and from the power of Satan to the power of God.

You're not to get under a burden of trying to make your past life smooth. That's why Jesus came so that old things of the old life will fall away and all things will become new. You're no longer under obligation to pay the bills of your old master the devil. Now you are free. You can pay restitution for the things that you have stolen. But you can't pay any restitution for the lives that you helped ruin by your drug dealing. Nevertheless, as Christ gave you a new life in him, so by your example of deliverance can show others what Christ can do for them. If they want it, they can have it too, but if not don't try to force it on them.

Apparently, this article is from the early days of the Jesus movement as the pastor Reverend Lyle Steenis recommends things that did not concern the young people of the Jesus movement.

The news back then was of addicts stealing from their parents in order to fund their drug habit. But many of the Jesus people came from well to do homes and did not have to steal. Plus those that lived on their own had their own dope distribution business. Other issues no Jesus person seemed to have included dating problems. Unlike normal teenagers the Jesus people were certainly not looking for sexual partners, boyfriends or girlfriends. They were simply taking 'a time out' in order to find the reality of enjoying God for a while.

They had found 'the pearl of great price' and were only interested in telling others about it. These people did not seem to be the least bit concerned about the issues of the day back then. They never talked about the Vietnam War, civil rights, Social Justice Issues, Richard Nixon or pedophile priests in the Roman Catholic Church.

They didn't have any mental problems as their actions were sensible. As dopers their sole concern was dope. So now as Christians their sole concern was Christ and pleasing Him by getting others saved.

My 15th article also comes from another offering envelope from the California Evangelistic Association, our church, Bethel Tabernacle. This note has a name and address on it: Terry May 152 Charlotte St, Hamilton, 26, Ontario. I do hope that you absorbed all of God that you found there at Bethel Tabernacle in Redondo Beach, California. If not you know about forty years later another similar move of God happened at the Toronto airport. After all these years and the thousands of people that passed through the Jesus movement, it's hard to remember you. But as I recall you were a tall guy about my same height. We were both skinny kids back then. You had a soft voice as if God got a hold of you and set you on your way to becoming a man of God. As you left we prayed that you might find a real church to equip you to do whatever God had for you.

In my wildest and highest positive confession of faith I picture you as a professional man of God now on TV and heading up a worldwide ministry complete with Bible schools and many evangelical churches busy turning entire nations from darkness to light and from the power of Satan to the power of God. Amen, I said it. If it does not reflect where you are now, do not be sad for yourself, consider my plight:

I had a bad motorcycle accident in 1976 and should have died, but God restored me to life as a cripple. Although I was now wheelchair disabled, I want to college, seminary and grad school and earned several college degrees. But thanks to affirmative action I remained unemployed. Even the church discriminated against me because to them 'wheelchairs do not inspire faith'.

Nevertheless, I and my attendant have been busy using the computer at the public library to write my memoirs of the Jesus movement in hopes that it might inspire some young person to do what I wanted to do. In any case please pray for me that God might give me a second chance. After all Kathryn Khulman got a second chance and became a wonder worker of miracles. Yes, with God all things are possible.

The notes on this offering envelope concern the church mentioned in Ephesians 5:25.

So, let's look at that: 'HUSBANDS, LOVE YOUR WIVES, EVEN AS CHRIST ALSO LOVED THE CHURCH, AND GAVE HIMSELF FOR IT'.

When people look at Christ, they look to his church. So the church represents Christ and therefore must be holy. Hitch hiking Christians create a schism in the body. When one member suffers all should suffer. But hitch-hiking Christians without relationships are not sufficiently attached to any local body.

When a message was given in tongues which said that God was angry with his people because of compromising convictions and rampart sin in the land.

Keep the enemy and sin out of the church. Assemblies must be cleaned up. The gates of hell shall not prevail against the church. God wants a glorious church without spot or wrinkle, so church must pull together.

'AS THE DAYS OF NOAH WERE, SO SHALL ALSO THE COMING OF THE SON OF MAN BE,' (Mathew 24:37). God is getting the church ready for the coming of the Lord. But first cleaning up must occur. 'IF GOD SPARED NOT THE ANGELS THAT SINNED, BUT CAST THEM DOWN TO HELL, AND DELIVERED THEM INTO CHAINS OF DARKNESS, TO BE RESERVED UNTO JUDGEMENT; AND SPARED NOT THE OLD WORLD, BUT SAVED NOAH THE EIGHTH PERSON, A PREACHER OF RIGHTEOUSNESS, BRINGING

IN THE FLOOD UPON THE WORLD; AND TURNING THE CITIES OF SODOM AND GAMORAH INTO ASHES CONDEMNED THEM WITH AN OVERFLOW, MAKING THEM AN EXAMPLE UNTO THOSE THAT AFTER SHOULD LIVE UNGODLY,' (II Peter 2:4-6).

Then the Pastor had more to say about the coming of the Lord. He mentioned the lamps of Mathew 24:37 and Joel's prophecies about the coming later day outpouring of latter day rain. From this he concluded that God was getting the church ready for the coming of the Lord. And of course, he declared how that we needed to be saved and ready to meet Jesus. Then he told us how that in the last days there would be scoffers. 'KNOWING THIS FIRST, THAT THERE SHALL COME IN THE LAST DAYS SCOFFERS, WALKING AFTER THEIR OWN LUSTS," (II Peter 3:3).

Then he concluded by quoting these three verses: 'IN MY FATHER'S HOUSE ARE MANY MANSIONS: IF IT WERE NOT SO, I WOULD HAVE TOLD YOU. I GO TO PREPARE A PLACE FOR YOU,' (John 14:2). 'YE MEN OF GALILEE, WHY STAND YE GAZING UP INTO HEAVEN? THIS SAME JESUS WHICH IS TAKEN UP FROM YOU INTO HEAVEN, SHALL SO COME IN LIKE MANNER AS YOU SAW HIM GO INTO HEAVEN', (ACTS 1:11). 'FOR THE LORD HIMSELF WILL DESCEND FROM HEAVEN WITH A SHOUT, WITH THE VOICE OF THE ARC ANGEL, AND THE TRUMPET OF GOD; AND THE DEAD IN CHRIST SHALL RISE FIRST; THEN WE WHICH ARE ALIVE AND REMAIN SHALL BE CAUSGHT UP TOGETHER IN THE CLOUDS, TO MEET THE LORD IN THE AIR: AND SO SHALL WE EVER BE WITH THE LORD,' (I Thess. 4:16, 17).

My 16th article came from a church ID card. On it were listed many different scriptures: 'HE THAT IS JOINED TO THE LORD IS ONE SPIRIT,' (I Corinthians 6:17). One spirit means one person in God. And 'IF THE UNBELIEVING DEPART, LET HIM DEPART. A BROTHER OR A SISTER IS NOT UNDER BONDAGE IN SUCH CASES. BUT GOD HAS CALLED US TO PEACE', (I Corinthians 7:15). This means to let your unbelieving partner leave. It does not mean to swap mates. Or that you are now free to have group sex like a pack of dogs. When evil departs, blessings come and these gifts come in different distinctives and diversities of operations. 'FOR TO ONE IS GIVEN BY THE SPIRIT THE WORD OF WISDOM; TO ANOTHER THE WORD OF KNOWLEDGE BY THE SAME SPIRIT: TO ANOTHER FAITH BY THE SAME SPIRIT; TO ANOTHER THE GIFTS OF HEALING BY THE SAME SPIRIT; TO ANOTHER THE

WORKING OF MIRACLES; TO ANOTHER DIVERSE KINDS OF TONGUES; TO ANOTHER THE INTERPRETATION OF TONGUES', (I Corinthians 6-10).

So then you are not to regard anyone to a human point of view. 'HENCEFORTH WE KNOW NO MAN AFTER THE FLESH', (II Corinthians 5:16).

Then according to II Corinthians 6:12 in the amplified: 'THERE IS NO LACK OF ROOM FOR YOU IN OUR HEARTS, BUT YOU LACK ROOM IN YOUR OWN AFFECTIONS FOR US'. Never the less according to Malachi 3:1 and Luke 7:27 the Holy Spirit makes a way for me.

'NO MAN, WHEN HE HATH LIGHTED A CANDLE, COVERS IT WITH A VESSEL OR PUTS IT UNDER THE BED, BUT SETS IT UP ON A CANDLESTICK THAT THEY WHICH ENTER MAY SEE THE LIGHT', (Luke 8:16). In other words, we are to shine and be bold.

'WHY TEMPT YE GOD, TO PUT A YOKE UPON THE NECK OF THE DISCIPLES WHICH NEITHER OUR FATHERS NOR WE WERE ABLE TO BEAR?' (Acts 15:10). Do not ever test God or His people about anything.

'I EXHORT THEREFORE, THAT, FIRST OF ALL, SUPPLICATIONS, PRAYERS, INTERCESSIONS AND GIVING OF THANKS BE MADE FOR ALL MEN', (I Timothy 2:1). After that you can pray some more for what you want. But remember to pray for other men's salvation first (II Timothy 2:4). Always pray more like this: 'I DESIRE THAT EVERY MAN PRAY EVERYWHERE BY LIFTING UP HOLY HANDS, WITHOUT WRATH OR DOUBTING', (I Timothy 2:8). **We also knew the value of praying God's word out loud and in tongues as we did every week in our Saturday Half–Day Pentecostal Prayer Meeting.**

'After I got home I watched Andrew Womack on Christian TV teaching about God's will. He mentioned that Elijah was fed by ravens. Then this revelation hit me and I remembered that ravens are an unclean bird. In this modern age of Christian Zionist's were there is much teaching about the law of Moses and Jewish tradition complete with prayer shawls and tzitzits, I can see right away where any Jew would have at least questioned God about being fed by Ravens, an unclean bird. Actually, many would have spent time arguing with God about this. So that's the reason why more doesn't get done for God. Too much arguing with the Master negates the Master's order and also depresses faith in the sovereignty of God, Who as Sovereign Lord can command whatever He wills. Elijah got blessed with provision to do the will of God and got up and went instead of wasting time arguing and questioning the Master. This is a good lesson for us all.

On the back side of this card is a scripture that says to use what you have learned, so let's now look at it: 'HOLD FAST THE FORM OF SOUND WORDS, WHICH YOU HAVE HEARD OF ME IN FAITH AND LOVE WHICH IS IN CHRIST JESUS', (II Timothy 1:13). Another Bible verse says: 'AND DAILY IN THE TEMPLE, AND IN EVERY HOUSE, THEY CEASED NOT TO TEACH AND PREACH JESUS CHRIST', (Acts 5:42). So they didn't quit, they kept at it as another scripture says: 'NOT SLOTHFUL IN BUSINESS; FERVENT IN SPIRIT, SERVING THE LORD. REJOICEING IN HOPE; PATIENT IN TRIBULATION; CONTINUING INSTANT IN PRAYER,' (Romans 12:11 & 12).

Obviously this passage in Romans goes on from here to the distributing to the necessity of the saints but the pastor did not want us to equate saints with bums and make ourselves busy by serving them.

Big Al and I were the main ones that distributed free fresh food to the saints (members of our fellowship). When we had an abundance of free food, Christians in the fellowship also distributed free food while witnessing at the airport, beach or elsewhere around Southern California. But we did not serve free food to the homeless under bridges or sleeping in boxcars. And certainly not to drunken stumble bums who had no respect for themselves, us or God.

He ended his sermon that day by quoting from 2 kings 2:20, about the prophet Elisha healing the waters, using the anointing to do for the people what they could not do for themselves.

My 17th article on a piece of scrap paper brought out a few points about 'seed faith' that were unknown at that time. Our pastor, Lyle Steenis. Had been a 'dirt farmer' in Kansas. He said that a farmer always selects the best seed to plant a crop. This is very important as not all Christian ministers are distributing for planting the very best seed. Some of their seed is contaminated by the doctrines of demons, false teachings, money making scams, denominational delusions, racial prejudice and un-American political bias and false theologies learned in Godless seminaries.

Plus even the good seed fails to produce a harvest when it is not mixed with faith. The faith of farmers includes care for the plant as it grows to maturity. Christians call that discipleship. Your care also shows your expectancy. As Galatians 6:9 says; 'LET US NOT BE WEARY IN WELL DOING, FOR IN DUE SEASON, WE SHALL REAP, IF WE FAINT NOT'.

Saint Paul mentioned in one of his missionary journeys: 'I PLANTED, APOLLOS WATERED; BUT GOD GAVE THE INCREASE', (I Corinthians 3:6).

It is important to note that God gave the increase. And this increase was of the same kind, not multiples of junk. We need patience to wait on the harvest. Evangelism breaks up the sods so that the hearts will take the good seed into them. Here intercessory prayer for souls is needed.

Here he begins to quote scriptures again: 'YE SHALLL RECEIVE POWER AFTER THAT THE HOLY GHOST IS COME UPON YOU AND YOU SHALL BE WITNESSES UNTO ME BOTH IN JERUSALEM AND IN ALL JUDEA, AND IN SAMARIA, AND UNTO THE UTTERMOST PART OF THE EARTH,' (Acts 1:8). 'THEREFORE MY BELOVED BRETHREN, BE YE STEADFAST, UNMOVABLE, ALWAYS ABOUNDING IN THE WORK OF THE LORD, FOR AS MUCH AS YE KNOW THAT YOUR LABOR IS NOT IN VAIN IN THE LORD', (Corinthians 15:58). 'VERILY, I SAY UNTO YOU, EXCEPT A CORN OF WHEAT FALL INTO THE GROUND AND DIE, IT ABIDES ALONE: BUT IF IT DIES, IT BRINGS FORTH MUCH FRUIT', (John 12:24).

Then from here several points are made. **You must have the Holy Ghost baptism in order to have the best seed and to labor responsibly for the Master**. Unless you are sacrificial, you will not bear much fruit. Let me enlarge that thought practically. You probably know that farmers get up very early. I remember when we used to have a cow that someone in the family, usually me had to get up about 4.00 am in order to milk it. Of course this detracts from your school time and other obligations your days require. We never thought it was sacrificial, but it was. Nevertheless we were healthy and well fed. Not everything growed right in the dust storms but we survived.

I still remember my parents exercising the authority of the believer before such was even popular. My dad would command a black dust cloud to become rain and it did. I never thought much of it, until we saw it rain right up to our fence and no further. Then my parents got scared as they realized that we were living only because God sustained us. And they felt that that was putting too much pressure on God. So we made plans to leave for California.

Before we review more, I'll share this revelation I just received this morning while getting ready for church. This revelation was because the Holy Spirit quickened a Bible verse to me that says: 'HE (JESUS, THE SON OF GOD) WAS MANIFESTED THAT HE MIGHT DESTROY THE WORKS OF THE DEVIL', (I John 3:8), but before that in that same verse it said that; 'HE THAT COMMITS SIN IS OF THE DEVIL'.

Evangelical Christians seize on this personal sin issue and miss the manifestation to destroy the works of the devil. Actually such sounds too revolutionary. It's better to be concerned about personal sins than the need of having to overthrow by destruction evil social structures, policies, institutions and governments even though a verse does say that the government shall be upon his shoulders.

In fact, the devil uses the scripture that says if I regard iniquity in my heart the Lord will not hear me. He uses this to keep Christians from praying against evil. Whereas Sampson, one of the heroes of the faith, who probably had more personal sins than any of us still prayed a questionable prayer of vengeance and still got God to help him accomplish his destiny by killing the Philistines who occupied Israel.

Yesterday as I finished my notes for that day there was a large crowd of protestors outside the library blocking the street. They were mostly deceived women protesting in favor of abortion. **Now I know firsthand that I can stop abortion just by fasting and praying against it regardless of my personal holiness. I prayed and fasted for Trump to win and he did. So I have a weapon that works and that I intend to use.**

My notes from yesterday mention that drought is the great destroyer. Whereas, **God sends the rain to the just and unjust. This idea that you must be just and lily white, drug free, incarceration free, and a tithe paying church member in order to get God's attention is false doctrine.**

God still rebukes the devourer according to his sovereign will not your personal holiness. But personal holiness is very good. The Bible does say that without holiness no man shall see the Lord. But it does not say that without holiness no man can please the Lord. If Adam and Eve walking naked in the Garden of Eden with God at the end of the day pleased God then I can too by what I do to obey Him.

When we began this article we realized upfront that: 'HE THAT SOWS BOUNTIFULLY SHALL ALSO REAP BOUNTIFULLY,' (II Corinthians 9:6). Here the amount sown makes the difference, not the quality of the seed. But the quanity of the crop is determined by the seed.

Pests do not bother the crops of the believing farmer. So then believing God has its rewards as there are no accidents with God. 'THEY WHO SOW IN TEARS SHALL REAP IN JOY AND SINGING,' (Psalm 126:5). 'HE THAT GOES FORTH WEEPING, BEARING PRECIOUS SEED, SHALL DOUBTLESS COME AGAIN WITH REJOICING, BEARING HIS SHEAVES WITH HIM', (Psalm 126:6).

After these few words of wisdom we move on to ***My 18th article*** Saint Paul who wrote most of this only wanted to finish his course with joy.

He didn't brag about the churches he had established, but about his trails. His life was not dear to him. He denied himself for the ministry. 'BUT NONE OF THESE THINGS MOVE ME, NEITHER COUNT I MY LIFE DEAR UNTO MYSELF, SO THAT I MIGHT FINISH MY COURSE WITH JOY AND THE MINISTRY WHICH I RECEIVED OF THE LORD JESUS, TO TESTIFY THE GOSPEL OF THE GRACE OF GOD', (Acts 20:24). Saint Paul also describes his many trails for the gospel's sake in II Corinthians 11:23-30. 'ARE THEY MINISTERS OF CHRIST? (I SPEAK AS A FOOL) I AM MORE, IN LABORS MORE ABUNDANT, IN STRIPES ABOVE MEASURE, IN PRISONS MORE FREQUENT, IN DEATHS MORE OFTEN. OF THE JEWS FIVE TIMES RECEIVED I FORTY STRIPES SAVE ONE. THRICE WAS I BEATEN WITH RODS, ONCE I WAS STONED, THRICE I SUFFERED SHIPWRECK, A NIGHT AND A DAY IN THE DEEP. IN JOURNEYINGS OFTEN, IN PERILS OF WATERS, IN PERILS OF ROBBERS, IN PERILS OF MY OWN COUNTRYMEN, IN PERILS OF WATERS, IN PERILS IN THE CITY, IN PERILS IN THE WILDERNESS, IN PERILS, IN THE SEA, IN PERILS AMONG FALSE BRETHREN. IN WEARINESS AND PAINFULNESS, IN WATCHING OFTEN, IN HUNGER AND THIRST, IN FASTINGS OFTEN, IN COLD AND NAKEDNESS. BESIDES THOSE THINGS THAT ARE WITHOUT, THAT WHICH COMES UPON ME DAILY, THE CARE OF ALL THE CHURCHES. WHO IS WEAK, AND AM I NOT WEAK? WHO IS OFFENDED, AND I BURN NOT? IF I MUST NEEDS GLORY, I WILL GLORY OF THESE THINGS WHICH CONCERN MINE INFIRMITIES'.

This is a very unusual series of statements to modern American Christians, who do not want to believe that at times we must suffer infirmity, lack of adequate funds, or even these above listed deficits in order to accomplish the ministry God has called us to. You theologians take note that the pre-tribulation rapture fits in here somewhere too. Moreover many modern Christians like to boast about the years of good health they have had and about them being debt free and even able to fly about in their own jets. **But with no Pre-Tribulation Rapture there will also be 'A Great Falling Away'.**

I guess that it's good to have stuff, but when you work for the Sovereign Lord, you take whatever he gives. And you certainly don't complain and grip and call it prayer. I am not saying to lay down and accept whatever comes.

But if you want to change your circumstances for the better exercise your faith and stop begging God's people to do for you what you refuse to do for yourself. Remember that I was once a professional beggar for over five years, so I know begging when I see it under the guise of prayer.

There has been much talk recently about 'waiting on the Lord'. As if such was due to a season in time in the Father's own power. For your consideration, may I submit to you Ecclesiastes 10:18: 'BY MUCH SLOTHFULNESS THE BUILDING DECAYETH; AND THROUGH IDLENESS OF THE HANDS THE HOUSE DROPPETH THROUGH'. If you want something, ask. Remember: 'YOU RECEIVE NOT, BECAUSE YOU ASK NOT', (1 John 5:12).

There is another exhortation that I need to give here. This comes from I Chronicles 25:2: 'AND HE DID THAT WHICH WAS RIGHT IN THE SIGHT OF THE LORD, BUT NOT WITH A PERFECT HEART'. Just because you are doing God's will outwardly, does not mean that you are inwardly perfect and beyond any correction.

MY 19th article concerns the peril of unsettledness. 'IF YOU CONTINUE IN THE FAITH GROUNDED AND SETTLED, AND BE NOT MOVED AWAY FROM THE HOPE OF THE GOSPEL, WHICH WAS PREACHED TO EVERY CREATURE WHICH IS UNDER HEAVEN: WHEREOF I PAUL AM MADE A MINISTER', (Colossians 1:23). Be well grounded, settled and steadfast. Don't let outside circumstances move you.

'BUT NONE OF THESE THINGS MOVE ME; NEITHER DO I ESTEEM MY LIFE DEAR TO MYSELF, IF ONLY I MAY FINISH MY COURSE WITH JOY AND THE MINISTRY WHICH I HAVE OBTAINED FROM THE LORD JESUS, FAITHFULLY TO ATTEST TO THE GOOD NEWS OF GOD'S GRACE', (Acts 20:24). AND DON'T WASTE TIME FOCUSING ON INWARD CONFLICTS OF WHAT'S GOOD OR EVIL OR WHAT YOU CAN AFFORD OR NOT OR PERSONAL DEFICIT PROBLEMS BEYOND YOUR ABILITY TO SOLVE'.

'THEREFORE, MY BELOVED BRETHREN BE YE STEADFAST, UNMOVABLE, ALWAYS ABOUNDING IN THE WORK OF THE LORD, FOR AS MUCH AS YE KNOW THAT YOUR LABOR IS NOT IN VAIN IN THE LORD', (I Corinthians 15:58). You must always keep busy serving the Lord, or else you will be using your free time for introspection and the personal evaluation of personal qualities that are only improved by use.

Actually, this presents the personal equation for happiness: If you will deny yourself and keep always abounding in the work of the Lord then you will finish your course with joy and find everlasting happiness. By doing this now you will always abide in the will of God here. Otherwise you'll be wavering like a wave of the sea according to James 1:6. And will become a doubleminded man according to James 1:8 that cannot please God. Count the cost of building before laying a foundation. Then run that ye might obtain. 'HAPPY ARE THEY WHICH ENDURE', (James 5:11).

After this I retrieved ***My Article 20*** from my notes. And about this time after church service, once each month I went to visit Kathryn Khulman ministering in the Shrine Auditorium in downtown LA. She said this once and I wrote it down for you: **'many church members who are Christians have given their souls to Jesus but have not yet dedicated their bodies to the Lord'. 'You need the baptism of the Holy Ghost to empower the use of your body for the Lord'.**

These notes concern presenting your body as a living sacrifice and make no reservation for the flesh to fulfill the lusts thereof. Don't join your body with a harlot, since your body is the temple of the Holy Ghost, the Spirit of God.

So many modern Christians feel that it would have been much easier to serve God in ancient times. However in the time of Paul, most young men were introduced to sex by Temple prostitutes, especially those who worshipped Diana the goddess of the Ephesians.

Back then having sex was considered a divine act or an act of devotion to some deity. After all, sex was supposedly created by the gods for men, so men were expected to enjoy it even at the expense of others. Thus there was no sexual exploitation of others either women or children or even animals back then.

But today sex is considered appropriate only after marriage in order to be approved by the True God. One cannot be filled with the Holy Ghost and still be having sex with prostitutes. There are other pursuits motivated by being filled with the Holy Ghost like spreading the gospel that are more important than having sex.

My Article 21 taken from my notes on the back of an offering envelope says: 'Don't be fearful of a storm if you're in a big ship with Jesus'. This problem is usually considered 'a lack of faith'. Even Jesus rebuked them for having no faith to recognize Who He (Jesus) was. So this faith thing was not just an impersonal force. Your faith in Jesus can overcome the storm and lead you into spiritual growth. But if your faith is not in Jesus alone it is ineffectual. So faith in your faith or some other thing does not fix your need.

This is just like 'the message of the cross'. It is not faith in the wooden beam that makes up the cross but faith that the sacrifice of Jesus on the cross was solely sufficient for your salvation and reconciliation to God.

Prayer also leads you into spiritual growth. But only the right kind of prayer: in Jesus name, secret prayer, without vain repetitions, but with worship and adoration, thanksgiving, and then clear requests.

Then it's on you to trust God. Recognize Him first. Then get the bad out of your life, since this can hold up your prayers from getting answered. Remember that your 'home walk' is very important. And prayer is very important too for you must seek God's face every day. In order to do this properly, you must get alone with Jesus every day. Let's look at how Jesus prayed in Luke 6:12. He went up a mountain to a solitary place and prayed all night before he made any important decisions. But after he had prayed, He did not hesitate to move out at once to obey God's will. He did not give the decision to move or not to a committee. He took decision making power upon himself.

It's probably good to let others put their 'two senses in' but not if it just serves to delay the action needed. On the other hand it's not good to get so busy serving God that you miss having adequate prayer time. Pray always with perseverance and all supplication for all saints. The prophet Daniel did this three times a day. Besides the times of prayer, there is also the proper method: Both in the Spirit and with the understanding also. Then there is also perseverance: 'THE EFFECTUAL FERVENT PRAYER OF A RIGHTEOUS MAN AVAILETH MUCH', (James 5:16). Praying, especially the habit of praying every day makes one into a spiritual person. And God tends to answer the prayers of such a spiritual person. Prayer keeps the church alive and revival depends upon the prayers of a living body of Christ (church). **Confusion comes into the camp when there is no joy from winning souls.** Consequently, people fail to pray and to obey and they don't stay up to date with God. They are not ready. 'If a man won't preach God will use donkeys and roosters.'

We must have reality in order to fulfill and fully give what God desires in Acts 3:6. In this Bible verse there is too much emphasis on not having silver or gold and not enough emphasis on having the power of God personally resident in you to do the mighty acts of God required daily. This brings out what Pastor Lyle Steenis called what's wrong with the church. Lack of prayer (Isaiah 64:7): 'THERE IS NONE THAT CALLETH UPON THY NAME'. 'NOR ANY THAT STIRS HIMSELF UP TO TAKE HOLD OF THEE'.

This is due to judgment, Luke warmness and the sins of unbelief which are still common today.

After he mentioned that Job's friends had nothing to offer, that's why they looked at Job speechless for seven days (Job 2:12 & 13). Then he proceeded to list the many shortcomings of every Christian and exhortations concerning them. Example: life is not what happens to you but the way you take it. Everyone has trouble and reversals in life. Even Job (God's blessed) lost a great deal. But God restored everything that the devil stole. What Job lost, God made up, until Job was rich again.

This shows that it is the will of God for his servants to be on top. If you serve God, 'He will open up the windows of heaven on you'. You just walk by faith but God answers according to his sovereign will. In other words this popular 'seed faith' teaching is not entirely true. If as a farmer you sow tomatoes, when the crop matures you will get tomatoes not corn or some other crop. If you sow money into a ministry you may get back good health which spares you medical bills. If you sow money does not mean that all God can give you back is more money. You don't give money to get rich in God's economy. You get rich by giving yourself first then all you have.

We must remember that there are no accidents in the Christian life. God does permit the devil to bring evil to everyone, especially the Christian in order to build the Christian up. You cannot become overcomers unless you have something to overcome. And unless you are overcomers you cannot inherit the kingdom of God. Don't be a coward, face up to the things of life. Remember to become fine gold, you must be tried in the fire. Job's friends didn't know how to help him, but right away they concentrated on Job's personal attributes as if he himself caused his problems. Today this is called: 'Blaming the victim'.

But we can be and we are 'MORE THAN CONQUERORS THROUGH HIM WHO LOVES US', (Romans 8:37).

My Article 22 concerns certain raps. Paul's rap began like this in Acts 17:16-21:'NOW WHILE PAUL WAITED FOR THEM AT ATHENS, HIS SPIRIT WAS STIRRED IN HIM WHEN HE SAW THE CITY WHOLLY GIVEN TO IDOLATRY. THEREFORE DISPUTED HE IN THE SYNAGOGUE WITH THE JEWS AND WITH THE DEVOUT PERSONS, AND IN THE MARKET DAILY WITH THEM THAT MET WITH HIM. AND CERTAIN PHILOSOPHERS OF THE EPICUREANS, AND THE STOICS, ENCOUNTERED HIM. AND SOME SAID, WHAT WILL THIS BABBLER SAY? OTHERS SAID HE SEEMETH TO BE A SETTER

FORTH OF STRANGE GODS: BECAUSE HE PREACHED UNTO THEM JESUS AND THE RESURRECTION. AND THEY TOOK HIM, AND BOUGHT HIM UNTO AREOPAGUS SAYING MAY WE KNOW WHAT THIS NEW DOCTRINE, WHEREOF THAT SPEAKEST IS? FOR THOU BRINGEST CERTAIN STRANGE THINGS TO OUR EARS WE WOULD KNOW THEREFORE WHAT THESE STRANGE THINGS MEAN. (FOR ALL THE ATHENIANS AND STRANGERS WHICH WERE THERE SPENT THEIR TIME IN NOTHING ELSE, BUT EITHER TO TELL OR HEAR SOME NEW THING).

Here we see clearly that Paul's rap was only about the Lord Jesus and his resurrection. The only knowledge needed for salvation. As it is written 'THAT IF THOU SHALT CONFESS WITH THY MOUTH THE LORD JESUS, AND SHALL BELIEVE IN THINE HEART THAT GOD HAS RAISED HIM FROM THE DEAD, THOU SHALT BE SAVED,' (Romans 10:9).

Other ministers had more inclusive raps too. Noah, for example was a preacher of righteousness. And Moses preached deliverance for Israel but judgment for Egypt. The truth that Noah preached provoked rain. Likewise the truth that Moses preached caused death of the first born Egyptian. So when results come because of the word preached, it's not just another rap or philosophy of no consequence. But if it's the word of God – Watch Out!

My 23rd article comes from notes on an offering envelope entitled: how to keep from being unfruitful. First verses are quoted by Rev. Steenis from I Peter 1:5-11 'WHO ARE KEPT BY THE POWER OF GOD THROUGH FAITH UNTO SALVATION READY TO BE REVEALED IN THE LAST TIME. WHEREIN YE GREATLY REJOICE, THOUGH NOW FOR A SEASON, IF NEED BE, YE ARE IN EVIDENCE IN HEAVINESS THROUGH MANIFOLD TEMPTATIONS. THAT THE TRAIL OF YOUR FAITH, BEING MUCH MORE PRECIOUS THAN GOLD THAT PERISHES, THOUGH IT BE TRIED WITH FIRE, MIGHT BE FOUND UNTO PRAISE HONOR AND GLORY AT THE APPEARING OF JESUS CHRIST. WHOM HAVING NOT SEEN, YE LOVE, IN WHOM THOU NOW YOU SEE HIM NOT, YET BELIEVING YE REJOICE WITH JOY UNSPEAKABLE AND FULL OF GLORY. RECEIVING THE END OF YOUR FAITH, EVEN THE SALVATION OF YOUR SOULS. OF WHICH SALVATION THE PROPHETS HAVE INQUIRED AND SEARCHED DILIGENTLY, WHO PROPHESIED OF THE GRACE THAT SHOULD COME UNTO YOU. SEARCHING WHAT, OR WHAT MANNER OF TIME THE SPIRIT OF CHRIST

WHICH WAS IN THEM DID SIGNIFY, WHEN HE TESTIFIED BEFOREHAND THE SUFFERING OF CHRIST AND THE GLORY THAT SHOULD FOLLOW.'

From these verses he singled out a few words that he concentrated on: Faith – 'WITHOUT FAITH IT IS IMPOSSIBLE TO PLEASE GOD', (Hebrews 11:1). Faith is needed to get saved and to get the Holy Ghost. Virtue - indicates holiness without which no man shall see God. And enables you to see every wart and sin that does so easily beset you. Knowledge – of his love and of God's judgments. Temperance – self-control, of eating and periods of rest, all things are lawful for me but not all things edify. Let your moderation be known unto all men. Not all things are expedient. Don't be brought into bondage. Patience - in your patience possess your souls. Godliness – be like God. Brotherly love – I Corinthians 13, 'IF YOU LOVE NOT YOUR BROTHER WHOM YOU HAVE SEEN, HOW CAN YOU LOVE GOD WHOM YOU HAVE NOT SEEN? Diligently apply yourself to these things and you shall never fall.

On that same offering envelope notes describe why Israel failed to conquer: 'AND THE LORD SAID UNTO JOSHUA, GET THEE UP: WHEREFORE LIEST THOU THUS UPON THY FACE? ISRAEL HAS SINNED AND THEY HAVE ALSO TRANSGRESSED MY COVENANT WHICH I COMMANDED THEM: FOR THEY HAVE USED IT OF THE ACCURSED THING, AND HAVE ALSO SOLD, AND HAVE DISSEMBLED ALSO, AND HAVE PUT IT EVEN AMONG THEIR OWN STUFF,' (Joshua 7:10, 11).

God won't save the world until you let him work in you. So you must take up your cross to do likewise and you need to get a burden. Don't be a law to yourself. God promised victory at Jericho and they got it. You can keep moving because blessing doeth good like a medicine. The sin of overconfidence is not faith based upon God's word but overconfidence in your own achievement. This is why Israel was defeated at Ai (Joshua 7:3, 4). By failing to keep the love of God in their heart therefore Israel coveted the spoils. And Achkan did not obey and disobedience is like witchcraft.

In revival must be stripped down for the race. Cannot be encumbered with a lot of junk. And must lay aside every weight and the sin which does so easily beset you. Achkan weighted down the people of God therefore he was put out of the camp. As a little leaven eleventh the whole lump.

This is very important. Once you focus on revival, it must be your main concern in life. Revival represents your obedience to the great commission. And if you love Jesus, you must do this for him as he has commanded.

Our 24th article comes from an undated copy of Youth Aflame about counterfeit conversions and carnal Christians which basically says what we have already declared. Their mailing address was Youth Aflame, P.O. Box 4044, Burbank, CA 91503.

Our 25th article is from notes written on an addition of HI CALL dated March 14, 1971. It is about a man who changed the frontier – the circuit riding preacher, Peter Cartwright. He was cut from the same mold as other frontiersman: rough, unpolished, strong, bold and not afraid of anyone – rowdies, woodsman, mountain men, church officials or even the devil himself. Peter carried a gun and used it if necessary. He alone evangelized much of the West. **He was the man that served God in his generation.**

Rev. Lyle Steenis preached words similar to this article he said that the Holy Ghost comes with unity and that we must be united to be militant. There is no need for any policed communion if we all have the Holy Ghost. If we are led by the Spirit, we must also have the Spirit and be under a spiritual shepherd. To avoid tragedies we must also have on the whole armor of God. And in order to win souls, we must see spiritual results. Don't be among those who cut up the church like was done in II Chronicles 28:24. The house of God and God's ministers must both be pure in order for revival to happen. Holy things must also be put in order as it is written in the word of God. And in every church the alters must be used for what they are meant for.

Always remember this: 'WHEN I SAY UNTO THE WICKED, OH WICKED MAN THOU SHALT SURELY DIE; IF YOU DO NOT SPEAK TO WARN THE WICKED MAN THOU SHALT SURELY DIE; IF YOU DO NOT SPEAK TO WARN THE WICKED FROM HIS WAY, HE SHALL SURELY DIE IN HIS INIQUITY BUT HIS BLOOD WILL I REQUIRE AT YOUR HAND,' (Ezekiel 33:8).

There is another major reason why revival does not come. Let's look at II Chronicles 7:14 'IF MY PEOPLE, WHO ARE CALLED BY MY NAME, SHALL HUMBLE THEMSELVES AND PRAY, AND SEEK MY FACE AND *TURN FROM THEIR WICKED WAYS*: THEN I WILL HEAR FROM HEAVEN, AND WILL FORGIVE THEIR SIN, AND WILL HEAL THEIR LAND'. **There can be no revival without personal repentance. Don't let your badness hold up God's goodness.**

A sure way to win souls is to weep before the Lord for them. I remember how that me and my wife were not able to have natural children of our own, so we wept for God to give us you and this revival and he did so, praise God! (Sayings of Pastor Steenis).

Our 26th article comes from a sermon outline about church bones. This vision is from the valley of dry bones, recorded in the book of Ezekiel. The dry bones represent the whole house of Israel so then **this replacement theology; that the church has replaced Israel is false.** For this prophecy speaks of a time when God's people: The Jews will be regathered from around the world and experience both physical and spiritual restoration to the Land of Israel.

Meanwhile there are at least five types of bones in the modern church. First comes the wish bones. Always wishing for something better that they don't have to work for. Then there are the funny bones always getting hurt like the crazy bone of your elbow. So these bones are very touchy and when hit have an electric pain. After these come the tail bones who are always behind in their donations and in their work for the Lord. Finely come the back bones which are the spiritual life that supports the church. These naughty bones have one thing in common: they lack the breath of God in them, so they are unconverted, so we need revival.

Let's stand and say together: 'OH YE DRY BONES HEAR THE WORD OF THE LORD', (Ezekiel 37:4). This is important as it is our group prophecy to the dry bones of America and the world who need God. This is why we must confess him before men.

Our 27th article is from another sermon outline about three kinds of medicine in the word of God. First comes preventive medicine: 'THY WORD HAVE I HIDDEN IN MY HEART, THAT I MIGHT NOT SIN AGAINST THEE', (Psalm 119:11).

Next comes curative medicine. This world is sin sick and since 'THE WAGES OF SIN IS DEATH', (Romans 6:23). Only God's cure will bring life. Through faith in the Lord Jesus Christ, the sinner is born again or given new life. This comes through God's word as Peter records in I Peter 1:2, 3.

And finally there is palliative medicine. 'THE WORD IS MY COMFORT IN MY AFFLICTION', (Psalm 119: 49, 50).

Our 28th article comes from an offering envelope on which three lines of a poem are recorded. It says: Now I'm living in a new creation. Now I'm drinking from the well of salvation. Now there is no condemnation, praise God, praise God! So apparently some of these young people that became Jesus people also received gifts and talents and blessings from God.

Our 29th article also comes from a sermon outline about taking up the cross. Our cross is something we assume voluntarily after that we have denied ourselves. Our cross is not imposed upon us by predestination, nor is it a personal trial. It is just part of the Christian compact of salvation for eternal life.

Our 30th article is also a sermon outline from that same paper. On the back it sadys shirker or worker. Moses had called for help in building the tabernacle and the people brought more than enough for the work. So then in this case the zeal of the workers far surpassed the laziness of the 'shirkers'.

After we got home we watched Rick Renner on Christian TV, he was talking about being touched by pagan gods before Christians got touched by the Holy Spirit in Corinth. In fact there's already a Greek word for this: Charis. From which we get charismatic. In this present era of unbelief called the post Christian era, many historians are not able to recognize **that Alexander the Great's many conquests was due to his possession by the pagan Greek false god Minerva, that female demon (world ruler) who had snakes for hair. All snakes have mouths that devour. So Alexander the Great was able to devour every nation and kingdom in the known world in his day.** At his end it is said that he cried because there were no more worlds to conquer.

This revelation about the past came to me on July 11, 2018. The rest below about the future came on July 16, 2018.

Most educated historians are aware of the Roman god of war called Mars. What that strong world ruler demon was able to accomplish through the Roman Empire should be self-evident. But for those who may question this: let's look to Mars the planet. Those who study planets say that Mars has no atmosphere. In that case Mars was either hit by an asteroid which exploded its atmosphere away or a demonic explosion destroyed the planet. There is no evidence of any impact, so obviously such was the result of 'THE DEVIL AND HIS DEMONS HAVE ONLY COME TO KILL, ROB AND DESTROY', (John 10:10). Yes, this is a revelation about the future that will be proven to be true someday.

Our 31st article comes from notes of exhortation on an offering envelope. The first exhortation says: You are the light, let the truth I've placed within you go forth to glory so you can be faithful to the crown of life. The second exhortation says: the person that is aware is responsible. The third exhortation says that: a trail is meant to establish, strengthen, and settle you after suffering, (I Peter 5:10). The fourth exhortation says: 'ALL THAT LIVE GODLY IN CHRIST JESUS SHALL SUFFER PERSECUTION', (II Timothy 3:12). Our fifth exhortation says that: 'I TRAVAIL IN BIRTH PAINS AGAIN FOR YOU UNTIL CHRIST BE FORMED IN YOU', (Galatians 4:19). Our sixth exhortation says 'BE THOU FAITHFUL UNTO DEATH AND I WILL GIVE YOU THE CROWN OF LIFE', (Revelation 2:10). Our seventh exhortation says 'FEAR NOTHING OF THESE THINGS THAT THOU SHALT SUFFER', (Revelation 2:10). Our eight exhortation says: to be faithful in Christian living is being faithful in the little things. Our ninth exhortation says to hold fast and let no one deprive you of you crown. Our tenth exhortation says that 'THE UNFAITHFUL ARE LIKE A BROKEN TOOTH OR A FOOT OUT OF JOINT', (Psalm 25:11).

There are excuses of the unfaithful which can be cured by the need of going to church, and 'THE ZEAL OF THINE HOUSE HATH EATEN ME UP', John and we must be faithful in Christian service. When David was inactive, he sinned. Likewise when John the Baptist doubted Jesus as Messiah he went to prison, a place of inactivity. **We must not be inactive if we're going to take dominion.**

We need to bear our cross too. This Jesus movement is not a one man show. Here the Holy Ghost is in control. He organizes. We must let the revival go according to God's originality, plan and purpose. To do this effectively we must pray in tongues and consecrate ourselves, live out our dreams as God's people, make our lives a witness and witness to others.

We also need to be laborers in God's vineyard by doing these things. Thus we will become faithful laborers in God's vineyard. And faithful men of good report. By so doing we can also bless the church. And we shall receive the reward for faithfulness. Every one of us wants to hear those words that say 'WELL DONE THOU GOOD AND FAITHFUL SERVANT, ENTER THOU INTO THE JOY OF THE LORD', (Matthew 25:21).

Our 32nd article is a piece of notebook paper on which are written a few more exhortations for a sermon. They include: 1. Take the purpose of Daniel. Daniel 1:8: 'BUT DANIEL PURPOSED IN HIS HEART THAT HE WOULD NOT DEFILE HIMSELF BY EATING OF THE KING'S MEAT NOR DRINKING THE KING'S WINE'. 2. Take the posture of Paul: I Corinthians 16:13: 'WATCH YE, STAND FAST IN THE FAITH, QUIT YOU LIKE MEN, BE STRONG'. And 3. Take the provision of Christ: Philippians 4:13: 'I CAN DO ALL THINGS THROUGH CHRIST WHO STRENGTHENS ME'.

On that same paper he gave another exhortation about your sin finding you out. This comes from Joshua 7:20-25: 'AND ACHAN ANSWERED JOSHUA, AND SAID, INDEED I HAVE SINNED AGAINST THE LORD GOD OF ISRAEL, AND THUS AND THUS HAVE I DONE. WHEN I SAW AMONG THE SPOILS A GOODLY BABYLONIAN GARMENT, AND TWO HUNDRED SHECKLES OF SILVER, AND

A WEDGE OF GOLD OF FIFTY SHECKLES WEIGHT, THEN I COVETED THEM AND TOOK THEM, AND BEHOLD THEY ARE HID IN THE EARTH IN THE MIDST OF MY TENT, AND THE SILVER UNDER IT. SO JOSHUA SENT MESSENGERS AND THEY RAN UNTO THE TENT, AND BEHOLD, IT WAS HID IN HIS TENT, AND THE SILVER UNDER IT. AND THEY TOOK THEM OUT OF THE MIDST OF THE TENT, AND BOUGHT THEM UNTO JOSHUA, AND UNTO, ALL THE CHILDREN OF ISRAEL, AND LAID THEM OUT BEFORE THE LORD.

AND JOSHUA, AND ALL ISRAEL WITH HIM, TOOK ACHAN THE SON OF ZERAH, AND THE SILVER, AND THE GARMENT, AND THE WEDGE OF GOLD, AND HIS SONS, AND HIS DAUGHTERS, AND HIS OXEN, AND HIS ASSES, AND HIS SHEEP, AND HIS TENT, AND ALL THAT HE HAD: AND THEY BROUGHT THEM UNTO THE VALLEY OF ACHOR. AND JOSHUA SAID, WHY HAST THOU TROUBLED US? THE LORD SHALL TROUBLE THEE. AND ALL ISRAEL STONED HIM WITH STONES, AND BURNED THEM WITH FIRE, AFTER THEY HAD STONED THEM WITH STONES. AND THEY RAISED OVER HIM A GREAT HEAP OF STONES UNTO THIS DAY. SO THE LORD TURNED FROM THE FIERCNESS OF HIS ANGER. WHEREFORE THE NAME OF THAT PLACE WAS CALLED, THE VALLEY OF ACHOR, UNTO THIS DAY'.

Then on the same paper he said to seek to be holy and useful for Jesus, seek not to pursue happiness. Then he made three more points: 1. Wound of contrition needed to become successful Christian: must have been afflicted with the knowledge that you were an undone sinner. Your sins killed Christ and you must feel this wound in order to love Jesus. 2. Wound of compassion needed for burden to help others. Christ wants us to suffer for them. He wants to love through us. 'WHO IS WEAK AND I AM NOT WEAK', (II Corinthians 11:29). Paul rejoiced in his suffering to fill up what was lacking in the suffering of others. 3. Wounded with desire for God. The person who has the most of God is the one seeking more. We don't want to hear messages of us dying for him, but him dying for us. We must suffer with Jesus to bring others to God and we must deny ourselves and bear his reproach too. **Obey whatever God says,** whether you understand it or not. Or else God may send some kind of judgment. God wants Christians to obey him. You know why so many Christians do not have the baptism in the Holy Ghost and speak with tongues simply because **'THE HOLY GHOST IS GIVEN TO THOSE WHO OBEY HIM', (Acts 5:32).**

Sometimes persecution also results from failure to obey. One time a group of Christians was told by God to move to greener pastures. They failed to do so. And because they disobeyed they lost their jobs and their houses were taken from them. In other words they were persecuted because of disobedience. Sampson lost the Spirit of God to do mighty deeds when his hair was cut, not because of his personal sins. So it's very important to obey your vows, especially vows to God. Remember that God said also that His Spirit would not always strive with man, (Genesis 6:3). So when you're Spirit filled and moving on in God to do his will, don't do anything to jeopardize that nor fail to obey Him.

When you come to the end of your horded resources then the giving of God has just begun. When I am weak, then am I strong. His strength is made perfect in our weakness. So then, God is glorified in our lack.

I see two final exhortations given in this article by Pastor Lyle Steenis many years ago and they are really important to this new move of God: 1. TRUE REVIVAL RESULTS FROM AND DEPENDS UPON PRAYER IN THE SPIRIT IN OTHER TONGUES. AND 2. THERE IS A TIME OF ABOUT FIFTY YEARS FOR A NEW MOVE OF GOD, AS AFTER 50 YEARS THE FIRE ENDS IN ALL HISTORICAL NEW MOVEMENTS OF GOD LIKE THE JESUS MOVEMENT.

There are three points I need to make now concerning the above exhortation. The most important point to me is that it has now been over fifty years since The Original Jesus Movement. So if you intend to have another revival you better get started. **First begin a prayer meeting where Spirit filled Christians pray in tongues not just to start the revival but to give it the prayer support it will need.**

The next point may seem unusual to most Christians. A revival starts off as an outward work. But if you give to others, God will give to you. Nevertheless this is not a time for introspection. God already knows what our faults are. **If we concern ourselves with the salvation and care of others, God will care for us by erasing our sins, correcting our faults and healing our shortcomings. So we need not waste our time in meditating and crying about our shortcomings and personal problems**. We need to learn how to give God the chance to be God. His word says that if we do for others, he will do for us! Let Him.

My concluding point may seem weird or even unfaithful to most holiness Christians. Although Sampson was a naughty sinner with many personal sexual sins, that I don't remember him ever repenting of, nevertheless he is still mentioned in the hall of faith of Hebrews 11. Because despite his sexual sins, he still fulfilled his destiny by faith. 'FOR WITHOUT FAITH IT IS IMPOSSIBLE TO PLEASE GOD', (Hebrews 11:6). 'AND WHATSOEVER IS NOT OF FAITH IS SIN', (Romans 14:23).

Our 33rd article comes from another piece of notebook paper which says: What kind of church does the Lord want? The first answer to this question is given in Ephesians 5:27; 'A GLORIOUS CHURCH'. And in Ephesians 5:26 God tells us how to achieve this: 'THAT HE MIGHT SANCTIFY AND CLEANSE IT WITH THE WASHING OF THE WATER BY THE WORD'. God has provided ministries to perfect the church, (Ephesians 4:11 & 12); 'AND HE GAVE SOME APOSTLES, AND SOME PROPHETS, AND SOME EVANGELISTS, AND SOME PASTORS AND TEACHERS'; FOR THE PERFECTING OF THE SAINTS, FOR THE WORK OF THE MINISTRY, FOR THE EDIFYING OF THE BODY OF CHRIST'.

If you don't have a perfect church it's because you have left your first love-Christ (Revelation 2:4). In fact the scriptures paint the true picture of Christ: First the vision of the living Christ. Revelation 1:7: 'BEHOLD, HE COMETH WITH CLOUDS, AND EVERY EYE SHALL SEE HIM, AND THEY ALSO WHICH PIERCED HIM; AND ALL COUNTRIES OF THE EARTH SHALL WAIL BECAUSE OF HIM, EVEN SO, AMEN'.

Our 34th article is taken from a small notepad that says: 'AND WHEN HE WAS COME INTO JERUSALEM, ALL THE CITY WAS MOVED, SAYING, WHO IS THIS', (Matthew 21:10). 'AND THE MULTITUDE SAID, THIS IS JESUS THE PROPHET OF NAZARETH OF GALILEE', (Matthew 21:11). 'THE STONES WOULD CRY OUT IF THE DISCIPLES HAD HELD THEIR PEACE', (Luke 19:40).

Then Jesus was asked if he heard what they said about him. He said that 'OUT OF THE MOUTHS OF BABES AND SUCKLINGS, THOU HAST PERFECT PRAISE', (Matthew 21:16).Then he went on to do miracles to be worthy of such praise. But the religious Jews rejected this and 'THE CHIEF PRIEST PLANNED TO PUT LAZARUS TO DEATH ALSO. BECAUSE ON ACCOUNT OF HIM MANY OF THE JEWS WERE GOING AWAY TO BELIEVE IN JESUS', (John 12:10 & 11). This shows the money bias of large congregations who want to stay in power more than obeying the will of God.

But the people refused to be discouraged, as 'THERE WERE CERTAIN GREEKS AMONG THEM THAT CAME UP TO WORSHIP AT THE FEAST. THE SAME CAME THEREFORE TO PHILIP WHICH WAS

OF BETHSAIDA IN GALILEE AND DESIRED HIM, SAYING, SIR, WE WOULD SEE JESUS', (John 12:20 & 21). This desire to see Jesus is the paramount desire of the Christian faith. And this also shows what I have been saying all along, that is: **Christianity is a Person. As it is written in first John 5:12,** 'HE THAT HATH THE SON HATH LIFE; AND HE THAT HATH NOT THE SON OF GOD HATH NOT LIFE'.

Then his many miraculous acts defined who he was. He healed a leper who said; 'IF IT BE THY WILL, THOU CANNEST MAKE ME CLEAN. AND JESUS MOVED WITH COMPASSION SAID I WILL', (Mark 1:44). And one touched the hem of his garment, saying if I touch him, I will be made whole, (Matthew 9:21). There is a song about this that says: *let me touch him, let me touch Jesus so that others may see and be blessed* and another song says; *he touched me and oh what joy fills my soul.*

When these miracles occurred it was said that this 'WAS NEVER SO SEEN IN ISRAEL', (Matthew 9:30) and that they never saw it done this way before. They concluded by saying that 'HE HATH DONE ALL THINGS WELL'**,** (Mark 7:37).

After this ***in Our 35th article*** were given many exhortations for the New Testament church. One was from Matthew 24:11 about how false prophets would arise to deceive many. And how that (Acts 20:29 & 30) grievous wolves would come into the flock. And from your own selves would men arise speaking perverse things to draw away disciples unto themselves.

Then he quoted I Timothy 4:1-5: 'NOW THE SPIRIT SPEAKETH EXPRESSLY, THAT IN THE LATER TIMES SOME SHALL DEPART FROM THE FAITH, GIVING HEED TO SEDUCING SPIRITS AND DOCTRINES OF DEVILS. SPEAKING LIES IN HYPOCRISY: HAVING THE CONSCIENCE SEARED WITH A HOT IRON; FORBIDDING TO MARRY, AND COMMANDING TO ABSTAIN FROM MEATS, WHICH GOD HATH CREATED TO BE RECEIVED WITH THANKSGIVING OF THEM WHICH BELIEVE AND KNOW THE TRUTH. FOR EVERY CREATURE OF GOD IS GOOD AND NOTHING TO BE REFUSED, IF IT BE RECEIVED WITH THANKSGIVING. FOR IT IS SANCTIFIED BY THE WORD OF GOD AND PRAYER'.

And the pastor cross referenced this with Matthew 24:11 which says that many false prophets will arise to deceive many.

And then he spoke about the need to try the spirits (I John 4:1). Then he went on to quote II John 1:9-11; 'WHOSOEVER TRANSGRESETH,

AND ABIDETH NOT IN THE DOCTRINE OF CHRIST, HATH NOT GOD. HE THAT ABIDETH IN THE DOCTRINE OF CHRIST, HE HATH BOTH THE FATHER AND THE SON. IF THERE COME ANY UNTO YOU, AND BRING NOT THIS DOCTRINE, RECEIVE HIM NOT INTO YOUR HOUSE, NEITHER BID HIM GOD SPEED. FOR HE THAT BIDDETH HIM GOD SPEED IS PARTAKER OF HIS EVIL DEEDS'.

Then Pastor Steenis concluded his sermon by quoting the last verses of Jude, from verse 17 on: 'BUT, BELOVED REMEMBER YE THE WORDS WHICH WERE SPOKEN BEFORE OF THE APOSTLE OF OUR LORD JESUS CHRIST: HOW THAT THEY TOLD YOU THERE SHOULD BE MOCKERS IN THE LAST TIME, WHO SHOULD WALK AFTER THEIR OWN UNGODLY LUSTS. THESE ARE THEY WHO SEPARATE THEMSLEVES, SENSUAL, HAVING NOT THE SPIRIT. BUT YE, BELOVED, BUILDING UP YOURSELVES ON YOUR MOST HOLY FAITH, PRAYING IN THE HOLY GHOST. KEEP YOURSELVES IN THE LOVE OF GOD, LOOKING FOR THE MERCY OF OUR LORD JESUS CHRIST UNTO ETERNAL LIFE. AND SOME HAVE COMPASSION, MAKING A DIFFERENCE: AND OTHERS SAVE WITH FEAR, PULLING THEM OUT OF THE FIRE, HATING EVEN THE GARMENT SPOTTED BY THE FLESH. NOW UNTO HIM THAT IS ABLE TO KEEP YOU FROM FALLING, AND TO PRESENT YOU FAULTLESS BEFORE THE PRESENCE OF HIS GLORY WITH EXCEEDING JOY, TO THE ONLY WISE GOD OUR SAVIOR, BE GLORY AND MAJESTY, DOMINION AND POWER, BOTH NOW AND EVER, AMEN'.

In a previous article about what kind of church the Lord wants I left this note in my Bible which I'll now impart to you: Marco polo described his visit to India and Cathay centuries ago. Of course few in the West believed him. As he died a Catholic Priest asked him to confess his accounts as lies or at most just stories, but Marco refused and said 'The half of what all I saw has never yet been told'. Likewise the half of the glory of our everlasting union with Christ in heaven has not yet been told. 'EYE HAS NOT SEEN NOR EAR HEARD, NEITHER HAVE ENTERED INTO THE HEART OF MAN THE THINGS WHICH GOD HATH PREPARED FOR THEM THAT LOVE HIM', (I Corinthians 2:9).

John saw the city, the heavenly Jerusalem in Revelation 21, let's read this account starting with verse 16: 'AND THE CITY LIETH FOUR

SQUARE, AND THE LENGTH IS AS LARGE AS THE BREADTH: AND HE MEASURED THE CITY WITH A REED, TWELVE THOUSAND FURLONGS. THE LENGTH AND THE BREADTH AND THE HEIGHT OF IT ARE EQUAL. AND HE MEASURED THE WALL THEREOF, A HUNDRED AND FORTY AND FOUR CUBITS, ACCORDING TO THE MEASURE OF A MAN, THAT IS, OF THE ANGEL. AND THE BUILDING OF THE WALL OF IT WAS OF JASPER: AND THE CITY WAS PURE GOLD, LIKE UNTO CLEAR GLASS.

So apparently there is plenty of room in the city for you. But this city is not like others, for it has a relationship with you as is recorded in Galatians 4:21. 'JERUSALEM ABOVE IS FREE, WHICH IS THE MOTHER OF US ALL'. And it is there where Jesus has purchased our habitation with the blood of his cross thus we have an everlasting inheritance. What about you, won't you make plans to relocate to this true land of milk and honey? The sufferings of this present age are not worthy to be compared with the glory that shall be revealed there.

God never appeared to man in an unhuman form, but always as a man. We are made in God's image to reflect his high ideals in all that we do. Thus, our conscience of our appearance tells us whose we are and guides us into what we should become to glorify God. And on the way to our fulfilment and eventual glorification we should stop to wash one another's feet as there is no advancement in the kingdom of God without humility and concern for others.

Our 36th article comes from an offering envelope in which two predestined people are mentioned with the words: God's draft. At no time did our pastor, Lyle Steenis, discuss the Vietnam War from the pulpit. This sermon about two men God drafted is the closest he ever got to that conflict. The first draftee he mentioned was Moses. And Moses tried to excuse himself by saying that he could not speak well enough to deliver Israel. (Exodus 4:10). Our second predestined person was Saul, who God didn't give the chance to talk back to. But knocked him off his ride and drafted him on the spot and told him how it was going to be.

Our 37th article comes from a piece of notebook paper saying: Psalm 24:3, 4 & 5: 'WHO SHALL ASCEND INTO THE HILL OF THE LORD? OR WHO SHALL STAND IN HIS HOLY PLACE? HE THAT HATH CLEAN HANDS AND A PURE HEART: WHO HAS NOT LIFTED UP HIS SOUL UNTO VANITY, NOR SWORN DECEITFULLY.

HE SHALL RECEIVE THE BLESSING FROM THE LORD AND RIGHTEOUSNESS FROM THE GOD OF HIS SALVATION'. Who shall ascend into the hill of the Lord? Or who shall stand in his Holy Place? He that hath clean hands and a pure heart: Who has not lifted up his soul unto vanity, nor sworn deceitfully. He shall receive the blessing from the Lord and righteousness from the God of his salvation'. Here we see that **righteousness and blessing are the result of obedience**, they are not earned by some religious calisthenics like even prayer before statues.

Psalm 94:12, & 10: 'BLESSED IS THE MAN WHOM THOU CHASTENEST OH LORD, AND TEACH HIM OUT OF THY LAW. HE THAT CHASTENETH THE HEATHEN SHALL NOT HE CORRECT? HE THAT TEACHES MAN KNOWLEDGE, SHALL NOT HE KNOW? The result of this is seen in verse 16 which says: 'WHO WILL RISE UP FOR ME AGAINST THE EVIL DOERS?', (Romans 9:15-23: 'FOR HE SAYETH TO MOSES, I WILL HAVE MERCY ON WHOM I WILL HAVE MERCY, AND I WILL HAVE COMPASSION ON WHOM I WILL HAVE COMPASSION. SO THEN IT IS NOT OF HIM THAT WILLETH, NOR OF HIM THAT RUNNETH, BUT OF GOD THAT SHOWETH MERCY. FOR THE SCRIPTURE SAYETH UNTO PHARAOH, EVEN FOR THE SAME PURPOSE HAVE I RAISED YOU UP, THAT I MIGHT SHOW MY POWER IN YOU, AND THAT MY NAME MIGHT BE DECLARED THROUGHOUT ALL THE EARTH. THEREFORE HATH HE MERCY, ON WHOM HE WILL HAVE MERCY, AND WHOM HE WILL HE HARDENETH. THOU WILL SAY UNTO ME, WHY DOES HE FIND FAULT? FOR WHOM HAS RESISTED HIS WILL? NAY BUT, OH MAN? WHO ART THOU THAT REPLIEST AGAINST GOD? SHALL THE THING FORMED SAY TO HIM THAT FORMED IT, WHY HAST THOU MADE ME THUS? HATH NOT THE POTTER POWER OVER THE CLAY, OF THE SAME LUMP TO MAKE ONE VESSEL UNTO HONOR AND ONE OTHER UNTO DISHONOR? WHAT IS GOD, WILLING TO SHOW HIS WRATH, AND TO MAKE HIS POWER KNOWN, ENDURED WITH MUCH LONGSUFFERING THE VESSELS OF WRATH FITTED TO DESTRUCTION: AND THAT HE MIGHT MAKE KNOWN THE RICHES OF HIS GLORY ON THE VESSELS OF MERCY, WHICH HE HATH AFORE PREPARED UNTO GLORY'. This part of scripture shows God's sovereignty over us all. Thus, Pastor Steenis said that God is our potter and we are the clay, so we can't resist HIS will.

'AND BY HIM ALL THAT BELIEVE ARE JUSTIFIED FROM ALL THINGS, FROM WHICH YE COULD NOT BE JUSTIFIED BY THE LAW OF MOSES', (Acts 13:39). So then, by Jesus all that believe in Him are justified from all things. In other words, 'Set Free'.

'HAVING THEREFORE OBTAINED HELP OF GOD. I CONTINUE UNTO THIS DAY, WITNESSING BOTH TO SMALL AND GREAT, SAYING NONE OTHER THING THAN THOSE WHICH THE PROPHETS AND MOSES DID SAY SHOULD COME: THAT CHRIST SHOULD SUFFER, AND THAT HE SHOULD BE THE FIRST THAT SHOULD RISE FROM THE DEAD, AND SHOULD SHOW LIGHT UNTO THE PEOPLE, AND TO THE GENTILES', (Acts 26:22, 23). Having obtained help from God I continue here to witness.

'I TELL YOU, NAY, BUT, EXCEPT YOU REPENT, YOU SHALL ALL LIKEWISE PERISH. I TELL YOU, NAY, BUT, EXCEPT YOU REPENT, YOU SHALL ALL LIKEWISE PERISH', (Luke 13:3 & 5).

'HE SPAKE ALSO THIS PARABLE: A CERTAIN MAN HAD A FIG TREE PLANTED IN HIS VINEYARD; AND HE CAME AND SOUGHT FRUIT THEREON, AND FOUND NOTHING. THEN SAID HE UNTO THE DRESSER OF HIS VINEYARD; BEHOLD THESE THREE YEARS I COME SEEKING FRUIT ON THIS FIG TREE, AND FIND NONE: CUT IT DOWN; WHY CUMBERETH IT THE GROUND? AND HE ANSWERED SAYING UNTO HIM: LORD, LET IT ALONE THIS YEAR ALSO, TILL I SHOULD DIG ABOUT IT, AND DUNG IT: AND IF IT BEAR FRUIT, WELL: AND IF NOT, THEN AFTER THAT THOU SHALT CUT IT DOWN', (Luke 13:6-9). We should all understand the meaning of this parable. It does not just mean to wait on God, since the times and the seasons are in His own power. But it also means 'If at first we don't succeed try and try again'. Some would also say that the dresser of the vineyard was securing his job and looking out for his own self-interest. Even if that were so the dresser's respect for the life of the fig tree shows that his Lord's decision to have him in charge of the vineyard was wise since after all **God's purpose here is to for the fig tree to be fruitful and multiply not to be cut down and stacked for wood.** Moreover, it should be noted that the vinedresser wanted to dig about the fig tree and dung it. *Not put toxic cancer causing fertilizer on it like 'round up' and hope for the best.*

'STRIVE TO ENTER IN AT THE STRAIGHT GATE: FOR MANY STRIVE TO ENTER IN AT THE STRAIGHT GATE AND WILL NOT BE ABLE', (Luke 13:24). This points out our futility. For us to try on our own results in failure. We can only enter in through Christ. And you don't need to strive to ask Jesus into your heart.

'FOR WHOSOEVER EXALTED HIMSELF SHALL BE ABASED, AND HE THAT HUMBLED HIMSELF SHALL BE EXALTED', (Luke 14:11). Whatever you do has consequences. If you play with fire you'll get burned. If you do the crime, you'll have to do the time. 'YOU RECEIVE NOT, BECAUSE YOU ASK NOT', (James 4:3). But if you ask Jesus into your heart he will come in and elevate you to your place in glory. On the way, he will baptize you in the Holy Ghost if you ask.

'IF ANY MAN COME TO ME, AND HATE NOT HIS FATHER, AND MOTHER, AND WIFE, AND CHILDREN, AND BRETHREN, AND SISTERS, YEA, AND HIS OWN LIFE, ALSO, HE CANNOT BE MY DISCIPLE', (Luke 14:26). This verse does not mean to despise and resent others including your own parents but simply to disregard others to the extent that you put Jesus first and consider Him the most important aspect of your life now. For those fleeing child support this verse does not justify your lack of responsibility. If you have brought children into this world it's your job to support them and to love and care for your wife too.

'BRETHREN, I COUNT NOT MYSELF TO HAVE APPREHENDED: BUT THIS ONE THING I DO, FORGETTING THOSE THINGS WHICH ARE BEHIND, AND REACHING FORTH UNTO THOSE THINGS WHICH ARE BEFORE, I PRESS TOWARD THE MARK FOR THE PRIZE OF THE HIGH CALLING OF GOD IN CHRIST JESUS: LET US THEREFORE, AS MANY AS BE PERFECT, BE THUS MINDED, AND IF IN ANYTHING HE BE OTHERWISE MINDED, GOD SHALL REVEAL EVEN THIS UNTO YOU', (Philippians 3:13-15). Here we are to forget the past and to look ahead. And God will reveal what must be covered.

'AND BE RENEWED IN THE SPIRIT OF YOUR MIND: AND THAT YE PUT ON THE NEW MAN, WHICH AFTER GOD IS CREATED IN RIGHTEOUSNESS AND TRUE HOLINESS. WHEREFORE PUTTING AWAY LYING, SPEAK EVERYMAN TRUTH WITH HIS NEIGHBOR, FOR WE ARE MEMBERS OF ONE ANOTHER. BE ANGRY, AND SIN NOT: LET NOT THE SUN GO DOWN UPON YOUR WRATH: NEITHER GIVE PLACE TO THE DEVIL. LET HIM THAT STOLE STEEL NO MORE: BUT RATHER LET HIM LABOR, WORKING WITH HIS HANDS THE THING WHICH IS GOOD, THAT YE MAY HAVE TO GIVE TO HIM THAT NEEDETH. LET NO CORRUPT

COMMUNICATION PROCEED OUT OF YOUR MOUTH, BUT THAT WHICH IS GOOD TO THE USE OF EDIFYING, THAT IT MAY MINISTER GRACE UNTO THE HEARERS. AND GRIEVE NOT THE HOLY SPIRIT OF GOD, WHEREBY YE ARE SEALED UNTO THE DAY OF REDEMPTION. LET ALL BITTERNESS, AND WRATH, AND ANGER, AND CLAMOUR, AND EVIL SPEAKING, BE PUT AWAY FROM YOU, WITH ALL MALICE: AND BE YE KIND ONE TO ANOTHER, TENDER HEARTED, FORGIVING ONE ANOTHER, EVEN AS GOD FOR CHRIST SAKE HAS FORGIVEN YOU', (Ephesians 4:23-32). Some of these exhortations in scripture are self-explanatory. But one issue mentioned in verse 28 shows the difference between hippies and the Jesus people. The Jesus people don't just work for themselves but also for needs to help others. Whereas hippies don't even work for their own needs but bum off others as if we're responsible to meet their needs. **This is devilish socialism, it is not Christianity to support bums.** The 'flower power' of hippies comes from the false god of transcendental meditation, whereas real FIRE power which you can feel comes from the Holy Ghost.

Our 38th article comes from a devotional about being kept. It starts by saying: 'HE WILL KEEP YOU AS THE APPLE OF HIS EYE', (Psalms 17:8). 'HE WILL KEEP YOU IN ALL YOUR WAYS', (Psalm 91:11). 'HE WILL KEEP THAT WHICH YOU HAVE COMMITTED UNTO HIM AGAINST THAT DAY', (II Timothy 1:12). 'HE WILL KEEP YOU AS A SHEPHERD CARES FOR HIS FLOCK OF SHEEP', (Jeremiah 31:10). 'HE WILL KEEP YOU IN PERFECT PEACE IF YOUR MIND IS STAYED ON HIM', (Isaiah 26:3). 'HE WILL KEEP YOU FROM THE HOUR OF TEMPTATION AND SUPPORT YOU IN THE TIME OF TRAIL', (Revelation 3:10, I Corinthians 10:13). 'HE WILL KEEP YOU FROM FALLING', (Jude 1:24). 'HE WILL KEEP YOU FROM EVIL', (John 17:15). 'OH KEEP MY SOUL AND DELIVER ME:......FOR I PUT MY TRUST IN THEE', (Psalm 25:20). Faith in God's keeping power is the link between our finite needs and God's infinite resources.

This same devotion article says something humorous for you prosperity preachers. Years ago this article appeared in a leading Florida newspaper. It was a prayer that said: 'Now I lay me down to sleep, I pray the Lord my cash will keep. Whatever I do, I want to know, that he will help my profits grow'. This prayer seems to contradict the clear teaching of God's word that says: 'WHATEVER YOU DO, DO ALL TO THE GLORY OF GOD', (I Corinthians 10:31). Actually this whole thing is a twisted version that thieves and bums love which says: 'LET NO MAN SEEK HIS OWN, BUT EVERY MAN ANOTHER'S WEALTH', (I Corinthians 10:24).

Our 39th article comes from notes on a piece of notebook paper about faith. He begins by defining faith from Hebrews 11:1, 'NOW FAITH IS THE SUBSTANCE OF THINGS HOPED FOR, THE EVIDENCE OF THINGS NOT SEEN'. Then he described how it comes in Romans 10:17: 'FAITH COMES BY HEARING, AND HEARING BY THE WORD OF GOD'. After this he said that we could contend for the faith as many scriptures encourage us to do by praying in the Holy Ghost: (I Corinthians 14:14), 'FOR IF I PRAY IN AN UNKNOWN TONGUE, MY SPIRIT PRAYS, BUT MY UNDERSTANDING IS UNFRUITFUL'. My records show that this message was from the early days of the Jesus movement.

Then he preached about the child Samuel from I Samuel, chapter 3. 'AND THE CHILD SAMUEL MINISTERED UNTO THE LORD BEFORE ELI, AND THE WORD OF THE LORD WAS PRECIOUS IN THOSE DAYS, THERE WAS NO OPEN VISION. AND IT CAME TO PASS AT THAT TIME, WHEN ELI WAS LAID DOWN IN HIS PLACE, AND HIS EYES BEGAN TO WAX DIM, THAT HE COULD NOT SEE; AND ERE THE LAMP OF GOD WENT OUT IN THE TEMPLE OF THE LORD, WHERE THE ARK OF GOD WAS, AND SAMUEL WAS LAID DOWN TO SLEEP; THAT THE LORD CALLED SAMUEL: AND HE ANSWERED, HERE AM I. AND HE RAN UNTO ELI, AND SAID HERE AM I, FOR THOU CALLEST ME. AND HE SAID, I CALLED NOT: LIE DOWN AGAIN. AND HE WENT AND LAY DOWN. AND THE LORD CALLED YET AGAIN, SAMUEL. AND SAMUEL AROSE AND WENT TO ELI, AND SAID, HERE AM I, FOR THOU DIDST CALL ME. AND HE ANSWERED, I CALLED NOT, MY SON LIE DOWN AGAIN. NOW SAMUEL DID NOT YET KNOW THE LORD, NEITHER WAS THE WORD OF THE LORD YET REVEALED UNTO HIM. AND THE LORD CALLED SAMUEL AGAIN THE THIRD TIME, AND HE AROSE AND WENT TO ELI, AND SAID, HERE AM I: FOR THOU DIDST CALL ME. AND ELI PERCEIVED THAT THE LORD HAD CALLED THE CHILD. THEREFORE, ELI SAID UNTO SAMUEL, GO, LIE DOWN: AND IT SHALL BE, IF HE CALL THEE, THAT THOU SHALT SAY, SPEAK, LORD, FOR THY SERVANT HEARETH. SO, SAMUEL WENT AND LAY DOWN IN HIS PLACE. AND THE LORD CAME, AND STOOD, AND CALLED AS AT OTHER TIMES, SAMUEL, SAMUEL: THEN SAMUEL ANSWERED,

SPEAK: FOR THY SERVANT HEARETH. AND THE LORD SAID TO SAMUEL. BEHOLD, I WILL DO A THING IN ISRAEL, AT WHICH BOTH THE EARS OF EVERYONE THAT HEARETH IT SHALL TINGLE. IN THAT DAY I WILL PERFORM AGAINST ELI ALL THINGS WHICH I HAVE SPOKEN CONCERNING HIS HOUSE: WHEN I BEGAN I WILL ALSO MAKE AN END. FOR I HAVE TOLD HIM THAT I WILL JUDGE HIS HOUSE FOREVER FOR THE INIQUITY WHICH HE KNOWETH: BECAUSE HIS SONS MADE THEMSELVES VIAL, AND HE RESTRAINED THEM NOT. AND THEREFORE, I HAVE SWORN UNTO THE HOUSE OF ELI, THAT THE INIQUITY OF ELI'S HOUSE SHALL NOT BE PURGED WITH SACRIFICE NOR OFFERING FOREVER. AND SAMUEL LAY UNTIL MORNING, AND OPENED THE DOORS OF THE HOUSE OF THE LORD. AND SAMUEL FEARED TO SHOW ELI THE VISION. THEN ELI CALLED SAMUEL, AND SAID, SAMUEL, MY SON, AND HE ANSWERED, HERE AM I. AND HE SAID, WHAT IS THE THING THAT THE LORD HATH SAID UNTO THEE? I PRAY THEE HIDE IT NOT FROM ME: GOD DO SO TO THEE, AND MORE ALSO, IF THOU HIDE ANYTHING FROM ME OF ALL THE THINGS THAT HE SAID UNTO THE. AND SAMUEL TOLD HIM EVERY WHIT, AND HID NOTHING FROM HIM. AND HE SAID, IT IS THE LORD: LET HIM DO WHAT SEEMETH HIM GOOD. AND SAMUEL GREW, AND THE LORD WAS WITH HIM, AND DID NOT LET NONE OF HIS WORDS FALL TO THE GROUND. AND ALL ISRAEL FROM DAN EVEN TO BEER-SHEBA KNEW THAT SAMUEL WAS ESTABLISHED TO BE A PROPHET OF THE LORD. AND THE LORD APPEARED AGAIN IN SHILOH: FOR THE LORD REVEALED HIMSELF TO SAMUEL IN SHILOH BY THE WORD OF THE LORD'. This shows that a child or even a young person like yourselves can be filled with the Holy Ghost and know the word of the Lord. In fact, the scriptures even promised such in Joel 2:28 & 29; 'AND IT SHALL COME TO PASS AFTERWARD, THAT I WILL POUR OUT MY SPIRIT UPON ALL FLESH; AND YOUR SONS AND YOUR DAUGHTERS SHALL PROPHECY, YOUR OLD MEN SHALL DREAM DREAMS, YOUR YOUNG MEN SHALL SEE VISIONS: AND ALSO UPON MY SERVANTS AND UPON MY HANDMAIDS IN THOSE DAYS WILL I POUR OUT OF MY SPIRIT'.

'AND IT SHALL COME TO PASS IN THE LAST DAYS, SAITH GOD, I WILL POUR OUT OF MY SPIRIT UPON ALL FLESH: AND

YOUR SONS AND YOUR DAUGHTERS SHALL PROPHECY, AND YOUR YOUNG MEN SHALL SEE VISIONS, AND YOUR OLD MEN SHALL DREAM DREAMS'. (Acts 2:17).

Acts 2:39; 'FOR THE PROMISE IS UNTO YOU, AND TO YOUR CHILDREN, AND TO ALL THAT ARE AFAR OFF, EVEN TO AS MANY AS THE LORD OUR GOD SHALL CALL'.

Our Fortieth article comes from an offering envelope about prophesying from Amos 7:13 where the prophets were forbidden to prophecy at Bethel, the king's sanctuary and seat of his kingdom. But Amos the prophet of God prophesied there anyway against Israel. The people said no, we don't want to hear it, but Amos was preaching repentance to benefit the people and avoid judgment, but the people refused to hear it and suffered the consequences.

Prophets sometimes speak hard sayings that are not liked but most of these objections are not based on understanding. Like when Jesus spoke about His flesh being meat indeed (John 6:55) and he said: 'EXCEPT YE EAT THE FLESH OF THE SON OF MAN AND DRINK HIS BLOOD, YE HAVE NO LIFE IN YOU'. (John 6:53). This was a very hard saying that displeased and offended many, so they left and walked no more with Him. So **be careful what you say and say nothing that the anointing does not confirm.**

Our Forty-first article comes from a piece of scrap paper about our relationship to Christ as God in Matthew 6:33. 'SEEK YE FIRST THE KINGDOM OF GOD AND HIS RIGHTEOUSNESS…'. God wants partners. He made Adam and Eve to have dominion over all the animals. They all were partners with God.

You're in the kingdom of God if you're a Christian because you're translated out of darkness into light. God has made you and saved you for a purpose. This is described in John chapter 14.

'LET NOT YOUR HEART BE TROUBLED: YE BELIEVE IN GOD, BELIEVE ALSO IN ME. IN MY FATHER'S HOUSE ARE MANY MANSIONS: IF IT WERE NOT SO, I WOULD HAVE TOLD YOU. I GO TO PREPARE A PLACE FOR YOU, AND IF I GO AND PREPARE A PLACE FOR YOU, I WILL COME AGAIN, AND RECEIVE YOU UNTO MYSELF, THAT WHERE I AM, THERE YOU MAY BE ALSO. AND WHITHER I GO YE KNOW, AND THE WAY YOU KNOW'.

Thomas saith unto Him, Lord, we know not whether thou goest, and how can we know the way?

Jesus saith unto him: 'I AM THE WAY, THE TRUTH, AND THE LIFE: NO MAN COMETH UNTO THE FATHER, BUT BY ME. IF

ANYMAN KNOW ME, HE SHOULD HAVE KNOWN MY FATHER ALSO: AND FROM HENCEFORTH YE KNOW HIM, AND HAVE SEEN HIM'. Philip said unto Him, Lord, show us the Father, and it sufficith us.

Jesus saith unto him 'HAVE I BEEN SO LONG TIME WITH YOU, AND YET HAST THOU NOT KNOWN ME PHILIP? HE THAT HAS SEEN ME HAS SEEN THE FATHER, AND HOW SAYEST THOU THEN, SHOW US THE FATHER? BELIEVEST THOU NOT THAT I AM IN THE FATHER, AND THE FATHER IN ME? THE WORDS THAT I SPEAK UNTO YOU, SPEAK NOT I UNTO MYSELF: BUT THE FATHER WHO DWELLETH IN ME, HE DOETH THE WORKS. BELIEVE ME THAT I AM IN THE FATHER, AND THE FATHER IN ME: OR ELSE BELIEVE ME FOR THE VERY WORK'S SAKE. VERILY, VERILY, I SAY UNTO YOU, HE THAT BELIEVETH ON ME, THE WORKS THAT I DO SHALL HE DO ALSO: AND GREATER WORKS THAN THESE SHALL HE DO; BECAUSE I GO UNTO MY FATHER AND WHATSOEVER YOU ASK IN MY NAME, THAT WILL I DO, THAT THE FATHER MAY BE GLORIFIED IN THE SON. IF HE SHALL ASK ANYTHING IN MY NAME, I WILL DO IT.

IF YOU LOVE ME, KEEP MY COMMANDMENTS. AND I WILL PRAY THE FATHER, AND HE SHALL GIVE YOU ANOTHER COMFORTER, THAT HE MAY ABIDE WITH YOU FOREVER. EVEN THE SPIRIT OF TRUTH, WHOM THE WORLD CANNOT RECEIVE, BECAUSE IT SEETH HIM NOT, NEITHER KNOWETH HIM: BUT YE KNOW HIM; FOR HE DWELLETH WITH YOU, AND SHALL BE IN YOU. I WILL NOT LEAVE YOU COMFORTLESS: I WILL COME TO YOU. YET A LITTLE WHILE, AND THE WORLD SEETH ME NO MORE, BUT YE SHALL SEE ME: BECAUSE I LIVE YE SHALL LIVE ALSO. AT THAT DAY YE SHALL KNOW THAT I AM IN MY FATHER, AND YE IN ME, AND I IN YOU. HE THAT HATH MY COMMANDMENTS, AND KEEPETH THEM, HE IT IS THAT LOVETH ME: AND HE THAT LOVETH ME SHALL BE LOVED OF MY FATHER, AND I WILL LOVE HIM, AND MANIFEST MYSELF TO HIM.'

Judas saith unto him, not Iscariot, Lord, how is it that thou will manifest thyself unto us, and not unto the world? Jesus answered and said unto him, 'IF A MAN LOVE ME, HE WILL KEEP MY WORDS: AND MY FATHER WILL LOVE HIM, AND WE WILL COME UNTO HIM,

AND MAKE OUR ABODE WITH HIM. HE THAT LOVETH ME NOT KEEPETH NOT MY SAYINGS: AND THE WORD WHICH I HEAR IS NOT MINE, BUT THE FATHER'S WHICH SENT ME. THESE THINGS HAVE I SPOKEN UNTO YOU, BEING YET PRESENT WITH YOU. BUT THE COMFORTER; WHICH IS THE HOLY GHOST, WHOM THE FATHER WILL SEND IN MY NAME, HE SHALL TEACH YOU ALL THINGS, AND BRING ALL THINGS TO YOUR REMEMBERANCE, WHATSOEVER I HAVE SAID UNTO YOU. PEACE I LEAVE WITH YOU, MY PEACE I GIVE UNTO YOU: NOT AS THE WORLD GIVETH, GIVE I UNTO YOU. LET NOT YOUR HEARTS BE TROUBLED, NEITHER LET IT BE AFRAID. YE HAVE HEARD HOW I SAID UNTO YOU, I GO AWAY, AND COME AGAIN UNTO YOU. IF YOU LOVE ME YE WOULD REJOICE, BECAUSE I SAID, I GO UNTO MY FATHER: FOR MY FATHER IS GREATER THAN I. AND NOW I'VE TOLD YOU BEFORE IT COME TO PASS, THAT, WHEN IT COME TO PASS, YE MIGHT BELIEVE. HEREAFTER I WILL NOT TALK MUCH WITH YOU: FOR THE PRINCE OF THIS WORLD COMETH, AND HATH NOTHING IN ME. BUT THAT THE WORLD MAY KNOW THAT I LOVE THE FATHER, AND AS THE FATHER GAVE ME COMMANDMENT, EVEN SO I DO, ARISE, LET US GO HENCE'.

Then Pastor Steenis said that you become a partner with Christ if and only if you abide in Him and his words abide in you. You cannot be led by the Holy Spirit unless you have the Holy Spirit and the Holy Spirit has you. And you can't bear fruit unless you abide in Him (Christ).

Our forty-second article is from another offering envelope on which are written a couple of exhortations: 1. In first touch just see men as trees walking but the second touch from Jesus sees men as needy human beings. And 2. Too many Spirit filled Christians are driving with only their parking lights instead of their headlights on because their battery is not charged up sufficiently with living water and prayer to light up the scene enough to do the right thing.

Our forty-third article also comes from another offering envelope (please forgive me for not having my own notepad in those days) in which Reverend Steenis says that **prayer keeps any revival alive**. And that **confusion in the camp results in the failure to win souls and the lack of joy.** Always be ready to preach the word. If a man won't preach God will use donkeys and roosters (other creatures). We must also have reality in order to fully give it away as recorded in Acts 3:6. You cannot give away what you do not have. The other side of this offering envelope declares what's wrong with the church which is our next article.

Our forty-fourth article begins with Luke warmness as the major cause of wrongs with the church. But I would probably say unbelief. Nevertheless his first scripture is from Isaiah 64:7 which says that: 'THERE IS NONE THAT CALLETH UPON THY NAME, THAT STIRETH UP HIMSELF TO TAKE HOLD OF THEE'. So we are not becoming good soldiers of Jesus Christ (II Timothy 2:4). Thanks to this Luke warmness many people have not even heard the gospel once and Jesus wants everyone to hear at least once.

Being lukewarm instead of being hot or cold is an environment which breeds the disease of sin. So we do not stir ourselves up to lay hold of the promise of God. We know that God keeps his word. 'YOU HAVE NOT BECAUSE YOU ASK NOT', (James 4:2) and 'GOD OWNS THE CATTLE ON A THOUSAND HILLS', (Psalms 50:2). So be a finisher and just get started. Don't just be a starter in this race. 'THEY THAT RUN IN THE RACE RUN ALL BUT ONLY ONE RECIEVES THE PRIZE. RUN THEREFORE THAT YOU MAY OBTAIN', (I Corinthians 9:24). You must believe God for any answer to your prayers. 'IF YOU ASK ANYTHING IN HIS NAME HE WILL DO IT'. 'WHATSOEVER IS NOT OF FAITH IS SIN', (Romans 14:23) so ask believing.

Much of this consolidating of denominations is because of Luke warmness and weakness in believing God's word. This causes the lack of sufficient fire to keep revival fires burning. There is no reward for idleness or indifference. **Thousands of churches have closed recently due to unbelief and Luke warmness.**

Nehemiah in the Old Testament once had a job to rebuild the wall of Jerusalem, the city of God. And it says that: 'THE PEOPLE HAD A MIND TO WORK', (Nehemiah 4:6). But if you do not work you will not accomplish your task. 'WHERE THERE IS NO VISION, THE PEOPLE PERISH', (Proverbs 29:18). **Moreover, once you see, you must act.** God commands his troops. The Ten Commandments are not ten suggestions. **A Christian's rewards are for obedience to God's 'marching orders.'**

Our forty-fifth article is from a page of notes torn out of some notebook. It contains many scriptures in a haphazard order. It begins by exhorting other preachers saying; speak slow, distinctly, and repeat. Many preachers are more concerned about their personal reputation of preaching a good message than having the people understand what they said and being able to apply it and grow thereby. Then we go on to obtain victory for revival.

He begins by saying that from II Chronicles 20:1-22 we see in the 22 verse praise before the battle. Likewise, there should be praise before revival or any major work of God that you want to see succeed. This is far more important than most realize. From what I see on Christian TV the Evangelist Jimmy Swaggart has a good handle on this which will not go unrewarded. Then as God does His part, our part will be easier.

Here are two songs which I wrote down from that time: 1. *'It only takes a spark to get a fire going. And soon all those around will warm up to its glowing. That's how it is with God's love once you've experienced it. You spread his love to everyone, you want to pass it on'.* And 2. *'I wish for you my friend, this happiness that I've found. You can depend on Him. It matters not where you're bound. I'll shout it from the mountain tops; I want my world to know, the Lord of love has come to me, I want to pass it on'.*

Then Rev. Steenis read from Luke 13 the parables about the lost sheep, the lost silver and the lost prodigal son. Then he brought out the need to overcome barriers like pride and unbelief in order to let God, the Holy Spirit move in revival. 'IT IS THE SPIRIT THAT QUICKENETH, THE FLESH PROFITETH NOTHING', (John 6:63).

Then he shared many scriptures like: II Peter 2, Luke 16, II Thess. 1:8 and 9 and 2:12, Hebrews 10:26-31, John 5:28 and 29, Galatians 5:19-24, I Corinthians 6:9 and 10, Luke 11:31 and 32, Romans 2:5-9 and Rom. 1:28-32 which we stood and read aloud. 'AND EVEN AS THEY DID NOT LIKE TO RETAIN GOD IN THEIR KNOWLEDGE, GOD GAVE THEM OVER TO A REPROBATE MIND, TO DO THOSE THINGS WHICH ARE NOT CONVENIENT: BEING FILLED WITH ALL UNRIGHTEOUSNESS, FORNICATION, WICKEDNESS, COVETOUSNESS, MALICIOUSNESS, FULL OF ENVY, MURDER, DEBATE, DECIET, MALIGNITY, WISPERERS, BACK BITERS, HATERS OF GOD, DESPITFUL, PROUD, BOASTERS, INVENTORS OF EVIL THINGS, DISOBEDIENT TO PARENTS, WITHOUT UNDERSTANDING, COVENANT BREAKERS, WITHOUT NATURAL AFFECTION, IMPLACABLE, UNMERCIFUL, WHO KNOWING THE JUDGMENT OF GOD, THAT THEY WHICH DO SUCH THINGS ARE WORTHY OF DEATH, NOT ONLY DO THE SAME, BUT HAVE PLEASURE IN THEM THAT DO THEM',(Romans 1:28-32). After that the altars were opened for our prayers. Many souls were saved and some were prayed through to their Holy Ghost baptism.

Our forty-fifth article is the back side or rear of the previous article. It was mainly concerned with being carried away with diverse and strange doctrines. Most of these concerned the physical appearance: 'THEY THAT ARE AFTER THE FLESH DO MIND THE THINGS OF THE FLESH', (Romans 8:5). Then he discussed the length of women's dresses and skirts. And compared that to the long hypocritical clothing of the scribes described in Mark 12:38. He also mentioned our need to receive both the poor and the rich without respect of persons as the scriptures describe in James 2:2&3. Then he mentioned the need for women to dress in modest apparel as indicated in 1 Timothy 2:9. But that verse does not say what modesty is. He concluded this exhortation about clothing by repeating 1 Peter 5:5, 'AND BE CLOTHED WITH HUMILITY'. It was found to be interesting that after this exhortation about being clothed with humility was stated the exhortation about being submitted to one another had been stated first. Thus the type of clothing one wears should be oked by the Christian community. Thus it would be unwise to wear bikinis or suggestive see through undershorts or blouses in church where people need to keep their eyes on Jesus instead of each other.

Then he closed his exhortation by also mentioning the length of one's hair from 1 Corinthians 11:14-16 and saying that that verse does not say how long. He also said that: 'FOR AS MANY AS ARE LED BY THE SPIRIT OF GOD, THEY ARE THE SONS OF GOD', (ROMANS 8:14). This went over very well as all of the Jesus people wanted to become sons of God.

There is also another exhortation on this page which says that if you support a minister who teaches lies and who is living in sin like divorce and remarriage then you are partaker of his evil deeds. So be very careful who you give your money to.

Another exhortation quotes Galatians 3:3: 'HAVING BEGUN IN THE SPIRIT, ARE YE NOW MADE PERFECT BY THE FLESH'? And Colossians 2:16: 'LET NO MAN THEREFORE JUDGE YOU…'. And, 'WE HAVE NO SUCH CUSTOM, NEITHER THE CHURCHES OF GOD'.

'ONE MAN ESTEEMS ONE DAY ABOVE ANOTHER. ANOTHER MAN ESTEEMS EVERYDAY THE SAME. LET EVERY MAN BE FULLY PERSUADED IN HIS OWN MIND', (Romans 14:5). This verse is primarily for the Sabbath keepers who like the Jehovah's Witnesses like to constantly harass Christians.

Our forty-sixth article is mainly about needed group support. Pastor Steenis noticed that many Jesus people were loners and kept to themselves. This was good in some ways especially in the area of gossiping about other peoples' problems. But it was a bad personal habit when it came to corporate or group prayer. Sometimes such would be needed in order to obtain a strong corporate anointing in order to break strong yokes.

I remember that he specifically stated several times the need for backup especially in prayer. He would use the football analogy of team sports and exhort us to get prayer partners. This was before the time of mentors which the Jesus people would not have liked. For they didn't like anyone telling them what to do. But they would listen to truth that they knew was for their own good.

I learned myself how important prayer backup was for revival. Several years ago I went to visit another church that I thought might be ready to come into 'the high calling of God'. So I went to their prayer room before the service and the door was locked. So I knew right away that these people were not yet ready for revival. I knew this from the Jesus movement. Because before every service there was always some young person praying in the Spirit for the souls that needed to be saved and filled. **So praying in the Spirit is an intrical part of revival.**

Some may wonder why these Jesus people prayed in the Spirit so fervently. This was because many of them had been delivered from dope with its hallucinogenic feelings. So when they came to God they wanted others to feel God in the Spirit. In other words this was a young person's feeling transference.

Sure it cost, like all dope and most feelings. Only this time instead of spending money, this overwhelming feeling of newness with God cost repentance from the old life and salvation in Christ with Spirit infilling.

Our forty-seventh article confirms that by saying that we cannot serve together effectively and properly unless our actions are based upon and motivated by the truth. As it is written: 'CAN TWO WALK TOGETHER EXCEPT THEY BE AGREED?' (Amos 3:3). To elaborate more on this: In this Jesus movement some Jesus people were concerned about the lack of having sufficient role models in the church. And Pastor Steenis remembered back then preaching in missions about Steven, the man of God.

This can be found in Acts chapter six. Back then there arose a controversy about Greek widows getting their fair share of ministering. This dependency was handled uniquely by the early church for instead of arguing and debating over this they appointed men of honest report, full of the Holy Ghost and wisdom to do this ministry. (Back in those days there was no Social Security nor welfare, so the church did this as a benevolence ministry). And one of those men busy in serving was Stephen. It is recorded in your Bible that

Stephen was a man full of faith and the Holy Ghost whom they appointed over this menial daily task.

Pastor Steenis told you back then according to verse three that Stephen had good business wisdom. And in verse five that he was full of both faith and the Holy Ghost.

Then in verse eight how that Stephen worked wonders among the people outside of his appointed ministry. That shows that you can become more in God by going beyond what's just expected.

Stephen was also skilled at disputing doctrines as verse 9 reveals. So you also should learn the major doctrines of the faith to protect you with truth from the Mormons and Jehovah's witnesses.

And then there were also trouble-makers who stirred up the people and set up false witnesses against Stephen, (please see Acts 6:12 & 13).

Then in verse 15 we see the part that Pastor Steenis liked best. That's when Stephen's face shown with the glory of God as the face of an angel.

Unfortunately for Stephen this may have been hazardous for Stephen because his face shown like Moses and happened as a result of his persecution for declaring the truth to the religious. Stephen didn't have any real problems until his dealing with the religious demagogues in the synagogues. Since they couldn't resist what he said, they lied on him. In other words they used false witnesses against him. Pastor Steenis supposed that some of you Jesus people have experienced this yourselves. We see in verse 12 that eventually these religious reprobates killed Stephen, the man of God. Then Pastor Steenis gave us his council: avoid any disputes with the religious who have already made up their minds to embrace the demonic doctrines of devils. **Don't witness to just anyone. Be sure you have the clearance and go ahead only as the Holy Spirit leads.**

Our forty-eighth article comes from a piece of typing paper about a major false theology to avoid. The pastor first mentioned that the main doctrine of devils invading the church was replacement theology. The idea that God is now through with the Jew. He said that we all saw how that God revisited the Jews in the 1967 six-day war. And according to his covenant with them He also restored some of their old lands including Jerusalem. So this idea and false theology that the church has replaced Israel is clearly false. Never-the-less do not argue this issue among the anti-Semitic, since it's your job to get people saved not to rescue them from stupidity. Cast out this demonic false doctrine first then preach the gospel.

Our forty-nineth article lists other major false theologies to avoid in order to get people saved. These include once saved, always saved or eternal security. The idea that just because you may have accepted Jesus as a child you're still saved and free to live in sin. But the truth is that if you live like the devil now you'll soon be living with him in hell. And the Baptist idea about Holy Ghost baptism; that such is not for today and God don't do that anymore. Sure enough He don't do that anymore in any Baptist church, that's for sure.

And the other major false Baptist theology that God don't heal anymore either since such died out with the apostles is also false.

How can any Christian expect to be in heaven with God when they have repeatedly insulted the Holy Spirit, Who is God?

Our fiftieth article concerns the lesser false doctrines which hinder your living for God and evangelizing the unsaved. These include: praying to dead saints for resolution of your personal problems, baptism for the dead to establish a genealogy of election, infant baptism by sprinkling, communion as a manifestation of the vow of poverty instead of being recognized as the monthly or weekly or daily Christian feast-day of the resurrection, tithing as modern-day indulgences, abortion not being modern day human sacrifice to the false gods of convenience, materialism and humanism, the false teaching of how that strangers and foreigners in the Bible should be recognized even though criminal aliens as citizens, the false doctrine that faith to make money is the same or equal to faith to get saved, the stupidity that impersonal sex like masturbation is not sinful, the assumption that a rapturist is not an escapist, the false conclusion that homosexuals are born that way, the false idea that sex with robots, animals and even children is not sinful, the illogical assumption that to unlearn bad behaviors beats deliverance from demons, the psychological false notion that most personal problems are caused by disease which can be healed by taking some pills. ***But the Jesus people took the 'Gos-pill'.***

They were told about all these false doctrines but I never heard them arguing with anyone about them. They just got people to the alters to pray and once the Holy Ghost came all issues or disagreements over them evaporated and even the disagreeable became happy so much so that the news media came to take pictures. In one case those pictures appeared in Look magazine world-wide.

In conclusion I must confess that had I known that these few articles composed a God given historical document I would have certainly kept better records. As I touch each one of these old articles, tears come to my eyes as I realize that it was my highest honor and blessing to be in the presence of the living God and the movement of His Holy Spirit for over three full years in the everyday lives of teenagers and common men and women who unexpectedly found God. By God's grace and for the good of mankind and America may it happen again!

It will, for God has shown me that I will not see death until two great awakenings happen. The first one, the Jesus Movement is now past, and we are expecting the second one to happen right away.

Apparently the second great awakening will happen after Russia is destroyed by its attempted invasion of Israel according to Ezekial chapter 38, then world wide Great Spiritual Awakening will happen!

This came to me by an open day vision on Friday Febuary 25, 2022. At that time, I was praying to God about Russia's invasion of Ukraine and complaining that the free nations of Europe remained uninvolved.

God told me that this invasion was a test case by Russia. Who felt that if it could get away with its invasion of Ukraine now and the free nations and America do nothing, then Russia sees itself free to invade Israel latter; once Israel starts exporting food, fruit, oil and gas to Europe.

MY PROPHECIES

After I wrote my first prophetic book the Lord told me that I was to be promoted from being just a congregational prophet in some church somewhere to being a revelatory prophet to the entire body of Christ.

This began the same way my congregational prophetic office began back in the Jesus Movement at Bethel Tabernacle in Redondo Beach, California. There I had to wait a whole year before I began prophesying in that church. Likewise I have waited a whole year now too before any revelatory prophecies have come my way. And when they came I was told to write them down for you all.

My first prophecy and perhaps the most important recent one began about midsummer 2016. At that time we were studying a subject from 1 JOHN 1:1 in Sunday school. Suddenly the verse began to come alive although I had read it many times before. Most can easily see that that verse tells us how we have seen and heard the gospel. But it goes on to mention how we have handled and felt the word of life, Jesus too. 'THAT WHICH WAS FROM THE BEGINNING, WHICH WE HAD HEARD, WHICH WE HAD SEEN WITH OUR EYES, WHICH WE HAVE LOOKED UPON, AND OUR HANDS HAVE HANDLED OF THE WORD OF LIFE', (1 John 1:1)**. Today almost no Christians recognize that we can feel God. And most Christians are taught to live by faith as the reformation declared.**

No one but Pentecostals are taught that feeling God is for today and part of the process of being reconciled to God commonly called the baptism in the Holy Ghost. So another reformation (awakening) is now needed in order to correct this false doctrine (that the Holy Ghost and His gifts died with the apostles and are not for today). This statement is false as God is NOT dead!

Some sophisticated theologians say that it would take a new doctrine to do this and to establish a new doctrine would require at least three different

Bible verses from three different Bible books. The one in I John 1:1 is already given and its explanation follows:

Explanation 1. When I was a young man I used to go to Kathryn Khulman's healing crusades at the Shrine auditorium in downtown LA. The song, 'He Touched Me' by Bill Gaither and his wife was one of Miss Khulman's theme songs. And as we sang it miracles started happening.

One day I got there+2 too late to find a good seat so I stood in back. Just as I entered the Shrine that day, Miss Khulman stopped the service as a miracle had just happened where I and some women were standing. Suddenly these women began to shriek and I looked around to see what was happening. Since I was just a few feet away from all this I saw it all first-hand. A young-women with a red dot on her forehead (apparently a Hindu) was holding a baby that had water on the brain and had a head as big as a watermelon. That baby's head shrank (something like 'trail stages' which dopers see) to the size of a football right in front of our eyes. Most of us fell on our faces realizing that now we were obviously in the presence of the living God since none of us had used any dope.

Back in the time of THE JESUS MOVEMENT many young people took dope to feel good and they came to Jesus to feel even better without the dangerous side effects of a criminal record and mental health, sin and employment problems.

The second major teaching about feeling God arose over doubting Thomas in John 20:26-28: 'AND AFTER EIGHT DAYS AGAIN HIS DISCIPLES WERE WITHIN, AND THOMAS WITH HIM: THEN CAME JESUS, THE DOORS BEING SHUT, AND STOOD IN THEIR MIDST AND SAID. PEACE BE UNTO YOU. THEN SAID JESUS UNTO THOMAS, REACH HITHER THY FINGER AND BEHOLD MY HANDS, AND REACH HITHER THY HAND AND THRUST IT INTO MY SIDE. AND BE NOT FAITHLESS BUT BELIEVING. AND THOMAS ANSWERED AND SAID UNTO HIM, **MY LORD AND MY GOD'.**

Your third scripture reveals that at another time in Matthew 28:9: 'JESUS MET THEM SAYING: ALL HAIL. AND THEY CAME AND **HELD HIM BY THE FEET, AND WORSHIPPED HIM'.**

Over a year latter this unusual prophecy was being given again as ***My second prophecy*** using another Bible story; shortly after the TV preacher was discussing virgins not prepared with adequate oil for the meeting of the bridegroom**. Those <u>not baptized in the Holy Spirit lack sufficient oil</u>**

to be ready to meet God, (Matthew 25). The Lord told me that this oil represents the Holy Spirit's ability to raise one to resurrection eternal life. So another reformation is now also needed to correct this false cecessionist doctrine; (that the Holy Ghost and his gifts are not for today for without this gift they fall for the false teaching like that tongues, prophecy and healing are not for today).

This explanation goes on to say **how dare some Christians even believe that after insulting the Holy Ghost and teaching against His gifts they can still enter heaven (His home)and have the audacity to expect Him to welcome them there even thou they have insulted Him with this false secessionist doctrine of those who believe their God is dead so His gifts must also be deceased as well.**

Without the Holy Spirit who raised Jesus from the dead how can any Christian really be raised to newness of life here and eternal life in heaven with God **So at least half the present Christian population will not be going to the marriage super of the Lamb and making heaven their home. THIS IS A VERY FRIGHTFUL REVELATION THAT I HOPE WAKES YOU UP.**

Explanation 2. These first two prophecies are just like the two parts of Pharaoh's dream that the prophet Joseph interpreted in Genesis 41:25 since the dream was double just like the two prophecies, therefore these dreams and these prophecies are both established by God and their fulfilment is certain and sure (Genesis 41:32).

Along about the end of Nov. 2017 ***My third prophecy*** came forth as there was much news about the abuse of women via sexual harassment, then I was told that all this complaining was making women look like rats, the enemies of men. And this will eventually serve to ensure that men will turn from women to each other in unnatural sexual unions called gay marriages (Romans 1:27).

On Thanksgiving Day My fourth prophecy came about government fraud concerning recruitment for the National Guard to supposedly stay in their home state to serve like in disaster relief. When this recruitment is really to have a standing army to fight in foreign wars just like President George W. BUSH did in Iraq. Jesus said that wars are due to come in Matthew 24:6. But He did not say that we should get involved in them.

Then ***My fifth prophecy*** came about our Pentecostal Church having moved away so we now must attend a Presbyterian church that does not believe as we do but nevertheless recites the Lord's Prayer every Sunday. Of course as Christians we believe in the Lord's Prayer too. The part I like the most is that part that says: 'THY KINGDOM COME. THY WILL BE DONE ON EARTH AS IT IS IN HEAVEN', (Mathew 6:9) of Mathew 6:9-15. Think how blessed that would be; no more crime, no more sickness and no more debts, wars, disasters or pain.

The part I like the least is that part which says; 'FORGIVE US OUR TRESSPASSES AS WE FORGIVE THOSE WHO TRESSPASS AGAINST US'. This may be fine for any mainline churches into personal relationships but as an evangelical Christian I believe that the blood of Jesus alone cleanses us from all sin, (1 John 1:7). So I want my forgiveness to be based on the blood of Jesus alone and not upon what I do or fail to do. I do not want God's forgiveness for me to be based on my forgiveness of others as if my personal relationships determine my relationship with God. As far as I know I have already forgiven others of whatever harm may come my way from them, so I now hold no grudges against anyone for anything.

There is another part of this prayer which I dislike; that is the unnecessary statement to lead us not into temptation. For where temptation is concerned; 'GOD CANNOT BE TEMPTED WITH EVIL NOR DOES HE TEMPT ANY MAN', (James 1:13).

The next part that I like the most says; 'DELIVER US FROM EVIL'. In this day of many telephone and computer scams we really need this protection to act as a fraud filter on our computers and with the people we contact everyday who want to entrap us in their web of evil, deceit and deception. Deception is first in the beginnings of sorrows, Matthew 24. (Sunday, Nov. 26, 2017).

(Sunday, Dec 10, 2017), ***My sixth prophecy*** came at this time saying there are four Biblical ways to obtain prosperity and to raise funds for evangelism. **1.** By paying tithes and giving offerings. (Luke 6:38), 'GIVE AND IT SHALL BE GIVEN UNTO YOU.' 2. Seed Faith (Matt. 17:20), 'IF YOU HAVE FAITH AS A GRAIN OF MUSTARD SEED.................... .'NOTHING SHALL BE IMPOSSIBLE'.

(Galatians 6:7) 'WHATSOEVER A MAN SOETH THAT SHALL HE ALSO REAP'. Anything means money, good health, long life or whatever you need or want for God's sake. 3. (Psalm 122:6), 'PRAY FOR THE PEACE OF JERUSALEM, THEY SHALL PROSPER THAT LOVE THEE'. 4. (II Chronicles 20:20), 'BELIEVE HIS PROPHETS SO SHALL YOU PROSPER'.

The above prophecy has been on my mind for 2 more days. I perceive that God has more to say about these ways of raising money to fulfill your mission.

In the first instance (Luke 6:7 & 8) God has blessed brother Hagee with tithes and offerings to move beyond his church to fulfill his mission to care for unwed mothers. Likewise, Dr. Ron Philips has been blessed also by this method of raising funds to fulfill that same type of mission for Abba House. And so has Jim Bakker with his Lori house. This part is ***My seventh prophecy.***

My eighth prophecy is about Brother Kenneth Copeland who has raised much money via seed-faith not for his personal prosperity but to fund mission outreaches to Africa and other places. I have heard from the missionaries in Africa and from Dr. Rodney Howard Brown how that he funds the mission outreach meetings of Rinehart Bonnke in Africa.

In addition, of course I have heard how that both Jewish Voice and Sid Roth and other messianic Jews like Rabbi Jonathon Con are **fulfilling their ministries by praying for the peace of Jerusalem and being blessed unexpectedly thereby (Psalm 122:6). Of course all these ministries benefit from believing God's prophets (II Chronicles 20:20)** on the part of the faithful to fulfill their missions. Praise God!

This prophecy asks God to deliver us from evil as a present tense verb. Thus a future or current evil is far worse than a past one which no longer influences people. Like condoning and advocating abortion. Which is far worse than sexually abusing or harassing some girl in grammar school. And to elect a democrat in favor of abortion and other sins like same sex marriage and the subsidizing of illegal alien bums is far worse than electing someone who stole a candy bar years ago. How one treats a girl or woman or personal property may be a personal sin. **But abortion is a social sin which can jeopardize the welfare of an entire society or nation**. What will the abortions of Houston, Texas cost America after costing Houston the flood? 'BE NOT DECEIVED, GOD IS NOT MOCKED WHATSOEVER A MAN SOWS THAT SHALL HE ALSO REAP', (Galatians 6:7).

My ninth prophecy (Wednesday night, Dec. 13, 2017). Abram lied to pharaoh that Sarai was his sister. Actually, Sarai was Abram's wife not his sister. I'm sure you've heard preachers say that all sins are the same. That is not true. There are such things as little white lies. Politicians say them as they run for office. Such sins may be considered inconsequential but real bad sins are called abominations. Like the one that says in (Leviticus 18:22) that 'YOU'RE NOT TO LIE WITH MANKIND AS WITH WOMAN KIND FOR SUCH IS ABOMINATION'.

My tenth prophecy (Thursday Dec. 14, 2017). There are other errors given from the pulpits of Christian Churches. A notable one from the Old

Testament is the erroneous belief that Moses was not allowed to enter the Promised Land because he struck the rock twice. Actually in any reading of the scripture in (Numbers 20:7-12) the meaning is clear. Here God told Moses exactly what to do. First he was to speak unto the rock (not unto the people to condemn them). And not to speak as if he and Aaron his brother were fetching water out of the rock themselves (whenever a supernatural event occurs like water out of a rock always give God glory)! Remember how it is written in (Isaiah 42:8) 'MY GLORY WILL I NOT GIVE TO ANOTHER'. Never confess in any way that a supernatural sign or event is your fault and fail to sanctify God thereby. Be careful that you don't assume more than what God has said for if so you will fall into the same trap that Moses did here by not fully obeying God's orders but demonstrating your anger instead.

It is very possible here that God wanted to demonstrate how creative miracles are performed – the same way that God spoke the world into existence (by an utterance of faith, commitment or decree as a sovereign).

My eleventh prophecy is by far the worst and the most dangerous error propagated from the pulpits of Christian churches today is the heresy of the Pre-Tribulation Rapture which keeps Christians from preparing for the last days. Most astute theologians like to come at this false teaching by exhaustive encirclement. However, realizing that all Christians must redeem the time I will just focus on one verse in Matthew 24:29. In this simple verse, the Lord Jesus says that 'IMMEDIATELY AFTER THE TRIBULATION OF THOSE DAYS. (Verse 30) THE SON OF MAN SHALL COME IN THE CLOUDS OF HEAVEN WITH POWER AND GREAT GLORY'. And those who have not prepared will experience 'The Great Falling Away'. So as a simple man not needing to engage in oral masturbation, I rest my case.

My twelfth prophecy says that some Christians feel that the God of the Old Testament is much sterner than the loving Jesus. For in the Old Testament the people of God were forbidden to eat unclean foods. However, when Jesus came God changed his mind and told Peter in Acts 11:7 to 'SLAY AND EAT' (the unclean). Back then we Christians could even eat food sacrificed to idols but not if it caused our brothers to be offended (I Corinthians. 8). Never the less by the end time of Revelations this was forbidden again (Revelation 2:14 & 20). Especially if anyone had the mark of the Beast upon them they could not even buy or sell food or anything (Revelation 13:17). Moreover, whoever received the mark of the Beast on his hand or his forehead shall be excluded from the first resurrection, (Revelation. 20:4).

Last summer last year I heard from God ***My thirteenth prophecy*** that God's man Donald Trump would be elected President of the United States of America. However, there would be many problems to overcome. Such as would the Christians get out to vote and would they vote for a rich man who some considered to be a philanderer with all his Miss America pageants. So I fasted (Isaiah 58:6) and prayed 3 days for this to happen and for Trump to win and he did. (I fasted Nov. 6, 7 and 8, 2016).

Now the most important aspect of the Trump agenda (tax cuts) required me to fast and pray again. So I did so Dec. 16-18, 2017 and ***My fourteenth prophecy*** came saying that God knows that it's very rare to fast and pray about issues that are not personal. In this case, as a senior citizen, my financial welfare was already assured. So I did not pray and fast for myself but for the people to have a substantial Christmas present, this greatly pleased God, since He is a giver too. I already know that some resent the rich and feel that money is the root of all evil. Never the less the Bible says in Ecclesiastes 10:19: 'THAT MONEY ANSWERS ALL THINGS'. So it's time for money to come your way too. What you do with it will be up to your conscience and not some bureaucrat's rules and regulations. Thus this extra money may be a test for some people. Of course more money may lead to increased domestic violence between substance abusers (like alcoholics, drunks and dopers) with members of their own families. But if it takes a fight to bring about rehabilitation and prevent the waste of money so be it.

I see that as the Bible says in I Corinthians. 6:19: 'YOUR BODY IS THE TEMPLE OF THE HOLY GHOST', so now you can spend more money on yourself. Buy yourself some good health books. See a doctor and a dentist. Take better care of yourself. Eat more nutritious food. Be aware of what your body needs for better health. I heard from one doctor that because America does not allow its land to lay fallow every seven years therefore it's now exhausted and lacks necessary nutriments like magnesium. So buy your vitamins and minerals and take them every day. Or better yet buy yourself a small farm and move away from municipal madness and cities with many social problems. Also use your extra money to realize your dreams and start a new business to make money and fund the gospel.

My fifteenth prophecy concerns you corporations that need to be thankful that the government has now recognized a corporation as a person with personal rights. So now use those rights and that increased money to expand your business, to hire more people, to pay your employees more and thus share the wealth. Since more money is coming to all, may all recognize that they are being blessed by God. Thank God that my fast for tax cuts is now over since any fasting causes me the inconvenience of diarrhea. Plus doctors don't like it when you skip taking meds for high blood pressure. But I have monitored my blood pressure each day and today Tuesday, December 19, 2017 my blood pressure is 116/68 which is fine for me.

My sixteenth prophecy says that although most Christian churches do not instruct their people to fast for any reason let alone non-personal and non-religious reasons. Certainly for political reasons or social issues or anything having to do with non-church issues like the government. Many say that there should be a separation between church and state. But the Bible also says (speaking of Jesus) that 'THE GOVERNMENT SHALL BE UPON HIS SHOULDERS', (Isaiah 9:6). And 'I'LL BE SEATED IN HEAVENLY PLACES WITH HIM', (Ephesians 2:6).

Moreover ***My seventeenth prophecy*** says from the Bible that 'YOU RECEIVE NOT BECAUSE YOU ASK NOT, ASK AND YOU SHALL RECEIVE', (James 4:2). And 'IF YOU ASK ANYTHING IN HIS NAME, YOU SHALL RECEIVE' (whatever you ask for) (John 14:13&14). So I have asked (fasted and prayed for several days). The proof that I will receive is the fact that I have already received several more unexpected revelations during this time. Here some of them are listed below:

My eighteenth prophecy says that Jesus first miracle of turning water into wine at the marriage of Cana of Galilee was a miracle of luxury as Jesus has come to not only erase one's sins and give the new birth but also 'TO GIVE US LIFE MORE ABUNDANTLY', (John 10:10).

My nineteenth prophecy here in Daytona Beach, Florida I have been seeing many turkey vultures up in the sky, circling around. A local TV channel has shown these same birds flying around the Orange County Courthouse in Orlando. These birds are attracted to death, but nothing has died around here yet. So death of some sort is due to come soon, at least during the lifetime of these birds. 'BE NOT DECEIVED THE WAGES OF SIN IS DEATH', (Romans 6:23).

My twentieth prophecy asks Have you ever heard that popular saying '<u>the force be with you'? </u>I don't want to scare you but this shows how far into the end times we have now come. The prophet Daniel describes the anti-Christ in Daniel 11:36-45. And in Daniel 11:38 it says that 'HE SHALL HONOR THE **GOD OF FORCES'.**

My twenty-first Prophecy *states* that in reviewing Daniel 11 in the previous revelation, a new revelation has come forth: most have heard that the Muslims terrorists like to kill Christians and Jews in order to have sex with 73 virgins in heaven. The scripture in Daniel reveals that the anti-Christ will be more religious than many Christians who are divorced and remarried. In other words he will not care for the desire of **women (Daniel 11:32) and so will be an asexual being. As such Muslim ideology may offend him and we know that he will kill many to show that he is god**. So if you have been worried about the Muslim invasion of Europe via its infestation of Syrian refugees with this naughty Muslim mindset get over it. For the anti-Christ will be more like a new age god than a 7th century emir of a caliphate of infidels.

My twenty-second prophecy came last night December 19, 2017 I listened some to Michael Savage on the radio. He was expounding on his research of President Trump's tax cut plan. I remember that he said that history shows that corporations will spend their excess money on stock buy backs and increased dividends for stock owners rather than expanding their business and hiring new employees. Then I turned the radio off and went to sleep. The next morning this revelation came: it was true once and still is that some big corporations are led by managers not entrepreneurs who take risks. But now the government has ruled that corporations are people too with personal rights and personal attributes. Among those attributes is ego. Now I graduated from Fuller Seminary, the only Seminary in the country with a graduate school of psychology approved by the APA. So I took a few graduate courses in ego development there. From those classes I see where every normal person would rather become something extra ordinary than just remain a dull, safe, nerd. But besides this there is another reason why Michael Savage's viewpoint does not apply here. Soon all will realize that God placed Trump in office as his man and not the Russians. And in such an atmosphere of God's favor Corporations are free to take risks, to become bigger by expanding and even go into new areas of business where they will need to hire new people (Isaiah 54:2).

In the old time of kings, a monarch's wealth was determined not by his gold or silver but by the number of subjects he had and the area or extent of his empire

Likewise God's kingdom is determined by the number of souls that are worshipping Him. God's wealth is not determined by the streets of gold or the splendor of His Kingdom. ***This is my prophecy twenty-three.***

Beyond this in ***My prophecy twenty-four*** it should be noted that along with my fasting has also come prayer, specific prayer for corporations to expand not only in their area of expertise but to go into new areas as well to have their own territories of dominance there by hiring more people to ensure their vision there. Now the Bible says in John 14:14 that 'IF YOU ASK ANYTHING IN MY NAME I WILL DO IT'. So I rest my case.

Then in ***My prophecy twenty-five*** I saw Kenneth Copeland on TV in which he was talking about **seed faith** from that scripture in **Mark 2:5.** Then I heard another prophet, Jeremiah Johnson also on TV **expounding the coming outpouring of God's Spirit upon all flesh from the prophecy of Joel.** Then putting them together this revelation came: **Since corporations are now people too God's promises also now extend to them as well. Anyone filled with the Spirit does the stuff that God wants done.** In a personal case that might mean starting a business to fund the end time harvest. A minister might also be blessed to start a new ministry. And a corporation may desire to realize its mission by extending itself into some new territory where it might build factories and ware- houses and hire new people to run it all.

Now we see by my prophecy twenty-five that I was right when I said that these corporations would spend their increased funds on people and their welfare. But I forgot to mention that their natural emphasis on giving to charities natural first fruit offerings that God commanded to Moses (Leviticus 5:8). In this light I would seek to evaluate any charity that I would donate to by the Evangelical Council of Financial Accountability.

Since more money is also coming to you according to ***My prophecy twenty-six*** I would review that book package about realizing dreams by Terri. com for just $35. When it comes read it and review it then sleep on it to get what the Lord wants you to do. Please remember that you only have one life to live therefore ask Christ to take your life and do something with it that brings honor to God.

My prophecy twenty-seven asks how can you give an alter call for getting reconciled to God in a church that has no altars? I think we're missing something here. Don't you think so?

Under the old covenant God told Moses in ***My prophecy twenty-eight*** **(Exodus 26:1-37)** to build an entire tabernacle down to the smallest detail in order to meet God with blood sacrifices. Since the blood sacrifice has already been paid by Jesus, we now get to meet God. 'WITHOUT THE BLOOD OF JESUS THERE IS NO REMISSION OF SINS' Hebrews 9:22)**.**

This morning December 23, 2017 ***My prophecy twenty-nine*** woke me up from my dream about dark religious experiences. At first I was with several men in some sort of Muslim experience. These people kept using a large black sheet to keep me from other Muslims and to supposedly protect me from evil spirits. Once I woke up this came: 'GOD IS LIGHT AND IN HIM IS NO DARKNESS AT ALL', (1John 1:5). So the black sheet was a very deficient and bad sign. I gathered instantly what I already knew that is that Muslims are not of God. Even though they sometimes wear white.

By My prophecy thirty I remembered from childhood that my mother once had a Jehovah's Witness landlord and once we went to visit his Kingdom Hall. This was back in the days before air conditioning and that place had no windows to open and it got very hot there. Plus it was dark inside. When my mother's mascara began to run she told me that we were not gonna go back there again. In addition, in a dark atmosphere no one was able to feel God or see any signs from Him. And besides she had been raised Catholic, so she remembered the commandment that says 'THOU SHALT HAVE NO OTHER GODS BEFORE ME', (Deuteronomy 5:7).

I just heard over TV their discussion over 'Francis and friends' about several different kinds of Bibles in ***My prophecy thirty-one*** they got a phone call which asked them which Bible was best. Of course they all said Jimmy Swaggart's Expositors Study Bible since they were all Jimmy Swaggart's employees. But the hidden treasure in that Bible is basically the King James Version with the notes of the famous evangelist Jimmy Swaggart.

Actually the King James Bible is the best known version. It is the only anointed Bible for it was composed for an anointed man-King James. No other Bible has the anointing quality of the King James Bible and this alone makes the King James Version the best. I can almost hear the majesty of it now, especially in the Jimmy Swaggart or fire edition. 'THY WORD OH GOD HAVE I HID IN MY HEART THAT I MIGHT NOT SIN AGAINST THEE', (Psalm 119:11).

In My prophecy thirty-two some teach that certain books of the Bible are only for Jews like the Old Testament and not for Christians like the New Testament. But the truth is as the old Sunday school song says; 'every promise in the book is mine every chapter every verse every line'. The Bible, all of it, is given to us as 'EXCEEDING GREAT AND PRECIOUS PROMISES', (II Peter 1:4).

Wednesday morning February 8, 2018 ***My prophecy thirty-three*** came saying when many of the sons of God came to present themselves before God, Satan also showed up. Whereupon God boasted to Satan about his servant Job. And God gave Satan permission to test Job first with finances, but then with his health as well. Most Christians do not believe that they will ever be tested or have to suffer in anyway. 'IF YOU DO NOT SUFFER WITH

HIM, YOU SHALL NOT REIGN WITH HIM', (II Timothy 2:2). This is easily confirmed by the names Christians call themselves. Back in Job's day Christians were called servants. In Jesus day they had moved on up to being called disciples. Some years ago, being lifted up with pride, they called themselves 'manifested sons of God'. Today, still having that same pride they call themselves 'Kings Kids'.

In ***My prophecy thirty-four*** as in **Genesis 17** Abram's name was changed to Abraham and later Sari became Sarah. As they confessed their new names their new promises came into manifestation too. Confession brings possession and always comes before possession. You must needs **speak forth out loud what you want God to do for you.** Therefore, people should pray out loud and often. 'YE RECEIVE NOT BECAUSE YOU ASK NOT, ASK AND YOU SHALL RECEIVE', (I John 1:5).

'DEATH AND LIFE ARE IN THE POWER OF THE TONGUE', (Proverbs 18:21). Consequently, you must speak forth good stuff and not stupid 'small talk' into reality in your life and renounce any bad habits that hinder you from becoming what God wants you to be. This is ***My prophecy thirty-five.***

On the night of December 28, 2017***My prophecy thirty-six*** came about Samson's sin and faith. The passivists that currently rule the church have made it their obligation to expose all of Samson's sins because they do not believe that God called any man to kill the Philistines. We Christians are to love our enemies (Luke 6:35). **But no verse commands Christians to love the enemies of God or those who follow a false god.** They believe that Samson's many sins disqualify him from doing God's will especially killing. But the prophet Elijah slew the 40 prophets of the false god Baal (II Kings 18:40). Just like today these people want to disqualify Trump for his past sexual sins with women. Samson's sexual sins as a young man are probably self-evident.

The real question here comes about after Samson is blinded and made to serve the Philistines. At no time does he ever repent for being with Delilah and for having his hair cut in violation of the Nazarite vow made at his birth. After his capture and subrogation, he continues to sin. One time he asked but really (lied) to the young boy who led him about that he needed to rest on the pillar of the temple to the Philistine god. And in his prayer to God he felt sorry for his blindness and asked God to throw down the Philistine temple to their false god because of it. Of course God gave him the power to fulfill his purpose even though his motivation was now vengeful, misguided and supposedly 'meanMy spirited', because it was also God's desire too **This**

proves that the power of real faith overshadows the disability of personal sin. Yes, the virtue of Samson's faith overcame the naughtiness of his personal sins. And because of the power of his faith he is now listed in the hall of fame for faith in Hebrews 11:32. In that light, I'd rather be celebrated for my faith in doing something explosive which pleases God then occupied trying to control some bad habit or subdue personal sins for the rest of my life like some monk. We are NOT commanded to only work on our personal sins as the blood of Jesus has already done that for us. But **now we are to occupy as Jesus destroys the works of the devil and gets us ready to rule and reign with Him. (Luke 19:13)(1 John 3:8).**

Apparently God has more to say about faith in ***My peophecy thirty-seven.*** Before I began, I remember Dr. Price over his TV program 'Ever Increasing Faith'. Dr. Price, a Black preacher exercises 'The Word of wisdom', a spiritual gift, that's why I watched him. He also took on to mentor a white Pentecostal preacher named Casey Treat who now ministers in Seattle. So much for this anti-Christian racist propaganda about how White and Black ministers are not able to see alike. So as it is written 'CAN TWO WALK TOGETHER EXCEPT THEY BE AGREED'? (Amos 3:3).

When the apostles asked Jesus to increase their faith, they made an enlightening though mistaken request. For 'EVERY MAN HAS A MEASURE OF FAITH', (Romans 12:3). To put it in more crude terms for everyone to understand: everyone who sits down on a toilet expects something to come forth. Jesus said that if you just had a little faith only the size of a grain of mustard seed. You could ask and that little faith could grow into the reality of the largest herb (as big as a tree), (Matthew 12:31&32). This shows how the apostles (disciples of Jesus) were mistaken about the amount of faith they already had.

According to ***My prophecy thirty-eight*** they could have asked the God-man Jesus to increase many human virtues like love for the lost or other qualities like wealth or health (like the health and wealth gospel). But their request centered on faith alone because they realized that faith was the essential ingredient in the miracles that they saw Jesus perform. And every disciple wants to be like their leader. So nowhere did they ever ask Jesus to increase any human virtue. Apparently though men they saw themselves on equal terms with the God-man Jesus when it came to personal virtues. But they recognized that Jesus could do miracles which they couldn't do. So they concluded that this was because they lacked sufficient faith to do so. 'THROUGH FAITH ALL THINGS ARE POSSIBLE', (Matthew 9:26).

But in reality they lacked sufficient risk taking and the expectation that after you do the will of God (like witnessing) you will receive the blessing or reward of obedience for doing so like saving souls.

I just heard one of my prosperity preacher friends over TV mention in ***My prophecy thirty-nine*** the case where Jesus after speaking told the professional fisherman (His disciples) to let down their nets to obtain the reward of fish. Then I realized something that most pastors do not see: **after speaking Jesus expected a blessing to confirm his words** likewise preachers who need more money or things for some ministry should **preach a message which outlines their vision from God and then take up an offering so that the people can confirm it as the will of God in this for them too. It is very important to give the people a reason to give** whereas most offerings are just taken up as a duty or obligation, just like paying tithes. A vision from God always overrules any religious obligation especially when it comes to giving. 'OBEDIENCE IS BETTER THAN SACRIFICE', (1 Samuel 15:22).

God has given me more to say about this in this same prophecy thirty-nine. When desiring to move on in God to accomplish more do not try to raise funds for the church by sharing all its expenses, especially staff salaries. But share your vision for that particular church for that people of God there and give the people there the opportunity to confirm your vision by taking up an offering. If it's more than enough, praise God! If not, declare a time of fasting and prayer for your vision to take root. Remember 'WHERE THERE IS NO VISION THE PEOPLE PERISH', (Proverbs 29:18).

In My prophecy forty came forth recently about my wheelchair scooter. Which one of my friends borrowed from me in order to get some food that the church was giving away. In transit to that church an automobile accident happened that was not his fault. And since he was banged up pretty bad and unconscious the other driver contaminated all the witnesses so they would see things her way. This aroused my anger since my wheelchair scooter is our only means of transportation to get groceries, pay bills, and buy stuff. So I filed a small claim for my wheelchair scooter which they damaged beyond repair. I was frustrated but as the case progressed this revelation came to me in a dream. It is from the second chapter of Mark in the Bible. Of course the Bible has been subject to many commentaries over the years. But no one has noticed this before as far as I know. So what I received is a clear revelation which should authenticate and substantiate my ministry here.

In this prophecy 40 the Lord Jesus had gone to do his ministry of preaching, teaching, working miracles and healing. A paralytic carried by four friends had shown up to be healed. Since the place was crowded, in order to get the paralyzed seeker to Jesus to obtain his healing they had to violate roman law, disregard property rights and break up the roof of that house to let the paralyzed 'drop in' on Jesus to get healed.

This prophecy 40 showed me that in order to get what you need from God sometimes it becomes necessary to disregard insurance rules and traffic laws. As with the healing of the paralytic my opponents in my wheelchair scooter case are attempting to use the obstacles of insurance rules and traffic laws as obstacles to keep me from obtaining justice. But the Lord wants me to hang in there as he told me that a wheelchair scooter is considered a wheelchair and a person in a wheelchair is considered a pedestrian. And a pedestrian is not subject to insurance rules and traffic laws. Most Christians know that faith without works is dead, but few understand that the works of God sometimes supersede man's folkways, customs or laws.

My prophecy forty-one, (Sunday, December 31, 2017). It is time to thank God for what He accomplished in 2017. In January, Trump was inaugurated and in December, his tax cuts became law. So now almost everyone including corporations have more money to fulfill their visions. 'MONEY ANSWERS ALL THINGS', (Ecclesiastes 10:19). Thank you Jesus for this Christmas present.

New Year's Day 2018. I heard over the news that this was the coldest New Years in a century in New York. And with more and more snow, apparently a little ice age has now begun according to ***My prophecy forty-two***. So much for the global warming hoax.

I remember that not long ago an expert from NASA wrote a scientific book about the coming little ice age. In addition, experts there confirmed his research. As a Floridian, I must say that if a little ice age is coming you will need to move away from all that bitter cold. If you move to Florida note, that we do not need your problems that are Democratic like Black Muslim infestations and Black and Latino gangs here. Keep your drugs including opioids and increased taxes to support illegal alien bums and their crimes away too. The scripture says to 'HAVE NO FELLOWSHIP WITH THE UNFRUITFUL WORKS OF DARKNESS, BUT RATHER REPROVE THEM', (Ephesians 5:11).

Actually according to ***My prophecy forty-three*** all Northern bums intoxicated with the Democratic policy of dependency should be compelled to enter reeducation camps to learn the Republican policy of self-sufficiency. 'IF ANY WILL NOT WORK NEITHER SHOULD HE EAT', (II Thess. 3:11).

Some of you may have heard about the Jews exodus from Egypt and journey to The Promised Land. They were led by Moses; the man of God not by some Democratic committee.

My prophecy forty-four points out that most of the cities ruled by the Democratic Party in the North have failed and we don't want that failure here. Moreover it's now time to make New Year's resolutions. So discard the Democratic Party, drugs and dependency and relearn how to obtain blessings for yourself and how to become a blessing to others.

In My prophecy forty-five I had a very unusual dream last night. In this dream a young bearded man dressed in work clothes was showing me around a large warehouse filled with used bicycles. From what I gathered he was the investor/owner of this enterprise. I was going to buy this and use it for the inner city. We were going to sell used and reconditioned bicycles as transportation for the poor. But I am wheelchair disabled and cannot work this business. Nor do I have the money necessary to buy it. Never the less to me this is a very familiar equation from God: my lack of money is always the obstacle I need to overcome to do God's will. So to overcome this I just need to fast for God's will to be manifest. My age and wheelchair disability means that I should probably give this away to someone more capable of handling it. I know that by prayer and fasting I can get the money to buy this business. But then I'll need to give it away for someone to run. Could that someone be you?

My prophecy forty-six says that even heaven is a walled city (Revelation 21:18). Today we would call it a 'gated community'. Actually it has twelve gates of pearls (Revelations 21:21). The Bible lists in Galatians 5:19-21 those who will be excluded from that city. It says that: 'THOSE WHO PRACTICE IMMORALITY, IMPURITY, INDECENCY, IDOLATRY, SORCERY, ENMITY, STRIFE, JEALOUSY, ANGER, SELFISHNESS, DISSENSIONS, FACTIONS, HERESIES, ENVY AND THE LIKE SHALL NOT INHERIT THE KINGDOM OF GOD'. So heaven excludes all sin against God. **It only includes those who believe that Jesus Christ is the Son of God and that He is the resurrection and the life.** As it is written 'HE THAT HAS THE SON HAS LIFE AND HE THAT DOES NOT HAVE THE SON OF GOD DOES NOT HAVE LIFE', (1 John 5:11&12). So then for the progressives who believe in unlimited inclusion of diversity or the universal salvation of all since all men are created equal it must be said that there will be no Muslims, Buddhists, Mormons, Scientologists, Hindus, Animists, infidels, sinners or reprobates in the kingdom of God. In fact there are certain angels of power who will be the guards of that city and whosoever is not written in the Lamb's Book of Life shall not be allowed to enter it (Revelation 21:27). **Democrats will weep as immigration exclusion becomes manifest for eternity.**

In My prophecy forty-seven I heard a famous faith preacher who is an expert in prayer discuss fasting yesterday on TV. After sleeping on his word this came. Being an expert in prayer does not make you an expert in all other areas. Usually when you pray you bring up your main needs and wants, as your prayer includes your petition. And backslidden preachers say that we fast to crucify the flesh or deprive it so that we will do the will of God. That idea comes from a guilty conscience not God. In Isaiah 58:6 God declares the fast that He has chosen. That fast loosens the bands of wickedness, undoes the heavy burden, lets the oppressed go free and breaks every yoke. In other words that fast is to bring about personal deliverance, revival and awakening to do the will of God on earth.

In My prophecy forty-eight in 2016 I fasted and prayed for Trump to win the election as the Republican platform was much closer to God than the Democratic one which was for the killing of babies (abortion). Of course Trump won and became President, thank you Jesus. At the end of 2017 I also fasted for Trump's tax cuts to bless people, corporations included with more money as 'MONEY ANSWERS ALL THINGS', (Ecclesiastes 10:19). Praise God it worked even though most preachers don't care for fasting to resolve political issues. I have just fasted again for God to keep Florida Republican and that these Democratic Porto Ricans get thrown out. These people destroyed the economy of Porto Rico and we certainly don't need them here to do the same thing to Florida. It should be required by law to renounce this ungodly (pro-abortion) Democratic mindset of dependency.

Today there are many non-Christians trying to act like Christians by doing good works and calling it social services. Even some governments do good works with your tax dollars as if they were godly. That's where we get free meals for school children from. Free clothes and food for the homeless and other such charities result from this too. People that participate in this feel that such reconciles them to God. But **good works do not reconcile anyone to God.** Christianity is not just for doing good works**. Christianity is a Person.** As it is written; 'HE THAT HAS THE SON HAS LIFE AND HE THAT DOES NOT HAVE THE SON OF GOD DOES NOT HAVE LIFE', (1 John 5:11 & 12) Moreover doing all these good works has a social drawback. It leads children and other people to lack sufficient motivation to improve their lot in life themselves. So in other words this **personal charity is just the first instalment on a life of perpetual dependency.**

In my prophecy forty-nine I just remembered the famous evangelist John G Lake. Back in the days of the bubonic plague he worked with some people suffering from this disease yet he himself never got sick. When people died from this plague he put his hand over their mouth to collect the foam from one of these infected. That foam was immediately examined under a microscope as it came from the victim's mouth. But once it touched the evangelist's hand the infecting virus died. John G Lake said to his questioners that Jesus had made him free from the law of sin and death. 'FOR THE LAW OF THE SPIRIT OF LIFE IN CHRIST JESUS HAS MADE ME FREE FROM THE LAW OF SIN AND DEATH', (Romans 8:2).

Today in My prophecy fifty January 10, 2018 I heard Joyce Meyer over TV in which she mentioned that too many people were just dating Jesus and not yet married to him exercising all the privileges that come with His name. I would go further than that by simply quoting a scripture that tells why there is a shortage of young converts in our churches today. That scripture is Romans 7:4 which says…'THAT YOU SHOULD BE MARRIED TO ANOTHER, EVEN TO HIM THAT IS RAISED FROM THE DEAD (JESUS) THAT YE SHOULD BRING FORTH FRUIT (NEW CONVERTS) UNTO GOD'.

Today in My prophecy fifty-one I also heard Rick Renner teaching about the armor of God. And how that the power of God clothes us in that armor. Here is a Pentecostal theological truth which many Christians ignore: the power of God only results from the anointing quality of Spirit baptized believers submitted to the Spirit of God. So instead of declaring this Pentecostal truth it's more popular today to refer to Spirit baptism (which could cause division in the body of Christ) instead of the power of God.

Last night My prophecy fifty-two came as I was listening to my radio program called coasttocoastam.com This had an expert talking about artificial intelligence. Which I tuned out and turned off as God began to speak to me. God mentioned an area in the Old Testament (2 Kings 6:6) where the prophet of God imparted a quality of life to an inanimate object by saying: 'THE IRON DID SWIM' And of course you know about the water turned to wine in John 2:7 & 8. Then there were also the times when Jesus fed the multitudes too. But today no one does these types of miracles even though it says: 'THE WORKS THAT I DO, SHALL YOU DO ALSO' (John 14:12).

In the Great Tribulation however both the beast and the false prophet will do them. In fact you will not be able to buy or sell without the mark of the beast. But most astonishingly the false prophet will be able to make the image of the beast to live and speak (Rev. 13:15). Most people do not understand that even our children are now being conditioned for this by TV cartoons in which animals and non-living objects like farm tools speak.

This will be a very freaky miracle as the image of the beast will be an inanimate object which will not age or get sick. Some will even say that this is better than the biological creation of God which both ages and dies. Only your knowledge of the Word and your possession of the Lord Jesus Christ will safe guard you from this deception and enable you to avoid the fires of hell as 'BOTH THE BEAST AND THE FALSE PROPHET SHALL BE CAST ALIVE INTO THE LAKE OF FIRE', (Rev. 19:20).

My prophecy fifty-three came while reviewing the above scripture for the above word I came across another word which needs to be said here. This word comes from Revelation 16:15 which discusses not only the coming of the Lord but also walking naked and failing to watch and pray. Since no preacher has mentioned the moral decline of this society to nakedness, I will. In the last days the wearing of garments will become less popular. Men and women will want to see what they are getting into, so nudity will become very popular. In fact the beautiful and the sexually gifted will want to become sexually active by showing themselves off as in advertising themselves for sex.

According to this same prophecy as today a grandfather feels the upper arm of his grandson to see how big his muscles have become. In that day a guy shall be felt to see how big his 'love muscle' has become. Some ignorant people say this will never happen. But those who have read their Bibles remember how that the children of Israel descended into a drunken orgy after Moses had been gone only 40 days. What do you think America's young men will be like after 40 years of no prayer or Bible reading in school and 50 years of legalized abortions nation-wide?

My prophecy fifty-four came on TV this morning as the man of faith Jerry Seville with his guest Richard Roberts. Jerry talked about some of his past victories in faith. Then Richard operated a word of knowledge. Then as most preachers do they began discussing sin and its consequences in everyone's life. But instead of dwelling on sin they agreed that **God is more concerned about moving ahead in faith than He is about anyone's personal sins.** For Jesus was given to erase the consequences of every sin. So why do we keep dwelling on them and everyone's shortcomings? All these negative feelings generate feelings of inferiority which result in 'low self-esteem which is very dangerous. Not because of the sin 'FOR ALL HAVE SINNED AND FALLEN SHORT OF THE GLORY OF GOD', (Romans

3:23). But because we allow that obstacle of sin to keep us from finishing the race that God has set before us, we thus allow that sin to deflate our faith and keep us from obeying God.

So the Lord Jesus asks this question ***in My prophecy fifty-five***; 'WHEN I COME WILL I FIND FAITH ON THE EARTH', (Luke 18:8). 'FAITH COMES BY HEARING AND HEARING BY THE WORD OF GOD', (Romans 10:17). **Therefore to increase faith just read the Bible out loud.** Just like I used to read out loud in grammar or elementary school. Remember now the value of childlike faith 'WHOSOEVER SHALL NOT RECEIVE THE KINGDOM OF GOD AS A LITTLE CHILD SHALL IN NO WISE ENTER THEREIN', (Luke 18:17).

I perceive God ***in My prophecy fifty-six*** has more to say about this. So I'll bring up one incident in the crucifixion of Jesus for a positive confession of faith alone without any ritual resulted in one person becoming reconciled to God or saved. That person was the criminal who was crucified with Jesus but asked to be remembered when Jesus came into His kingdom **(Luke 23:43).**

In My prophecy fifty-seven I have received some additional truth which those who are into ritual will dislike. Nevertheless here it is: this criminal in Luke 23:43 never repented nor confessed his sins. He did not do penance. He was not baptized by any method either sprinkling or total emersion. Nor was he baptized in any specific name, either Jesus only or in the name of the Father, the Son and the Holy Ghost. All he did was confess out loud who Jesus was (the King) by asking to be included in his kingdom. This is honoring God and ascribing to Him by faith the ability to transform a criminal into a citizen of the kingdom of God.

So the Spirit in the Bible says: 'THAT IF YOU SHALL CONFESS WITH YOUR MOUTH THE LORD JESUS AND SHALL BELIEVE IN YOUR HEART THAT GOD HAS RAISED HIM FROM THE DEAD YOU SHALL BE SAVED', (Romans 10: 9 & 10).

On January 14, 2018 ***My prophecy fifty-eight*** came while I was reading some more in my new book: Right People, Right Place, Right Plan by Janzen Franklin when I also had 60 minutes on TV to see about North Korea's nuclear arsenal. About the time the segment about North Korea came on I also reached the bottom of page 17 in my book where Janzen Franklin talked about his mom paying him $20 to sing the 'king is coming'.

About that time the number 20 came into clear focus. 20 was the age a young Hebrew had to be in order to fight in the army of God. So 20 usually means war. This nuclear arsenal part of 60 minutes which came on at that exact time seems to be saying who the war will be within the natural. But in the Spirit 20 indicates that Janzen Franklin began his war against Satan when he got the $20.00 from his mom and it will continue throughout his life. As far as war with North Korea I recommend you start watching the Jim Baker show and get ready for what's coming naturally but in the Spirit go to a Spirit Filled Church to get prepared spiritually. Save money, store food, stay prayed up, get out of debt, get out of the anti-Christian pro-abortion Democratic Party with its global agenda of fake news like global warming and move South as it's going to get cold. Their 'fake news' has angered God. And we know from history that if sinners in the hands of an angry God repent awakening results. But if there is no repentance then mass destruction comes. **So what comes depends upon your repentance from sin and obedience to God's will.**

So the Holy Spirit says ***in My prophecy fifty-nine***: 'REPENT AND BE CONVERTED SAYS THE LORD AND THE TIMES OF REFRESHING SHALL COME FROM THE PRESENCE OF THE LORD', (Acts 8:19).

My prophecy sixty came on Wednesday morning January 7, 2018 as I continued reading in Janzen Franklin's new book: <u>Right People, Right Place, Right Plan</u> under the chapter heading 'a feel for God's voice' page 25 Janzen reports how that US treasury agents were trained to determine real from counterfeit bills by studying and handling the real bill. They did this for so long that they acquired by experience '<u>a feel for the real</u>'. And thus it was easy for them to discard the fake or counterfeit.

This also happens in Jimmy Swaggart's ministry especially in his messages of the cross. Where the study centers upon what the Lord Jesus has done to secure our salvation. Being this well rooted in the truth gives you the insight and prerogative to expose non-Christian cults.

I suppose that it is not very unusual for this issue to come up again as there are no coincidences in God. But he does repeat truth that has not yet been absorbed by his people. From 1 John 1 we understand that or should be **<u>feeling God is part of the conversion process, or should be</u>.** As far as I know Jimmy Swaggart has been the only evangelist that has done this. Perhaps his obedience to this has now resulted in a worldwide television network. Christian people acquire many ways to increase their blessings. <u>But expounding the whole truth of God's word is the best method known (after preaching Jesus as Savior go on to preach Jesus as the baptizer in the Holy Ghost too).</u>

My prophecy sixty-one then came in the form of a personal rebuke. God said to me: 'I KNOW THAT YOU ARE A SEMINARY GRADUATE

AND A COLLEGE GRADUATE BUT MOST OF MY PEOPLE HAVE NOT EVEN GRADUATED FROM HIGH SCHOOL AND MANY ARE MEMBERS OF TRIBES THAT LIVE IN REMOTE HUTS AND ARE ILLITERATE. FOR THEIR SAKE I WANT YOU TO GO BACK TO WHAT YOU HAVE ALREADY WRITTEN AND PLAINLY AND CLEARLY IMPART EXACTLY WHAT THE HOLY SPIRIT HAS TO SAY ABOUT EACH ISSUE. THEN I WILL TELL YOU MORE LIKE THIS CLEAR FAITH WHERE CATTLE WERE JUST DUMB BEASTS WITHOUT HUMAN BRAINS SAW SPOTS ON A PIECE OF WOOD IN THEIR TROUGHS AND GAVE BIRTH TO SPOTTED CATTLE. THUS JACOB BECAME VERY RICH'. (Genesis 30). So much for those anti-prosperity preachers of vows of poverty. Some people feel that positive confessions from God's word are too dangerous to say out loud as the devil might use his power to find and abuse them. But the devil is not Omni-present and he cannot find you if you are 'HIDDEN WITH CHRIST IN GOD', (Colossians 3:3).

Then ***My prophecy sixty-two*** came on Friday morning January 19, 2018. A few days ago when I heard on the news about that horrible case of child abuse in Southern California I thought right away about that Bible verse in 1 Timothy 5:8 which says that 'IF ANY PROVIDE NOT FOR HIS OWN ESPECIALLY THOSE OF HIS OWN HOUSE HE HAS DENIED THE FAITH AND IS WORSE THAN AN INFIDEL'. This is a very strong judgmental word. So I decided to hold my peace for a more pleasant one to manifest. Today January 19, that word came forth and it's a very good word. The number of abused children is 13. And 13 is the prophetic number which converts bad news to good news. And in the Old Testament when the people of God were deprived God sent abundance. Sometimes this happened in the form of rain but once it also happened in the form of prepared food, ready to eat. That's just like real revival. As those 13 were released I thought of ***the power of God which breaks every yoke and sets the captives free. This indicates that 2018 will be the beginning of a time of revival and awakening. Praise God!***

I woke up this morning (Monday, January 20, 2018) as ***My prophecy sixty-three*** came with a very unpleasant Bible Verse on my mind. It was from 1 Timothy 4:14 that says: 'ALEXANDER THE COPPERSMITH HAS DONE ME MUCH EVIL, MAY GOD REWARD HIM ACCORDING TO HIS WORKS'. Here we see Paul being judgmental as the passivist say and not turning the other cheek. The Democrats especially believe we should include evil for diversity's sake. But the Bible says 'TO HAVE NO FELLOWSHIP WITH THE UNFRUITFUL WORKS OF DARNESS, BUT RATHER TO REPROVE THEM', (Ephesians 5:11). Additionally the Bible also says in (2 Corinthians 6:14) 'BE NOT UNEQUALLY YOKED TOGETHER WITH UNBELIEVERS FOR WHAT FELLOWSHIP HAS RIGHTEOUSNESS WITH UNRIGHTEOUSNESS, OR WHAT COMMUNION HAS LIGHT WITH DARKNESS?' The above clearly applies in the case of absorbing into our society illegal aliens.

From my own experience in ***My prophecy sixty-four*** let me share this: after I graduated from Fuller Seminary in California I could not get any ministerial job because I am wheelchair disabled and 'wheelchairs do not inspire faith'. So after I graduated I was kicked out of student housing there. And wound up living on the streets of Southern California since I could not afford the high cost of rents out there. I then also decided to use my wheelchair as an asset instead of a deficit by begging.

Out on the streets you get more dirty than usual. So, everyone including me has to take a shower to stay clean. So, I went to the mission to take my shower, but every time I got outside the mission door to line up for my shower there would always be a fight with these illegal Mexican alien bums trying to force me out of the shower line. So, when the mission people showed up I had to blow my whistle to get in. Once in, more trouble came my way as these illegal Mexican Indian bums tried to steal my shower spinet and force me away from the showers. Whereupon I had to pretend to have soap in my eyes so I couldn't see to avoid running over these reprobate feet. But since I am a Christian I didn't like this much at all. So from taking 3 showers a week, I took only 1 on Monday while most of these reprobates slept in. From my personal experience I know that these illegal alien Mexican Indian bums lack any moral development or manners or sense of educate and decency. They have not been socialized enough to be included in our society.

Take for example this shower scene. Immediately after drying off, it was time to get dressed with new clean clothes supplied by the mission. But these illegal alien Mexican bums would choose clothes according to color like Indians and not their own size. So they failed to get their size in anything shirts or pants. If their pants were too long these illegal alien Mexican bums would fold up the cuffs of the pants they got to make them appear as if they fit them. This naughty factor kept me with long legs and other wheelchair people and Anglos from getting our size pants. The liberal missions would not help the normal American street people but would bend over backwards for these illegal alien Mexican Bums. In fact most missions had a policy about clothes that said 'first come first serve' therefore no wheelchair person could get his size pants. Since these illegal alien Mexican bums had already taken all the pants that were not even their size, thus the Anglos had to wear 'high water' pants too.

Thanks to the lack of moral decency on the part of these illegal alien Mexican bums I hope that their dreams become a nightmare as we don't need them in our country. I have just said what needed to be said about this issue. 'SINCE THERE IS NOTHING NEW UNDER THE SUN', (Ecclesiastes 1:9). Now let's see what the Holy Spirit of God said through His prophet Moses. Since some may consider my statements too 'mean spirited.'

The Spirit of God said through Moses in Deuteronomy 28 that there would be blessings for obedience of God's commandments but curses for disobedience. And He would send strangers (aliens) to be your heads and you to be their tails. To American street people this means that these illegal Mexican alien bums lack common sense but will still be our bosses if we don't get rid of them now. And in verse 28 the Bible says: 'AND THE LORD WILL SMITE YOU WITH MADNESS'. **What is shutting down the government that serves 330 million Americans for illegal alien bums if it is not madness?**

My prophecy sixty-five asks why are Christian prayers so short, because you run out of things to ask for. Since you only think of your prayer time as a time of petition. Whereas prayer time should be a time of conversation with God. 'ENTER HIS GATES WITH THANKSGIVING', (psalm 100:4) not begging. Thank God for His Person, His glory, His goodness, His blessings, His word, His health, His wealth, His salvation plan, His kingdom, His plans for your life, His resurrection power, His anointing's, His gifts, His faith, His earth, His heaven, His revival, His exposure of evil, His inspiration, His strength, His energy, His power, His gentleness, His peace, His wisdom, His knowledge, His holiness and all of His qualities you can think of. After building Him up then ask your petitions. Remember 'YE RECEIVE NOT, BECAUSE YOU ASK NOT, ASK AND YOU SHALL RECEIVE', (James 4:2). Then praise Him some more by going on to pray in the Spirit and glorify Him in some unknown tongue.

My prophecy sixty-six says that many Christians have trouble with prosperity as they do not know the word of God and think that poverty makes them more holy but poverty is a curse. Christians go from salvation through the development called discipleship I submit to you that the last stage of Christian development has to be prosperity in order to make one comfortable to live in a mansion and walk on streets of Gold there and have all of the attributes of the glorified resurrection body including the splendor, luxury and magnificence of it all.

My prophecy sixty-seven happened some years ago while I was going to the mission to eat we passed a Large Catholic Church. It was surrounded by many police cars from all over Florida and some from other states too. There was a parade which passed us. This ceremony was for a prison guard who had been killed by an escaped convict from the prison. Many distinguished guests also showed up for the funeral. Although I wasn't prepared to go (I had not shaved) nevertheless I received the words that God wanted said there. I still remember what I should have said although I am not a Roman Catholic. The word said: 'IT IS GOOD THAT YOU HAVE SHOWED UP TO GIVE HONOR TO WHOM HONOR IS DUE. OF ALL THE TIMES YOU WILL GO TO CHURCH THIS YEAR THIS IS THE MOST IMPORTANT BECAUSE IN AS MUCH AS YOU HAVE DONE IT UNTO THE LEAST OF THESE MY BRETHREN YOU HAVE DONE IT UNTO ME', (Romans 13:7) (Mathew 25:45).

I saw on the TV news ***My prophecy sixty-eight*** (January 24, 2018) a segment about how Florida had received a grade of F for rejection of tobacco use. Almost all the agencies concerned with health and public welfare contributed to that grade. Even the Bible says that 'YOUR BODY IS THE TEMPLE OF THE HOLY GHOST AND WHOEVER DEFILES THAT TEMPLE HIM WILL GOD DESTROY', (1 Cor. 3:17).

In this tobacco tax issue there is a complicated problem for as the excise tax on cigarettes goes up so does food stamp fraud and embezzlement as the poor want their cigarettes too. So which sin is worse hurting your own health, increasing medical expenses due to your smoking or smoking itself which leads to the demise of society?

I also saw on the TV morning news ***My prophecy sixty-nine*** the segment about the school shooting in Kentucky. While the experts were talking about guns and violence I noticed how unusually fat the students and even the athletes were. Then this word from the Bible came before me which said: 'LAY ASIDE EVERY WEIGHT AND THE SIN WHICH SO EASILY BESETS YOU AND RUN WITH PATIENCE THE RACE WHICH GOD HAS SET BEFORE YOU', (Hebrews 12:1). Most health professionals say that an epidemic of obesity is coming to America. This will cause many health problems from susceptibility to common diseases like colds and flu to high blood pressure resulting in strokes, heart attacks and death.

According to ***My prophecy seventy*** unfortunately there is no word for prosperity in the King James Bible. But abundance is a synonym for prosperity. Many Christians see the possession of a large luxurious and expensive airplanes like the Gulf Stream 5 to be an exorbitant display of wealth. They fail to understand that God would give this to some Christians as a result of their faith to reach the masses for Christ. I have found a very common Bible verse that uses a synonym for prosperity in saying: 'I HAVE COME THAT YOU MAY HAVE LIFE AND HAVE IT MORE ABUNDANTLY', (John 10:10). More abundantly equals increase too. To have life more abundantly could mean many things. It not only means wealth but also health and long life. Wealth in the form of going first class with jets, TV studios, satellites and TV cameras to spread God's word worldwide. Health could also mean Christian immunity to certain diseases and gifts of healing, the laying on of hands and miracles. Abundance could also mean inspiration for the authors of Christian books and composing Christian worship songs and long life too.

Now there are no volcanos in Florida. According to ***My prophecy seventy-one.*** It was mentioned before in this book that **an erupting volcano indicates hell needing to expand itself in order to make room for more victims.** In 1513 Ponce De Leon discovered Florida on Easter Sunday morning, a day the Spanish called 'the feast of flowers'. So that's where Florida got its name. When Florida was claimed for Ferdinand and Isabella, the king and queen of Spain, at that Catholic mass **Florida was also recognized as a gift from God as the land of resurrection. Therefore resurrection revival/awakening will come to Florida in these last days.** Despite the fact that the mass was Roman Catholic, it was also an act of faith which will not go unrewarded.

My prophecy seventy-two declares which fruit of the Spirit is the most important or most valuable one to have? The Fruits of the Spirit are listed in Galatians 6:22. Love is first. But I would not want to have more love for that would put me in competition with God as God is love. Besides if I had more love I would have to love criminals although I do not want to be the victim of any crime. I would have to love child molesters, rapists and con men. Look I'm human, Therefore you cannot increase love just as you cannot increase faith. For 'EVERYMAN HAS RECEIVED A MEASURE OF FAITH', (Romans 12:3).

I have chosen faith as the most important fruit of the Spirit because the scripture says that 'WITHOUT FAITH IT IS IMPOSSIBLE TO PLEASE GOD', (Hebrews 11:6). And 'HE THAT COMES TO GOD MUST BELIEVE THAT HE IS AND THAT HE IS THE REWARDER OF THEM THAT DILIGENTLY SEEK HIM'.

I was watching TV this morning as ***My prophecy seventy-three*** came on Friday, January 25, 2018). Katie Souza was discussing travel through time on Christian TV. Since I was once a missionary, I know missionaries that have done this. Actually all Christians which have become part of the divine nature can do this too. But before we get into the exercise of spiritual attributes, gifts and manifestations, **it is necessary to first receive the baptism in the Holy Spirit. Then the Spirit of God can do as he pleases with your body.**

Note when Philip was translated he did not pray for his translation. Nor did he ask for this ability. **It simply came as part of Philip's duty to evangelize. And as a result of Philip being baptized in the Spirit.**

This revelation also states that Jesus is the Son of God but Muslims do not believe nor allow anyone to teach that Jesus is the Son of God. For to them God doesn't need a son to do his work. The Muslim Koran pronounces a curse on those who believe their Jesus is God's Son. In fact, the Muslim dome of the rock in Jerusalem has these words inscribed around the inside of its dome 'far be it from God that he should have a son'. With this kind of anti-Christian hate speech this mosque should have been destroyed in 1967 that the new Jewish temple may have been built there. For Jewish temples are for God's service not for the exhibiting of anti-Christian hate speech.

My prophecy seventy-four goes on to say that to Christians the New Testament says in 1 John 5:12: 'HE WHO HAS THE SON OF GOD HAS LIFE AND HE THAT DOES NOT HAVE THE SON OF GOD DOES NOT HAVE LIFE'.

My prophecy seventy-five reveals that Muslims do not believe that Jesus died on the cross for our sins. Or that He is in anyway our Savior. But the Bible in the Old Testament calls Jesus as God 'THE HOLY ONE OF ISRAEL OUR SAVIOR', (Isaiah 45:15). The King James Version of the amplified Bible says in 1 John 2:2 that 'HE (JESUS) IS THE ATONING SACRIFICE FOR OUR SINS AND NOT OURS ONLY BUT ALSO FOR THE SINS OF THE WHOLE WORLD'. And Jimmy Swaggart Expositors Study Bible, King James Version says in Colossians 1:20: 'AND HAVING MADE PEACE (with God) THROUGH THE BLOOD OF HIS CROSS BY HIM (Jesus) ALL THINGS ARE RECONCILED TO GOD'.

Then ***My prophecy seventy-six*** reveals that Muslims claim that Jesus will return as a radical Muslim. The Bible however says in Revelation 19:19 that Jesus returns to rule and reign 'OVER EVERY NATION KINGDOM, TRIBE AND TONGUE', (Revelation 19:16). 'AND WHOSOEVER IS

NOT FOUND WRITTEN IN THE BOOK OF LIFE WILL BE CAST INTO THE LAKE OF FIRE', (Rev. 20:15).

But Muslims also claim in ***My prophecy seventy-seven*** that their Mahdi out ranks our Lord Jesus. But the Bible says that: 'JESUS HAS A NAME ABOVE EVERY NAME', (Philippians 2:9). 'WHEN HE RETURNS YOU SHALL BE REWARDED AS HE SHALL GIVE TO EVERYMAN ACCORDING TO HIS WORKS', (Revelation 22:12). 'JESUS AS GOD INCARNATE WAS MANIFESTED IN THE FLESH, JUSTIFIED IN THE SPIRIT, SEEN OF ANGELS, PREACHED UNTO THE GENTILES, BELIEVED ON IN THE WORLD, RECEIVED UP INTO GLORY', (1 Timothy 3:16).

In My prophecy seventy eight in a democratic society where social engineering occurs after a generation social changes need to be reevaluated. One of those legalistic social changes was brought about by the liberal Warren court in the case of Gideon vs Wainwright. Back in the 60's a man named Gideon sued the state of Florida about him not being represented by adequate legal counsel at his trail while the state had a state's attorney. It was ruled back then that this was unfair and every accused should have an attorney at taxpayer expense. But now America is broke and since two wrongs do not make a right I submit to you that instead of giving each side legal counsel to stir the case up into legal ambiguity it would be far better and wiser to review and judge each case based on its facts or merits. Reverse that court decision by laying off every public defender and state's attorney and close all the law schools. And save America lots of money. Always remember that Fidel Castro the former communist dictator of Cuba was a lawyer who was comfortable screwing the Cuban people out of their property and God given freedoms.

Oh my God, we can't do that, as representation by legal council is now 'settled law' and can't be changed. If so then the 'settled law' which used to say that a Black man was only 3/5 of a person should not have been changed either. It's high time to change these laws that favor lawyers and supposed human rights and Muslim sharia law at our expense and outlaw school prayer and Bible reading destined to turn our children into sexually active perverts and abortionists of the new 'one world order'.

Social Security will soon be under funded thanks to the slaughter by legalized abortion of over 60 million future American taxpayers thanks to our 'settled law' pro-abortionist Democrats.

In ***My prophecy seventy-nine*** Muslims also believe that Jesus comes again to enforce Sharia Law all over the world. This would require the Lord

Jesus to be a celestial cop with a badge and police power to arrest with mace, a stun gun and a service revolver to then abuse with police brutality any non-Muslims.

My prophecy eighty reveals that many Christians are doing Sunday school Bible studies on increasing the attributes of the fruit of the Spirit. Look these qualities of the fruit of the Spirit listed in Galatians 5:22, come about automatically once one is baptized in the Spirit and filled with the Spirit. Thus more prayer time should be spent in praying in the Spirit instead of asking repeatedly and begging and pleading for some qualities that automatically are bestowed on one who becomes a full gospel Christian by being baptized in the Holy Spirit.

Likewise in ***My prophecy eighty-one*** many Christians spend too much of their prayer time asking for needs which God already knows about. 'GOD ALREADY KNOWS WHAT WE HAVE NEED OF BEFORE WE ASK', (Matthew 6:8). 'MANY PAGANS BELIEVE THAT THEY WILL BE HEARD FOR THEIR MUCH SPEAKING', (Matthew 6:7). All we should do is ask, then use the rest of our prayer time to glorify God and thank Him for his blessings.

My prophecy eighty-two says you can keep your kids in church by having them needing to help you rejoicing. Like singing, playing a guitar or banjo, fiddling, banging on drums or doing piano. If you do not involve them in doing the ministry with you they will feel no obligation to stay and will leave.

My prophecy eighty-three reveals that Muslims claim that Jesus will return to earth at some Mosque in Damascus. He will arrive just in time to meet the Muslim Mahdi there to prepare for the final war. The scriptures however say that 'JESUS FEET WILL STAND THAT DAY ON THE MOUNT OF OLIVES WHICH IS BEFORE JERUSALEM ON THE EAST', (Zachariah 14:4). Also Isaiah 17:1 says that 'DAMASCUS SHALL BE TAKEN AWAY FROM BEING A CITY AND SHALL BECOME A RUINOUS HEAP'.

My prophecy eighty-four says that Muslims also believe that the Zionist empire of Israel will fall and cease to exist since Jesus never really liked the Jews anyway. How stupid this false teaching about Jesus is for anyone can see for themselves from any Bible that the New Testament beginning in Matthew 1:1 lists the genealogy of Jesus clearly showing his Jewish ancestry.

My prophecy eighty-five says that contrary to what Muslims believe, Israel is due to expand to the original borders that God gave to Abraham in Genesis 15:18 & 19: 'ABRAHAM WILL BE GIVEN ALL THAT LAND

FROM THE RIVER OF EGYPT TO THE GREAT RIVER, THE RIVER EUPHRATES'. All this land includes Judea and Samaria plus all of Lebanon, all of Jordan, all of Gaza all the Sinai and part of Syria along with part of Iraq.

I recently heard in ***My prophecy eighty-six*** the false doctrine which encouraged Christians to present their subject or problem before the courts of heaven to be handled by angels. But the Bible says 'THERE IS ONE MEDIATOR BETWEEN MAN AND GOD, THE MAN CHRIST JESUS', (1 Timothy 2:5). And **there is no Bible record of angels ever holding court.**

My prophecy eighty-seven reveals that an educated group of supposedly sophisticated Christians once said that since they had moved beyond the cross therefore they were going to remove all crosses from their church. But as a Christian it is not possible to remove the cross which was and still is your main touch stone for reconciliation to God. Every Christian church that I know of has a cross at the highest point of its building. Some even have crosses in their windows and painted inside. The Roman Catholics even have 'stations of the cross',

According to ***My prophecy eighty-eight*** Christian math is not logically based on numbers alone. But Christian math like other Christian qualities is based on faith. Thus it is written: 'ONE SHALL CHASE A THOUSAND AND TWO SHALL PUT TEN THOUSAND TO FLIGHT', (Deuteronomy 32:30). The increase of persons of faith by just two increases the result by 10 times. How's that for increase?

For those into faith let's consider ***My prophecy eighty-nine*** which states that according to II Peter 1:5-8: 'ADD TO YOUR FAITH VIRTUE AND TO VIRTUE KNOWLEDGE AND TO KNOWLEDGE TEMPERANCE AND TO TEMPERANCE PATIENCE AND TO PATIENCE GODLINESS AND TO GODLINESS BROTHERLY KINDNESS AND TO BROTHERLY KINDNESS LOVE, FOR IF THESE THINGS BE IN YOU AND ABOUND THEY SHALL MAKE YOU THAT YOU SHALL NEITHER BE BARRON NOR UNFRUITFUL IN THE KNOWLEDGE OF OUR LORD JESUS CHRIST'.

My prophecy ninety is for those seeking revival the scripture says: 'IF I BE LIFTED UP FROM THE EARTH I WILL DRAW ALL MEN UNTO ME', (John 2:32). Many preachers are lifting up many things like current events, false doctrine, pet Bible verses, end time prophecy assumptions like the pre-tribulation rapture, anti-sematic anti-Jewish propaganda, freedom from debt, gay marriages, finance investments, prosperity, credit and every topic under the sun but the Lord Jesus Christ and Him crucified. Paul said: 'I AM DETERMINED TO KNOW NOTHING AMONG YOU BUT JESUS CHRIST AND HIM CRUCIFIED', (1 Corinthians 2:2). As I said before and say again Christianity is a Person the Lord Jesus Christ. As it is written: 'HE THAT HAS THE SON, HAS LIFE, AND HE THAT DOES NOT HAVE THE SON OF GOD DOES NOT HAVE LIFE', (1 John 5:12).

According to ***My prophecy ninety-one*** once T.L. Osbourne asked Kenneth Copeland if he wanted to be rich. Kenneth said yes. And brother Osbourne said then find an anointed minister who has received a vision from God about a local church and get in there and do whatever you can to make his vision come to pass. This is confirmed by the scripture which says: 'SEEK YE FIRST THE KINGDOM OF GOD AND HIS RIGHTEOUSNESS AND ALL THESE THINGS (including wealth) WILL BE ADDED UNTO YOU', (Mathew 6:33).

My prophecy ninety-two says that the American dream for Americans cannot be realized if we 'CAST OUR PEARLS BEFORE SWINE', (Mathew 7:6) and try to rescue everyone from debt and poverty by building up the welfare state at our expense and fail to recognize the Bible example of Jesus having Peter 'take money' to pay the taxes for Jesus and Peter alone out of the fishes mouth and not for the other apostles (Mathew 17:27). **At no place did Jesus ever take up a 'love offering' to pay the people's debts or to engage in the socialistic share the wealth policy.**

My prophecy ninety-three says if the first apostles, like Peter and John had no gold or silver and said so in the Bible verse that says 'SILVER AND GOLD HAVE I NONE', (Acts 3:6). How can some modern ministers have vast fortunes?

The ministry of James Robeson also puts in wells for the children to have more free time to go to school, since they no longer have to fetch polluted water. So send your dollars to these Christian ministries instead of the secular halfhearted charities **as 'only what's done for Christ will last'**.

My prophecy ninety-four says that there is another sign that the last days will soon culminate in the Lord's coming. This sign is both unpleasant and homosexual. If you remember from the Bible Lot was accompanied by angels who forced him to abandon Sodom just before God destroyed it. When the angels first visited Lot the men of the city wanted to commit homosexual rape on the angels. I know that they were handsome young men, but fully clothed in long white robes. So everyone must have known that they were angels and after they were propositioned by the men of Sodom the angels smote them with blindness **(Genesis 19:11)**. Actually similar events are happening now and Sodom was destroyed right in the midst of its sex party.

My prophecy ninety-five reveals that a new sex party is coming as some adult companies have developed new drugs which cause the Vienna sausage size male genitalia of immigrants to grow and expand to be like the huge genitalia of the Nephilim. This sort of thing is already being set up by a school counseling practice called 'gay conversion therapy'. Therefore it will soon be time to make like Lot and leave as the diabolical becomes normal.

My prophecy ninety-six says don't let a negative confession warp your personality to the extent of becoming a self-fulfilling prophecy. Prophecy comes by anointing and it's always true. Negative confessions like 'you'll never amount to anything' are not prophetic words which I should heed but un-anointed words of no value that limit your growth without justification or reason.

Others cannot evaluate your intelligence nor your ability. You can be whatever God wants you to be. God does not limit you by outward appearance for 'WITH GOD ALL THINGS ARE POSSIBLE', (Mark 10:27). No person knows you as well as God does and God never jumps to negative conclusions about anyone. Don't listen to hate speech but only to words of edification, help, hope and encouragement.

In ***My prophecy ninety-seven*** we see that from the baptism of the Holy Ghost and fire the fire purges one's past sins and it cleanses one from all sicknesses and delivers one from all the work of demons including bad habits, bad attitudes and depression. The fire consumes ones past to the extent that you have nothing left but God. Then the Holy Ghost Imparts the Supernatural Life of God, Christ's Love, His Faith, His Power, His Gifts, His Callings, His Vision, His Plans, His Purpose, His Joy, His Peace, His Gentleness, His Meekness, His Temperance, His Long Suffering (Galatians 5:22) and all the armor of God (Ephesians 6:13-18). So then you are empowered, endued, and enabled to do what God wants done.

In ***My prophecy ninety-eight*** praise is obviously the main gifting of the Evangelist Jimmy Swaggart. He knows something about singing the right kind of songs that please God and get's people saved. I have heard mainly hymns and spiritual songs via his telecast which lift up Jesus, and Jesus said: 'IF I BE LIFTED UP FROM THE EARTH I WILL DRAW ALL MEN UNTO ME', (John 12:32).

My prophecy ninety-nine says that the poorest person in this life is not the one who hasn't saved anything in life but the one who has no savior for eternal life. For as it is written 'WHAT DOES IT PROFIT A MAN TO GAIN THE WHOLE WORLD AND LOSE HIS OWN SOLE'? (Mathew 16:26).

My prophecy one hundred says that there is much misunderstanding among modern Christians about loving your enemies. The Bible does say to 'LOVE YOUR ENEMIES',' (Mathew 5:44). But the Bible does NOT say anywhere to love the enemies of God. In fact 'WHEN THE LORD JESUS RETURNS, HE WILL FIGHT AGAINST HIS ENEMIES' (Zachariah 14:1).

My prophecy one hundred and one says that as far as Christian revival is concerned remember: 'I CAN DO ALL THINGS', (win wars against Muslim Jihadists, expose corruption, perform miracles, impart healings, feed multitudes, command storms to dissipate, make it rain, supply people with jobs and get people saved, sanctified, build and ready to serve God) 'THROUGH CHRIST WHO STRENGTHENS ME', (Philippians 4:13).

The Lord Jesus also said in that same revelation: 'THE WORKS THAT I DO WILL YOU DO ALSO AND GREATER THAN THESE SHALL YOU DO', (John 14:12).

My prophecy one hundred and two says 'EXCEPT THE TRUMPET GIVES A CERTAIN SOUND WHO SHALL PREPARE THEMSELVES FOR THE BATTLE?', (1 Corinthians 14:8). Your trumpet call has been given to you via my prophetic book, what will you now do about it?

My prophecy one hundred and three says that back in the 70's if one needed an abortion they went to California. If that didn't work they went to Mexico. If that didn't work they went to Houston, Texas which had the largest abortion clinic in America back then. Some feel today that that is why Houston was judged by the flood. But an even worse story is the fact that Houston has offered people free abortions due to distress of having to raise a child in the midst of having to deal with a flood too. So since there is no repentance from abortion there will be NO revival in the Houston area but only more judgments. 'For THE WAGES OF SIN IS DEATH', (Romans 6:32) not revival.

According to ***My prophecy one hundred and four*** as Christians we do not believe in the hyper-religious idea of sinless perfection since 'THERE IS NONE GOOD BUT GOD', (MARK 10:18). However many of us have learned how to overcome everyday sins. I submit to you that most of our problems with sin come from our lack of education as to the tense of the verbs about sin and our lack of understanding as to what the cross of Christ has already done for our sin problem. As an educated Christian I could speak from a seminary, bible school or college perspective. But instead I'll speak from what we all learned in grammar school. The Bible lists in (Galatians 5:19-21) the current works of the flesh or present day sins many deal with. The Bible says in (I Cor. 6:9-11) how we were delivered from such sins and all other unnamed or future sins by the blood of Jesus, (I John 1:7). Thus **the blood of Jesus shed on the cross of Christ is the change agent that turns current sins into the past.** 'Are is the present tense of the verb to be. Whereas 'were' is the past tense of that same verb. As it is written: 'OLD THINGS ARE PASSED AWAY, ALL THINGS HAVE BECOME NEW', (II Cor. 5:17). Speaking of sin God has given us a good example of faithfully and victoriously overcoming sin in these last days. Jesus said: 'AS IT WAS IN THE DAYS OF NOAH SO SHALL IT BE IN THE LAST DAYS', (Mathew 24:37).

My prophecy one hundred and five on Valentine's Day Feb. 14, 2018. Florida's Governor Rick Scott said regarding the school shooting in South Florida to be an act of pure evil. In that regard evil must be conquered and rooted out. It is not the job of any school to continue to employ the deceptive world view of diversity. One who has been expelled for violence should not be allowed back on the campus to be more violent with revenge. **It is unwise to have the unsuccessful with the successful.** An expelled student should have somewhere to obtain his education other than the same public school. **The idea of forced integration of reprobates with normals in our society is the mental disorder of liberalism.**

We do not allow child molesters to live in our neighborhood or near our schools and we should also exclude violent offenders from doing so. Much crime in any neighborhood can be traced back to domestic violence. If someone cannot treat their own family members' right they should be thrown out of society and pastors should throw such reprobates out of the church of God lest they also abuse the saints.

My prophecy one hundred and six reveals that everyman should have a body guard. Jesus had Peter who had a sword (Mark 14:47). And everyplace of social gathering should have an armed man's man to ensure order. Even neighborhood bars have this. Schools, shopping centers, grocery stores, laundromats, parks, public playgrounds, libraries and even churches should have police or private armed protection because the unsuccessful in our society are determined to work out their vengeance for their own mental deficits on the rest of us.

In the old days history tells us that horse thieves and even pick pockets were hung even though those crimes only concerned stealing. What about all these sexually abused crimes that are being tolerated? And all these mental health violent crimes that are being tolerated too? It's time for Christians to stand up and demand that God's kingdom come, that His will be done on earth as it is in heaven. It's also time for our society to have a Christian awakening to throw off all this diversity trash that forces us to accommodate evil and revive our old freedom of association that excludes evil. This is still America remember, the land of the free.

My prophecy one hundred and seven reveals that as it is written: 'WHAT YOU DO IN SECRET SHALL BE SHOUTED FROM THE HOUSETOPS', (Luke 12:3). Hopefully the investigation of Russian meddling in the election of 2016 has now concluded without the indictment of any Trump Administration Officials. While the FBI has wasted all this time on this, the shooter of that school in south Florida was ignored when he first came to the attention of law enforcement 5 or 6 weeks before the shooting and the wasting of 17 lives there. So the governor of Florida, Rick Scott has asked that the FBI Director to resign for the sake of all those families who lost their children at that school unnecessarily.

My prophecy one hundred and eight said last night before the evening news came on a political ad appeared. This ad was for the abortionist democrat Philip Levine who spoke against the BP oil spill as if it was an environmental problem that he alone could control. Actually not all of us old retired people have Alzheimer's and dementia. Some of us have very good memories. We remember that the BP oil tragedy happened right after the Muslim President Obama let it be known that his UN ambassador would no longer side with or support Israel at every opportunity. I suppose it's alright to have policies you want to enforce. But Israel has a renowned weapon called the God of Israel. And any Jew like Phillip Levine should have known this. The BP oil disaster (judgment from the God of Israel) happened right after the Muslim Obama stabbed Israel in the back.

I went to visit a mainline Christian church and some there knowing that I watched Jimmy Swaggart's broadcast every morning said to me that Jimmy Swaggart puts too much emphasis on the cross. Whereupon ***My prophecy one hundred and nine***, a word of wisdom suddenly came forth saying: 'At the highest point of every church building there is a cross either on the top of the church rotunda or the top of its steeple. Then this word came forth: 'HE THAT HAS THE SON HAS LIFE AND HE THAT DOES NOT HAVE THE SON OF GOD DOES NOT HAVE LIFE', (I John 1:9). So Christianity is a Person, the Lord Jesus Christ. And that Person gives the symbol for what He has done for Christianity. And that symbol is the cross. The cross needs to be emphasized for it was the place of the blood sacrifice of Jesus. Though the cross may offend some nevertheless the blood of Jesus will offend more. The God of Israel has always required a blood sacrifice for sins both in the Old Testament by the priests and in the New Testament by the Lord Jesus who sacrificed Himself' 'ONCE FOR ALL' (Hebrews 10:10).

In ***My prophecy one hundred and ten*** a very embittered young Black Man said he could no longer be a Christian since he did not want to worship a White Man's God, so he began buttering up to the Muslims. Actually, Jesus is not a White Man but the God man. The Black Man really wanted to become a Muslim not for religious reasons but sexual one s. After all Muslims can have four wives and such keeps you sexually active.

According to ***My prophecy one hundred and eleven*** in examining what Muslims have contributed to Blacks, it should be realized that slavery happened not due to White exploitation but with Muslims raiding non-Muslim villages to steel their men and sell them into slavery. It can easily be seen that this practice is still happening today with all the evidence from burned out villages where tribes people once lived.

Jesus was once asked by his disciples who do men say that I am? ***In My prophecy one hundred and twelve.*** Since his disciples were obviously his friends they did not respond by saying what Jesus enemies would have said. You know, things like you cast out devils by Beelzebub or you heal on the Sabbath like any transgressor of Moses law. Plus you stink, your hair is too long and you spoke to that Samaritan woman because you were trying to pick her up to become her sixth husband. Intimate things like this would only have been brought up by marriage partners.

Peter gave the true answer when motivated by the Holy Ghost he said: 'THOU ART THE CHRIST, THE SON OF THE LIVING GOD', (Matthew 16:16).

In ***My prophecy one hundred and thirteen*** Jesus was discussing His second coming and said that: 'AS IT WAS IN THE DAYS OF NOAH SO SHALL ALSO THE COMING OF THE SON OF MAN BE', (Mathew 24:37). He went on to say that 'IN THE DAYS BEFORE THE FLOOD THEY WERE EATING AND DRINKING, MARRYING AND GIVING IN MARRIAGE UNTIL NOAH ENTERED THE ARK AND THE FLOOD DESTROYED THEM ALL'. But there are many things about the days of Noah that Jesus did not mention. A main reason for the flood was to destroy the hybrid race of sin. Many men at this time were descendant from the fallen angels who left heaven for the daughters of men. This union resulted in men of renown who were exceptionally evil (Genesis 6:1-5). So this means that extra-terrestrials will come again to earth to make the human race worse and worse until destruction comes again to all humanity.

My prophecy one hundred and fourteen is about a clairvoyant who had worked with many police departments across America said over a radio interview that people were becoming more and more evil. He said that he used to go out to eat when he was younger but now he feels evil even at the best restaurants. Of course the food is contaminated with many toxins but the environment is also charged with the animosity of hate.

Our God is a speaking God Who spoke the worlds into existence. As you want God's will to be in your life you've got to speak God's will revealed in his word from your mouth. Confess it in order to possess it.

My prophecy one hundred and fifteen came on Tuesday morning, Feb. 27, 2018. Apparently God has more to say about this. There is some confusion as to what the future holds for some prophets have said that good times are here again to make America great again. While other prophets known as prophets of doom have said that we are already in the time of sorrows in which many bad things are due.

Matthew answers this. It says in Matthew 24:37 'THAT AS IT WAS IN THE DAYS OF NOAH SO SHALL IT BE IN THE DAYS WHEN JESUS COMES AGAIN'. Now the days of Noah was a time of great prosperity, back then there were even sons of God extraterrestrials and giants in the earth. Noah himself was a preacher of righteousness and he preached while building the arc for 120 years. God fellowshipped with Noah and took care of him and his house.

So this is the period we are in now. Only the extraterrestrials and the giants have not yet appeared but they will. We also know from Matthew 20:16 & Matthew 19:30 'THAT THE FIRST SHALL BE LAST AND THE LAST SHALL BE FIRST'. That order also holds true for prophecy. Mathew 24:37 'THE DAYS OF NOAH' SHALL HAPPEN BEFORE THE WARS, FAMINES AND EARTHQUAKES of Mathew 24:6-9. I hope that clears things up for you.

After this awakening from Bible history we know will come a time of sudden war, calamity and persecution to drive Christians throughout the earth preaching the full gospel. So then these wars, famines and earthquakes are not only just signs of judgment but also of apocalyptic catastrophes like title waves too to force Christians to spread God's word. For those who still expect the pre-tribulation rapture I hate to bust your balloon but **in order to spread God's word Christians must still be here in order to do so, unless you want 'The Great Falling Away'.**

My prophecy one hundred and sixteen came to me on my way back from the city hall here on Monday, March 12, 2018. In this revelation I suddenly realized that the deception Jesus mentioned in Mathew 24 concerned Him and his return not so much about everyday deceptions but only about Jesus alone. As it is written in Mathew 24:5 'FOR MANY SHALL COME IN MY NAME SAYING I AM THE CHRIST AND SHALL DECIEVE MANY'. God has revealed to me that the many mainly compose the over one billion adherents to the false religion of Islam. Therefor to speak clearly and forthrightly on this deception about Who Jesus really is I'll include my chapter about Muslim Jesus vs. Jesus Christ already composed for a previous prophetic book.

Most other common everyday deceptions did not exist in Jesus day. Back then there were no telephones. Hence no telephone scams. Back then there were no computers to be hacked into. Nor was there any social media full of fake news.

Since Christianity is basically a Person, the Lord Jesus Christ and not just another teaching or ideology, the deceptions that really count are personal not social, financial nor ideological.

March 15th midday***, an unusual prophecy one hundred and seventeen*** about Joshua having the sun stand still so that he might win a battle – no preacher certainly no passivist preacher has ever mentioned that conflicts like wars are important to God, so important that He will even change nature's laws in order for His will to happen.

My prophecy one hundred and eighteen came on March 16th and concerned unlimited faith healing, not just healing for certain things. For many this was an unusual revelation as it emphasized a certain Bible verse Matthew 10:1 Where the Lord Jesus gives power to heal all manner of sickness and all manner of disease not just certain conditions that a ministry might emphasize.

My prophecy one hundred and nineteen came on March 20th and said that the main reason why the pre-tribulation rapture is wrong is **because it requires all Christians to vacate instead of still obeying God's word to continue to take dominion over the largest missionary sending nation that has evangelized the world and the largest food producer that has fed the world.** What souls will you save in heaven and who will you feed up there? Moreover if you can't save souls yourself then your own soul will be lost in 'The Great Falling Away'.

My prophecy one hundred and twenty came on March 21, 2018 saying it's rare to receive a revelation that contradicts the current theological viewpoint of most Christians about the pre-tribulation rapture. For when it fails to happen then there will be 'A Great Falling Away'.

'LET GOD BE TRUE, AND EVERY MAN A LIAR', (Romans 3:4). I received this morning the three words that say: 'THESE ARE THEY' from Revelation 7:14 describing an entire multitude which no man could number of people saved out of the Great Tribulation. So this contradicts the idea that Billy Graham's Christians will never get to witness and save souls themselves but must depart in the rapture of Revelation four. Additionally, this false doctrine also says that there will be no more awakenings nor revivals again until Jesus comes again supposedly in Revelation 4.

MY REVELATIONS

My revelations are different from my prophecies for a prophecy is about a person, place or thing whereas a revelation is only about revealing the true meaning of the word of God and the testimony of Jesus.

1. Does the fire of the Holy Ghost only equal spoken tongues? There has been some dispute in the body of Christ among Pentecostal Christians about fire as to whether it is fire to purge us from sins, as in just spoken tongues or fire to advance God's kingdom.

In Mathew 3:11 most full gospel churches say that being baptized with the Holy Ghost and fire means having the Holy Ghost's fire to purge you out of your sins. Actually this conclusion is not biblically based. For the remedy for personal sins is the blood of Jesus shed on the cross of Christ and nothing else, not counseling, prayers, devotions, talking in tongues or some other manifestation of Spirit filled Christian in-filling or Holy Ghost baptism. **The Holy Ghost, his gifts and His 'fire power' are to evangelize by signs and wonders and to take dominion by force, to conquer, to overcome evil, and to occupy.**

This same Revelation was given again in other words on January 3, 2019. It said: many people feel that they can break free from sin via New Year's Resolutions. But a New Year's Resolution like other human will power may be able to break bad habits like being late for class or work, drinking or smoking or some other personal or social problem or short coming, but **only the blood of Jesus shed on the cross of Christ cleanses one from all sin,** not counseling, nor human will power, nor some psychotropic medication and not even the development of good new habits to compensate for the old naughty ones.

The common denominational Pentecostal practice of just speaking in tongues alone does not accomplish expanding God's kingdom. These denominations feel that any new doctrine which goes against fire as spoken tongues only, needs to be confirmed as a new doctrine by at least three scriptures. So here they are; ACTS 2:3 'AND THERE APPEARD UNTO THEM CLOVEN TONGUES LIKE AS OF FIRE, AND IT SAT UPON EACH OF THEM', ACTS 2:19 'AND I WILL SHOW WONDERS IN HEAVEN ABOVE, AND SIGNS IN THE EARTH BENEATH; BLOOD AND FIRE, AND VAPOR OF SMOKE' AND HEBREWS 1:7 'AND OF THE ANGELS HE SAYETH, WHO MAKETH HIS ANGELS SPIRITS, AND HIS MINISTERS A FLAME OF FIRE'.

Of course many unbelieving theologians try to discount these words from God with their commentaries. They in fact confuse the issues presented and ask stupid questions. Like how can cloven tongues of fire sit on a person without burning them? Or how can a vapor of smoke be a sign and a wonder and not just air pollution? Or how can angels be flames of fire instead of denominationally dead and deceived preachers?

Now we all need to accept the fire power of God the Holy Spirit which will enable us to bring in this great awakening in order to give the Lord Jesus Christ the nations he deserves for his inheritance rather than just a few carnal denominational nerds that cackle like hens and bray like mules.

No I am not condemning tongues. For as a spiritual gift it does have a very important purpose especially in prayer. Praying in tongues can accomplish many things. In fact whole books have been written just about this unseen and unrecognized power that Spirit filled Christians possess. As in The Beauty of Spiritual Language by Jack Hayford. **The point I am trying to make here is that tongues is no substitute for evangelism which any awakening must accomplish.**

2. ABORTION – The curse of our time.

On Labor Day 2018 Jim Bakker had several end time prophetic people discussing ancient false gods on his show when suddenly this revelation hit me: a main reason why the democrats want illegal aliens to come into America is because they are descendant from those same Latin American Indians who sacrificed their children to false gods. And one's heredity supposedly over rules Catholic indoctrination. So they will easily adopt the ideology of the Democratic Party which is also a false religion that worships its false god of expediency by the infant sacrifice of abortion. But abortion now violates the commandment of God that says: 'THOU SHALL NOT KILL'.

Later that same year, on May 29, 2018 I received a very unusual revelation about abortion. As a man I had always thought that abortion was mainly a woman's issue so it was not my major concern in life. But I remembered from prison those few men who have been convicted of manslaughter for shaking babies that would not stop crying. Today those few men have now become many and that manslaughter is now called: 'Shaken baby syndrome'. Some of you who may have gone to Sunday school as children remember from Bible reading how that Cane slew Able and then God asked Cane where Able was. And Cane said I don't know, 'AM I MY BROTHER'S KEEPER'? 'AND GOD REPLIED THE BLOOD OF YOUR BROTHER ABLE CRIES TO ME FROM THE GROUND', (Genesis 4:10).

The crying, no the constant whaling of 60 million aborted babies has infuriated God and He is about to shake America in judgment. Instead of a 'shaken baby syndrome' we are soon due to have a shaking of the land of the abortionist. So if you live in a blue state where the abortionist democrats control things especially abortion vote those reprobates out of office or else move away for your own good. Under the circumstances, which is more probable a woman's right to choose or God's right for vengeance? If I were you I wouldn't dare put God to the test. For as it is written: 'VENGEANCE IS MINE, I'LL REPAY, SAYS THE LORD', (Romans 2:19). Remember God is the creator so what do you think He feels like when someone destroys His creation?

3. Modern Christians are unprepared for these end time wars.

I recently met an old China man from Taiwan who refused to become a Christian because he felt that another war with the communists was on the way and passive Christians would only emasculate and feminize His Chinese people to the extent of not adequately preparing them for war. **Moreover this church mindset of the pre-tribulation rapture as a fairy tale of escape does not prepare my people for any of the end time wars that the Bible says are coming but only for The Falling Away that false doctrine will cause**.

For example let's just consider Sampson and how the Christian church has tried to twist his warrior nature and divine calling into that of a monk. Now Sampson was a wonder worker in whom the power of God resided. But Sampson was naughty and sinful and confided to the enemy of God the secret of his power. Therefore the Spirit of God departed from him although he did not realize it at the time. So Sampson was captured by the Philistines who then put out his eyes for revenge and then had him milling grain like an ox for his punishment.

At a famous meeting of the Philistine Lords to worship Dagon, their false god, they exhibited Sampson to mock him and his God. But as you know,

GOD IS NOT MOCKED, (Galatians 6:7). Apparently God was angrier about this than Sampson's personal sins. So there is no record that Sampson ever repented for his naughty lifestyle. In any case Sampson did not have 'Job's comforters' quoting for him Psalms 66:18 that says; 'IF I REGUARD INIQUITY IN MY HEART THE LORD WILL NOT HEAR ME'. So he continued to sin when he asked the young lad who led him about to take him to the pillars of the Philistine Temple that he might rest against them. Here Sampson lied for Sampson was not seeking rest but to get to those pillars that held up the weight of that temple that he might push them over. For he prayed anyway and still believed that his God, the God of Israel would once again give him the power to destroy the enemies of God. Yes there is a verse in the New Testament that says that we are to love our enemies, but **no Bible verse says to love the enemies of God at all**.

This proves that faith despite personal sin pleases God. This is probably why Sampson is listed in the hall of fame for faith in Hebrews 11. And this proves also that if you have a gift from God to do something (like in Sampson's case he was gifted to kill the Philistines) **always complete it.**

4. Actually many things besides end time wars will be happening during the tribulation that Christians deceived by the pre-tribulation rapture false doctrine are not prepared to handle.

Much of this results from the deceived believing that tribulation equals wrath. They even quote several Bible verses to confirm their viewpoint: 'WE SHALL BE SAVED FROM WRATH THROUGH HIM', (Romans 9:5), …'EVEN JESUS, WHICH DELIVERED US FROM THE WRATH TO COME', (I Thesalonians1:10) and 'FOR GOD HAS NOT APPOINTED US TO WRATH', (I Thessalonians 5:9).

When I studied Greek at Fuller Seminary, the Greek word: thlipis usually means tribulation. Of the fifty-five times it appears in your King James Bible forty-Seven of those times it is translated: tribulation. The rest of the times it may mean affliction, burden, persecution or anguish. **But in no case does it ever indicate wrath. So by taking it out of context they have used it to validate their pre-tribulation rapture theory.** Actually many scriptures validate that Christians will be here and should expect tribulation. Some of those Bible verses are: 'IN THE WORLD YOU SHALL HAVE TRIBULATION', (John 16:33), 'WE MUST THROUGH MUCH TRIBULATION ENTER INTO THE KINGDOM OF GOD', (Acts 14:22), 'FOR UNTO YOU IT IS GIVEN IN THE BEHALF OF CHRIST, NOT ONLY TO BELIEVE ON HIM, BUT ALSO TO SUFFER FOR

HIS SAKE', (Philippians 1:29) and 'THE SERVANT IS NOT GREATER THAN HIS LORD IF THEY HAVE PERSECUTED ME, THEY WILL PERSECUTE YOU ALSO', (John 15:20).

But the one Bible verse that makes this issue crystal clear is the one that states in Revelation 7:3: 'HURT NOT THE EARTH, NEITHER THE SEA, NOR THE TREES, TILL WE HAVE SEALED THE SERVANTS OF OUR GOD IN THEIR FOREHEADS'. **This happens midway through the tribulation period signifying that the saints will still be here then making the pre-tribulation rapture theology into a rip off and not a blessed hope at all but a false doctrine causing 'The Great Falling Away'.**

5. About March of 2016 I asked God who to vote for in the Florida primary. He said Trump. Of course I was aghast and wondered how a super-rich playboy could be the best candidate. Never the less as I had learned by experience don't question, always obey God. So I voted for Trump and to get others to join me I decided to do an Esther fast.

This Esther fast is for only three days to resolve political power problems. In the process I decided to reread the book of Esther in my Bible. Of course, we Christians know that famous verse about Esther in Esther 4:14 about 'COMING TO THE KINGDOM FOR SUCH A TIME AS THIS'.

There I found out something very unusual that preachers never mention I guess because it goes against their theology. That is Esther got her chamber maids to join her in this fast to change the king's mind from killing all the Jews.

Now her chamber maids were non-Jewish and even non-Persian. They were from different parts of the Persian Empire and worshipped different gods. Never the less they joined Ester in her fast to the Hebrew God and won, (Esther 4:16). Because back in those days if you really honored a person, you would also pray or fast to their God. So I fasted my three days and got others to join me despite their views on abortion or other liberal policies. **So, I found out that the idea that you must be devout, holy and godly in order to get God and people to see things your way is false. Anyone can ask for anything in faith believing. God will honor your faith not your holiness. So, Trump won anyway.**

6. Pluralism: There is a modern idea that there are many ways to God in this pluralistic society and that Jesus is not the only way. To this the Bible answers; 'I AM THE WAY, THE TRUTH, AND THE LIFE AND NO MAN COMES TO THE FATHER BUT BY ME', (John 14:6).

7. Diversity. In Ester's day this was a common practice among kingdoms, but today many say that we Christians should incorporate many different types of people into our fellowships to show diversity, but the Bible says in II Timothy 3:1-5; 'THAT IN THE LAST DAYS PERILOUS TIMES SHALL COME, FOR MEN SHALL BE LOVERS OF THEIR OWN SELVES, COVETOUS, BOASTERS, PROUD, BLASPHEMERS, DISOBEDIENT TO PARENTS, UNTHANKFUL, UNHOLY, WITHOUT NATURAL AFFECTION, TRUCE BREAKERS, FALSE ACCUSERS, INCONTINENT, FIERCE, DESPISERS OF THOSE THAT ARE GOOD, TRAITORS, HEADY, HIGH MINDED, THE LOVERS OF PLEASURE MORE THAN LOVERS OF GOD; HAVING THE FORM OF GODLINESS, BUT DENYING THE POWER THEREOF; FROM SUCH TURN AWAY'.

8. Transgender. Some deceived ultraliberal democrats say that one's sexual orientation changes from day to day with circumstances according to their feelings. But the Bible says that; 'IN THE BEGINNING GOD CREATED THE HEAVENS AND THE EARTH, (Genesis 1:1). 'AND GOD SAID, LET US MAKE MAN IN OUR OWN IMAGE, AFTER OUR LIKENES, (Genesis 1:26). SO GOD CREATED MAN IN HIS OWN IMAGE, IN THE IMAGE OF GOD CREATED HE THEM, MALE AND FEMALE CREATED HE THEM, (GENESIS 1:27). **What you are then sexually is the result of your creation NOT your feelings.**

9. Socialism. Some say that socialism comes from the early Christian church when 'THEY HELD ALL THINGS COMMON', (Acts 2:44). But the early Christian church did that only for certain people in the Christian community like widows, **they did not share with non-Christians nor did they support Roman bums. So this modern idea of socialism should not be blamed on the Christian church**.

If anything, this economic perversion today is the result of deceived idealistic ultra-liberal democrats who are trying to act like Christians without really being saved from their own sins. So then, this is just another scam or fraud upon the people. It is now manifesting itself in getting retired people and adults with families to pay for the exorbitant costs of a liberal college education for bums. Since the current debt from a college education cannot be dissipated by any other loan modification therefore young college students want socialism to remove them from having to pay for a lifetime of college debts. This one issue is the main reason why millennials want it.

In expanding this; of course, bums do not like to work. They'd rather live at home and get their parents to support them. Even a popular health plan gets young people under medical coverage if they continue to live at home and go to some college until they are twenty-six years old.

10. Gay marriage. After God made Adam and Eve, not Adam and Steve he gave them his first commandment which said: 'BE FRUITFUL AND MULTIPLY', (Genesis 1:23). So, with God procreation is apparently his main concern for mankind. And not psycho-social feelings of supposed love which are really the alternative lifestyle of disguised lust. Obviously, this form of lust does not result in necessary population increase. Therefore, it not only offends God but also harms the social security trust fund by not resulting in adequate pay-ins to support our retirees. So, this so called sexual freedom actually can produce social unrest problems instead.

Christians are supposed to be a blessing to our society, not selfish and into a self-indulgent lifestyle. Gay marriage by court order is a social disgrace. But for a pastor to perform a gay wedding in church is an abomination. By so doing those into this form of sexual deviance get others to approve of and participate in their sins.

11. What's happening? - Nothing.

Nothing is a negative confession. Many Christians say that they are waiting on God or 'that they don't want to get ahead of God'. When the truth is that God is waiting on us. If we move out in faith to do the work of God, God will move with us to confirm his word with signs and wonders. As it is written in Mark 16:20; 'AND THEY WENT FORTH, AND PREACHED EVERYWHERE, THE LORD WORKING WITH THEM, AND CONFIRMING THE WORD WITH SIGNS FOLLOWING.'

12. Is the cross of Jesus Christ the main message of Christianity?

Unlike other religions, Christianity is a vicarious religion. That means that it is not based on your works but on the works of the Lord Jesus on the Cross of Christ. Without His blood sacrifice there is no forgiveness of your sins. As it is written: 'WITHOUT THE SHEDDING OF BLOOD THERE IS NO REMISSION', (Hebrews 9:22).

This is the foundation of the Christian faith that all doctrines are built on. **Without what Christ did on the cross there is no salvation.**

This is why every Christian church service mentions the Lord Jesus at least once in their service. Even Kenneth Copeland the faith and prosperity preacher opens every service with prayer in Jesus name and closes every service by saying that Jesus is Lord**. This makes Christianity real.**

13. I was glancing through this prophetic book, under the section about articles of sermons from the Jesus Movement and I found this old record from Mathew chapter twenty-five. This portion of scripture has come to me several times before but I did not interpret it properly then. I guess because what I realized then is just too dangerous for Christians to accept now. Nevertheless 'LET GOD BE TRUE AND EVERY MAN A LIAR', (Romans 3:4). In this case we will see many lying doctrines from the deceived New Testament churches. And an end time truth from God's word that will not only amaze but also offend many.

These truths will come out for all to see as I dissect this portion of scripture. In Matthew 25 we see that this parable about 10 virgins who were going to meet Jesus, the bridegroom. Five were wise and five were foolish. They that were foolish took their lamps without any oil in them. But they that were wise took their lamps full of oil and flasks of extra oil too.

We better stop here to interpret this scene: the virgins are all Christians. The oil is representative of the Holy Spirit. Since only half of the lamps were full, that indicates also that only half of the Christians were full of the Holy Ghost. And were left behind because of their lack.

Some Christians assume that this lack is no big deal. But because of it half of the Christians lacked the spiritual gift of the word of wisdom to be sure that their lamps were full of oil.

All the Christians slept that means that even the Spirit filled Christians failed to 'WATCH AND PRAY'. But the other Christians who went shopping at night were worse off. **You can't receive gifts from God whenever you want you must take what he offers when he offers that to you.**

Now in the eighth verse we begin to see a phrase different from what we learned in Sunday school. Remember in Sunday school we were taught to share and give. But **here the wise told the foolish to shift for themselves**. Actually the idea of buying the oil of the Holy Ghost is a repugnant idea. Something like what that magician tried to get Peter to do for him in exchange for some money in Acts 8:18.

But the worst part of the whole story is that while the other Christians were busy buying the oil for their lamps the bridegroom, Jesus came and He denied them access to his wedding even though they were virgins or Christians themselves.

This brings out a point that no one has ever made before: that is that the Holy Ghost is in heaven and you cannot live there if you offend Him

by saying stupid things like God don't do that anymore or that's not for today or that died out when the last apostles died. It would be far better to offend some lukewarm Calvinist denomination then the Spirit of the living God! 'IF THAT SAME SPIRIT THAT RAISED CHRIST FROM THE DEAD DWELL IN YOU, HE SHALL ALSO QUICKEN YOUR MORTAL BODY'. (Romans 8:11). But IF ANY MAN HAVE NOT THE SPIRIT OF CHRIST THEN HE IS NONE OF HIS', (Romans 8:9).

Actually, this entire false teaching comes primarily from Calvinism which did not like the old Catholic doctrine of Christians suffering and needing to suffer. So they latched on to the pre-tribulation rapture theory when it first came out, even though it lacked Biblical support. The word of God says that: 'THE LORD GOD WILL DO NOTHING WITHOUT REVEALING HIS SECRET TO HIS SERVANTS, THE PROPHETS', (Amos 3:7). **No prophet ever confirmed or initiated this teaching at first, so it must be false.** But the Pentecostal Christian churches also adopted this heresy just because it sounded good somewhat like an old-fashioned twisting of the prosperity message. (Even the old timers wanted to escape poverty) But you still cannot take a spiritual trip without spiritual or Biblical support. **This false doctrine was not spiritual nor Biblical because it was not ever confirmed by any spiritual gift like prophecy at first.**

We also now see clearly how that many lukewarm Pentecostal Christian Churches forbade the Prophet David Wilkerson to preach from Revelations in their churches since that Bible book alone points out the error of Calvinism and this pre-tribulation rapture heresy.

When the Apostle John wrote some exhortations and revelations from the Lord Jesus to several of the churches that existed in that day. (Today the area of all these churches is now Muslim so they also failed to take dominion). He told several of them to repent or else the Lord would remove their lampstand (In other words no eternal security). This is brought out again most clearly in Revelation 22:18 & 19.

It is very dangerous to mess with, twist and circumvent the clear word of God. In fact; 'GOD HAS MAGNIFIED HIS WORD ABOVE HIS NAME', (Psalms 138:2) and those who subtract its warning may have their names subtracted from the book of life, (Rev. 22:18 & 19).

14. 'WHERE THE SPIRIT OF GOD IS, THERE IS LIBERTY', (II COR. 3:17). But now America has kicked God out of schools. So, when the Spirit of God leaves so does liberty. And liberty is replaced by demonic instruction, bullying, hostility, demonic disease masquerading as mental illnesses and school shootings since the wages of sin is death, even the death of students. Among those evil manifestations of demons is also drug overdose which also kills students.

On the national level, when the Spirit leaves this society in comes the contaminants of false philosophies like income inequality, global warming (climate change) and the one world order. Out goes decency and in comes depravity. Out goes sanity and in comes insanity. Out goes men and women and in comes the bisexual transgender. Out goes good hygiene and in comes filth. Out goes middle class values and in comes the ghetto with its prison values of oral and anal sex etc. Out go ladies and in comes bitches. Out goes manners and in comes pornography. Out goes respect and in comes delinquency. Out goes prosperity and in comes socialism (masqueraded poverty). Out goes restraint and in comes violence. Out goes personal relationships and in comes sterile technology known as cell phone communication. Out goes reading books like the Bible and in comes texting via cell phones. Out goes Sunday church and in comes 'Meet the Depressed'.

My friends; anyplace without the Spirit of God is not worth living in. For the Spirit of God gives a life worth living. Whereas His absence results in abortion and death.

To restore liberty some feel political contributions can assure this. **But true liberty (a life worth living) needs to be restored by a spiritual rebirth or revival**. Political accomplishments are only the beginning of a change from bad to good and may not last if reprobates continue to exercise political power and change the laws that benefit people to those that benefit the evil with their false visions for America. **Without a spiritual revival the liberty to achieve the American dream will NOT happen**. So please pray for America and for this coming election that Christians will get out and vote their values so that we can live in a great America once again before tribulation begins.

15. A commentator on Christian TV said that the Muller report had just given President Trump six more years. Then I remembered from watching the Sid Roth supernatural program on Christian TV where a notable, national prophet had spoken against the Muller team in the Spirit. As you know this is very alarming. So apparently the Muller team of investigators promptly finished their job and disbanded and went away while the getting was still good. Even demonic democratic professionals do not like to mess around with God looking over their shoulder.

In any case, this commentator went on to say that the democrats needed to accept their loss of 2016 and stop trying to blame others for it.

Now is national celebration time with America returning to the Moon and going on to Mars, having the lowest unemployment for Blacks ever and also having the lowest unemployment for Hispanics ever recorded. America is becoming great again and democrats need to attend the party of celebration and stop being the party pooper.

But even though this good news moves me to celebrate too, I intend to do my Esther fast again like I learned from the Florida Primary of the Presidential Election several years ago. Back then I learned by first-hand experience that it was possible to bring about political change not only by voting myself but by also fasting for three days to get other Christians to also join me in voting to bring about political change and eventual revival.

16. As I was watching Christian TV, a show about revival came on BVOVN called Revival Radio in which they discussed the historical backgrounds of periods of revival. One of the Spirit filled participants mentioned a little-known fact from history. From what he said his grandfather had been the pastor of a small church in Oklahoma who decided to begin having tent revivals. Their first evangelist was the healing evangelist Oral Roberts.

Of course, Kenneth Hagen also lived back in those days along with many other men of God. All these men of God got along very well back in the days of the Voice of Healing. It seems that this was so because of unity expressed in Psalm 133. They did not ever speak against each other. Nor have theological differences, since they all spoke from shared experiences.

I also experienced this when we had a plural ministry at the Maranatha House after some foreign mission ministry and The Jesus Movement. Today however most ministers play ministerial monopoly, in other words they alone speak and everyone else is eliminated for one reason or another. This does not work out too well when God wants someone to prophesy a word of confirmation, exhortation or comfort.

Then this participant returned to talking about his grandfather. Apparently back then one's manners where much more evident. Since he also lived with his grandfather he knew from first-hand experience that his grandfather never raised his voice at home. Nor did he ever hear his grandfather cuss or use gossip about any other minister. So apparently, they had more unity then than now. Back then all these men shared the same spiritual experience without different theological interpretations. Today there are many theological disputes as to what any spiritual experience may mean. Consequently, 'CAN TWO WALK TOGETHER EXCEPT THEY BE AGREED? (Amos 3:3). The way to have more unity is for all to preach the same thing. I also submit to you that the resulting theological gobbledygook of our day is because of the failure to properly recognize the Person behind these expressions instead of just some vain theology.

17. Even Peter thought that Jesus was merely a man anointed of the Holy Ghost at first. Even at the transfiguration where Jesus appeared in glory accompanied by Moses and Elijah Peter wanted to build tabernacles for these three heroes of the faith. He failed to recognize the divinity of Christ but wanted to get into a building program. Watch this when pastors want to build. Only after the sermon Peter preached on Pentecost did he make it clear that Jesus was both Lord and Christ.

18. Only at this time did the apostle John confirm that Jesus is divine when he wrote in his gospel that in the beginning was the word and the word was with God and the word was God. Moreover, the word was spoken which brought the worlds into existence.

19. This brings up my oldest and most important revelation. It began when I was a child going to school. Back then, many Jehovah's witnesses, Mormons and even some Christians with their four spiritual laws gave me a bunch of junk to study to supposedly find God.

I once heard a radio preacher back in those days say that the Bible is a book of love letters from God to man. But you cannot marry love letters. There must be two people. So with God one Person is Jesus, the other person is you, not the Bible. So then, real Christianity is a Person, The Lord Jesus Christ. Not even a teaching even if it has Biblical support. As it is written: 'HE THAT HAS THE SON HAS LIFE AND HE THAT DOES NOT HAVE THE SON OF GOD DOES NOT HAVE LIFE, (I John 5:12).

Well then which accomplishment of Jesus is most important: his Cross, miracles, healings, resurrection or second coming? All of these issues have importance and different Christian ministers emphasize different points. But a knowledge of history shows the answer to be: Under Moses the blood sacrifice was required. In the New Testament the blood sacrifice on the Cross of the Lord Jesus was his main or primary mission. As recorded by John the Baptist: **'BEHOLD THE LAMB OF GOD WHO TAKES AWAY THE SIN OF THE WORLD', (John 1:29).**

Well then what about the verse that says that 'THE LORD JESUS IS MADE UNTO US WISDOM, AND RIGHTEOUSNESS, AND SANCTIFICATION, AND REDEMPTION', (I CORINTHIANS 1:3). Which is the most important? Redemption, (Colossians 1:14 and Ephesians 1:7). But don't ignore sanctification (the conquest of your own sin nature) as this once saved always saved propaganda is a false theology.

Wasn't Jesus a mere man anointed by the Holy Ghost? No Jesus was the God Man. His works including miracles were as a man anointed by the Holy Ghost. But his Person was always divine, He never stopped being God the Son. Let's now see which non-Jew recognized that first.

20. Preachers, teachers and theologians have already gone into all the prophecies concerning Jesus so I will not repeat them and claim their conclusions as my own. As a prophet I like to be original and tell you truth that you may have read many times from the Bible but still have never grasped. I suppose this was because when the Bible mentioned the wise men coming to the manger you assumed that it was just part of the nativity scene. But the wise man were followers of a star that showed them important things. You might say that they were followers of coasttocoastam.com before radio and computers were even invented or that they knew all about ancient aliens before TV and its history channel.

In any case they asked another king, Herod where the king of the Jews was to be born. They were concerned to find him since they wanted to worship him. None of these scholarly theologians who have been experts at giving us all this Calvinist trash about 'once saved always saved', predestination and election can seem to grasp that you do not worship what is not God. So they must have known something about this Child. Actually since this Child had His own personal moving star, He had to be a 'Star Child'. This meant that the baby Jesus was God manifested in the flesh and these wise men knew it and gave gifts accordingly. When they recognized Him as such that meant that He was both extra-terrestrial and divine.

Of course, you have heard about the transfiguration of Christ recorded in your Bible, (Matthew 17:2). Were Peter, James and John saw who the Lord Jesus Christ really is.

Years ago when I was a congregational prophet this word came to me but the Baptists from Dallas Theological Seminary kicked me out of that Vineyard Church in Anaheim, California before I got a chance to publically pronounce it. The Lord told me that I'd still get to give it to a world-wide audience. So here it is: 'CHRIST IS MORE DAZZLING THAN DIAMONDS SPARKLING, HE IS MORE MAGNIFICENT THAN GOLD SHIMMERING IN THE SUNLIGHT OF NOONDAY AND MORE RADIANT THAN SILVER MOLTON IN THE FIERY FURNACE. BY HIM ALL THINGS WERE MADE AND THROUGH HIM DO ALL THINGS CONSIST AND HE UPHOLDS ALL BY THE WORD OF HIS AWESOME POWER. HOLY, HOLY, HOLY LORD GOD ALMIGHTY WHICH WAS AND IS AND IS TO COME. HEAVEN AND EARTH CANNOT CONTAIN YOUR GLORY THAT'S WHY THE WHOLE UNIVERSE WITH OTHER WORLDS HAVE BEEN MADE'! This is the word of the Lord. Thanks be to God.

FIRST END TIME PLAGUE: COVID 19

I must also say a few things about this Corona Virus. First, I must impart what I know by supernatural knowledge that comes from my spiritual gifts. **Both Christians and non-Christians have been victims of this COVID 19 so the idea that Christians would be raptured before any bad events like this Corona Virus or any other tribulation is false thanks to that false doctrine of the pre-tribulation rapture.**

Much of what I say the deceived will see as controversial but it will be truth that you need to face. Among those is the truth that 'IT RAINS ON BOTH THE JUST AND THE UNJUST', (Matthew 5:45). So you both were here while this judgment rained down on us all both saints and sinners. Moreover, 'JUDGMENT BEGINS WITH THE HOUSE OF GOD', (1Peter 4:17). But it does not stop there.

Because of the theological indoctrination of the so-called Christian advisors of President Trump, President Trump also became victim of this false belief in the pre-tribulation rapture, therefore he saw this Corona Virus as just a medical issue requiring social distancing (while co-conspirators see such as a way to more clearly identify individual cell phones for individual 666 identity) and work stoppage as the medically insane took it upon themselves to paint a very dark picture of horror for President Trump. **So severe as to cause the closing down of jobs throughout America and change America from a first-rate capitalist economy into a socialist one without a single vote.** In the process America has acquired a four trillion-dollar debt and a socialist recovery that shall eventually be ruled over by the antichrist for no democratic president can rule over a hungry herd without a weapon of some sort. So, Biden and the baby killing Democrats will try to rule for our welfare but will fail, as baby killers cannot care for adults.

This Corona Virus has caused many governments to also close their borders therefore the migrant workers that our farmers need to pick the harvest will not be coming**. This is how famine comes our way**. So the fact that famine may be our next judgment should be obvious.

But for now, you can safeguard yourself from this plague by repenting if you had any part in the sins which caused it, like abortion and same sex marriage.

To build up your immunity or self-confidence against this plague first as Christians or if not a Christian yet, become one then remember from God's word that: 'THERE SHALL NO EVIL BEFALL THEE, NEITHER PLAGUE COME NIGH THY DWELLING', (Psalm 91:10).

Then by proper nutrition, eating from the Mediterranean diet with lots of olive oil, broccoli, and raw onions and taking supplements like vitamins A, B, C and D and other things like magnesium, turmeric and zinc to build up your immunity.

Several homeopathic physicians have also recommended that you get on a gluten free diet, with no bread nor wheat products**. Taiwan eats rice and has had no Corona Virus deaths since March.** Along with these please be sure to get your free flu shot every year **and most importantly ask for the free pneumonia shot too. This pneumonia shot is very important because all these flulike viruses kill by pneumonia and taking this pneumonia shot keeps you from becoming a statistic to this type of virus.**

So for those of you who need to go back to work to support your families **I'd get my Corona vaccine and free flu and pneumonia shots first then go back to work. For I'd rather be abused by this virus than starve to death.**

Knowing this, Trump's medical advisors deceived him by insisting on social distancing when they knew that such dissipates 'herd immunity' and instigates the closing down of America's economy. (Now there are approved drugs for the treatment of COVID 19 like what President Trump got that are now being kept from the American people). When the real reason for the virus was a spiritual one of judgment for infanticide especially in New York and gay sex especially by mardi-gras in New Orleans, Louisiana not any other major medical, social or economic problems at all.

Mardi-gras sparks my memory about some truth that concerns this Corona Crisis. As a teenager I surfed with a group of high school students early in the morning while the surf was still 'glassy'. A local 'beach bum' with a dark suntan would sometimes join us. This guy was older than us. He was a full-grown young man and while we wore surfer trunks, he wore a male bikini bathing suit that showed off the size of his huge love muscle. Many young guys go to the beach to show off their muscles too so we were not phased at all by this even though it was somewhat strange to us. After all you see everything at the beach.

One day this dude told us that he had to go to New Orleans for Mardi-gras. He had to raise his support by 'sharing' himself with these gay Catholics who would be giving up meat and gay sex for Lent. And as a male prostitute he had to get out there before Lent started. Most of us could not see giving up surf here in Daytona Beach for the filthy air of New Orleans and the lack of good surf in Louisiana so we paddled on out to catch another wave and let him go do his own thing which most of us did not understand anyway. But now you know that there has been over sixty years of this evil. So God must have gotten tired of it all and since the Roman Catholic Church would not shut it down, God has and will by this Corona Virus or something else in the future if need be.

There have been several positive points to this Corona Crisis and its stay at home order. Former employees have gotten closer to their pets and to their family members too. Parents have learned how to help their children do schoolwork again. Every dad has time to help his wife with the housework. Teenagers have learned to stay at home and honor their parents not to just go out to do their own thing.

Some people have even learned how to do new things like how to work a computer and read a Bible (like the Expositor's Study Bible) with understanding. And some sophisticated people have learned how to judge a Christian TV program as to which topic is really Bible based and which is just church propaganda. You know TV producers of Christian programs do not take the time to identify which denomination or church supports which TV program. So, we even have preachers declaring different viewpoints on the same Bible verses and since no one ever corrects their misinterpretations we're just left to our own confusion, distrust and lack of understanding. 'THESE THINGS OUGHT NOT SO TO BE', (James 3:10).

Once these stay at home orders expire as a free Christian you need to change this foolishness by going back to work and insisting on having your constitutional rights restored. Then vote against forcing the Federal Government to bail out states that have by deception screwed their people out of adequate and earned state retirement and other benefits.

There have also been some very negative conclusions from this Corona Crisis, some of which are unconstitutional. Like ruling against church attendance. And coming against your right to work. Plus moving from a capitalist economy to a socialist one to supposedly solve this Corona Crisis by throwing money at it without even attempting to find out why it came or how to get rid of it.

Beyond this Corona Crisis there is no mention in the book of Revelation in your Bible of any government ever shutting down the economy for any of the horrible events recorded there. So why was it done for this virus? **It should never be done again**. I feel anointed to say this: **If Jesus is a king then He must have a kingdom to rule over. Tell the Democrat Joe Biden that a mob of unemployed paupers does not compose any kingdom worth having.**

From what I remember Daniel was the only prophet that Jesus ever mentioned in the New Testament ('WHEN YE THEREFORE SHALL SEE THE ABOMINATION OF DESOLATION SPOKEN OF BY DANIEL THE PROPHET STAND IN THE HOLY PLACE', (Matthew 24:15). Of course, Daniel was privileged to see many things. And then he was told to seal up in his book of visions of what had been revealed to him. This book was to be unsealed and its contents revealed at the time of the end.

Many theologians say that the time of the end is now. So then how could it have been in the 1830's when the Adventists falsely revealed The Pre-Tribulation Rapture which most Christian denominations then adopted despite the fact that it was based upon 'unsealed' theory.

Since most of President Trump's Christian advisors are from these same Christian denominations that believed in this false doctrine of the pre-tribulation rapture and so had nothing to say to President Trump about this Corona Virus because they believed that all Christians would escape this virus and any other tribulation or anything else bad by going to heaven first because their viewpoints were poisoned by this 'unsealed' theory of the pre-tribulation rapture.

Since these pre-tribulation rapturists had nothing to say to President Trump about this Corona Virus therefore President Trump mistakenly adapted the socialist solution of the medically insane instead of sticking with his strong suit (the economy) and acquiesced to shut down the greatest economy the world has ever known. Such will not happen again.

The medically insane also believe that as a medical disease this Corona Virus may repeat itself just like any other flu in the fall of the year. So the deceived democrat Biden wants us to wear masks and maintain social distancing to supposedly ward off this Corona Virus as a medical issue **instead of the plague which his abortion policy has caused.**

Whereas an anointed Christian advisor who sees this Corona Virus as a curse from God which it is for the abominations of abortion and same sex marriage would know how to stop this plague just like Moses and Aaron did when they stood between the living and the dead in Numbers 16:48 and the plague was stayed. So God could take it away for now and send it again in some other form of judgment later on. Maybe even years later like the 19 years from 9/11 to COVID 19 now, or to about ten years in the future until the asteroid Apophis crashes into the earth in 2029.

But I have heard how that this Corona Virus is increasing now with more deaths, so this points out its need to have been stayed by some prophetic spiritual people full of the Holy Ghost and power like real prophets not just stupid dispensational preachers of theologically insane false doctrines that most of President Trump's so-called Christian advisors were indoctrinated with in lukewarm denominational Bible schools.

Since I live in Florida where many hurricanes happen, I remember how that a few years ago a Pentecostal minister named Dr. Rodney Howard Brown kept a hurricane from his River Ministry in Tampa, Florida. This is the exact type of prophetic anointing we need now to combat this Corona Virus throughout the United States of America instead of adopting more socialist restrictions that do not seem to work since this virus is air-born and spreads through the air, (You know from the Bible that the devil who is doing this for God is: 'THE PRINCE OF THE POWER OF THE AIR', (Ephesians 2:2).

So now President Trump has suffered three deceptions. The first one concerned the Democrats lies about Russia to bring about President Trump's impeachment. The second one was when these Christian theological advisors thanks to their false doctrines failed to tell President Trump the truth. **(That the 'Beginnings of Sorrows' may be happening now and are due to increase after President Trump leaves office). In that light, it may be wise to keep President Trump in office as long as possible.** (After this warning President Trump's adoption of these bad medical policies which counteracted his economic policies would not have been adopted as he would have realized that his terms of office was to be the good time of prosperity before the bad times come). The third one was when the medically insane deceived Trump about how to end this Corona Crisis. By keeping America shut down and adopting their foolish policies. instead of stopping this plague just like Moses and Aaron did (or any modern prophets could do today) when they stood between the living and the dead in Numbers 16:48 and the plague was stayed.

In baseball at three strikes that puts you out. But America is not baseball. So, I intend to fast for Trump to win the Presidency again so that your future employment is assured. **After all, if Trump with God's help could turn the depressed economy of the food stamp president into America's boom economy one time. I expect him to overcome all these man-made obstacles and serve the American people to do again as he did before. When he accomplishes this again with God's help we'll all know that it has been God Who has intervened to help us and many of us will need to repent for blaming Trump for everything bad while failing to give abortion and same sex marriage and the democrats the blame that they deserve.**

I strongly feel this way. Because unlike most people who get jealous over the nice things' others are able to get, I get happy when I see others blessed even if it's a new car that I as a disabled person cannot drive.

An examination of the deaths caused by this Corona Virus shows that over half of all the deaths in the cities of America have been those of Afro-Americans. Since most Afro-Americans vote for abortionist democrats, the real cause of death is easily seen as 'THE WAGES OF SIN IS DEATH', (Romans 6:23). So it's dangerous to vote against God's laws.

In this crisis some things like abortion clinics and liquor stores are seen as essential while churches and the economy are not.

Thank God that this book is not politically correct but also discloses an unknown truth behind the old adage that the rich get richer while the poor get poorer. This is especially true in any financial crisis where the stock market goes down.

Most of the superrich including some democrats like Speaker Nancy Pelosi have stock market options trading agreements in addition to their stock brokerage account. This options agreement enables them to buy OEX stock option PUTS as the stock market is going down so that their bank balance goes up. That's right, while you are losing, they are making money. Therefore millionaires become billionaires.

And those of you with 401Ks lose your retirement funds and whatever was invested by that fund in the stock market. This mainly happens because wage earners are not allowed to trade options by the discriminatory rules of the Securities and Exchange Commission of the US government who supposedly believes in equal opportunity for all.

The Bible does say 'THERE IS A TIME FOR EVERY PURPOSE UNDER THE SUN', (Ecclesiastes 3:17). But nowhere does it say that you need to embrace poverty as if it were to be your lot in life. Or to be sure to vote for Biden so you can familiarize yourself with food stamps again.

There are two actions to take in this case. For the Christian you can ask God to restore to you what the devil has stolen from you and you should start 'CASTING ALL YOUR CARE UPON HIM FOR HE CARES FOR YOU', (1 Peter 5:7). For the secular non-Christian, you can go to court once they reopen and sue these retirement funds of various companies and even some unions who claimed falsely to secure your retirement. But they failed with all that money that they once controlled to secure your retirement and now you have to find another job which you can do at your advanced age.

Your former employer probably has corporate lawyers. Let them handle your suits for justice, since they lost their matching funds in your retirement account themselves.

This action for your retirement savings and investment needs to be taken right away and set into law. Because in these end times this virus and even worse will happen again because the people have not yet repented from their national sins of legalized abortion and legalized same sex marriage. 'BE NOT DECIEVED, GOD IS NOT MOCKED', (Galatians 6:7). So the Bible verse I received back in January, before this Corona Crisis happened still stands, still applies and it still says: 'FOR THIS PURPOSE THE SON OF GOD WAS MANIFESTED THAT HE MIGHT DESTROY THE WORKS OF THE DEVIL', (1 John 3:8).

No church today preaches that Jesus is or will become a destroyer of the evil works of the devil. We usually attribute tragic events to the devil even though they are seen as acts of God. In any case, my prophetic books are published to hopefully restore a healthy fear of God to the people even you, so that you can get delivered, forgiven, saved, sanctified, filled, thrilled, endued, equipped and empowered to turn this current darkness all around us into the light of God's new day for you, America and the world.

Many unions are insisting that their members be protected from this Corona Virus with masks and sterile coverings with medical gloves. They should also insist that their members not vote for any abortion or gay rights candidates. For now we know that this Corona Virus (COVID 19) is judgment from God for those abominations in particular.

When God created man out of the dust of the earth, he breathed into his nostrils the breath of life and man became a living soul.

Not long ago a young man called his dad on the telephone in New York and said that he couldn't breathe and dropped over dead. Job said in the Bible that 'THE LORD GIVES AND THE LORD TAKES AWAY, BLESSED BE THE NAME OF THE LORD', (Job 1:21).

So here we see how that God gave the breath of life at first but has now taken it away via this Corona Virus (COVID 19). Despite what all the ungodly and backslidden preachers say on TV (they're on Daystar and TBN) about this Corona Virus being from the devil, we now know better because in January 2020 God gave me this Bible verse by revelation: 'FOR THIS PURPOSE THE SON OF GOD WAS MANIFESTED THAT HE MIGHT DESTROY THE WORKS OF THE DEVIL', (1 John 3:8). And those works include abortion and same sex marriage causing this Corona Virus or COVID 19.

We also know that Jesus was never recognized as a destroyer. Nevertheless, as I revealed in my other prophetic book; Jesus as a mature star child had to show His 'invincibility'. Most kings (king of the Jews) usually do this by war. So, a coming war would probably be the next judgement if famine were not already resultant from this Corona Virus.

But keeping people confined to their own homes has also produced some very unpleasant side effects. Among those is the need to get out of one's home and get noticed by protesting in any issue real or imagined. Let's face it the unemployed have a lot of free time to protest. For Black people even if their issue is real like discrimination or police brutality it's better to protest in daylight to also absorb vitamin D from sunlight then go out at night when the bad show up to keep you from work, or making money for your own needs? For

'MONEY ANSWERS ALL THINGS', (Ecclesiastes 10:19). So President Trump has been busy getting America's workers (White, Black, Brown, Yellow and Red) back to work rather than participating in pseudo psychological discussions about race and police brutality. Let's face it, we all know that the police can be brutal, after all that's their job to keep people in line but not to violate people's God given constitutional rights.

Nevertheless, some people under the influence of demons of resentment, demons of hatred, demons of revenge, and demons of conflict and war will want civil war in order to get even for the violation of their civil rights, including unjust racial discrimination and murder. Remember that demons usually work in teams. So just in case a civil war is coming your way. I am including my chapter on **THE AMERICAN CIVIL WAR** from my other prophetic books so that you may get prepared for it. Meanwhile famine is already in the works due to closed borders and the lack of healthy migrant farm workers to bring in our harvest. For those who still cannot see God and Jesus as a destroyer (1 John 3:8) let me refer you to the Bible book of Revelation.

While Jesus is the only savior and no one comes to the Father but by Him and every promise of God is ye ye and amen, and as divine He can change these 'beginnings of sorrows' or even the apocalypse by repentance.

There are other supernatural entities who have the power to get vengeance and destroy. Just two of these are Medusa goddess of destruction who's head of hairs was really snakes that bit people. And Mars the Roman false god of war. Some say that these false gods were just myths. If so then how do you explain Rome's complete conquest of the known ancient world?

Men are getting ready to explore the planet Mars. Look the god of Mars will not like fallen, deceived and wicked men who have disrespected other divinities like Jesus and have trampled underfoot the blood of the covenant and have done despite to the Spirit of grace to come to his world to infect it with their evil. And since Mars is not governed by Christian values man dare not invade his dominion. (save this book so other generations will know why that future Mars landing crashes).

There is a book, Conviction Machine written by a former federal prosecutor Sidney Powel in which he discusses all the civil rights the federal courts have unconstitutionally taken from us. Other civil and constitutional rights have also been taken from American citizens by this Corona Crisis. Particularly the obvious abuse of your right to work. And the forced order in a supposedly free society to stay home while the US Constitution supposedly guarantees life (no abortion), liberty and the pursuit of happiness (freedom to go to church and work). How can you possibly have the liberty to pursue happiness if you must stay home as though imprisoned by some virus?

Before this Corona Virus assaulted our constitutional rights, there was the 9/11 tragedy which also eroded our constitutional rights.

As a wheelchair disabled man before I am allowed to board any commercial plane the TSA must strip search me in a room where they stick their finger up my anus to be sure I have no weapons. Of-course this intimate personal examination involves what you could call molestation. This is why I don't travel by air much anywhere. So please don't invite me anywhere to speak or display my books unless you can provide me with a private jet compliments of one of our prosperous prosperity preachers.

Some naughty criticisms of our prosperity preachers masquerading as disguised jealousy has recently come forth. Just because you have a small home in the suburbs from God's blessings does not mean that another man's fulfilled vision for a new Gulfstream jet for ministry is beyond the abundant life and a lavish display of luxury and just a foolish waste of money. Remember God is not a socialist or communist where all blessings must be the equal. You can name and claim a house and someone else can do the same for a luxurious jet and both get blessed. The quantity or value of a blessing does not define its quality. The Giver gives as He sees fit, your job is to thank Him for your results and not to try and disqualify the other recipient for receiving what you think is too much.

Another main medical objection to this Corona Virus quarantine with masks and stay at home orders says that this disease is not spread primarily by people at all but through the air just like any other respiratory diseases. So closing down the economy for this was just stupidity. And closing down the church for this is insidious.

Other controversies and criticisms about this Corona Crisis have come forth. One brought by William Koenig, you remember the author of Eye To Eye reveals that President Trump's peace plan to divide Israel's land for peace results in this Corona Crisis. President Trump decided to extend Israeli sovereignty to the Golan Heights after recognizing Jerusalem as the capital of Israel. With that extension of Israeli sovereignty he included the settlements in Judea and Samaria but gave the rest of the land to the Palestinians. This displeased the God of Israel as he wants inheritance of land to come only through Isaac and not Ishmael and sent this Corona Crisis to confirm his will. Now this COVID 19 plague will increase and get worse as long as his will concerning His land gets ignored and unrecognized.

April sixteenth reveals that Trump's medical expert was deceiving him and should be fired because he has a patent on one of these viruses. In other words, he intends to make money off people getting sick and dying.

Another one of these points of unfounded hatred against TRUMP for supposedly failing to protect the people from COVID 19 was disproved by a female doctor Simone Gold on August 10, 2020 over coasttocoastam.com radio when she, an ER physician, said that when Trump was taking the malaria drug, hydroxychloroquine a few months ago, he was doing the right thing, since that drug combined with zinc does cure this Covid 19.

The economic shutdown of the American economy was thanks to the communist propaganda of a doctor Tedros Adhamon of the World Health Organization who told this BS to the Deep State Doctor Fauci who then told it to President Trump who unfortunately acted upon it. Unfortunately, the con artist Dr. Fauci supposedly already has a patent on a drug that hopes to cure this virus. The World Health DR. knows malaria well but he is not an expert in any pulmonary virus, so his advice was at least lacking.

Another major concern with the 'stay at home' orders of this Corona Virus is the personal assault of demons called: ''familiar spirits'. As a former deliverance minister, I know how that **familiar spirits have had a field day thanks to this Corona Virus. Because they have been able to spread to all members of the family those conditions or problems that 'run in the family'.** These conditions or problems may include: disingenuous theologies to the basic fundamental truths of the Christian faith such as: replacement theology (that gentile Christian blessings have now replaced those of the Jews and that this antisemitism will continue until the deception of the pre-tribulation rapture), amillennialism (that there will be no thousand year reign of Christ upon the earth), Christians can have bad habits but Christians cannot have demons, (This is the false belief that Christians cannot have demons). Eternal security (once saved always saved). and the false teaching that the Holy Spirit and His gifts like speaking in tongues are not for today (Cessation theology).

Familiar spirits also put bad family habits on us, like drunkenness, smoking, telling lies, bearing false witness, criminal behavior and unbelief: that I'll never amount to anything and am not able to go to college or learn a trade that pays well or become any better in this life than my parents.

Obviously familiar spirits and other demons are far more dangerous than any disease. In fact, many diseases can be vaccinated against. In America and in Europe all vaccines must be free of mercury by law. So The World Health Organization under the auspices of Bill Gates forces those Black nations in Africa to use these contaminated vaccines or else they will not be given any HIV vaccine. So it seems to me that this is just genocide-a desire to eliminate the Black race far worse than-any police department having police brutality. My Black brothers probably will have more to say about this racism. I already said what I need to say in my other prophetic book: **REPORATIONS FOR SLAVERY.**

There is another issue here that comes from technology. Bill Gates wants to save the world via the technology of vaccinations. While Dr. Bill Ankerberg is saving Nigeria by audio recorders of the gospel.

President Trump's deceived dispensational Christian advisors were afraid to speak out against medical foolishness and just like many modern theologians do not believe that Christians can have demons. But I know by personal experience that comes from ministering to many charismatic groups all over Florida that demon inspired mental problems (depression, anxiety, anger, violence, addiction, sexual perversion, police bullying kleptomania, police brutality and bureaucratic harassment) and emotional issues (marriage problems, inferiority complex, suicide, loneliness, poverty mindset, feelings of superiority, lack of love, racism, lack of a giving spirit, selfishness, self-centeredness, not able to sleep or get any rest, nightmares) and even physical or social issues like (hard heartedness, unemployment, hives, hemorrhoids, varicose veins, constipation, gluttony, inability to gain weight) various diseases (high blood pressure, diabetes, cancer, COPD, HIV, pneumonia, the common cold, flu, Corona Virus, meningitis, TB,) ailments, pains, injuries and disabilities can be dealt with and healed by both the power of the blood of Jesus and the power in the name of Jesus whose healing power reflects His divinity.

Last night I had a prophetic dream that showed me that there is more to add to this demonic abuse resulting from COVID 19. Of-course the most serious problem is the increase of suicides due to the inability to provide adequately for your own family thanks to all these lack of work lay-offs due to this COVID 19 virus. These other short comings also involve imposed poverty due to the stupid social distancing and personal isolation viewpoints of the medically insane.

Of course, a stimulus stipend which has caused inflation was given each family to supposedly prevent their slide into poverty. But $1200.00 is too little for that goal to be achieved. Some people were also considered 'essential' and had to have expensive laptop computers, food, water, phone service, internet hookup, cable and all manner of expenses.

Let's face it the unemployed have a lot of free time to protest. Even if their issue is real like discrimination or police abuse. It's better to go back to work, to make money for their own needs. For 'MONEY ANSWERS ALL THINGS', (Ecclesiastes 10:19). So President Trump has been busy getting America's workers (White, Black, Brown, Yellow and Red) back to work rather than participating in pseudo psychological discussions about race and police brutality. Let's face it, we all know that the police can be brutal, after all that's their job to keep people in line but not to violate people's God given constitutional rights.

There is a God of justice and those who believe in God are willing to let Him handle justice issues like unwarranted police brutality. But those who see God as either a myth or a 'White man's God' would rather riot and loot instead with municipal Democratic Party support.

There is a major misunderstanding about looting as if it were just stealing by the frustrated and those who feel that society has disinherited them. But looting is really the taking of spoils which a victorious army does after it has won a battle. So, it must be acknowledged that Civil War has begun just as the prophets foretold and we Christians can pray and vote against it for our own welfare and the good of our nation.

Back during the charismatic movment the children of Christians needed deliverances too. These deliverances involved basic illnesses like flu, many birth defects and even downs syndrome.

Back then however we did not have to deal with diseases that should have been vaccinated against like measles, chicken pox, typhoid, tuberculosis, smallpox, diphtheria and whooping cough.

One modern physical problem we now have but did not have back then is autism. This disorder should have triggered alarm bells because of its anti-God nature.

A doctor was recently asked about the beginning symptoms of autism. He said that if a baby does not seem to smile or laugh at all by 6 months then they should be brought in for autism screening.

Smiling reveals 'THE LOVE OF GOD SHED ABROAD IN YOUR HEART BY THE HOLY GHOST', (Romans 5:5). Laughing indicates 'THE JOY OF THE LORD WHICH IS OUR STRENGTH'.

Let's first consider love or more specifically the lack of love and the inability to smile. If one cannot smile at the opposite sex then their possible future mates will feel that you could not possibly love them. So, this alone could cause you to remain unmarried and dependent on your parents for the rest of their lives.

But that problem would not usually show itself until the teen years. Prior to that need, your main need is for strength. Especially psychological and moral strength and personal strength of character so that you can't be bullied in life. Without this personal strength it's easy to become the victim of social misfits, perverts (pedophiles) and drug dealers.

This points out a major deliverance truth: that is **most modern American and European and Asian Christians have never been delivered from anything by anyone at any time**.

The prevalence of demons in everyone's life should now be crystal clear. Blacks coming as slaves from Africa were dominated by which doctors in their villages and practiced voodoo. Whites in Europe were subject to antisemitism by Martin Luther. And also by the false doctrines of John Calvin. Other non-Christian peoples (like Muslims) should not have been allowed into America. (The Indians were also non-Christian but there is no evidence that they were demon possessed or gave demons to the cowboys.

Christians who believe in Jesus still have bad habits like smoking and drinking booze, driving drunk, participating in extramarital affairs, having sex with animals and their own children, gay relationships and all manner of naughtiness including over-eating, gluttony and eating disorders.

Many sophisticated people like judges, police psychologists and defense attorneys try to avoid made up crimes based on mere suspicion which are really the result of the demons of unbelief. That's what we have here that people are protesting about. Only US Treasury agents are to determine whether or not a currency is counterfeit, not a local police department. For the local police to arrest anyone for suspicion of counterfeiting or any other undetermined and unsubstantiated crime is not worthy of arrest and should be thrown out of court.

Obviously, it is wrong to then kill the suspect already in custody for a supposed crime that may not even have been real. Consequently, I submit to you that all so called crimes that have no visible means of support and are based on mere suspicion alone should be discarded as invalid. Let's cut down on the unnecessary high cost of incarceration. While Blacks make up less than forty percent of Americans, they constitute half of all prisoners.

Unlike most people who are not wheelchair disabled with a speech impediment from a head injury I know by personal experience the hassles you get from the police who might feel that you are drunk and want to arrest you for public intoxication. That's what we have here in one particular case that the people are demonstrating about.

In this case a young Black man was found sleeping in his car at a fast food drive-in. As peacekeepers the police woke him up to do a personal welfare check. But seeing this man was OK, the police moved from being peacekeepers to becoming investigators. This needs to be stopped by law.

Usually this happens when someone is stopped for a traffic violation. After this violation the police usually ask for the driver's license. Not to just see if the defendant has a license to be on the road but to also check for any warrants in order to pacify taxpayers who want their money's worth.

Since this case did not involve driving or any traffic violations, the police who moved from being peacekeepers to investigators decided to ask the young

Black man if he would take a breathalyzer for them, so they could determine if they might arrest him for public intoxication (legally they had no right to ask him for this), Please note that the effectiveness of the police is determined by their number of arrests and not by the amount of community or family peace problems that they are able to solve.

Of course he failed the breathalyzer test so they proceeded to take him into custody even though he told them before that his sister lived nearby and they could let him go sleep in her house.

Once they tried to put the handcuffs on him, he became upset and grabbed the police officer's Taser and ran off as he did not want to go to jail. As he ran away he shot the Taser at the police to stop them but he was shot by return fire with a police gun that killed him.

Obviously, this was an unwarranted waste of human life as a taser is not a deadly weapon to be responded to with via police gunfire. Likewise many other crimes are based on mere suspicion alone and not even worthy of any arrest. (There should be no arrest unless the police officer himself sees a crime in progress).

Speaking of racism from history we get: The author Eugene Beranger described the condition of Blacks in the North at this civil war time in his book**:** North of Slavery. He writes: **'In virtually every phase of existence (In the North), Negroes found themselves systematically separated from Whites. They were either excluded from railway cars, omnibuses, stage coaches, and steam boats or assigned to special 'Jim Crow' sections; they sat, when permitted, in secluded and removed corners of theaters and lecture halls; they could not enter most hotels, restaurants, and resorts, except as servants, they prayed in 'Negro pews' in the White churches, and if partaking of the Sacrament of the Lord's Supper, they waited until the Whites had been served the bread and wine first. Moreover, they were often educated in segregated schools, punished in segregated prisons, nursed in segregated hospitals and buried in segregated cemeteries.'**

This quickens my memory of my experience with this exact type of abuse I had when I had just graduated from Fuller Seminary in 1985. And I began sleeping with the homeless since I could not afford the high rents out there in expensive southern California and could not get any church job to pay rent anyway since 'wheelchairs do not inspire faith'.

One night as I was sleeping outside, a local police officer kicked me awake and wrote me a ticket for trespassing. But I knew the Bible well and that I was on public land. So once that policeman left, I laid that ticket down before the Lord to pray over it just like the king of Israel had done when he was threatened by the king of Assyria. But since I was too tired to think up a long religious prayer, I simply quoted the part of the twenty fourth Psalm which says that: 'THE EARTH IS THE LORDS'. And asked God to judge between his word and trespassing and do whatsoever to Him seemed best and rolled over and went back to sleep.

God has magnified his word even above His own name. So anything compared to the supremacy of God's word, like some dumb human law over trespassing on God's land does not hold up well. And in fact, it is automatically put down.

That morning I caught the bus to go to the mission to eat my oatmeal. The bus passed the police station with its flag at half-staff. So I asked the mission director what had happened. He said that a local police officer had had a fire-arms accident and had shot and killed himself. It was written up in the paper that he gave to me. Afterward for some reason I looked to see the name of that officer if it matched the name on my ticket. **It matched.** Of course, I was horrified. And I thought that it was an overreaction by God to put someone to death just for a mistake over trespassing, but I said nothing and held my peace. For I had learned in that seminary never to question or criticize our Sovereign Lord about things I didn't understand.

Then I remembered how strongly God feels about his word. And that as the Sovereign Lord his acts are not for me to evaluate, judge, or correct. So I just thanked him and forgot about it all until now.

But if anyone tries to do this deliverance from demons stuff today especially in any lukewarm denominational church they are labeled a fanatic. Other unbelieving ministries try to cover up the congregation's need for real deliverance with all manner of delusions including false dream interpretations to false prophetic viewpoints.

Few today have taken the time to realize and grasp that demons are very much alive and are involved in many unfortunate ways with many things in our personal lives, society and even our churches.

Casting out demons was a pillar in the ministry of Jesus. In the over three years that Jesus ministered on the earth fully one-third of his teachings involved deliverances. Beloved where then did all the demons go?

None of the demons were cast into outer space nor even hell**. All of the demons that were ever here on earth at any time (like even the times of Jesus) are still here now as demons do not die.** So the same demons that were cast out by Jesus or one of his disciples are here now perhaps even in you or some relative. **They have just been (reincarnated) as once one dies they go into another living person.**

Usually when all the family members are invited to a wake where one of the other family members dies, the demons that were in that person jump to other living members of the same family. This is easily proven because whenever you attend a séance the demons that were in that relative speaks about what they and you knew because the demons were familiar spirits once in your relative speaking again to you and not your relative at all. Besides wakes demons also gain access by human emotions such as fear, anger and substance abuse.

This is a very unusual doctrine that you do not hear in most churches even though they know it is true. Most Christians do not believe in any form of reincarnation at all, but this is **the doctrine of the reincarnation of demons**. The same demons that Jesus dealt with 2000 years ago are still here, in like kind, today and much of the pressure on our lives comes from these same demons of darkness that surround us and are operating in our world. So we must obey Jesus order to cast them out, 'IN MY NAME SHALL THEY CAST OUT DEVILS', (Mark 16:17).

Now the passivists that rule the church would much rather council demons or the afflicted person than to cast out demons. Since you can't cast out demons but by the Holy Ghost anointing to do so. No one ever cast out demons before Jesus. Now any discussion of the Holy Ghost is very unpopular in most denominational churches as any deliverance is just too demonstrative and does not well follow preaching from Readers Digest.

Most Christians feel that they should relate to demons as to other people. But demons are evil spiritual entities they are not to be treated like personal relationships just as other people. So **the admonition to forgive your enemies does not apply at all to demons.** After all demons just consider humans to be monkeys and want no forgiveness for anything from us. In fact, our God does not care for demons illegally squatting on any of His creatures.

Our God is a speaking God, therefore speak to these demons and command them to leave. That's the way to drive them out.

But if you are not anointed enough to do that you could get another Christian to help you. Remember though Jesus said: 'I HAVE GiVEN YOU AUTHORITY OVER ALL THE POWER OF THE ENEMY', (Luke 10:19). Even so we have nothing to be afraid of, for Jesus has prepared the way for our victory through His victory at the cross. This does mean that since Jesus did His job, we must also do ours. As it is written: 'THIS KIND (of demon) DOES NOT GO OUT EXCEPT BY PRAYER AND FASTING', (Matthew 17:14-16).

Fasting strengthens us in our resistance to evil and also increases your awareness of the Spirit of God in you. Until you stand up in the righteousness of Jesus and then command the spirits to go, they will not leave. So, you must speak to them and command the demons to leave. Just like Jesus did where it is written: Jesus 'CAST OUT THE SPIRITS WITH A WORD', (Matthew 8:16).

In order to maintain our deliverance, we must keep on fighting those demons that once abused us lest they return. The word that brought about your deliverance has the power and authority that when exercised with your persistence shows the devil who is in control. Remember that Jesus did not come to tolerate demons as if they were to become included as part of our diverse society.

The Lord told Moses in Numbers 33:51-53 'SPEAK TO THE SONS OF ISRAEL AND SAY TO THEM, WHEN YOU CROSS OVER THE JORDAN INTO THE LAND OF CANAAN, THEN YOU SHALL DRIVE OUT ALL THE INHABITANTS OF THE LAND FROM BEFORE YOU, AND DESTROY ALL THEIR FIGURED STONES, AND DESTROY ALL THEIR MOLTEN IMAGES AND DEMOLISH ALL THEIR HIGH PLACES; AND YOU SHALL TAKE POSSESSION OF THE LAND AND LIVE IN IT, FOR I HAVE GIVEN THE LAND TO YOU TO POSSESS IT'. After this was done God told Moses in Deuteronomy 7:2 'WHEN THE LORD YOUR GOD DELIVERS THEM BEFORE YOU AND YOU DEFEAT THEM, THEN YOU SHALL UTTERLY DESTROY THEM. YOU SHALL MAKE NO COVENANT WITH THEM AND SHOW NO FAVOR TO THEM.

Obviously, this does not sound like the loving of your enemies for we are to show no mercy in our battles against evil. Remember that there is no verse that says to love the enemies of God. Moreover 'WHEN THE LORD JESUS RETURNS, HE WILL FIGHT AGAINST HIS ENEMIES' (Zachariah 14:1).

In this particular case going back to dealing with autism I would under the circumstances make it my highest priority to contact any Christian faith healer or Christian miracle worker who has the spiritual expertise to deal successfully with this problem as it is not just a medical or mental problem but a spiritual one.

A leading psychologist once said that their research had shown that autism was in some ways the result of fear from having to deal with dangerous personal relationships with unsocialized (unconverted) bad people. He also shared a very unusual psychological revelation about the divinity of Christ.

In his revelation he showed how that Jesus was from the divine family of God. Because as you know God the Father is surrounded by four living beasts who worship Him all the time saying: 'HOLY, HOLY, HOLY, LORD GOD ALMIGHTY WHICH WAS AND IS AND IS TO COME,' (Revelation 4:8.). Then Jesus said that: 'EXCEPT YOU EAT THE FLESH OF THE SON OF MAN AND DRINK HIS BLOOD YOU HAVE NO LIFE IN YOU', (John 6:53).

If everyday people said these things we would call them egotistical or that egotism runs in their family. But since they are both divine we would realize that they both have a right to boast about their greatness. After all the boxer Casus Clay (Mohammad Allie) could boast everyday about how great he was because he won every fight. And Jesus and God the Father can boast about themselves because as supernatural they have no equals.

Fear and demonic oppression are going to intensify as we move deeper into the end times and today there is not enough truth being taught about demonic activity. So, I was told by God to write this prophetic book.

But demons of fear are only one kind of demons. There are also demons of unforgiveness, resentment, hatred, lust, adultery, sodomy, divorce, inferiority, poverty, condemnation, judgment, lying, anger, addiction to either booze or dope, selfishness, murder including abortion theft including robbery and unbelief including doubt (the lack of faith).

Another Corona Crisis viewpoint is that it supposedly started in China as a biological weapon. Well you can see for yourself that it was instrumental in America's economy being closed down while the Chinese economy is booming again. How's that for the Deep State being two faced and having ulterior motives?

Speaking of Deep State deception; from the medically insane subversives, their fake news now has many people believing that the Corona Virus must be increasing again as its testing confirms. But the medical truth is that the testing only reveals weather or not the Corona Virus antibody is present. The presence of antibodies could indicate the development of 'herd immunity' and not just an increase in sickness. Thus the Deep State has found another way to attack Trump for his supposed mishandling of this Corona Crisis. Thus, their propaganda hopes to show that the Corona Virus is increasing because of TRUMP and his policies. When the truth is that this Corona Virus is being defeated the same way small pox was by 'herd immunity.'

If after taking this test one's results are positive but the patient remains asymptomatic should prove to any realistic person that although the patient has been infected by the virus nevertheless remaining a- symptomatic proves that their 'herd immunity' to the virus is under their control and not that since they were once exposed to this virus now they can pass it on undetected.

Thanks to the Deep States' fake news some people even have the mistaken idea that a change in administrations brought about by voting for the abortionist Biden will somehow change America's destiny for the better. But 'you do not change horses in mid-stream'.

Moreover in ministry you don't even interrupt ones calling for a supposed serious sin that offends some denomination. As I see it TRUMP was elected to be President of the USA in 2016 as God's man. That mission has not yet been completed as it is not finished. **Therefore, I would vote to reelect TRUMP so that he gets to fulfill his mission for our benefit as before. With President TRUMP we had the lowest Black and Hispanic unemployment ever recorded. Remember that when you go to vote.**

But the major truth that I want to leave with you is that we have already had two instances when Americans failed to repent of their sins of legalized abortion and legalized gay sex. The first one was 9/11 now the second one is this Corona Crisis. Another opportunity to repent and get right with God will come as the asteroid Apophis like the one that wiped out the dinosaurs crashes into earth in 2029. Please note that the Star Child, Jesus now the invincible King of the universe will still get his vengeance!

Since America is a diverse society composed of many conmen, thieves, reprobates, convicts, dopers, illegal aliens, lying politicians and even a few bastards, I'd rather have a few more bastards than millions upon millions of more paupers thanks to the socialist policies of the now President Joe Biden, the abortionist, the V. P. of the former food stamp president.

Actually this abortion issue is much more important than I have related so far. It is definitely highly possible that America could be destroyed for not only practicing this 'SHEDDING OF INNOCENT BLOOD' (Proverbs 6:17) themselves but also giving this evil as a right to the whole world.

The democrats and especially Joe Biden have not repented from killing over sixty million babies by their legalized abortion policy. Although in his political campaign he nevertheless maintains that he will protect and provide for America's seniors, the democrats including Biden have actually removed by murder the sixty million plus taxpayers that Social Security will need in order to remain solvent.

When I was a young man I went to a local prayer meeting here in Daytona Beach, Florida. There a visiting minister from southern California shared how that a young Hebrew had to be at least twenty years old in order to fight in the army of God. Apparently, the God of the Hebrews has also adopted this by waiting twenty years after the warning of 9/11 before He fights in full judgment against the abominations of abortion and same sex marriage.

Of coursem, this means that from 9/11/2001 until 9-11-2020 makes up the 19 years of COVID 19. But the full judgments of other viruses, economic collapse and national earthquakes among other judgments are due to begin next year on 9-11-2021.

But if the abortionist democrat Joe Biden gets elected expect worsening judgments right away. In that case me and the kid already have our passports ready to fly away. I was once a missionary in Honduras and my son Patrick was a missionary to Brazil. So we may just return to minister as God wills.

Speaking of passports, the US state department had been seizing them in Afghanistan and returning them only if the wealthy Americans pay again. Some say that conditions in America could not possibly get that bad, especially from a democratic political decision. **But to vote against God and His word is more dangerous than I want to endure.**

As a respected prophet for many years, God usually speaks to me in current small natural issues to indicate future events. Like when that small Sycamore tree that was abused by 9/11 and replaced with an evergreen in a ceremony called Hope withered and died anyway to indicate America's coming death in some form of judgment from God within twenty years.

Most of us Americans are wearing masks today and maintaining social distance. Unfortunately this current COVID 19 pandemic is being used by the demonic democrats to exercise social control over our society. They order churches and synagogues to remain closed which pleases the atheists and socialists while at the same time they keep abortion clinics open as being essential. It is now easy to see which political party is really a servant of the devil. This is just like the devil to use a pandemic supposedly only about health as a deceptive means of curtailing the worship of God. As you read further in my prophetic books you will see how that this pandemic is only the beginning of what our sins will cause to come our way.

There is a place in scripture where the Lord Jesus after His resurrection also practiced social distancing when he said; 'TOUCH ME NOT', (John 20:17). But this was not to avoid contamination from a dread disease but to avoid interference with his glorification and ascension over his enemies and all things visible and invisible 'WHETHER THEY BE THRONES, OR DOMINIONS, OR PRINCIPALITIES, OR POWERS', (Colossians 1:16).

I hope that this also proves that Christianity is a Person, (Only a person can sit on a throne, not a denomination or a committee). As it is written: 'HE THAT HAS THE SON HAS LIFE AND HE THAT DOES NOT HAVE THE SON OF GOD DOES NOT HAVE LIFE', (1 John 5:12).

So, by my other prophetic book (**JESUS, THE REAL STAR CHILD**) I have shown you how that Jesus was a Star Child from birth, with His own star. And that His first miracle was to prove His divinity. And by His cross He became our savior as the Lamb of God, Who takes away the sins of the world. And by His resurrection He became the Lord of Glory. And when Jesus comes again He comes as the King of the Universe. 'EVEN SO COME QUICKLY LORD JESUS', (Revelation 22:20).

Usually the gift of prophecy foretells the future. But once in a while it along with the word of knowledge can reexamine and retell the past which people have forgotten. When examining past plagues in history, it's easy to see that the first plagues were named for the Emperors of Rome, like the Cyprin Plague of 250 AD.

Shortly after this time were several smallpox epidemics which Constantine, the new emperor solved when he came to power by abolishing the worship of the old angry Roman Gods of war, famine and death in favor of Christianity which loved and cared for sick Romans and even healed some. ***This is how Christianity got its start in the Roman world***.

I'm sure you've all heard about the Roman Catholic Church. While it has changed some over the years, **the Lord Jesus Christ has not changed. He still heals the sick, cares for sick people and rescues soles from hell**. May we Christians through Him also turn this evil plague of COVID 19 into a blessing like another Great Awakening. Now: **'UNTO THE KING ETERNAL, IMMORTAL, INVISIBLE, THE ONLY WISE GOD, BE HONOR AND GLORY FOR EVER AND EVER, AMEN', (1 Timothy 1:17).**

COVID 19: VACCINE OR REPENTANCE

After writing my other prophetic books: **'WHAT TO EXPECT', 'ANOTHER JESUS MOVEMENT', 'RAPTURE RIPOFF', 'REPARATIONS FOR SLAVERY', 'JESUS THE REAL STAR CHILD', 'COVID 19 TRUTHS REVEALED', 'WEALTH TRANSFER'** and **'END TIME PLAGUES',** I felt that I was due for a period of rest. But instead suddenly the Spirit of God let me know via a prophetic dream around May 1, 2021 that I was not yet done writing and had more to write about **COVID 19: VACCINE OR REPENTANCE** to not just tell the truth about it but also to correct professional and denominational error.

This particular prophetic dream informed me that the current plagues sent to America and the world for the abominations of abortion and same sex marriage would mirror how God had dealt with national sins before, when He sent ten plagues upon Egypt in the days of Moses not only for the slavery of the Hebrew people but also for the failure of the pagan Egyptians from worshipping their false gods while not allowing the worship of the one true Hebrew God,

As a prophetic book, my prophetic manuscript would also question the erroneous interpretation of some current professional and denominational widely held theological beliefs like the pre-tribulation rapture and the so called expansive scriptural view point that 'GOD DOES NOTHING WITHOUT REVEALING HIS SECRET TO HIS SERVANTS: THE PROPHETS', (Amos 3:7).

When we all know that many so called prophetic ministers on TV have condemned this COVID 19 plague as if it were just another respiratory disease like the flu or a mischievous act of the devil that America did not deserve and could be cured of by vaccinations alone without any need for any repentance; certainly not any repentance for the abominable sins of abortion and same sex marriage which President Biden's democratic political policies and anti-Christ progressives support.

The prophets recognized here where the so called secular prophets who have claimed that what God sent, this COVID 19 plague is actually a work of the devil, that can be cured by vaccinations alone.

But when it comes to God's judgments, no one knows exactly how long each plague will last nor what type of curse they will become. Even the Lord Jesus in Matthew 24 spoke about what would come, but not in any order as prophecy is not exact because: 'WE KNOW IN PART AND PROPHECY IN PART, (1 Cor. 13:9).

Although this prophetic book concerns Christian End Time Prophecy, it is not about an esoteric eschatology so much as the hidden issues of the day. This book discloses truths that God wants known. As an example, the ever increasing deficit comes about in part from the throwing out of free spying by Christian Prophets in favor of expensive secular 'military industrial' spying by spy satellites, wire-tapping of phones, computer hacking, tapping into the internet and cell phones, and drones complete with 'octopus' agencies like Homeland Security, FEMA, NASA, TSA, CIA, FBI, ATF and IRS keeping their eyes on your every move thanks to your taxes.

This came about during the cold war when former President Eisenhower used to visit a Christian Prophet in Pasadena, California about once each month to find out what God saw behind the 'iron curtain'. His advisors told him that his policy was relying too much on Christianity and the Christian Prophets. So, they encouraged him to acquire a more 'military industrial' means of spying like the new U2 spy plane. Eisenhower adopted this idea but it blew up in his face as the U2 spy plane was shot down over the Soviet Union and its pilot, Francis Gary Powers was held hostage.

Nevertheless, this policy grew right along with your taxes. Today the Soviet Union has fallen apart but now America not only spies on other nations with these technological instruments but on its own citizens as well.

Are allowed by their lies thanks to Muslim false doctrine to conceal, disguise and hide their personal beliefs, ideas, feelings and opinions Muslims like Obama about anything and everything in order to achieve personal success for the Muslim cause. Like ruling over Christians or even hiring other Muslims like Valerie Jarrett as public employees to abuse Christians and promote Iran's nuclear arms as well. To make my disclosure about Muslim lying clearer, it must be reiterated that as long as a Muslim is in a country where Islam is a minority, then the Muslim

(in this case, Obama's) deceptiveness about anything and everything is officially expected and sanctioned by the 'evil religion of Islam' (the Muslim faith). That's why we should throw all the Muslims out!

What judgment now awaits Obama and his many czars for telling thousands of lies about 'everything under the sun' to the American people in two terms of office? With President Biden now serving out Obama's third term to do the same evil that former President Obama did resulting in the same entitlements for deserved plagues and **joining former President Obama to dump Christianity has bequeathed America and the entire world to deceptions, wars, delusions, deficits, disasters and many more plagues, Watch out!**

Just at that moment I turned on the TV to see a Christian TV program that God wanted me to see as it told me just what I needed to know in order to obey Him.

This Christian TV Program was entitled: ***Joni table talk*** in which the wife of a famous TV evangelist on a TV talk show interviewed various people who were notable in current events to give the people of God more information about the issues of the day.

Last year I remember how her topic was COVID 19 and she was discussing with her doctor guest a medicine to supposedly heal this plague. At that time hydroxychioroquine with zinc was brought up as a possible cure. And it did work to cure President Trump of his Corona Virus infection.

According to the Bible however a plague is NOT healed by any medicine but by repentance only. That Christian TV show failed to bring this out. But to me such was obvious as I remembered how that: 'ALL SCRIPTURE IS GIVEN BY THE INSPIRATION OF GOD AND IS PROFITABLE FOR DOCTRINE, FOR REPROOF, FOR CORRECTION, FOR INSTRUCTION IN RIGHTEOUSNESS THAT THE MAN OF GOD MAY BE COMPLETE, THOROUGHLY EQUIPPED FOR EVERY GOOD WORK', (II Timothy 3:16, 17).

So here is what the scripture says about this plague topic: 'WHEN I SHUT UP HEAVEN AND THERE IS NO RAIN, OR COMMAND THE LOCUST TO DEVOUR THE LAND, OR SEND PESTILENCE (**plagues**) AMONG MY PEOPLE, IF MY PEOPLE WHO ARE CALLED BY MY NAME WILL HUMBLE THEMSELVES AND PRAY AND SEEK MY FACE, AND TURN FROM THEIR WICKED WAYS (**repent**), THEN WILL I HEAR FROM HEAVEN, AND WILL FORGIVE THEIR SIN AND HEAL THEIR LAND', (II Chronicles 7:13 & 14).

Back in those days, the last year of President Trump's term, many promises were made and apparently kept by President Trump about developing a vaccine for this CORONA VIRUS.

Thanks to the reprobate DR. Fauci (the masked robber of American free enterprise) such vaccines were to be developed even though it is illegal to use an experimental vaccine for a medical problem that already has a known and established medical cure that is recognized worldwide. Perhaps DR. Fauci was more concerned about making some more money off his patents on various vaccines than the welfare of the American people.

To DR Fauci's surprise and elation many have now required that school children also be vaccinated against this COVID 19 before they return to school this fall as required by the teacher's union. Another requirement about needing a booster shot has also materialized. And Dr. Fauci once said that this COVID 19 is not over yet and may even require a booster shot.

But in this electric age of increased technology I would like to submit to you (parents especially) this recommendation:

Recently I was watching the Jim Bakker Show on Christian TV where they discussed a new product called): the SIGNAL RELIEF PATCH. From what I understand this patch that you apply to your skin relieves pain. Since I don't have much pain, I ignored this product at first. But then the Lord started revealing more truth to me:

The electrical design of this patch apparently redirects nerve impulses to such an extent that they relieve one's pain. Taking this same concept into consideration it may also be possible to redirect nerve impulses in such a way as to modify unwanted and unholy behaviors like addiction and to even redirect or to force the organs of the body to make needed hormones to help form antibodies to attack this virus.

I understand that to the medical community this may sound far-fetched. But a patch is not that much different from a prayer clothe which has been used in the healing of the sick. In fact, one Bible verse says: 'GOD DID EXTRORDINARY MIRACLES THROUGH PAUL SO THAT WHEN HANKERCHEIFS OR APRONS THAT HAD BEEN TOUCHED BY HIS SKIN WHERE BROUGHT TO THE SICK THEIR DISEASES LEFT THEM AND EVIL SPIRITS CAME OUT OF THEM', (Acts 19:11 & 12). This my friends is absolutely wonderful it not only shows healing from disease but also deliverance from demon oppression. **And it should be well known that many Americans need deliverance.** That is deliverance from headaches, depression, anxiety, lack of get up and go, lack of love, insufficient self-esteem, lack of memory, unreasonable fear, mixed up desires, lack of proper emotional response, deception, hostility, hot temper with increased anger, unreasonable hatred, delusions, hallucinations, fits and convulsions.

There must also be deliverance from resentment over medicines, medications and mandates that don't work. Deliverance from animosity over plumbers and other repairman who don't fix your pipes right and over electricians that screw up your wires.

Christians who believe in Jesus still have bad habits like smoking and drinking booze, driving drunk, participating in extramarital affairs, having sex with animals and their own children, gay relationships and all manner of naughtiness including over-eating, gluttony and eating disorders.

However professional medical doctors, like Dr. Fauci can't make more money off any vaccines unless he discounts any other medicine that may work to cure the invading virus. So, then the real issue is more money.

In any case, a few months later Joni interviewed as her guest; Robert F. Kennedy Jr. who had been busy researching fraud dealing with this issue.

(I remember specifically that he had somewhat of a raspy voice somewhat like my own). Some of the fraud discovered back then was about the increased or added amount of sugar in most breakfast cereals and some of this fraud also had to do with various recommendations about certain diets that could supposedly cure this CORONA VIRUS. One of these was the gluten free diet. Which seems to be working in Taiwan and especially some in South India where they mainly eat rice as a gluten free staple. While this diet does reduce blood pressure and one's weight it is not a medicine and does not heal (which I already told you about in my previous prophetic book entitled: COVID 19: TRUTHS REVEALED).

In that book I also stated that this CORONA VIRUS or COVID 19 is also a curse or plague sent by God for sin (and I named the sins: ABORTION and SAME SEX MARRIAGE). And not just another disease that vaccines or booster shots can cure.

About this time I also remember that when I graduated from the University of South Florida in 1982 I went to take the Graduate Record Exam to see what I had learned and what grad school I might be able to get into. That morning a student had left his stereo on and it was playing an old surfer tune: The Little Old Lady From Pasadena. Pasadena, California was the location of the seminary that God wanted me to attend. So I took that song as my sign to go to Fuller Theological Seminary.

When I arrived there a young student receptionist told me that they would train me but I probably would never be able to get any church job, 'since wheelchairs do not inspire faith'. I ignored that negative confession since I wanted to become a college counselor anyway and not just another professional Christian minister.

I subsequently graduated from the Seminary in 1985 and went on to another grad school to take my psychology classes in education that I would need in order to earn my college counseling credential.

I remember while at that other grad school a learning psychologist who was visiting them from some Ivey League School told most of the future college teachers there and me that a behavioral psychologist had recently discovered that if you want someone to really learn and remember your information you need to be sure to repeat it so that it makes a deeper impression on their brain. So that's what I intend to do here even though some of my critics may call my repeat information redundant. Thus this whole chapter is going to be repeated again later in this prophetic book.

There is one more cataclysmic point he had to make (this will anger most authors of books). He said that if you have an important point to make, make it right away. Then repeat it later in your lesson or manuscript. Do not beat around the bush like most writers of mysteries or researchers into discoveries do. Teach your main point up front and then repeat it later in your lesson or manuscript if you want your students to remember it.

When God gave Moses the Ten Commandments and Moses gave them to the people of Israel, he also told the children of Israel what blessings would come their way if they would obey them.

But if they disobeyed God's commandments and statutes Moses began to list in Deuteronomy 28:15 the curses for the children of Israel to expect from God: 'BUT IT SHALL COME TO PASS, IF YOU DO NOT OBEY THE VOICE OF THE LORD YOUR GOD, TO OBSERVE **CAREFULLY** (this word is far more important in the spiritual dimension than the slang words of everyday unconcerned speech) ALL HIS COMMANDMENTS AND HIS STATUTES WHICH I COMMAND YOU TODAY THAT ALL THESE CURSES WILL OVER TAKE YOU': (Curses have power behind them, the power of God and curses are the exact counterpart of blessings so they are very dangerous).

'CURSED SHALL YOU BE IN THE CITY AND CURSED SHALL YOU BE IN THE COUNTRY', (Curses have real power to follow you wherever you go and as blessings are nationwide, so shall curses be too).

'CURSED SHALL BE YOUR BASKET AND YOUR KNEADING BOWL.' (in other words famine with no bread will follow you everywhere so the stores will be empty if not closed as a result of these curses).

'CURSED SHALL BE THE FRUIT OF YOUR BODY' (sterility, inability to have children just like these COVID 19 vaccines are causing),

'AND THE PRODUCE OF YOUR LAND' (No need for migrants to work your fields that no longer produce crops nor exist),

'THE INCREASE OF YOUR CATTLE AND THE OFFSPRING OF YOUR FLOCKS'.

'CURSED SHALL YOU BE WHEN YOU COME IN, And CURSED SHALL YOU BE WHEN YOU GO OUT', (Doesn't that remind you of what could be causing 'drive by shootings' where you get shot everywhere, every day and nothing that you do (like taking vaccines) will stop the curse).

'THE LORD WILL SEND ON YOU CURSINGS, CONFUSSION AND REBUKE IN ALL THAT YOU SET YOUR HAND TO DO' (That's why illegitimate President Biden's executive orders are worthless unless you stupidly obey them, this is an example of Biden being cursed for his disobedience).

'UNTIL YOU ARE DESTROYED AND UNTIL YOU PERISH QUICKLY, BECAUSE OF THE WICKEDNESS OF YOUR DOINGS' (**like restarting that Iran nuclear agreement and turning Blacks against Whites and spending the people's money which Biden has stolen by a fraudulent election**).

'IN WHICH YOU HAVE FORSAKEN ME' **(So judgment starts now and not until the end of your stolen presidential term).**

'THE Lord WILL MAKE THE PLAGUE CLING TO YOU', (President Biden you cannot escape it by fleeing to your basement).

'UNTIL HE HAS CONSUMED YOU FROM THE LAND WHICH YOUR GOING TO POSSESS'.

'THE LORD WILL STRIKE YOU WITH CONSUMPTION, WITH FEVER, WITH INFLAMATION, WITH SEVERE BURNING (could this also mean nuclear war? After the sickness that God sends comes first).'

'WITH THE SWORD' (this is symbolic of war)

'WITH SCORCHING' (symbolic of cities burning due to riots and forest fires due to drought).

'AND WITH MILDEW' (symbolic of floods).

'THEY SHALL PURSUE YOU UNTIL YOU PERISH AND YOUR HEAVENS WHICH ARE OVER YOUR HEAD SHALL BE BRONZE' (When the heavens become brass your prayers go unheard).

'AND THE EARTH WHICH IS UNDER YOU SHALL BE IRON', (Too hard to break up and plant).

'THE LORD SHALL CHANGE THE RAIN OF YOUR LAND TO POWDER AND DUST' (in old times called the dust bowl, now it's valley fever).

'FROM THE HEAVEN IT SHALL COME DOWN ON YOU UNTIL YOU ARE DESTROYED' (If God is offended then you are destroyed).

'THE LORD WILL CAUSE YOU TO BE DEFEATED BEFORE YOUR ENEMIES' (China and Iran and who else). The communist Soviet Union was once our enemy, does that now make Russia ours too by default)? and (We know that Russia is an enemy to the progressive democratic communists of America).

'YOU SHALL GO OUT ONE WAY AGAINST THEM AND FLEE SEVEN WAYS BEFORE THEM AND YOU SHALL BECOME TROUBLESOME TO ALL THE KINGDOMS OF THE EARTH'. 'YOUR CARCASSES SHALL BE FOOD FOR ALL THE BIRDS OF THE AIR AND THE BEASTS OF THE EARTH, AND NO ONE SHALL FRIGHTEN THEM AWAY', (This already happened once before but it will happen again as a result of the battle of Armageddon).

THE LORD WILL STRIKE YOU WITH THE BOILS OF EGYPT, WITH TUMORS, WITH THE SCAB, AND WITH ITCH **FROM WHICH YOU CANNOT BE HEALED'.** (God controls all sickness and disease and healing too).

'THE LORD WILL STRIKE YOU WITH MADNESS AND BLINDNESS AND CONFUSSION OF HEART' (President Biden may even be removed from office thanks to the 25th amendment due to his dementia and the loss of his mental faculties and the loss of his sanity)

'AND YOU SHALL GROPE AT THE NOONDAY, AS A BLIND MAN GROPES IN DARKNESS'. (If God is against us, due to our retained sins, who can be for us?).

'YOU SHALL NOT PROSPER IN YOUR WAYS', (so apparently all those schemes to defraud Ukraine and share the bounty with Hunter Biden will be of no avail along with the desire to rip off the American taxpayer to pay for imaginary infrastructure like child care, homes for the homeless, free college, free food for children while their fathers spent surplus money on dope and booze, and bailing out cities that have been run into the ground by Democrats).

'YOU SHALL BE ONLY OPPRESSED AND PLUNDERED CONTINUALLY AND NO ONE SHALL SAVE YOU'. (What kind of future is Biden and his progresses giving to America and the world? Where no one, not even Jesus will save us? Because we've become too hard-hearted to ask God for help).

'YOU SHALL BETROTH A WIFE, BUT ANOTHER MAN SHALL LIE WITH HER'. **(Sounds like the Muslims with multiple wives have seduced Biden).**

'YOU SHALL BUILD A HOUSE, BUT YOU SHALL NOT DWELL IN IT' (Sounds like the Chinese communist plan of building vacant cities).

'YOU SHALL PLANT A VINYARD, BUT YOU SHALL NOT GATHER ITS GRAPES' (Migrants usually do that work but America's COVID 19 and other curses have scared them away as your plans to prosper will fail).

'YOUR OX SHALL BE SLAUGHTERED BEFORE YOR EYES, BUT YOU SHALL NOT EAT OF IT', (Stupid vegetarian policies shall deceive you and you shall also move to forbid animals grazing on Federal lands).

'YOUR DONKEY SHALL BE VIOLENTLY TAKEN AWAY FROM BEFORE YOU' (As is commonly done in war time when it becomes part of the spoils). 'AND SHALL NOT BE RESTORED TO YOU' (May mean that there will be no treaty to suspend conflict and end this war).

'YOUR SHEEP SHALL BE GIVEN TO YOUR ENEMIES' (As is the usual practice of dealing with the spoils of war). 'AND YOU SHALL HAVE NO ONE TO RESCUE THEM' (**No war against God and His word has ever been won by any man at any time. Let Biden's Democratic progressives know that).**

'YOUR SONS AND YOUR DAUGHTERS SHALL BE GIVEN TO ANOTHER PEOPLE AND YOUR EYES SHALL LOOK AND FAIL WITH LONGING FOR THEM ALL DAY LONG', (This only happens as the result of conquest, where your enemy wins the war, so without God America like Israel will be helpless before her enemies).

'AND THERE SHALL BE NO STRENGTH IN YOUR HAND', (Does this foreshadow the onset of feebleness)?

'A NATION WHOM YOU HAVE NOT KNOWN SHALL EAT THE FRUIT OF YOUR LAND AND THE PRODUCE OF YOUR LABOR, AND YOU SHALL BE ONLY OPPRESSED AND CRUSHED CONTINUALLY'. (Communist China already owns a lot of farmland in America, will they eat while you go hungry?).

'SO YOU SHALL BE DRIVEN MAD BECAUSE OF THE SIGHT WHICH YOUR EYES SEE', (It might be better to wear a blindfold than to continue wearing a face mask).

'THE LORD WILL STRIKE YOU IN THE KNEES AND ON THE LEGS WITH SEVERE BOILS **WHICH CANNOT BE HEALED**, AND FROM THE SOLE OF YOUR FOOT TO THE TOP OF YOUR HEAD'. (You will not be able to get down on your knees to pray as God sees through your hypocrisy).

'THE LORD WILL BRING YOU AND THE KING WHOM YOU SET OVER YOU TO A NATION WHICH NEITHER YOU NOR YOUR FATHERS HAVE KNOWN, AND THERE YOU SHALL SERVE OTHER GOD'S – WOOD AND STONE', (Biden and his communist progressives could lead us into serving underground aliens from Mars if they are found there).

'AND YOU SHALL BECOME AN ASTONISHMENT, A PROVERB, AND A BYWORD AMONG ALL THE NATIONS WHERE THE LORD WILL DRIVE YOU'. **(Instead of being praised by history for doing a good job, Biden will be rebuked by history for leading America into communism and ruin).**

'YOU SHALL CARRY MUCH SEED OUT TO THE FIELD BUT GATHER LITTLE IN FOR THE LOCUST SHALL CONSUME IT'. **(So, get ready because another plague is coming due to the hardness of your heart).**

'YOU SHALL PLANT VINEYARDS AND TEND THEM, BUT YOU SHALL NEITHER DRINK OF THE WINE NOR GATHER THE GRAPES; FOR THE WORMS SHALL EAT THEM'. (How's that for an agricultural policy that feeds the world where your efforts to bring in the harvest fail because of your retained and unconfessed sins like abortion and same sex marriage).

'YOU SHALL HAVE OLIVE TREES THROUGHOUT ALL YOUR TERRITORY, BUT YOU SHALL NOT ANNOINT YOURSELF WITH OIL; FOR YOUR OLIVES SHALL DROP OFF' **(Due to Biden's global warming freeze).**

'YOU SHALL BEGET SONS AND DAUGHTERS, BUT THEY SHALL NOT BE YOURS; FOR THEY SHALL GO INTO CAPTIVITY'. (Obviously going into captivity does not happen unless you lose a future war. So wars will come).

'THE ALIEN WHO IS AMONG YOU SHALL RISE HIGHER AND HIGHER ABOVE YOU, AND YOU SHALL COME DOWN LOWER AND LOWER', (This is what the evil change from former President Trump's immigration policy to Biden's is now costing America**, thanks to the sins of Biden and his evil Democratic progressives).**

'HE SHALL LEND TO YOU, BUT YOU SHALL NOT LEND TO HIM; HE SHALL BE THE HEAD, AND YOU SHALL BE THE TAIL'. (How's that for a future that your children will be proud of especially if they are White. White children are learning in school today about how they must lose now because of supposed White privilege in the past). 'MOREOVER, ALL THESE CURSES SHALL COME UPON YOU AND PURSUE AND OVERTAKE YOU, UNTIL YOU ARE DESTROYED, BECAUSE YOU DO NOT OBEY THE VOICE OF THE LORD YOUR GOD, TO KEEP HIS COMMANDMENTS AND HIS STATUTES WHICH HE COMMANDED YOU'. (There is no mystery here for Biden and his Democratic progressives know that 'THE CURSE CAUSELESS WILL NOT COME', (Proverbs 26:2), therefore they must be responsible for not only their sins but causing yours too).

'AND THEY SHALL BE UPON YOU FOR A SIGN AND A WONDER, AND ON YOUR DESCENDANTS FOREVER'. (But Israel shall be restored anyway, (Romans 11:25-27).

'BECAUSE YOU DID NOT SERVE THE LORD YOUR GOD WITH JOY AND GLADNESS OF HEART, FOR THE ABUNDANCE OF EVERYTHING'. (All these curses will come upon you because you will not serve God).

'THEREFORE YOU SHALL SERVE YOUR ENEMIES, WHOM THE LORD WILL SEND AGAINST YOU, IN HUNGER, IN THIRST, IN NAKEDNESS, AND IN NEED OF EVERYTHING, AND HE SHALL PUT A YOKE OF IRON ON YOUR NECK UNTIL HE HAS DESTROYED YOU'. (And if you will not serve God then you will serve your enemies).

'THE LORD WILL BRING A NATION AGAINST YOU FROM AFAR, FROM THE END OF THE EARTH, AS SWIFT AS THE EAGLE FLIES. A NATION WHO'S LANGUAGE YOU WILL NOT UNDERSTAND, A NATION OF FIERCE COUNTENANCE, WHICH DOES NOT RESPECT THE ELDERLY NOR SHOW FAVOR TO THE YOUNG', (Sounds like a nation without social justice like Communist China to me).

'AND THEY SHALL EAT THE INCREASE OF YOUR LIVESTOCK AND THE PRODUCE OF YOUR LAND, UNTIL YOU ARE DESTROYED; THEY SHALL NOT LEAVE YOU GRAIN OR NEW WINE OR OIL, OR THE INCREASE OF YOUR CATTLE OR THE OFFSPRING OF YOUR FLOCKS, UNTIL THEY HAVE DESTROYED YOU'. (Even the homeless here fare better than you there).

'THEY SHALL BESEIGE YOU AT ALL YOUR GATES UNTIL YOUR HIGH AND FORTIFIED WALLS, IN WHICH YOU TRUST, COME DOWN THROUGHOUT ALL YOUR LAND, AND THEY SHALL BESEIGE YOU AT ALL YOUR GATES THROUGHOUT ALL YOUR LAND WHICH THE LORD YOUR GOD HAS GIVEN YOU'.

'YOU SHALL EAT THE FRUIT OF YOUR OWN BODY, THE FLESH OF YOUR OWN SONS AND YOUR DAUGHTERS WHOM THE LORD YOUR GOD HAS GIVEN YOU, IN THE SEIGE AND DESPERATE STRAITS IN WHICH YOUR ENEMY SHALL DISTRESS YOU', (Here cannibalism becomes part of your curse as the civilized take on the customs of jungle head hunters).

'THE SENSITIVE AND VERY REFINED MAN AMOUNG YOU WILL BE HOSTILE TOWARD HIS BROTHER, TOWARD THE WIFE OF HIS BOSOM, AND TOWARD THE REST OF HIS CHILDREN WHOM HE LEAVES BEHIND SO THAT HE WILL NOT GIVE ANY OF THEM THE FLESH OF HIS CHILDREN WHOM HE WILL EAT, BECAUSE HE HAS NOTHING LEFT IN THE SEIGE AND DESPERATE STRAITS IN WHICH YOUR ENEMY SHALL DESTRESS YOU AT YOUR GATES'. (Here we see where starvation causes severe mental health problems which turn you against your own family to the point of your criminal response to them) [Cannibalism].

'THE TENDER AND DELICATE WOMAN AMONG YOU, WHO WOULD NOT VENTURE TO SET THE SOLE OF HER FOOT ON THE GROUND BECAUSE OF HER DELICATENESS ON SENSITIVITY, WILL REFUSE TO THE HUSBAND OF HER BOSOM, AND TO OUR SON AND HER DAUGHTER HER PLACENTA WHICH COMES OUT BETWEEN HER FEET AND HER CHILDREN WHOM SHE BEARS: FOR SHE WILL EAT THEM SECRETLY FOR LACK OF EVERYTHING IN THE SEIGE AND DESPERATE STRAITS IN WHICH YOUR ENEMY SHALL DESTRESS YOU AT ALL YOUR GATES'. (The word Placenta brings up a possible side effect to these vaccines which medical researchers have discovered. It appears that the vaccines cause the body to synthesize COVID 19 which then forms antibodies to attack. Unfortunately this synthesized COVID 19 is molecularly like the human placenta. And we do not know until a woman reaches children bearing age that her placenta will not be attacked too. If so, she will be sterile and unable to have children, **for this reason one should NOT vaccinate his daughters under any circumstances).**

'IF YOU DO NOT CAREFULLY OBSERVE ALL THE WORDS OF THIS LAW THAT IS WRITTEN IN THIS BOOK, THAT YOU MAY FEAR THIS GLORIOUS AND AWESOME NAME, THE LORD YOUR GOD, THEN THE LORD WILL BRING UPON YOU AND YOUR DESCENDANTS **EXTRAORDINARY PLAGUES** ------GREAT AND PROLONGED PLAGUES-------AND SERIOUS AND PROLONGED SICKNESS,'(The modern apostate super sensitive and love only oriented church composed of the lukewarm liturgical, the dead denominational, the extinct ecclesiastical and the carnal pseudo-Christians all suffer from a psychological deficit that makes them believe that God only expresses positive emotions like love, joy and peace. Thus, they fail to understand that a balanced Person, like God also has an all-encompassing personality including social justice, judgment and punishment).

(The current Israeli and Palestinian conflict with neighbor against neighbor reveals that this liberal diversity inclusion mindset has been wrong as God is not pleased with those who serve false Gods living among His people. In my previous prophetic books I told you that this would eventually happen not only in Israel concerning religion but also in America concerning race which has not happened yet. But this White privilege propaganda like Affirmative Action on steroids will eventually provoke a race war. So I warned all Americans via my former prophetic books to relocate to live in an area that is composed of people that are at least 90% your own race, for your protection. Typically, I should not need to argue this point as it is well seen in the above Bible verses).

(Moreover 'the never Trumpers' and many Democrats are so deceived about their own goodness that they falsely accuse others like former President Trump guilty of lying about the stolen election of 2020 to cover up the Bush administration's lying about Iraq having weapons of mass destruction used by them to trick America into the Iraq War).'

'MOREOVER, HE WILL BRING BACK ON YOU ALL THE DISEASES OF EGYPT THAT WHICH YOU WERE AFRAID AND THEY SHALL CLING TO YOU'.

(So much for that false doctrine that says that God never sends sickness upon his people or that this COVID 19 plague could not possibly be from God**. COVID 19 is from God and you need to face it and repent of the sins which caused it).**

'ALSO EVERY SICKNESS AND EVERY PLAGUE, WHICH IS NOT WRITTEN IN THIS BOOK OF THE LAW WILL THE LORD BRING UPON YOU UNTIL YOU ARE DESTROYED'.

'YOU SHALL BE LEFT FEW IN NUMBER, WERE AS YOU WERE AS THE STARS OF HEAVEN IN MULTITUDE, BECAUSE YOU WOULD NOT OBEY THE VOICE OF THE LORD YOUR GOD'.

'AND IT SHALL BE, THAT JUST AS THE LORD REJOICED OVER YOU TO DO YOU GOOD AND MULTIPLY YOU. SO THE LORD WILL REJOICE OVER YOU TO DESTROY YOU AND BRING YOU TO NOTHING; AND YOU SHALL BE PLUCKED FROM OFF THIS LAND WHICH YOU GO TO POSSESS'.

'THEN THE LORD WILL SCATTER YOU AMONG ALL PEOPLES, FROM ONE END OF THE EARTH TO THE OTHER, AND THERE YOU SHALL SERVE OTHER GODS WHICH NEITHER YOU NOR YOUR FATHERS HAVE KNOWN – WOOD AND STONE'.

AND AMONG THOSE NATIONS YOU SHALL FIND NO REST, NOR SHALL THE SOUL OF YOUR FOOT HAVE A RESTING PLACE; BUT THERE THE LORD WILL GIVE YOU A TREMBLING HEART, FAILING EYES AND ANGUISH OF SOUL'.

'YOUR LIFE SHALL HANG IN DOUBT BEFORE YOU; YOU SHALL FEAR DAY AND NIGHT AND HAVE NO ASSURANCE OF LIFE'.

'IN THE MORNING YOU SHALL SAY: 'OH THAT IT WERE EVENING', AND AT EVENING YOU SHALL SAY: 'OH THAT IT WERE MORNING' BECAUSE OF THE FEAR WHICH TERRIFIES YOUR HEART AND BECAUSE OF THE SIGHT WHICH YOUR EYES SEE'.

'AND THE LORD WILL TAKE YOU BACK TO EGYPT IN SHIPS, BY THE WAY OF WHICH I SAID TO YOU: 'YOU SHALL NEVER SEE IT AGAIN.' 'AND THERE YOU SHALL BE OFFERED FOR SALE TO YOUR ENEMIES AS MALE AND FEMALE SLAVES, BUT NO ONE WILL BUY YOU'. (This last verse points out a few very interesting points about God that we never heard about either in the seminary or in psychology school. So here they are by revelation: 1. Just like in prophecy it is possible to go back in time and change the outcome of your status, for our God is not bound by time constraints. And 2, being presented to your enemies by God as slaves can happen because of your sins. And 3. Not having been bought and adopted into the plantation lifestyle would have been horrible for your ancestors if you are an Afro-American and remain unappreciated, unloved & unwanted).

(The victors of the American Civil War got to write the story of what slavery was like in the South. Of course, they lied. For most plantation slaves were members of the plantation family and were treated accordingly. They all ate with silver wear as stainless steel had not yet been invented. They all wore costume fitted clothing that was made right on the plantation by another slave. They were all medically inspected every time the medical doctor or the vet came around. They had to be kept free from disease so that they could bring in the crop).

(The slaves did so well on the plantations that when the Northern armies came in the Yankee soldiers stole the slave silver ware and other goodies from the slave cabins and rapped the Black women there. So much so that if the Black men had been armed the results of that Civil War would be different today).

(The current prejudicial viewpoint now taught in school about the so called wrongs of 1619, common core and critical race theory are all wrong).

(The truth is that the slaves were in fact rescued by the plantation owners as I said before in my former prophetic books).

(For the plantation was a family where slaves were treated as children. That's why a male slave was called boy and a female slave was called girl no matter how old they were).

(These slaves and their descendants are not entitled to reparations from Whites just as you do not pay your own adult children for what they did as kids).

(Moreover, those most responsible to pay reparations are those Muslim raiders and their descendants from oil rich Muslim nations who stole the Blacks from Black villages in Africa and then sold them into slavery).

Speaking of racism from history we get: The author Eugene Beranger described the condition of Blacks in the North at this civil war time in his book**:** North of Slavery. He writes: **"In virtually every phase of existence (In the North), Negroes found themselves systematically separated from Whites. They were either excluded from railway cars, omnibuses, stage coaches, and steam boats or assigned to special 'Jim Crow' sections; they sat, when permitted, in secluded and removed corners of theaters and lecture halls; they could not enter most hotels, restaurants, and resorts, except as servants, they prayed in 'Negro pews' in the White churches, and if partaking of the Sacrament of the Lord's Supper, they waited until the Whites had been served the bread and wine first. Moreover, they were often educated in segregated schools, punished in segregated prisons, nursed in segregated hospitals and buried in segregated cemeteries'.**

This quickens my memory of my experience with this exact type of abuse I had when I had just graduated from Fuller Seminary in 1985. And I began sleeping with the homeless since I could not afford the high rents out there in expensive southern California and could not get any church job to pay rent anyway since 'wheelchairs do not inspire faith'.

One night as I was sleeping outside, a local police officer kicked me awake and wrote me a ticket for trespassing. But I knew the Bible well and that I was on public land. So once that policeman left, I laid that ticket down before the Lord to pray over it just like the king of Israel had done when he was threatened by the king of Assyria. But since I was too tired to think up a long religious prayer, I simply quoted the part of the twenty fourth Psalm which says that: 'THE EARTH IS THE LORDS'. And asked God to judge between his word and trespassing and do whatsoever to Him seemed best and rolled over and went back to sleep.

God has magnified his word even above His own name. So anything compared to the supremacy of God's word, like some dumb human law over trespassing on God's land does not hold up well. And in fact, it is automatically put down.

That morning I caught the bus to go to the mission to eat my oatmeal. The bus passed the police station with its flag at half-staff. So I asked the mission director what had happened. He said that a local police officer had had a fire-arms accident and had shot and killed himself. It was written up in the paper that he gave to me. Afterward for some reason I looked to see the name of that officer if it matched the name on my ticket. **It matched.** Of course, I was horrified. And I thought that it was an overreaction by God to put someone to death just for a mistake over trespassing, but I said nothing and held my peace. **For I had learned in that seminary never to question or criticize our Sovereign Lord about things I didn't understand.**

Then I remembered how strongly God feels about His word. And that as the Sovereign Lord his acts are not for me to evaluate, judge, or correct. So I just thanked him and forgot about it all until now.

Then a few months later she interviewed another doctor about this COVID 19 issue again, only this time they discussed the vaccine and what it could cause.

Of course, since these vaccines against COVID 19 are new they lack the necessary medical history required to ensure their safety.

Most vaccines are made from a small particle (live, dead, or in some compound) of the invading virus so that the body can make the necessary anti-bodies needed to destroy it. But in this case these new vaccines are all artificial and trick the body in several ways. The first way is to cause the body to make or manufacture a likeness to the virus itself. Unfortunately, here the likeness is that of the human placenta. The human placenta is a necessary part of reproduction. Without it babies cannot grow and experience birth and consequently families do not happen.

So, then women of childbearing age become infertile. Therefore, if you wanted a family you'll have to remain disappointed if you get vaccinated.

Of course, this presents a sexual problem, as we see it now. In the Bible it discusses how that man will eventually become very devious in their sexual expression.

'THIS KNOW ALSO THAT IN THE LAST DAYS PERILOUS TIMES SHALL COME, FOR MEN SHALL BE LOVERS OF THEIR OWN SELVES, COVETOUS, BOASTERS, PROUD, BLASPHEMERS, DISOBEDIENT TO PARENTS, UNTHANKFUL, UNHOLY, WITHOUT NATURAL AFFECTION, TRUCE BREAKERS, FALSE ACCUSERS, INCONTINENT, FIERCE, DESPISERS OF THOSE THAT ARE GOOD, TRADERS, HEADY, HIGH MINDED, LOVERS OF PLEASURE MORE THAN LOVERS OF GOD, HAVING A FORM OF GODLINESS BUT DENYING THE POWER THEREOF FROM SUCH TURN AWAY', (II Timothy 3:1-5).

Since men are attracted to women. This attraction is family oriented as most normal men want to have their own miniature kingdom where they reign as king. With no chance of having a family the only purpose of having sex is pleasure and not reproduction.

There are several kinds of sexual expression, vaginal, oral and anal intercourse. Most men like these different methods of having sex. But previously men only had vaginal sex. Now in this day of choice and what feels best for you entices men on to try new methods to reach a more pleasing organism.

Since most men desire to have sex they usually look for extra marital sex especially if their own wife is old and cold. Obviously heretofore most men have desired sex with another woman. But that is due to change. As you remember from reading the scripture recorded above with sex men also desire to show dominance. Several synonyms for dominance are used in those few Bible verses. For a man to show dominance will become more important psychologically in these last days. Even though it has always been an intrical part of male sexual expression as in 'the missionary position' of old.

It is hard for any man to show forth dominance to any woman who feels depressed over her inability to be able to have children. For this depressed woman her feelings of loss cancel her expressions of romance. And she then contaminates the aroused man and encapsulates him with her negative feelings of inadequacy. Consequently, this drains the man's feelings of dominance.

To revive their dominance in these last days some ungodly men will seek to have sex with another man. Preferably a passive gay man who will reinforce the normal man's sense of dominance. It should also be noted that gay sexual partners are usually more enthusiastic about having sex than a depressed woman. Since gay men are also men they are stronger than any woman and can enthusiastically do whatever their sexual partner wants.

This brings up a very important point for you to consider. I am sure that you are aware of the current immigration crisis America is facing at its southern border. I just got this spiritual impute about this issue from God yesterday, the first of May, 2021.

This happens to be a very clear prophecy as no one has ever put these points of truth together at any time. The evil Biden Administration has been informed by clairvoyants, remote viewers and other secular shaman that this COVID 19 vaccine will have consequences which this illegal immigration of Hispanic children will supposedly resolve.

Since after being vaccinated against COVID 19 American women of child bearing age will remain infertile and unable to have children. Therefore, the devil is giving to America illegal Hispanic children via immigration.

On the 21st of May 2021 I received the necessary confirmation of my comments about these vaccines. This came from that Christian TV show: **Joni Table Talk.** On that show they had a special guest: Professor Gahill who had a PhD in immunology. Along with her assistant she conveyed that **these new vaccines lacked sufficient medical history to justify their use.** In fact, her assistant even mentioned that the lockdowns had caused 'a pandemic of malpractice'. And further said, that if another disease plague comes within two years there will be 'a die off' of all those who have received these new vaccines. Since the Bible book of Revelation also predicts much death, I would also council my students to take mortuary science to become essential workers as master morticians.

This new crisis of increased and expanded death will also result in the defeat of President Biden's reelection too.

FAKE NEWS

Does the murder of thousands of Cubans produce a more equitable society? (the current exposure of communism's ugly face in Cuba should turn every freedom loving person like Catholic Christians off especially when it is realized that Biden's order to the Coast Guard about the dangers of crossing the Florida Straights from Cuba to Florida is merely propaganda, Fake News and hate speech designed to keep more Cubans especially Black ones who will Vote Republican out of Florida).

Of course, since these Black voters are not Democratic, they will be held in low esteem. Obviously then this current news story about the Cubans, President Biden and crossing the Florida straits from Cuba to Florida is plain Fake News.

Let's look at how most of these deceptions come about. Of course, you realize that **Fake News is really just the latest name for the art of lying.** And lying as an art is taught in most law schools. And most politicians are lawyers too. To lie as you know is to supply others with convincing misinformation based on various forms of psychological deceptions called logical fallacies listed below:

AD HOMINEM: This type of logical fallacy begins the same way my Christian analysis began. That is the Person of the Lord Jesus Christ stated a super ego statement that said: 'I AM THE WAY, THE TRUTH AND THE LIFE'. (John 14:6).

In other words, His statements are true because He is the Truth and not questioned in Christianity because He has no character flaws at all.

Whereas other people do have very common flaws which supposedly lead to the fallacy of their argument or the positions they hold.

Actually, in history this issue is handled the same way. In the time of the Romans, a Roman coin had on its head side, the Roman emperor, while on the other side appeared the Latin word; PROVIDENT, which means PROVIDER. The reigning Caesar was considered the person who made the rules too and as sovereign he had no character flaws to question his policy.

So then **AN APPEAL TO AUTHORITY** could also be made here because of the position the person (Caesar) holds.

Unfortunately, in today's democracies we question everything so that the real truth is very hard to arrive at. Each side has a dissenting opinion, even the Supreme Court of the United States usually has one.

Speaker Pelosi seems to be very upset over the capitol fiasco that occurred on Jan. 6 to destroy the house that democracy built. But her concerns should not be the paramount concern of this year. For God so loved the world that he did not send us a democratic committee of many opinions and theories.

In the future the Bible says that there will be no democracy per se, but the absolute rule of the anti-Christ who is not just a force or power of evil but a specific evil person known as the devil incarnate.

On the news last night Senator Rand Paul was interviewing Dr. Fauci about 'gain of function' research that America paid for that he admitted to. But now he tried to lie out of it. All of this is recorded in my former prophetic book so that you can see which version of the truth is real.

Besides all this I am more apt to believe Senator Rand Paul because of his stand against abortion, although abortion is not relevant to this topic. If I were to focus on abortion too along with these other concerns that would be called **THE PACKAGE DEAL FALLACY**. But here I just used **AD HOMINUM** to discredit DR. FAUCI. But lying to Congress will cost Dr. Fauci 5 years. And although he has now been discredited, the Biden administration still intends to use him as its CHIEF MEDICAL ADVISOR. So being lifted up with megalomania DR FAUCI now sees himself as the embodiment of truth that 'going by the science' confirms. Has anyone even suspected that this abuse of immigration alone is keeping people from being vaccinated

AD POPULUM: This fallacy appeals to positive ideals like Patriotism, Religion or Liberty and is very popular among politicians. But it can also appeal to those politicians who express a counterpoint of negative fears, like the fear of getting vaccinations which many like to call Fake News when it is really just a safety concern over an experimental drug that has no long term record of recorded valid use without unpleasant side effects. And should be taken as a matter of course whenever an experimental drug is evaluated. **A recent study out of Israel shows that a vaccinated person is 6 X more likely to catch COVID than an unvaccinated person.** This of coarse is contrary to what you hear on the TV Fake News.

It should be noted that if you should die from taking an experimental drug like this COVID 19 vaccine, the life insurance that you may have will no longer pay. **Remember that before you get your shot.**

The twelve most vaccinated countries have the most COVID 19.

In any case this fallacy is really a side issue and not really the main concern being discussed. In this case the main issue being discussed must be true since most people believe it to be so regardless of the questions it may raise otherwise it will detract from the information actually being discussed.

In this particular case with the onset of the 'D' variant from India of this corona virus much fear has induced people to get anti-COVID 19 vaccinations to their own detriment.

Let's consider this practically: 1st, India is a crowded country without any room for Social Distancing. 2nd, this 'D' variant of the corona virus mainly affects school age children. So if your children are grown up or if you have no children this 'D' variant of the corona virus should not affect you. But it may be wise for you to voluntarily wear a mask if you ever encounter school children in your daily routine, like when riding the bus with school kids, playing the sports at the parks that school kids also use or visiting a library that school kids also use.

If you are NOT vaccinated against this corona virus before you let fear overcome you and grab you to get your vaccination, please do this: 1st, pray and ask God what to do. Be sure you ask your medical doctor too. **Then if you must get a vaccination go to your doctor where they get free flu shots and get a free pneumonia shot as all these flu viruses including COVID 19 kill by pneumonia. This one medical truth alone is well worth the price of this prophetic book.**

Some truths like the following one: (in Africa the four leaders who were recently assassinated were those that opposed vaccinations) are beginning to show evil behind so called 'medical truth'.

All this information has also jogged my memory about these actual psychological logical fallacies. The next one is called: **HASTY GENERALIZATIONS.** In these logical thoughts one jumps to a conclusion, like I must get a vaccination based on biased or insufficient evidence (that Dr. Fauci tried to lie out of in his recent interview with Senator Dr. Rand Paul).

Along with this same kind of faulty reasoning comes what the **BAND WAGON FALLACY** says that because these vaccinations are popular just like in **AD POPULUM** they must be the right thing to do.

Then I also remembered **THE RED HERRING FALLACY** in which the issue of vaccination by an experimental drug with no long-term record of safety was represented as a cure for COVID 19 when **the medical authorities of Israel say that 80% of those who are spreading this 'D' variant of COVID 19 have already been vaccinated against it.**

But to correct this **THE SLIPPERY SLOPE FALLACY** says that if you go ahead and get your vaccination against it anyway then good things like your good health, longer life span, new job, job promotions, new home, better neighborhood, new second car and other goodies will come.

From here **THE MORAL EQUIVELANT FALLACY** attempt to reinforce those already mentioned by equating things that are not really compatible. How can a manufactured disease like COVID 19 which is equal to its manufactured vaccination cure this corona crisis when 80% of those vaccinated against COVID 19 wind up getting it again?

I just heard on the Fake News radio that the states of Missouri, Florida and Texas have just had the highest incidents of new COVID 19 infections. Apparently Fake News wants to blame this on the Republicans. But when you look at this from a Christian perspective you see that this supposed conflict is not just about a disease like COVID 19 but spiritual warfare.

Thank God that Missouri has the world-wide Christian influence of the Jim Bakker show with its PTL TV network and other media outlets too numerous to mention. Florida influences the world from the Christian perspective by Dr. Rodney Howard Brown's TV evangelism and schools. And Texas has both the Christian influence of Kenneth Copeland's VICTORY TV network, Bible School and new TV news show: FLASH POINT which keeps faithful Christians informed rather than deceived by Fake News.

From my college notes (yes I do save things) I see several others psychological logical fallacies some of which may no longer be in use now.

They are**: STRAW MAN FALLACY** which is most commonly used in the courtroom to confuse someone's testimony and make it appear to be an argument that was never really made by your opponent.

POST HOC FALLACY: Most commonly used in court to confuse the jury by saying that if A happens before B, then A must have caused B.

GENETIC FALLACY: No longer used in this diverse society, but once said that a person's ideas, theories, thoughts or opinions are based on that person's origin, race or social position within that society.

EITHER/OR FALLACY: The reducing of an argument to an either or choice of over simplification to avoid many questions in court.

DIVINE FALLACY: Rarely used today in this age of unbelief. But once held that the best way to resolve a disagreement was to attribute it to some supernatural power like a demon which possessed the person and therefore was responsible for the crime.

DISMISSIVE FALLACY: Excluding something from the testimony simply because it seems absurd and does not conform to common sense. But common sense is highly subjective and maybe weird, strange or unusual but that does not make it false.

When evaluating some new information you can easily discard the false by knowing how to spot the deceptive techniques employed. As you know people will fight documents, photographs, text, audio and video in order to make the false appear genuine and even original.

DENOUNCING THE HYPOCRISY: of those with whom we disagreed is the go to strategy for anyone to use when in commenting on controversial topics. This is very easy in this case with President Joe Biden because **Biden has taken almost every position every issue since he has been in the US Congress.**

MIXING FACT WITH FICTION: is also very popular with President Joe Biden as it's just the way he thinks and unfolds what he thinks is to be shared as the truth. Example: over the past year, President Biden has claimed that the Obama Administration 'never locked people up in cages', Politico has affirmed this statement to be false. Moreover President Joe Biden stated that: 'Immediately after the Iraq War started, I came out against it'**. When the truth is that Joe Biden voted for this war.**

OMMITING SELECTED FACTS: President Joe Biden said that he went to law school on a full academic scholarship and ended up in the top half of his class. When the truth is Biden graduated 76th out of 85 students and did not win top honors at any time. He also claimed to have visited Nelson Mandela in prison when such never happened. He has also cast himself as a civil rights activist, when **Biden voted against civil rights** because he did not want his children going to school with 'jungle monkeys'.

The last type of academic psychological fallacy is **REPEATING UNTIL IT BECOMES TRUTH**: This was once the leading propaganda technique of the Nazis and now of the Biden administration. It is still used today mainly among politicians. President Joe Biden used it long ago when he claimed he went to Afghanistan to honor a heroic naval officer.

Speaking of Afghanistan your President Biden's decision to leave that country failed to honor the Americans who had sacrificed their blood for that nation's democracy. ***WE SHOULD NOW KNOW THAT AS SOCIALISTS SPEAKER PELOSI AND PRESIDENT BIDEN ONCE SAID THAT YOU***

CAN'T KEEP WASTING TRILLIONS OF TAX DOLLARS ON ANY FOREIGN WAR THAT YOU'RE NOT DESIGNED TO WIN WHILE YOUR HOPING INSTEAD TO WASTE THOSE SAME TRILLIONS OF TAX DOLLARS ON SOCIAL PROGRAMS THAT WILL GET YOU REELECTED. Why doesn't the news media report that? Such would surely change the upcoming election.

Another truth that mass media is trying to hide as Fake News is the occultic prophecy of Ben Laden who once said that the best way to take down America was to assassinate President Obama so that Biden would take over to destroy the country. This personal plan was found written in a rolled up Muslim prayer rug among Ben Laden's other papers years ago.

Foreign wars have bad consequences anyway, when former President Obama abandoned Iraq, the terrorist gang Isis rose up and now that Biden has done the same in Afghanistan, the Taliban are rising up at our expense.

Your President Biden has told several more lies about Afghanistan. One is that he wants you to believe about his concern for all Americans to get out of that country safely. When in fact many Americans have been beaten as infidels by the Taliban and hindered from getting out by Biden's own State Department as well as our helpers and allies too.

Another lie that we saw on the TV nightly news was where President Biden lied about his abandonment of Afghanistan and how that such has not insulted nor hurt any of our allies. So, the British Parliament voted to censure President Biden for lying.

Not being satisfied with these lies he failed to mention that his sudden abandonment of the conflict in Afghanistan had left behind over $2billion of military hardware so that now the Taliban in Afghanistan has more military helicopters than Australia. In fact, more military hardware has been left behind then 185 other nations in the UN, which Ukraine could have used.

After abandoning all those weapons in Afghanistan, the Democrats no longer have any right to tell us to turn in our guns. No doubt you saw on the TV news how that church leaders in Australia were arrested and abused by the COVID 19 medically insane authorities since they no longer had any guns to protect themselves. This same problem also showed up at the airport in Afghanistan where the local people are disarmed but the Taliban are fully armed.

Your President Biden closed down the US embassy first after he decided to withdraw from Afghanistan and once that happened there was no longer any safe place where Christians in Afghanistan could find safety. So the Taliban has now begun to execute the Christians door to door.

The State Department says that it is helping Americans escape from Afghanistan but really it is lying about all the documents and papers that Americans need in order to do so. And the fact that when it left the $2 billion Embassy it left behind computer information about every former informer on the Taliban. This is mainly called BIO-METRIC DATA identifying Christians and America's helpers. So now the Taliban can go door to door to execute their Christians, informers and enemies too.

Speaking of Biden's State Department, they are keeping US Special Forces from rescuing Americans, Christians and helpers outside the airport so that they could be escorted under armed guard to their planes unlike the British, French, German and Dutch armed forces are doing.

BEFORE I SAY MORE ABOUT LYING LET ME GIVE YOU THIS FURTHER TRUTH ABOUT THE TALIBAN: YOU HAVE NEVER SEEN THE TALIBAN ON TV GETTING VACCINATED AGAINST COVID 19 ALTHOUGH THIS PLAGUE IS WORLD-WIDE. TAKING BATHS IS NOT POPULAR IN AFGHANISTAN AND THEIR HYGIENE LEAVES SOMETHING TO BE DESIRED TOO. PLUS, THEY LIVE AS MUSLIMS, WHICH WE KNOW IS A FALSE RELIGION. SO IT SEEMS THAT THIS COVID 19 IS A PLAGUE SUSCEPTIBLE MOSTLY TO AMERICANS DUE TO THEIR SINS OF ABORTION AND SAME SEX MARRIAGE. THE TALIBAN DO NOT TOLERATE SAME SEX MARRIAGE AND CONSIDER A MARRIED WOMAN'S GIVING BIRTH TO BE A BLESSING.

Speaking about women in Afghanistan it should be noted that in that culture a married women is the authority in her family. She decides if their son is to join the army. So under these circumstances it is not considered wise for girls to go to school to learn how to read so they can read the KORAN and see through its false teachings and keep their men from joining the Taliban and becoming Muslim. That's why girls going to school are killed.

Your President Joe Biden recently lied to the American people on TV when he said that he had decided that Americans must leave Afghanistan by August 31st When in fact it was the Taliban that told Biden that they would only honor his original date of August 31st as any later date would increase the intolerable occupation.

But the main incident of presidential lying that most Americans remember was about Obama Care. It used to say **'If you like your doctor, you can keep him'.** Now President Biden and his progressives want to expand supposedly now truthful Medicare in spite of all the lies we remember to 'serve' every American with expended socialism.

Speaking of socialism, it should be noted that it has killed many millions of people from China and Russia to North Korea and Cambodia.

There are so many erroneous zones with President Joe Biden that it's impossible to find any erogenous zones on him at all. No wonder like other socialist democrats he supports the gay community (LGBTQ+) just like all these deceived sexual deviants who have been spaded.

The Biden administration also expects all Americans to buy their delusional narrative about crime and the necessity for defunding the police (especially the Muslim anti-sematic Alexandria Ocasio-Cortez).

Critical Race Theory is another issue that America is being told by the Biden administration is not happening yet. When in fact 3rd graders are being forced in public schools to deconstruct their racial and sexual identities then rank them according to their power and privilege,

Critical race theory which is opposed to the basic teachings of Dr. Martin Luther King Jr. that people should be judged according to the content of their character and not the color of their skin has been replaced by President Biden with reverse or anti-white racism that's being taught to your children in school especially if they are white.

Your President Joe Biden seems to be less concerned with deadly discrimination against women by the Taliban in Afghanistan then the supposed racial discrimination against Blacks in America.

As a person with a psychology degree I know that this teaching of reverse racism is very dangerous as it results in low self-esteem and self-confidence in those who we expect to invent the stuff and make the things that will make our future better than today. ANY SUCH ABUSE AGAINST ANY RACE DEPRIVES AMERICA OF ITS FULL MEANING AS A NATION WITH FULL JUSTICE AND LIBERTY FOR ALL.

Moreover this naughty teaching has a highly detrimental aspect that is: its pseudoscientific dogma teaches that whiteness is malignant, voracious, insatiable and perverse thus resulting in more gays or conditioned homosexuals.

Instead of submitting to all this anti-white propaganda of the Biden administration and seeing their children indoctrinated before their own eyes they are starting homeschooling to teach the same values to their children that their parents taught them.

YOUR PRESIDENT JOE BIDEN SEEMS TO BE LESS CONCERNED WITH THE VIOLENT DISCRIMINATION AGAINST

WOMEN BY THE TALIBAN IN AFGHANISTAN THAN THE NON-EXISTENT RACISM AGAINST BLACKS IN AMERICA.

IN THE AFGHANISTAN CULTURE WOMAN ARE GIVEN AUTHORITY IN THE FAMILY. THE MOTHER DECIDES IF HER SON IS TO JOIN THE ARMY. SO THESE PEOPLE DO NOT WANT GIRLS TO GO TO SCHOOL TO LEARN HOW TO READ, BECAUSE THEN THEY WILL READ THE KORAN AND SEE THROUGH ITS FALSE TEACHING THAT JUSTIFY MOST WRONGS INCLUDING THE MUSLIM FAITH.

Also most recently the Biden administration has borrowed a number of passages that were copied and pasted into the 'meteorologist" Joe Biden's climate change fiasco (**it should be realized that many unbelievers that Christ is God call tribulation events like the California wildfires climate change instead of tribulation resulting from their own sins).**

Most of this climate change 'bull spit' comes from the Obama administration. After cursing climate change former President Obama bought a multi-million-dollar mansion in the sea coast town of Martha's Vineyard. So former President Obama and the Democrats believe more in what Obama's money bought than in what he and the Democrats now say.

Let's now compare just a few of these with former President Donald Trump. These Biden people are spending like there's no tomorrow and our taxes are going to go 'up up and away'.

Former President Donald Trump on the other hand gave us a tax cut that created over 2½ million new jobs that led to the lowest Black and minority unemployment ever recorded.

Former President Donald Trump has kept his word about his promises more than any other ex-President.

President Joe Biden lies constantly about everything and the media does not ever question any of it. I guess that they want to see us saddled with Cultural Race Theory, Obama care, the Green New Deal, removal of voting safeguards, endless tax hikes, statehood for Puerto Rico and D.C. and teaching your children sexual discovery with newly changed sexual identities. About the border, Biden says that it's the same as it has always been, nothing has changed. That's why he hasn't gone to visit it.

This morning while the library computer was being updated I reviewed one of their reference books about propaganda and misinformation entitled: <u>THE REFERNCE SHELF.</u>

On page 113 this reference book makes a very stupid statement that we need to look at. It discusses a supposed flap on Facebook, YouTube and some television networks from the Trump campaign suggesting that Joe Biden had pressured Ukraine into squelching the investigation of his son Hunter by having the prosecutor fired so that Hunter could keep the millions from that energy company.

Of course, they say that their political facts in this case show that the Obama administration in which Joe Biden was Vice President and several US allies had pushed for the removal of that prosecutor because of his slow moving on corruption. This idea is an insult to the intelligence of anyone knowing anything about diplomacy. You do not insult nor question the authority of the employees of another nation that you are trying to establish good relations with. I hope that my common-sense answer has helped you to better sort through all the 'bull spit' and find the real truth.

Nevertheless, we know that true political information rarely changes any partisan attitudes. But in things like health, misinformation can really change view points and their subsequent behaviors. So I expect to see an increase in vaccinations especially among younger people who are more tech-savvy in assessing and distributing digital and technical information but still susceptible to Fake News especially in the area of medical truth.

Unfortunately for the liberal news media one fact that is usually hidden by fake news got unveiled on last night's CBS evening news. This news story was about a young Black football player who was in children's hospital in New Orleans, Louisiana suffering from COVID 19. In the interview he stated that several weeks ago he had received a COVID 19 vaccination because he wanted to play football for his high school and letter in his senior year there. Plus he wanted to be able to greet his many fans without being a health hazard.

There is much propaganda today about the necessity of getting your vaccination in order to beat this pandemic. But in his case we see where his circumspect vaccination for COVID 19 to avoid infecting the people actually served to act as a portal for this COVID 19 health catastrophe.

Perhaps I failed to make myself clear enough when I discussed COVID 19 before. So here is the plain truth as I see it: despite what the experts say, **COVID 19 is not just another disease but a biological weapon. As such there really is no vaccination against it. Else why did those thousands of people who mistakenly took this vaccination die from COVID 19? (This vaccination has killed over 10,000 people so far).**

Both Israel and the UK per capita have vaccinated more people than the us and have now had more COVID deaths than us as of 8/28/2021. (So you should avoid blood transfusions now too).

Actually it appears that the so called vaccination against COVID 19 is really a portal for it. In other words, by taking the vaccination you actually open yourself up to receiving full blown COVID 19, many thousands of deaths confirm this truth despite Fake News failing to report such.

As I said before, President Joe Biden during the over forty years that he was a Senator from Delaware he took almost every side on every issue ever discussed. Now he is doing likewise with this issue of having to wear a mask. And Dr. Fauci has now joined him in this fiasco.

For the sake of peace however I would wear a mask if the authorities said so. Look at it this way, wearing a mask is more of a psychological sign of agreement than a medical sign of any kind indicating either health or sickness. After all we know medically that only surgical masks really work.

This brings up spiritual timing (first mentioned by that prophet: Roberts Lardon in his book on that subject). Some Christian theologians are now arguing about when the four horse men of the Apocalypse will start ridding. When will the moon turn red. And when will Jesus be coming again?

It is written that: 'IN THE LAST DAYS YOU WILL NOT BE ABLE TO BUY OR SELL WITHOUT THE MARK OF THE BEAST, HIS NAME OR THE NUMBER OF HIS NAME', (Revelation 13:17). Also consider this: right now you cannot buy or sell without the beast's mask (especially if you are buying groceries in a food store). **So that actually the mask equals the number of the beast, his name or his mark for all practical purposes. Now can you see where we are at prophetically?**

Let's look also at the forest fires and wild fires out West. Most unchristian secular people, sinners, reprobates, social democrats and other bums call these catastrophes the result of climate change instead of our obvious approach to or residence in tribulation. Those of you who have ever lived in California have heard of 'earthquake' weather too. So you know to expect earthquakes just like Jesus said in Matthew 24. And you know that earthquakes are increasing in number and getting worse just like the tribulation says they would.

Let's also consider prophetic wars, they must also come according to scripture when Joe Biden promises peace and safety. 'FOR WHEN THEY SAY PEACE AND SAFETY, SUDDEN DESTRUCTION COMES', (I Thess. 5:3). Wake up the issue here is not just wars. But an unforeseen end time war that winds up hurting you.

Let's also consider this COVID 19 with its many varieties and fake vaccinations that do not protect you from it but actually make you susceptible to it. No doubt you have heard of the thousands of vaccinated people who got COVID 19 anyway. Obviously then this COVID 19 is not just another corona virus like the flu, but an end time plague that Jesus said to expect in the tribulation of the last days. The Lord Jesus said in Matthew 24 that all these plagues and tribulation must come before He comes again.

Unfortunately, the false doctrine of the pre-tribulation rapture has deceived most Christians away from accepting and preparing for these end time plagues. Obviously, these lukewarm Christians have joined secular sinners in calling these plagues 'climate change' instead of admitting their need for repentance and reconciliation to God.

Let's also look at the devil that most Christian theologians believe will run the tribulation period of much demonic activity. Actually that demonic activity is already alive and well in the democratic party thanks especially to abortion. Now 'THE DEVIL HAS COME TO KILL, ROB, AND DESTROY', (John 10:10).

Thanks to Biden and his progressive Democrats their international policy is to fund world-wide abortions. And to rob the American tax payer to fund a delusionary, socialist infrastructure agenda amounting to billions of dollars. Biden and his stupid socialists have adopted a stupid foreign policy which insults premier Putin of Russia who controls many supersonic missiles which can deliver the largest nuclear arsenal on earth. And the Democrat Biden's stupid tolerance of communist China's continued violation of human rights, religious freedom and other nations sovereignty has jeopardized America's position of leadership authority in the world and put the peace of the world at risk.

Speaking of socialism since I have both a degree in Theology and one in Psychology I'll now use the one in Psychology to relate my feelings about this issue. As you know socialism just by voting it in alone leaves no room for your ego development (resulting in self-esteem, self-worth or any feeling of accomplishment). You must have a satisfactory sense of accomplishment that comes from inventing something or writing something and then being able to sell it for a profit big enough to employ many people in a capitalist society thus making yourself and others rich. In other words and to put it more plainly socialism is a great goal if you want to become a zombie. Most unemployed, homeless people who already have a do nothing attitude and would fit in easily to a socialist society where you don't need to care about anyone, even yourself.

Socialism just by voting it in leaves no room for any mans ego development, like the satisfactory sense of accomplishment that comes from inventing something and the being able to sell it for a profit big enough to employ people and make yourself and other rich. In other words and to put it more plainly: socialism is a great goal if you want to become a zombie. Most unemployed and homeless people already have a do nothing attitude and would fit in easily in a socialist society where you don't need to care about any one, not even yourself

So then having to wear masks goes against being yourself especially in a socialist society where everyone must look the same and where everyone is supposedly equal. Personal gifts like singing, swimming and surfing etc. put constitutional concepts that all men are created equal into jeopardy. Socialism is not only bad for your country but also leads you to your personal abandonment of any life goals as a person supposedly created in the image of God.

In a capitalist society becoming a bum is mainly your choice based on your psychological deficits like depression, low self-esteem, substance abuse, etc. But in a socialist society everyone including the most intelligent or mechanically inclined is poor just like today's Cubans in communist Cuba who all make $20.00 a month, even physicians and street sweepers.

It should also be noted that the Biden administration has intercepted boats of people leaving Cuba and returned them there to be prosecuted by its communist government while welcoming in illegal immigrants with COVID 19, TUBERCULOSIS, MALERIA and all manner of disease to be bused all over America at your expense infecting us with COVID 19 and every other disease known to man.

I submit to you that this is being done because most Cuban immigrants will vote Republican as they have endured socialized democracy first-hand. While most other Latinos will vote for the Democrats who give them free stuff that we free-born Americans pay increased taxes for.

There is also a very unpleasant political reason behind this which you probably will not want to hear. That is: these illegal Latino immigrants are coming in and NOT being vaccinated against COVID 19 nor any other disease because they are expected to all survive to take over once the older vaccinated Americans all die off. As unlikely as it seems could this really be why most Americans are being forced to get their vaccinations? You know one of Karl Marx's main truths was to replace the population of those who would not accept communism (socialism).

The most important way to evaluate any vaccinations is to look at it historically. By that I mean real history not that cultural race theory nor 1619 propaganda.

In my personal history I was vaccinated against polio in the early 1950's from what I remember. Back in those days we lived on a suburban mini farm right outside Kingsport, Tennessee. My family had a black and white TV like everyone else and they saw on it how that polio was becoming a very dangerous disease with children incarcerated in 'iron lungs'. Of course, this scared them, so they took me to school to get my Salk vaccine (Dr. Jonas Salk was the inventor of the polio vaccine (in a socialist society there are no inventors nor medical doctors for everyone is an equal bum).

Unlike today's COVID 19 vaccine this polio vaccine acted perfectly like all vaccinations should. With this polio vaccine there were no 'breakthrough' problems either. That is where after getting the polio vaccination you still were susceptible to catching this polio disease. Neither did you take the polio vaccination by faith, hoping for the best. This polio vaccine had a 100% success rate as seen on black and white TV with Douglas Edwards (remember him).

We had black and white TV back in those days not only because of technology but because we lived in a black and white culture back then. You might remember how there were no shades of grey back then with double meanings that could cost you your life, like transgender or gay marriage.

In this present depressing age many parents have not been able to pay their back rent and have had to move back in with their parents and grandparents. Some thankfully have been able to recall these successful polio vaccinations and have communicated to their children their own very suspicious attitudes about this COVID 19 vaccine that doesn't seem to work as well with Dr Fauci's ever increasing abominable oral masturbation.

As you probably know this corona virus better known as COVID 19 is really a form of flu which is a respiratory virus. Back years ago when I was a naughty young man, serving the year 1968 in The Florida State Prison for forgery an epidemic occurred with this Hong Kong flu. Many inmates remained in their beds too sick to do anything, even to eat. Me and about 200 other men never caught the disease although it was all around us.

On my mother's side (God Bless her soul) they were Italians from Sicily. That big island in the Mediterranean Sea where all the early plagues came through before hitting Europe. These included the Black death and Smallpox. And apparently, I am descendant from these survivors. In other words, I must have high natural immunity to any flu. I have caught colds but no flu that I can remember. So I have never had a flu shot and do not intend to get a vaccination for COVID 19 not only for natural immunity but also for living by faith as a Christian and practicing repentance instead.

Looking at death again, it's very depressing if your own child or other relatives are vaccinated against this COVID 19 and then die from it.

In the 'black and white days' folks knew the scriptures well since Christianity was more popular back then. But now their children do not know the Bible verse that says: 'GOD HAS DELIVERED ME FROM ALL MY FEARS', (Psalm 34:4). This is still true whether you know it or not. **And fear of the ungodly abortionist Democrats is keeping the unvaccinated from getting their vaccinations.**

The experts say that any breakthrough vaccination causes you to spread the virus. So which is better getting the vaccination or not?

Many older folks are retiring to Florida. And these people remember what the polio vaccine accomplished and what this 'half assed' COVID 19 vaccination could result in. Not longer life with many of God's blessings but sickness, hospitalization, being put on a ventilator and not being able to visit your family again but having to face death with all its uncertainties. So skeptical Americans are also very concerned about having to take another shot against this COVID 19. (My niece's mother-in-law took her second shot and died from it within less than a week).

In my former prophetic book I said that this COVID 19 was a manufactured biological weapon and not a natural disease from bats. Therefore, vaccinations to this COVID 19 do not act like 'normal' vaccines.

I already mentioned that some people have died from a 'breakthrough' experience from this 'half-assed' vaccine resulting in death.

Most Christians believe that they are already ready to make heaven their home because that's where the Lord Jesus lives and 'TO BE ABSCENT FROM THE BODY IS TO BE PRESENT WITH THE LORD'. (II Cor. 5:8).

To most Christians this sounds very good. But to secular unbelievers and demonic Democrats, this brings up many unpleasant questions. And any long-term viewer of Christian TV that many unbelievers watch to get away from violence and fake 'soap operas' say different things using the same scriptures. Like when they discuss belief they fail to mention that, 'EVEN THE DEVILS BELIEVE AND TREMBLE'. (James 2:19).

So to most people heaven is not a sure thing and they are afraid to take these COVID 19 vaccinations accordingly. I could describe heaven to some extent but there are already Christian books that discuss it well.

No doubt you have heard that saying that says: 'Everyone wants to go to heaven but nobody wants to die' Since heaven is a toss-up, most people would rather not have to face this issue, but once a person dies the possibility of going to hell must be faced. This of course is a very uncomfortable proposition. And there are already many Christian books about this subject available to all too. But I would add to it a prophetic truth that is: volcanic eruptions erupt to make more room in hell to accommodate those many who shall soon be rushing into it. And the many forest fires about you reduce your surroundings to ashes to inform you that hell is where you are going. As in behind the hidden meaning behind 'ashes to ashes'.

Those who discover 'deep truth' (this reminds me that on this day, August 18, 2021 I received the revelation which said that if we are just branches it's our job to bring forth fruit not to play 'roots' and try to discover all the hidden unknown truths about God, like to believe that it's like eclosion, the process of a monarch butterfly emerging from its cocoon as a full-grown butterfly as opposed to ecdysis where a snake sheds its skin). So, for the event of January 6 at the US capitol rather than use the words rally or protest the socialists Democrats would rather use the word riot or insurrection to put blame on the protestors.

But several months ago before this insurrection propaganda took hold I saw on the Flash Point TV show on the Victory channel the video of former President Trump's exhortation to his supporters. He encouraged them to go and be seen and speak at the capitol 'PEACFULLY'.

A peaceful protest is not an insurrection. Neither is an insurrection accompanied by and invited in by police authorities. On the Flashpoint video I saw the local police authorities escorting military clothed rightest groups of people into the capitol building. Such does not constitute an insurrection, certainly not against the peaceful protestors and supporters of President Donald Trump.

The misuse of words by the abortionist and socialist Democrats to describe this scene that most Americans have not fully seen is fake. To call a peaceful protest a violent assault by Trump supporters that laid siege to the Capitol an insurrection is also Fake News. The idea that these abortionist and socialist Democrats felt that they needed to use such strong language to keep the Trump supporters from being seen in a heroic light is also false.

There is another point about the Capitol building that needs to be said. Unlike City Halls or County Commission Chambers the Capitol building is not opened to the public, where as a constituent you get the right to address and speak to your representatives. Thus, it's locked doors and police guards prove that it is not the house that democracy built. And now the abortionist and socialist Democrats have taken it

and the government over to waste your stolen tax dollars on their stupid social programs. In the old days our ancestors used to hang horse thieves and during this century thieves of intelligence or spy information to aid our enemies were put to death too. What will we now do that the abortionist and socialist Democrats who have by evil means stolen and turned our fresh water spring lake into an open sewer known as the Washington Socialist Swamp?

The Biden administration has also spread more Fake News by saying: 'The November 3rd election was the most secure in American history' and that 'Automatic recounts or canvases' were unnecessary because there was 'no evidence of either wrong doing or mistakes that casts any doubt on the outcome of the national election results'.

Then the Biden administration goes on to say that: 'And unusual second round of examinations by the various states in looking at certain ballots, election records and election systems (machines) used to conduct the election of 2020 is unnecessary'.

And following this the Biden administration claims that 'this sort of activity raises concerns regarding potential intimidation of voters'. So the Supreme Court and other courts failed to hear the evidence of this Democratic skullduggery when it was first presented to them by the Trump administration. I wonder what they will now say when this evidence of democratic skullduggery, lying and falsification of ballots and records is presented to them by the various states that have been victims?

Supporters of the Biden administration like to say that this national election of 2020 saw a record turnout of more people than were registered to vote and were attracted to Joe Biden so much so that it did not matter if they violated the law to stuff ballot boxes with unsigned ballots.

Finally the truth has come out that more people voted in the 2020 election nationwide than were really eligible to vote. Many said that the election of 2020 had the highest voter turnout in over a century. Of course fraud is easily seen here as no one was that excited about voting for Joe Biden.

According to the records President Trump won 74 million votes in that election, that only leaves 67½ million votes remaining for Biden. **This means that about 13 million ballots of votes were falsely created and counted for Biden**. Revolutions have been fought over less and taking into account how Biden has hurt this country and what End-Time prophecies say what should we now do to remedy this and return America to God?

Some have said that Joe Biden is the worst President that America has ever had. They go on to blame all this on a repeat of the bad Obama days plus the onset of socialism. But let's begin with God. Americans were disappointed in President Joe Biden when he decided to omit God in the National Day of Prayer of May, 2021.

First of all, President Joe Biden is an abortionist Democrat. That means he is a baby killer. This way he is free to kill off all conservative Americans to make room for illegal aliens to do what KARL MARX the communist recommended; that is, kill off the established Americans and replace them with illegal aliens who will see things more from our communist perspective.

(YOU COULD SUBSTITUTE SOCIALIST FOR COMMUNIST AS THEY ARE BOTH THE SAME. ONLY COMMUNISM KILLS A DEMOCRATIC NATION BY REVOLUTION WHEREAS SOCIALISM KILLS BY SUICIDAL VOTE).

Of coarse elections do have consequences and Joe Biden has emerged from his basement like Rip Van Winkle who turned his clock back to 2016 (the bad Obama years). Unfortunately, 'The Way We Were' might be a nice song but it cannot describe our socialist future nor how to play the right political games in order to get there. Why go to an era of no prosperity and no peace abroad anyway?

Former President Trump, as you remember had major policy successes in this area (both with increased employment and the decrease of illegal aliens). Please don't forget that former President Trump's 'Remain in Mexico' policy was an effective means to stop the endless stream of caravans of illegals invading the US. Plus, former President Donald Trump put more Black and Brown people to work than any other President.

Former President Trump provided Americans with access to affordable healthcare and he drove down the price of prescription drugs.

Speaking of drugs, I just remember that taking the vaccination cancels your right to due process under law.

President Biden on the other hand has cancelled former President Trump's executive order keeping medicines affordable (you socialist Democrats note that: the price of insulin for diabetics alone has now gone from $60.00 a month to $320.00 a month).

Critical race theory which is opposed to the basic teachings of Dr. Martin Luther King Jr. that people should be judged according to the content of their character and not the color of their skin has been replaced by President Biden and now reverse or anti-white racism is being taught to your children in school especially if they are white. As a person with a psychology degree I know that this teaching of reverse racism is very dangerous as it results in low self-esteem and low self-confidence in those who we expect to invent the stuff and make the things that will make our future better than today. ANY SUCH ABUSE AGAINST ANY RACE DEPRIVES AMERICA OF ITS FULL MEANING AS A NATION WITH FULL JUSTICE AND LIBERTY FOR ALL.

Despite President Biden's best efforts at disinformation or Fake News over half of Americans still believe that changing one's gender identity or sexual identity is morally wrong (even though a fake news Soros pole indicated otherwise). Millennials (ages 18-34) feel stronger about this than most of us. Perhaps they realize that sex is a gift from God that no one has the right to reject. And that you make due with what you have.

President Biden believes that all election fraud should be labeled 'domestic terrorism'. And any entity that aligned itself with the audit of election outcomes should be targeted as an enemy of the dually elected government. According to this about 100 million American voters should be considered dissidents, rebels or white-supremacists.

He believes this in spite of the fact that ¾ of Americans support election integrity laws with voter ID. President Biden is also working with social media platforms like Facebook to identify white males conservatives as domestic extremists. Then the social media platforms see these extremists as anti-authority terrorists or white supremacists and should be treated as the Patriot Act describes against Muslim terrorists. Under this sort of political hostility the old adage: 'If you see something, say something' arises to turn all Americans into domestic spies that rat each other out.

President Biden has also engaged in evil undemocratic practices like permitting the US military to be used in civilian law enforcement to help detain US citizens without judicial review. Some of this comes from President Biden's Omnibus Counterterrorism Act of 1995. So Biden has been against your personal freedoms for many years. All of this should have been brought out before he was elected the first time. I'm bringing it out now to be sure that he doesn't get elected the second time.

A man who identifies as a woman in sports takes away many opportunities for a woman to excel (such as scholarships, college offers, increased self-esteem and increased self-worth. And from feeling good about herself the increased desire to find a suitable mate and eventually marry and start a great family. Most Americans feel that it is unfair to make women compete against transgender athletes. But your President Biden considers these laws against such to be the 'ugliest, most un-American laws'.

President Biden feels that school children should be allowed to change their gender without their parent's permission. President Biden also wants to allow gender-confused males to have full access to girl's bathrooms and girl's locker rooms, to play girls sports as girls without having to use any hormones or undergoing sex change surgery.

Your President Biden's stupid Green New Deal will spend about 2 trillion on this so called 'infrastructure'. And Biden's American jobs plan will pay for it via the largest federal tax increase since 1942.

Your President Biden also proposes to spend 174 billion on electric vehicles. He fails to realize however that these electric vehicles depend on small earth rare products that come mainly from China where they are produced mostly under slave labor.

This happened just as **French President Emmanuel Macron announced at his Davos conference that capitalism was now dead thanks to Biden's 'GREAT RESET'. Whereupon the President of Communist China laid out the marching orders for Biden to follow in this transition.**

Analysts also predict that President Joe Biden's American Families Plan would add about 21 million dollars to our current welfare plan with most of that money going to families of middle and upperincome families as opposed to poor kids. This agrees with the projected economic growth of 1.9 percent like the stagnant Obama nomics years when Biden was Vice President. Oh yes, because of all this wasteful spending on social issues any deterrent defense posture is now dead.

The Biden administration also proposes doubling the size of the IRS to an $80 billion budget increase to prevent any illegal leaking of tax dollars in keeping with Marxist class warfare policies.

The Biden administration also wants to spend $225 billion on subsidized daycare as an interictal part of its $2 trillion American Family Plan. This of course is on top of the proposed $200 billion that the Biden administration wants to spend on universal preschool childcare where young students will be taught masturbation and 'sex therapy' to tone down the aggressive and hyperactive behavior of Black boys with high crime rates.

Two-parent households with two preschool-age children would qualify for this if they had incomes below $130,000 and so would single parent households below $113,000.

President Joe Biden thus wants to Europeanize the American welfare state by installing a universal government preschool, free community college and child care.

Occupational licensing and expanded decree requirements for daycare workers will create higher costs leading to higher wages, more taxes and more single mothers unable to earn the required degree so remaining on welfare. Thus expanding President Biden's welfare state.

The United Auto Workers endorsed Joe Biden in the 2020 election. So by March of 2021 Ford announced it was shifting its production of new electric vehicles from Ohio to Mexico.

President Joe Biden supports abortion (the human sacrifice of baby killing) under any and all circumstances including late term abortion and putting the unwanted to death as in (euthanasia).

President Joe Biden wants to pack The Supreme Court to get his way on the issues of the day despite what the Constitution requires.

President Joe Biden wants to ban semi-automatic fire-arms although his drug addicted son, Hunter purchased a gun by lying on his background check. This is nothing new to Biden who has had 3 positions on defunding the police as well. Once he even called them 'systematic racists'. Thanks to all this Democratic and unamerican propaganda more Blacks have been killed so far this year than last year. Biden's defund the police movement has thus become very unpopular even with Blacks. As a result the cities are seeing a large Black crime surge.

Your President Biden tried to buy the necessary votes needed for his three and a half trillion-dollar socialist boondoggle called The Green New Deal from moderate senator Joe Mansion by nominating his wife as co-chair of The Appalachian Regional Commission. A federal job worth $160,000.00.

Your President Biden plans to bring many thousands of illegal Muslim immigrants into the country and he promised to also teach your children in public schools Sharia law in order to accommodate them so that they will vote for the Democrats.

Right after a Never Trump Muslim immigrant from Syria with Isis sympathies massacred 10 white people at a supermarket, your President Biden proposed the disarming of the native-born population to deprive them of the ability to fight back (of course this also deprived them of their constitutional rights). Being from Florida I know that the FBI (under the Obama-Biden administration) knew in advance the Muslim shooter at the Pulse night club (Omar Mateen) who killed 49 supposedly gay people who Muslims hate. Why is your President Biden allowing haters into America?

Your President Biden's Bureau of Alcohol, Tobacco and Fire Arms believes it has the authority to confiscate, ban and register any class of fire arms it wants without consulting Congress. And your President Biden's proposed rule-making about rifles, rifle barrels and a stabilizing brace hopes to ensure the forced registration or destruction of millions of privately owned fire arms to ensure the removal of 99% of the fire arms in circulation. Your President Joe Biden is well on his way to accomplishing this as in June 2021 Biden proposed expanded background checks for any gun purchases. As your President Joe Biden intends to control peoples right to own guns. **But the Supreme Court may have to stop Joe Biden weather it wants to or not.**

Of course, your President Biden feels that the terrorist hate group, Antifa is an ideological group not a terrorist group. And since it supports Democrats it must be OK. And when anyone during the election looked up Antifa, Biden's campaign page would appear.

Your President Joe Biden's immigration policy is far worse than was ever suspected. Immigrant children are forced to sleep either in crowded cages or hot, filthy tents. Thus, they are not able to practice any social distancing neither are they given any vaccinations against COVID 19 nor any other prompt medical care. Their only daily provision is some stale food to eat. As for hygiene, they only get 1 shower a week. Those in cages are not allowed outdoors. You might say that your President Biden has reopened Obama era concentration camps for illegal immigrants and illegal immigrant children, in other words: 'babies in cages'. On top of all this abuse the National Sherriff's Association now estimates that at least half of all illegal immigrants are COVID positive. But these illegal immigrants not only have COVID but many other dangerous diseases as well. As it stands now by the end of June, 26,000 of these infected people have squatted on America.

Your President Joe Biden has also cancelled a Trump era operation that focused on deporting illegal child sex traffickers and sexual predators. So now many of these children have been rapped and will eventually want to rape others themselves, So, then your President Joe Biden has reduced our clean society into a polluted one with all manner of filth and human residue having the audacity and the nerve to claim the right to citizenship.

Thanks to the corrupt immigration policies of your President Joe Biden the drug cartels of Mexico are now making more money off these contaminated people than they ever made off smuggling drugs into America (the going rate for smuggling humans is $10,000 per person amounting to over a billion dollars).

Your President Biden by reversing Trump era border policies has now given the Mexican cartels the opportunity to exploit illegal immigrants for their own enormous financial gain. When Americans hear about the humanitarian disaster at the border they need to remember that it had been fueled by and subsidized by the Biden administration's failure to secure the border.

There is another rather unpleasant problem with these illegal immigrants. Those who try to freelance, that is cross the border on their own without paying the cartel are usually shot on sight.

Unfortunately, a form of socialist government is now coming to America. Some of you may remember when Adolf Hitler was elected chancellor of Germany. He was a national socialist better known as the NAZI's concerned for the welfare of the German workers. That means that eventually he had to get rid of the non-workers in German society in order to make the Socialist ideal work.

Some theological experts now say that Hitler is a forerunner of the anti-Christ. In that case he will be appearing very soon as socialism takes over most democratic nations as they become socialist themselves. The socialist form of government is just like all others when it comes to money. The socialist have no money. So, in order to distribute money to those they feel are worthy, they must seize it from the 'hangers on'. In Hitler's day the 'hangers on' were considered to be: the criminals, the mentally retarded and mentally ill along with the insane, the handicapped and deformed, bums and gypsies and of course the Jews.

Today the criminals will include the illegal aliens (it is estimated that about 12,000 criminal illegal aliens each month will not be deported during Biden's term and will be able to vote by the Democrats 'For the People Act'). the mentally handicapped will include the autistic, bums will include the homeless and of course as an anti-God remedy of society's social clean-up will include the Christian capitalist both gentile and Jew. **And if the anti-Christ will be appearing soon then Jesus must be coming again soon too.**

The second coming of Jesus will be 'AS IT WAS IN THE DAYS OF NOAH', (Matthew 24:37). 'THE THOUGHTS AND INTENTS OF MANS HEARTS WAS ONLY EVIL CONTINUALLY', (Genesis 6:5). 'AND IT REPENTED GOD THAT HE HAD MADE MAN', (Genesis 6:6). 'SO HE SENT THE FLOOD', (Genesis 7:1). Obviously, the flood caused the first world-wide shut-down.

Now this second world-wide shutdown is being caused by COVID 19 which I told you before is a plague for the sins of abortion and same sex marriage and not just another corona virus. *you get rid of plagues by repenting not by taking vaccinations.*

Many Christians are so busy rejoicing that this COVID 19 plague will not come near their dwellings that they have failed to see that the shutdown it caused means prophetically that the issue is not now safety from plagues like this corona virus but **the immediate coming of the anti-Christ preceding the coming again of the Lord Jesus Christ.**

I need to say one more thing about this COVID 19 plague that supposedly began in the WHOAN BIOMEDICAL WEAPONS LAB IN CHINA where it contaminates through the air.

The war currently happening between Russia and Urkraine is really over Ukraine's biomedical weapons labs which Russian missles destroyed six of. So Russia could stop fighting now if Ukraine did not intend to back up its recommissioned and restored weapons labs with NATO. Since the natural air flow over Russia goes from West to East, Russia feels that it can take no chances of having its people polluted by Ukraines weapon's labs which FAKE NEWS fails to report on.

Moreover, the fake news report that Russia has threatened to use nuclear weapons makes no sense since the fallout from such would drift into Russia itself.

FAKE NEWS OF CNN, MSNBC, ABC, CBS, NBC AND OTHERS INCLUDING MOST CHRISTIAN TV NETWORKS TOO EXCEPT CTN'S 'JONI SHOW' AND VICTORY'S 'FLASH POINT' HAVE AGREED TO SUPPRESS THE TRUTH ABOUT VACCINE INJURY IN ORDER TO PROMOTE VACCINATIONS. REMEMBER, NO VACCINE CAN IMPROVE UPON NATURAL IMMUNITY FROM REPENTANCE AND YOU CAN'T GET RID OF PLAGUES BY VACCINATION BUT ONLY BY REPENTANCE FROM THE ABOMINABLE SINS OF ABORTION AND SAME SEX MARRIAGE.

RAPTURE RIPOFF I

The second coming of the Lord Jesus Christ really matters in New Testament theology as it is mentioned approximately 300 times in the New Testament or about once in every 25 verses.

There is not a single passage in the entire New Testament that clearly says that there is coming an immediate pre-tribulation rapture.

In fact, on page 69 of his book: NO FEAR OF THE STORM, DR. Tim LaHaye says**: 'one objection to the pre-tribulation rapture is that no one passage of scripture teaches the two aspects of his second coming separated by tribulation.'** So, this truth is well known. Yes, **the timing of the rapture has no scriptural support despite what many denominational Christians are taught**. It is not my purpose in this book to only attack this false doctrine but to also show that the people of God are not going to be removed from participating in the end time harvest of last days revival that is coming.

As you know **all revivals require repentance.** Repentance by grace and mercy have yet to work, so now we will see and experience shaking because without a great shaking there will not be the great repentance that is now needed.

The pre-tribulation rapture doctrine has produced a lot of laziness, slothfulness and plain indifference among God's people as to fulfilling the great commission. So we are about to see the book of Revelation come to life right before our eyes with us in it participating fully in what it describes.

I received the following bombastic revelation on October 12, 2020: it is known from the scriptures that this tribulation period is called 'The time of Jacob's Trouble'. As if the Great Tribulation was only for the Jews. From that our gentile ancestors got the anti-Semitic viewpoint that only the Jews will suffer tribulation but we gentiles will be rescued by pre-tribulation rapture.

This prejudicial view point was first formed with the help of the Adventist about the early 1830's. That time was a great time of serious religious persecution in early America. You might remember how that the Mormons, an American religious cult which began in New York state was persecuted all the way to Utah back then.

So, the pre-tribulation rapture is just anti-Semitic propaganda or hate speech. Anyway, **the main purpose of this false doctrine is to keep us from doing the exploits of winning souls for Christ by preaching the message of the cross as the great commission mandates.**

Former President Thomas Jefferson sent a letter containing the words 'separation of church and state' to reassure a Baptist church that they would have religious liberty in this new republic. Over a century later the Supreme Court of this republic used that same letter to throw prayer and Bible reading out of the public schools throughout America.

This was done despite the Constitution which says that Congress shall make no law regarding the establishment of a religion nor prohibiting the free exercise thereof. Of course, constitutional law forbade Congress from doing such but not the courts with activist judges.

Likewise, the churches of America have used letters which Saint Paul wrote to the Thessalonians about their resurrection, the antichrist and the end of days to assure them of peace and safety for now thanks to what was to become the pre-tribulation rapture. **When actually there is no Bible verse to substantiate any pre-tribulation rapture.**

While the Lord Jesus told his disciples in Matthew 24, Luke 21 and Mark 13 exactly how His second coming would happen. But the churches wanting to avoid unpleasantness like conflict liked the letters more than Jesus' first-hand witness which included tribulation.

For those of you into the veracity of letters you should know that Enoch, the seventh from Adam wrote in the first chapter of his book (that was excluded from the Bible by the elite because it was too supernatural) **that there would be no pre-tribulation rapture.** He made this observation long before Jesus ever came the first time. Now it is said that Enoch walked with God so much so that God took him home to heaven without him ever having to see his death. Apparently, God may have told him a few things about the future that we do not now know.

As it stands now I would much rather put confidence in the writings of Enoch than those of St. Paul. But the personal witness of the main character (Jesus) in any event in any court carries far more weight than any letters.

The second coming of the Lord Jesus Christ is mentioned about 300 times in the New Testament of your Bible. That means that this truth appears about once in every 25 verses. So its importance should be self evident. **Bad teaching about the second coming including a pre-tribulation rapture is causing a tremendous amount of damage to the body of Christ as it is imparting only 'the blessed hope' but fails to make adequate preparations for the tribulation and antichrist that precedes it.**

One of the leading points of disagreement concerning the letters of St. Paul to the Thessalonians concerns the word: 'air' as opposed to the words of various prophecies and the words of Jesus Himself about His coming again to the Mount of Olives. This bad English theology was adopted before the study of Greek words became common place. So most Christian people felt that coming in the air and coming to a mountain were two different things. But there is no Bible verse that says that Jesus is coming three times. Actually, as Jesus comes to the Mount of Olives He must pass through the air in order to reach the mountain. **So, this does not describe two different events but 'one and the same'.**

Excuse me, but the preceding conclusion was just a little bit of logic common to psychological reasoning. So, I'm on the right course in obeying God. But now I intend to use a few more Greek words.

Throughout the New Testament the Greek word: ('PAROUSIA') is constantly used in passages regarding the second coming of Jesus. The rapture will happen at the second coming ('PAROUSIA') or official state-visit of the Lord Jesus Christ, King of the Universe. **Thus, it cannot be a pre-tribulation rapture as it comes immediately after the end of the seven-year tribulation period according to Jesus in Matthew 24.**

Unfortunately, many denominations and churches require strict adherence to their particular doctrinal positions that are taught in their Bible schools and seminaries. So, I do not expect adequate respect for either Greek words or psychological reasoning. But in these last days it is absolutely imperative that we all use our brains to think for ourselves.

I am sure that all of you Christians have heard about revival and that it must soon happen. I remember that Leonard Ravenhill said in his book: Why Revival Tarries that **revival starts with repentance**. Along that line America needs to repent of ROE vs. WADE (Abortion) and needs to overturn the Affordable Care Act and Obama Care too.

As a man of God I have experiential knowledge as to how God looks at things. Since God is the creator, He considers the killing of His creation an insult to His Person.

Likewise, some like former Vice President Joe Biden feel that this Corona Virus must be cured to cover up his abortion policy before America can go back to work and return to normal.

Along that line may I submit additional facts from my chapter of **COVID 19 TRUTHS REVEALED:** COVID 19 is not a disease but a plague caused by sin, the sins of abortion and same sex marriage. Therefore, if Joe Biden really wants to solve this problem, he needs to close down all the abortion clinics. Making people wear masks is a deceptive afterthought because: only surgical masks worn by doctors' work and these reprobates that impregnated these lowlife women should have worn condoms instead. So now we all get to wear masks (they don't work) because they failed to wear condoms. How's that for social justice?

Likewise, before revival can happen, repentance must occur. Once this repentance does happen the body of Christ must be trained to be the army of God fit for God's service. And not fit to study a false doctrine as if it were designed to lead us on into the high calling of God.

Once one has a vision of Jesus the living Lord they become more interested in pleasing God than having the most pleasant theology like pre-tribulation rapture come into manifestation. And the best way to please God begins with repentance. And without a great shaking there will not be the great necessary repentance that is required.

This repentance is due because the vast majority of Christians in America today believe in the pre-tribulation rapture. Even though it is without Biblical support. Since grace and mercy have not worked to lead men to repentance for believing in this false doctrine therefore now we will experience shaking. **Too bad, immediately when any correction comes from God repent right away in order to avoid worse tribulation.**

This pre-tribulation rapture error has also caused another very serious problem. That is, as a result, most Christians are not preparing spiritually mentally, emotionally and physically for the end time events and happenings that the Lord Jesus mentioned in Matthew 24. Thus, this pre-tribulation false doctrine has produced a lot of laziness, slothfulness and indifference among God's people. So, if you are sitting around waiting for the pre-tribulation rapture to pull you out of your current situation you just might miss out on everything that God has planned for you right now in the area of doing exploits. As some have said that this is the greatest time of victory that the church has ever known is coming by the power of the Holy Spirit Who will shake this world to its core.

The Bible also speaks of a time of trouble that will take place immediately before the Lord Jesus returns. This period of time is referred to as The Great Tribulation or 'The Time of Jacob's Trouble'. From this we get the anti-Sematic viewpoint that the tribulation is only for the Jews and we gentiles get rescued by pre-tribulation rapture from it. So the pre-tribulation rapture is just anti-Sematic propaganda or hate speech.

Traditionally there are 4 main schools of timing regarding the rapture. The first one, most commonly believed by most Christians is the pre-tribulation rapture. Which means that before any tribulation at all the Lord Jesus is scheduled to come and rescue us from hard times.

The mid-tribulation view is the second one which is becoming more popular today.

The pre-wrath view is next and it too has gained in popularity.

The fourth view is the post-tribulation or Biblical view which is the only one that the Lord Jesus spoke of in Matthew 24.

Getting back to the first Greek word 'PAROUSIA' mentioned in Strong's Bible Dictionary we see in the King James Bible that this word is used 24 times in the New Testament and 16 of those times are about the second coming of the Lord Jesus. This word is also used in the rapture section of most Bibles (1 Thessalonians 4:14-17) as appears below: 1 Thessalonians 4 : 14 'FOR WE BELIEVE THAT JESUS DIED AND ROSE AGAIN, EVEN SO THEM ALSO WHICH SLEEP IN JESUS WILL GOD BRING WITH HIM'.

: 15 'FOR THIS WE SAY UNTO YOU BY THE WORD OF THE LORD, THAT WE WHICH ARE ALIVE AND REMAIN UNTO THE COMING ('PAROUSIA') OF THE LORD SHALL NOT PREVENT THEM WHICH ARE ASLEEP'.

: 16 'FOR THE LORD HIMSELF SHALL DECEND FROM HEAVEN WITH A SHOUT, AND THE VOICE OF THE ARCHANGEL, AND WITH THE TRUMP OF GOD: AND THE DEAD IN CHRIST SHALL RISE FIRST':

: 17 'THEN WE WHICH ARE ALIVE AND REMAIN SHALL BE CAUGHT UP TOGETHER WITH THEM IN THE CLOUDS TO MEET THE LORD IN THE AIR AND SO SHALL WE EVER BE WITH THE LORD'.

Now ('PAROUSIA') is also used in 1 Corinthians 15:21-23 which appears below. But first I must say that clouds indicate how the Lord travels, through the air without any airplanes or missiles. 'FOR SINCE BY MAN CAME DEATH, BY MAN CAME ALSO THE RESURRECTION OF THE

DEAD'. 'FOR AS IN ADAM ALL DIE, EVEN SO IN CHRIST SHALL ALL BE MADE ALIVE'. 'BUT EVERYMAN IN HIS OWN ORDER: CHRIST THE FIRST FRUITS: AFTERWORD THOSE THAT ARE CHRIST'S AT HIS COMING': ('PAROUSIA').

Later on, in the same chapter this is what 1 Corinthians 15:51-53 says: 'BEHOLD, I SHEW YOU A MYSTERY; WE SHALL NOT ALL SLEEP, BUT WE SHALL BE CHANGED', 'IN A MOMENT, IN THE TWINKLING OF AN EYE, AT THE LAST TRUMP: FOR THE TRUMPET SHALL SOUND, AND THE DEAD SHALL BE RAISED INCORRUPTIBLE, AND WE SHALL BE CHANGED'. 'FOR THIS CORRUPTIBLE MUST PUT ON INCORRUPTION, AND THIS MORTAL MUST PUT ON IMMORTALITY'.

In Matthew 24 we find the Greek word 'PAROUSIA' again.

'AND AS HE SAT UPON THE MOUNT OF OLIVES, THE DISCIPLES CAME UNTO HIM PRIVATELY, SAYING, TELL US, WHEN SHALL THESE THINGS BE?

AND WHAT SHALL BE THE SIGN OF THY COMING ('PAROUSIA'), AND OF THE END OF THE WORLD'?

First the Lord Jesus discusses personal deception regarding Him by saying: 'LET NO MAN DECIEVE YOU, FOR MANY SHALL COME IN MY NAME SAYING I AM CHRIST AND SHALL DECIEVE MANY', (Matthew 24:5). Of course, after this Jesus spends much of the rest of the chapter describing those things which must take place prior to His return. (Notice also that He is not coming secretly). 'FOR AS THE LIGHTNING COMES OUT OF THE EAST, AND SHINETH EVEN UNTO THE WEST; SO, SHALL THE COMING ('PAROUSIA') OF THE SON OF MAN BE', (Matthew 24:27).

We are also told that His coming ('PAROUSIA') will happen 'IMMEDIATELY AFTER THE TRIBULATION OF THOSE DAYS SHALL THE SUN BE DARKENED, AND THE MOON SHALL NOT GIVE HER LIGHT, AND THE STARS SHALL FALL FROM HEAVEN, AND THE POWERS OF THE HEAVEN SHALL BE SHAKEN':

'AND THEN SHALL APPEAR THE SIGN OF THE SON OF MAN IN HEAVEN:

AND THEN SHALL ALL THE TRIBES OF THE EARTH MOURN', 'AND THEY SHALL SEE THE SON OF MAN COMING IN THE CLOUDS OF HEAVEN WITH POWER AND GREAT GLORY', (Mathew 24:29&30).'AND HE SHALL SEND HIS ANGELS WITH A

GREAT SOUND OF A TRUMPET, AND THEY SHALL GATHER TOGETHER HIS ELECT FROM THE FOUR WINDS, FROM ONE END OF HEAVEN TO THE OTHER'.

Obviously these sayings of Jesus do not fit in with the pre-tribulation rapture viewpoint. But one point needs to be made. The Lord Jesus as the head of His disciples has the absolute right to tell them just how He is going to return. And they have the duty to believe whatsoever He says.

In I Thessalonians 4, I Corinthians 15 and Matthew 24 all say that the rapture happens at the 'PAROUSIA' as I have now proven.

Here is more from Matthew 24:37-41

37. 'BUT AS THE DAYS OF NOAH WERE, SO SHALL THE COMING ('PAROUSIA') OF THE SON OF MAN BE'.

38. 'FOR AS IN THE DAYS THAT WERE BEFORE THE FLOOD THEY WERE EATING AND DRINKING, MARRYING AND GIVING IN MARRIAGE, UNTIL THE DAY THAT NOE ENTERED INTO THE ARK',

39. 'AND KNEW NOT UNTIL THE FLOOD CAME, AND TOOK THEM ALL AWAY; SO, SHALL ALSO THE COMING ('PAROUSIA') OF THE SON OF MAN BE'

According to the Lord Jesus, speaking personally to His disciples, His coming ('PAROUSIA') occurs 'IMMEDIATELY AFTER THE TRIBULATION OF THOSE DAYS'.

He goes on to state what must happen before He comes again. This information is mainly given not just to fulfill prophecy but to enable the people of God to avoid any deception and get prepared to do exploits.

The Apostle Paul tells us once again that the rapture happens at the ('PAROUSIA'). And Paul lists for us certain events that must happen beforehand in II Thessalonians 2:

3. 'LET NO MAN DECIEVE YOU BY ANY MEANS: FOR THAT DAY SHALL NOT COME, EXCEPT THERE COME A FALLING AWAY FIRST, AND THAT MAN OF SIN BE REVEALED, THE SON OF PERDITION'.

I believe that the falling away happens because the pre-tribulation rapture fails to occur and most Christians find themselves unprepared for any tribulation or hard times at all or for doing any exploits like winning souls as it was never preached to them.

4. 'WHO OPPOSES AND EXALTS HIMSELF ABOVE ALL THAT IS CALLED GOD, OR THAT IS WORSHIPPED: SO THAT HE AS GOD SITS IN THE TEMPLE OF GOD, SHOWING HIMSELF THAT HE IS GOD'.

Thus, the apostle Paul states that the antichrist goes into the temple to show himself off to be God. Obviously then these few verses in second Thessalonians prove that at least 3 things must happen before Jesus returns, II Thessalonians 2:3 **'THERE MUST COME A FALLING AWAY' first,** Then, in verse 3, '**THE MAN OF SIN MUST BE REVEALED'**, then 3 in verse 4, **'HE MUST SHOW HIMSELF TO BE GOD IN THE TEMPLE OF GOD'.** So, the modern church propaganda that Jesus could come at any time utilized by many denominational evangelists to supposedly win souls by scaring them into a quick confession of faith is both disingenuous and fraudulent.

Matthew 24 records Jesus telling us that the manifestation of the abomination of desolation spoken of by Daniel the prophet begins the period of the great tribulation after which the rapture takes place at the coming ('PAROUSIA') of the Lord, (Matthew 24:29-31).

Going back to II Thessalonians 2 the apostle Paul tells us that the final confrontation between Jesus and the antichrist comes at the 'PAROUSIA'.

8. 'AND THEN SHALL THE WICKED BE REVEALED WHOM THE LORD SHALL CONSUME WITH THE SPIRIT OF HIS MOUTH, AND SHALL DESTROY WITH THE BRIGHTNESS OF HIS COMING ('PAROUSIA'). The brightness of His coming kills. That's why 'NO ONE CAN SEE GOD AND LIVE', (Exodus 33:20).

We also know from Revelation 19 and elsewhere that the final confrontation between the Lord Jesus and the antichrist comes at the very end of the tribulation.

In all of these passages that we have looked at so far, we are told that the 'PAROUSIA' or rapture takes place at the end of the tribulation, (Matthew 24 and II Thessalonians 2).

Before this event or after we see the abomination of desolation the Lord Jesus tells us in Matthew chapter 24 exactly what is to happen.

This period of time is called: 'The great tribulation, or in the Greek the word: 'THIPSIS' Example, Matthew 24:

29. 'IMMEDIATELY AFTER THE TRIBULATION ('THLIPSIS') OF THOSE DAYS SHALL THE SUN BE DARKENED, AND THE MOON SHALL NOT GIVE HER LIGHT, AND THE STARS SHALL

FALL FROM HEAVEN, AND THE POWERS OF THE HEAVENS SHALL BE SHAKEN':

30. 'AND THEN SHALL APPEAR THE SIGN OF THE SON OF MAN IN HEAVEN:

AND THEN SHALL ALL THE TRIBES OF THE EARTH MOURN, AND THEY SHALL SEE THE SON OF MAN COMING IN THE CLOUDS OF HEAVEN WITH POWER AND GREAT GLORY'.

In verse 29 of Matthew 24 we see where tribulation in the King James Version is translated from 'THLIPSIS' in the Greek.

As we see no rapture can come before the 'TRIBULATION OF THOSE DAYS'. **But the rapture does come immediately after the tribulation just as your Bible declares.**

When we review the other Gospels we see these exact events recorded in Mark 13:

24. 'BUT IN THOSE DAYS, AFTER THAT TRIBULATION, THE SUN SHALL BE DARKENED, AND THE MOON SHALL NOT GIVE HER LIGHT,

25. 'AND THE STARS OF HEAVEN SHALL FALL, AND THE POWERS THAT ARE IN HEAVEN SHALL BE SHAKEN'.

26. 'AND THEN SHALL THEY SEE THE SON OF MAN COMING IN THE CLOUDS WITH GREAT POWER AND GLORY'.

27. AND THEN SHALL HE SEND HIS ANGELS, AND SHALL GATHER TOGETHER HIS ELECT FROM THE FOUR WINDS, FROM THE UTTERMOST PART OF THE EARTH TO THE UTTERMOST PART OF HEAVEN'.

Here there is no TRUMPET mentioned but it is still describing the same event as what we read in Matthew 24. Here is the same event as described in Luke 21:

25. 'AND THERE SHALL BE SIGNS IN THE SUN, AND IN THE MOON, AND IN THE STARS; AND UPON THE EARTH DISTRESS OF NATIONS, WITH PURPLEXITY; THE SEA AND THE WAVES ROARING';

26. 'MEN'S HEARTS FAILING THEM FOR FEAR, AND FOR LOOKING AFTER THOSE THINGS WHICH ARE COMING ON THE EARTH: FOR THE POWERS OF HEAVEN SHALL BE SHAKEN'.

27. 'AND THEN SHALL THEY SEE THE SON OF MAN COMING IN A CLOUD WITH POWER AND GREAT GLORY'.

Here also a trumpet is not mentioned. Now when you talk to those people who believe in the pre-tribulation rapture, they are not able to take you to a single verse in the Bible that says that the rapture will happen before the tribulation because no such Bible verse exists.

If there was going to be a pre-tribulation rapture the Lord Jesus would have told us about it when he listed that things we should watch for. It would have been at the beginning of Matthew 24, Mark 13 and Luke 21 instead of at the end of those chapters.

The Lord Jesus was very clear in telling us that the rapture will happen 'AFTER THE TRIBULATION OF THOSE DAYS'.

I feel a revelation coming on and must say this: For those of you who may have forgotten, the Lord Jesus is the pre-emanate One. 'AND HE IS THE HEAD OF THE BODY, THE CHURCH: WHO IS THE BEGINNING, THE FIRST BORN FROM THE DEAD; THAT IN ALL THINGS HE MIGHT HAVE THE PREEMINENCE', (Colossians 1:18). 'YE CALL ME MASTER AND LORD AND YE SAY WELL FOR SO I AM', (John 13:13). 'THEREFORE LET ALL THE HOUSE OF ISRAEL KNOW ASSUREDLY, THAT GOD HATH MADE THIS SAME JESUS, WHOM YOU HAVE CRUCIFIED, BOTH LORD AND CHRIST', (Acts 1:36), 'AFTER THIS I LOOKED, AND BEHOLD, A DOOR WAS OPENED IN HEAVEN: AND THE FIRST VOICE WHICH I HEARD WAS AS IT WERE A TRUMPET TALKING WITH ME; WHICH SAID, COME UP HITHER, AND I WILL SHEW THEE THINGS WHICH MUST BE HERAFTER'. 'AND IMMEDIATELY I WAS IN THE SPIRIT: AND, BEHOLD, A THRONE WAS SET IN HEAVEN, AND ONE SAT UPON THE THRONE'. 'AND HE THAT SAT WAS TO LOOK UPON LIKE A JASPER AND A SARDINE STONE, AND THERE WAS A RAINBOW ROUND ABOUT THE THRONE, IN SIGHT LIKE UNTO AN EMERALD'. 'AND ROUND ABOUT THE THRONE WERE FOUR AND TWENTY SEATS AND UPON THE SEATS I SAW FOUR AND TWENTY ELDERS SITTING CLOTHED IN WHITE RAINMENT: AND THEY HAD ON THEIR HEADS CROWNS OF GOLD'. 'AND OUT OF THE THRONE PROCEEDED LIGHTING AND THUNDERINGS AND VOICES: AND THERE WERE SEVEN LAMPS OF FIRE BURNING BEFORE THE THRONE, WHICH ARE THE SEVEN SPIRITS OF GOD'. 'AND BEFORE THE THRONE THERE WAS A SEA OF GLASS, LIKE UNTO CRYSTAL: AND IN THE MIDST OF THE THRONE, AND ROUND ABOUT THE THRONE,

WERE FOUR BEASTS FULL OF EYES BEFORE AND BEHIND'. 'AND THE FIRST BEAST WAS LIKE A LION, AND THE SECOND BEAST LIKE A CALF, AND THE THIRD BEAST HAD A FACE LIKE A MAN, AND THE FOURTH BEAST WAS LIKE A FLYING EAGLE'. 'AND THE FOUR BEASTS HAD EACH OF THEM SIX WINGS ABOUT HIM AND THEY WERE FULL OF EYES WITHIN: AND THEY REST NOT DAY OR NIGHT SAYING; HOLY, HOLY, HOLY LORD GOD ALMIGHTY, WHICH WAS, AND IS, AND IS TO COME', (Revelation 4:1-8). This is the typical greeting of the Lord Jesus Christ, The Son of God.

I remember that at the transfiguration when Peter wanted to get into a building program, the Father interrupted saying: 'THIS IS MY BELOVED SON IN WHOM I AM WELL PLEASED, HEAR YE HIM', (Matthew 17:5). This should prove that Jesus has the first word and the last word on this or any other issue. 'I AM ALPHA AND OMEGA, THE BEGINNING AND THE END, SAITH THE LORD, WHICH WAS, AND IS, AND IS TO COME, THE ALMIGHTY', (Revelation 1:8).

Nevertheless, I still want to review Paul's message in I Thessalonians 1-4 again. I Thessalonians 4:

14. 'FOR IF WE BELIEVE THAT JESUS DIED AND ROSE AGAIN. EVEN SO THEM ALSO WHICH SLEEP IN JESUS WILL GOD BRING WITH HIM'.

15. 'FOR THIS WE SAY UNTO YOU BY THE WORD OF THE LORD, THAT WE WHICH ARE ALIVE AND REMAIN UNTO THE COMING OF THE LORD SHALL NOT PREVENT THEM WHICH ARE ASLEEP'.

16. 'FOR THE LORD HIMSELF SHALL DECEND FROM HEAVEN WITH A SHOUT, WITH THE VOICE OF THE ARCH ANGEL, AND WITH THE TRUMP OF GOD: AND THE DEAD IN CHRIST SHALL RISE FIRST'.

17. 'THEN WE WHICH ARE ALIVE AND REMAIN SHALL BE CAUGHT UP TOGETHER WITH THEM IN THE CLOUDS, TO MEET THE LORD IN THE AIR: AND SO SHALL WE EVER BE WITH THE LORD'.

First, I feel another revelation coming on: this one reveals why clouds accompany the divine ones. If you remember right after the creation, God used to walk with Adam and Eve nude in the cool of the day. At that time before the fall of man there was no such thing as sexual sin. And God liked to show off His creation as being exact replicas of Himself. But after the fall of man everyone had to wear clothes. Adam and Eve wore fig leaves and then skins and God wore clouds as clothes. I hope this adds to your understanding of these verses.

Getting back to Matthew 24 we see the same words: Matthew 24:

29. 'IMMEDIATELY AFTER THE TRIBULATION OF THOSE DAYS, SHALL THE SUN BE DARKENED, AND THE MOON SHALL NOT GIVE HER LIGHT, AND THE STARS SHALL FALL FROM HEAVEN, AND THE POWERS OF THE HEAVENS SHALL BE SHAKEN':

30. 'AND THEN SHALL APPEAR THE SIGN OF THE SON OF MAN IN HEAVEN: AND THEN SHALL ALL THE TRIBES OF THE EARTH MOURN, AND THEY SHALL SEE THE SON OF MAN COMING IN THE CLOUDS OF HEAVEN WITH POWER AND GREAT GLORY'.

31. 'AND HE SHALL SEND HIS ANGELS WITH A GREAT SOUND OF A TRUMPET, AND THEY SHALL GATHER TOGETHER HIS ELECT FROM THE FOUR WINDS, FROM ONE END OF HEAVEN TO THE OTHER'.

The similarities here are very obvious: First Jesus comes in or with the clouds, then, second, there is the sounding of a great trumpet, and third, there is a worldwide gathering of all believers unto Jesus.

Now let's look at a few more Greek words. The Greek word translated for clouds is 'NEPHELE'. This word appears in I Thessalonians 4:17 and in Matthew 24:30.

Another Greek word for trump or trumpet is the Greek word: 'SALPIGX' which is also used in both 1 Thessalonians 4 and Matthew 24.

Another Greek word is: 'OURANOS' which is translated heaven in I Thessalonians 4:16 and in Matthew 24:30, 31. Since they both describe the exact same event they must be simultaneous which describes both the rapture and the second coming which comes at the end of the tribulation.

So since these same Greek words are used to describe the same events in both instances (the rapture and the second coming) it must be concluded by any reasonable person that these events are one and the same and not one separated from the other by a seven years of tribulation.

For those that insist that the scriptures indicate two different events, logic itself indicates that if two events equal in this case the same event with the same Greek words describing it, then they must at least be equal to each other if not one and the same event.

From here other theologians and scholars like to discuss the last trump in I Corinthians 15:52 and the rapture appearing in the book of Revelation but since I have already made my point, I'll now go on to submitting to you the psychological proof that I spoke about in my introduction.

While I was going to Fuller Seminary I also worked as a volunteer Christian rehabilitation drug counselor for New Start which was a new drug rehabilitation program overseen by a pastor I knew from our Jesus Movement church in Daytona Beach, Florida. My immediate supervisor there was a young Christian psychiatrist. This guy could prescribe medicine but did not do so as he was also a homeopathic physician.

I mentioned that he was also a Christian, but a peculiar kind that I did not know of since the original Jesus Movement in Southern California. As all medical doctors he could prescribe pills, but did not do so, as he felt that the only pill one ever needed was the gospel. Likewise, although he could counsel he did not do so. He felt that the Lord Jesus could tell people what they needed to hear and obey. He believed: 'TO CAST ALL YOUR CARE UPON HIM (Christ) AS HE CARES FOR YOU', (I Peter 5:7).

Most of our young people being rehabilitated just like in the original Jesus Movement did not cry on his shoulder about their personal problems as they didn't seem to have any question that they had been delivered from drugs and the unconverted lifestyle.

He also felt that most psychiatric illnesses and addictions were not really mental health issues at all but brain health problems from a vitamin deficiency (like low vitamin D) or some bad habit (like smoking) that evidenced the lack of proper socialization. The failure to understand that: 'ONCE I BECAME A MAN, I PUT AWAY CHILDISH THINGS', (I Cor. 13:1). And the inability to understand that deliverance meant total and all-consuming deliverance.

As most Christian rehabilitation programs, we were into the doing of devotions, prayer and Bible reading. But he, as a physician was mainly into health problems. He liked to keep our young people in the rehabilitation program busy overcoming smoking. At first, we thought this was strange, but he explained more about it to us. 'YOUR BODY IS THE TEMPLE OF THE HOLY GHOST'. 'AND WHOSOEVER DEFILES THIS TEMPLE, HIM WILL GOD DESTROY', (I Corinthians 3:17). It seems that cigarettes are some of the most toxic substances that you can buy. Cigarettes burn some 7,000 chemicals which are poisonous, here is just 10 of them: Acetic acid, Ammonia, Arsenic, Benzene. Butane, Cadmium, Formaldehyde, Methanol, Tar and Toluene.

It's common knowledge that the tobacco industry still promotes smoking despite the Surgeon General's warning against it. And even encourages psychiatric patients with schizophrenia can benefit by self- medicating with cigarettes. So today 80% of those with schizophrenia smoke as if smoking were the smoke signal of approaching reprobate.

Before I go on to reveal some more psychological truths I must say that I also have a college degree in psychology. After I graduated from Fuller Seminary in 1985, I went on to another graduate school to earn my counseling credential. I wanted to become a professional counselor in hearing and realizing that 'wheelchairs do not inspire faith' and that no church job would be available to me anyway because of discrimination so I went on to another graduate school to earn my counseling credential.

As you know prayer was removed from the public schools in 1962. About the same time President Kennedy was assassinated in 1963 the reading of the Bible was also expelled from school. But psychological truths remained under many different headings. So now let's look at the rapture from its psychological perspective to confirm my views as spoken by the Lord Jesus in Matthew 24 and to better understand that, let's first layout a few psychological truths.

According to the psychoanalytic view, the personality consists of three main systems; the id, the ego and the superego. These are the names for various psychological processes in counseling psychology which operate one's personality functions. The id is the biological component. The ego is the psychological component of compromise and the superego was the spiritual component but now without God it is considered the social component as if we could have a righteous family that treats everyone well without God.

I have just received another revelation about this next issue: That is that God (in this case Jesus) is the energy Being of supremacy. The Freudian perspective considered humans to be energy systems whose personality dynamics consist of ways in which psychic energy is distributed to the id, ego and superego. One system gains control over the others according to what the person has absorbed according to their unique experiences in this life. And behavior as such is determined by psychic energy alone. **Therefore, God can still regulate behavior.** Also, God still has an ego as you can see from Revelations 4:1-8 where He sits on the throne and is worshipped too.

Of course, one dangerous infidel who advised President Trump to shut down America's economy in order to avoid millions of deaths was the medically insane counselor, Dr. Fauci who got false information from the communist doctors of the World Health Organization.

This entire issue brings to light a very important point: that is if God has called you to exercise your specific gift for the benefit of mankind always stay with this commission never let the advice of others distract you, you see what it has cost President Trump.

I remember from The Jesus Movement how that the anointing or what the psychologist like to call psychic energy imparts the needed spark that results in sudden change from bad to good. This is why the ex-dopers in The Jesus Movement insisted that new converts also get baptized in the Holy Spirit. This was not a salvation requirement but a congregational one for ex-dopers to get the necessary spark from the Spirit of God to ensure transformation to a new, happy life, free from sin and addictions. This is why I became a Christian counselor and a drug counselor.

But there has also been another rapid change due to this COVID 19. Therefore I am including my **'COVID 19 TRUTHS REVEALED'** chapter after **'PESTILENCES'** that I wrote for another prophetic book. This came to my mind as I was watching the last presidential debate where both candidates seemed to be unaware of the main cause of COVID 19 and how to heal Americans from it. In my chapter on this topic I will show how that COVID 19 is not just another disease requiring a vaccine but a plague caused by sin which God can take away or remove according to II Chronicles 7:

13. 'IF I SHUT-UP HEAVEN THAT THERE BE NO RAIN', (California and Colorado should take note of this), OR IF I COMMAND THE LOCUST TO DEVOUR THE LAND, OR IF I SEND PESTILENCE AMONG MY PEOPLE', (like COVID19).

14. 'IF MY PEOPLE, WHICH ARE CALLED BY MY NAME, SHALL HUMBLE THEMSELVES, AND PRAY, AND SEEK MY FACE, AND TURN FROM THEIR WICKED WAYS, THEN WILL I HEAR FROM HEAVEN, AND WILL FORGIVE THEIR SIN, AND HEAL THEIR LAND'.

Most evangelical theologians who advised President Trump were pre-tribulation rapture apostates and did not believe that this COVID 19 could possibly be a plague sent from God for the sins of abortion and same sex marriage. But that's just what it was and is and someday soon someone in political power needs to admit it and repent for it or God will strengthen and increase this plague or send worse tribulation our way.

After that the problem of fracking for oil and 'climate change' was addressed. Of course, Biden being a politician lied about his stand on this issue. He really wants to close down the oil industry and all fossil fuels in order to begin his 'green new deal' solar enterprise. He has not told us that such will cost millions of jobs and trillions of dollars. I hope all the states that produce oil like Pennsylvania, Texas, Oklahoma and Alaska were listening to that debate. And the states like Louisiana which refine oil and have oil pipelines running through them also noticed this lie.

In fact, untruthfulness lies at the heart of all too many of the problems we face as individuals, as a nation, and as a global community of nations.

Spiritually dealing with lies can be solved by the Spirit of Truth.

But the psychological method would rather detect deception by polygraph examination. In which various nervous responses can supposedly detect whether or not one is telling the truth. However, the truth is that people do lie, and they lie a lot. Some behavior research suggests that on the average, we lie about ten times in every 24-hour period. That means that there is very little respect for truth and even less for God. Anyone will lie to you about anything if he believes it's in his own best interest to do so.

Unfortunately, there is no such thing as a human lie detector, neither is there any such thing as a mechanical lie detector that always works. But there is one way to be partially correct if you want to know if someone is lying: that is you need to ignore and not process any of their truthful statements. Otherwise you will wind up swallowing their bad diagnosis, interpretation, or viewpoint along with whatever good that they say.

The reverse of this is also true, take for example President Trump, people have been so turned off to his manners, language like a construction worker and unorthodox texting that they failed to recognize any good which he had done. I'm sure that you have also heard about white supremacy and how it was attributed to President Trump. But what the news media has failed to mention is President Trump's aid to historical Black colleges and universities, plus his criminal justice reform, establishment of opportunity zones in Black neighborhoods and record minority employment.

Another very interesting point was made in a book I was examining in the library. I was attracted to it because as a psychological book it also quoted scripture which is very unusual for any secular book. This new book was entitled: 'The Information Age' by two college professors. In it they state: 'The gospel of John tells us that Jesus was brought before the Roman Prefect of Judea, Pontius Pilate, after the Jewish leaders of Jerusalem accused Him of attempting to usurp Roman power and declare Himself a king. But when Pilate questioned Him, Jesus demurred. He did not proclaim Himself king but merely a witness to truth'.

This of course left an out for Pontius Pilate who went on to question Jesus about what is truth? You see, in the ancient world under the influence of Greek philosophies, especially the upper class, all believed truth to be relative or subjective except for mathematics. And today most believe in relative truth; that is my truth, your truth and his truth. But there is no universal truth for all supposedly. Unfortunately, this type of response is equally a part of the long history of those in political power. Right now, I feel another prophecy coming on. This one is about dreams.

Dreams where held in very high esteem in the ancient world. Back in those days no one could say I had a pizza dream. Because there was no fast food back then. So, Pilate washed his hands of this murder, just as his wife had said her dream told her. Back then all believe that it was possible for them to hear from God via dreams. But today most Protestants believe from their false doctrine that God only speaks to sinners about their need for repentance. But the prophet Joel said: 'AND IT SHALL COME TO PASS AFTERWARD THAT I SHALL POUR OUT MY SPIRIT UPON ALL FLESH AND YOUR SONS AND YOUR DAUGHTERS SHALL PROPHECY AND YOUR OLD MEN SHALL DREAM DREAMS, 'Joel 2:28

The authors of this book then go on to tell us why real truth according to the ancient Greek skeptics is questionable at best as we can never truly know anything about this world or even if there are truths out there to know. This fatalistic idea was also adopted by the 18th century philosopher David Hume. Which he called: 'the problem of induction.'

He said that since the sun will eventually run out of hydrogen gas to fuel it, it will explode in upon itself and take the earth with it. So then this fatalism cancels all truths man may have discovered. So, Hume concluded that we cannot really know anything about this world. Thus, science cannot always be right as 'WHETHER THERE BE PROPHECIES, THEY SHALL FAIL', (I Corinthians 13:8 & 9). 'FOR WE KNOW IN PART AND PROPHECY IN PART'.

Apparently, we do care about the truth of our beliefs which enable us to live successfully in this world. **What we strongly believe to be true determines the choices we make in this life.** That's why it's important to get rid of false beliefs in order to fulfil the will of God for our lives.

One major false belief is the deception among pre-tribulation rapture Christians that God will take away from the earth both the Holy Spirit and the church before the tribulation begins. If that were true then how could millions of people be saved during the seven years of tribulation? 'AFTER

THIS I BEHELD, AND, LO, A GREAT MULTITUDE WHICH NO MAN COULD NUMBER OF ALL NATIONS AND KINDREDS AND PEOPLE, AND TONGUES, STOOD BEFORE THE THRONE, AND BEFORE THE LAMB,.....', (Revelations 7:9). This would be the time of the great awakening revival. 'THESE ARE THEY WHICH COME OUT OF GREAT TRIBULATION', AND HAVE WASHED THEIR ROBES, AND MADE THEM WHITE IN THE BLOOD OF THE LAMB', (Revelations 7:14). So if you're 'pigging out' at the marriage supper of the Lamb. Your supper appointment resulting from this pre-tribulation rapture has just caused you to miss out on doing any exploits (like saving any souls) for the great evangelical awakening.

But if the Holy Ghost were to be taken out from the earth too then no one could be saved: As it is written: 'NOT BY WORKS OF RIGHTEOUSNESS WHICH WE HAVE DONE. BUT ACCORDING TO HIS MERCY HE SAVED US, BY THE WASHING OF REGENERATION, AND RENEWAL OF THE HOLY GHOST', (Titus 3:5).

Another one of these false Christian beliefs involves rescuing the homeless. When the homeless would much rather have their cigarettes and their booze than a monthly house or car payment along with other responsibilities. Before the homeless squatted on American cities with the stench of public defecation there were the infidels of public spiritual infestation from the Unification Church, Moonies, Children of God, Hare Krishna and other infidels with backslidden and nominal Christians now.

Back in the days of the Jesus Movement we usually dealt with religious cults by simply laying our hands on them and praying for them. This way the Spirit of God on us would come on them. And they would become so shocked that we would not need to argue false doctrine out of them. As we had a strong Pentecostal prayer base behind us.

This helped a great deal as Moonies and other weird religious groups were also exploiting American kids for financial gain. Those who joined these weird religious groups were expected to donate to them all their personal possessions including stereos, musical instruments and cars.

Then the kids were expected to do fundraising activities. Which involved the selling of flowers, American flags, fortune cookies, candles, handkerchiefs, sunglasses and other stuff for 'charity'. This proved to be a method for these religious parasites to feed on the idealistic feelings of American kids.

Perhaps their worst false teaching was about becoming their disciple by rejecting, renouncing and defaming their parents. By calling them on the phone and telling them that they were evil and now they have found a better and more spiritual home.

To disrespect your parents is very dangerous as it may limit your lifespan. The first commandment with promises says: 'HONOR YOUR FATHER AND YOUR MOTHER THAT YOUR DAYS MAY BE LONG UPON THE LAND WHICH THE LORD YOUR GOD GIVES YOU', (Exodus 20:12).

All of this added up to what the professional cult deprogrammers term as the same indoctrination as the North Koreans used on prisoners of war. Most passivizes didn't like this deprogramming and felt it was too harsh. But you recognize evil as needing to be burned thus 'You fight fire with fire'.

But today most churches do not recognize evil nor have any Pentecostal prayer base that works, especially where deliverance is concerned. This is very important because most of these people were demon possessed as they only speak in a monotone, have a blank stare in their eyes, as if they were focusing on something far away, wore fake smiles, had no sense of humor or spontaneity, but always focus on themselves as if they were better than anyone else.

They engage in false positive confessions by chanting earthly concepts of a secular nature. They never praise Jesus or God. And make no mention of the things of God, or His creations or His will. They chant egotistical sayings like this:

I am my own best friend.
I enjoy my own company.
I spend time alone every day.
I enjoy getting to know myself.
I have no need of drama.
I have peace.
I am responsible for my own happiness.
I enjoy nature, relaxation and meditation.
I cultivate my inner sanctuary.
I am grounded in the present moment.
I have no mental disorders.
I can reason and recognize truth.
I am comfortable with myself.
I enjoy the silence of my mind.
I have plenty of time.

I allow myself to spend time doing nothing.
I can find safe harbors for me.
I am not rushed for anything.
I have enough money and time to spend it.
I am in the right place at the right time doing the right thing.
I have no need to procrastinate.
I love myself unconditionally.
I am worthy.
I am beautiful.
I am perfect just as I am.
I am free from entanglements.
I nourish myself with healthy food every day.
I enjoy giving myself to others.
I accept things I cannot change.
I am honest, trustworthy and kind.
I am reliable and helpful.
I deserve to be loved and liked.
I let go of toxic relationship.
I enjoy meeting new people.
I only attract positive people to my life.
I am not governed by bad moods or bad thoughts.
I trust people as my new friends.
I am friendly and hold no grudges or suspicions.
I take an active interest in others.
I take the time to put a smile on everyone's face.
I do what I can to help the less fortunate.
I let go of bad feelings from the past and focus on present possibilities.
I am positive, connected and do express love to all.
I am non-judgmental and forgiving.
I forgive myself and others as needed.
I accept mistakes as a part of being human.
I am kind and gentle toward everyone I meet.
I see what I can do to contribute to worthy causes.
I have no need to bully anyone.
I hold no shame or guilt.
I use positive language.
I abstain from gossip and character assassination.
I give and receive compliments.

I give others the benefit of any doubt.
I move from surviving to thriving.
I am grateful for my mind, body and spirit.
I treat life as the ultimate gift.
I sincerely appreciate whatever support I get.
I thank people often.
I pay my bills on time.
I appreciate all forms of life on this planet.
I focus on what I have to give.
I honor all that is good about me.
I am grateful for my past.

Today of course without deliverances we argue and debate with those who make these egotistical positive confessions about themselves especially if they are non-Christian and not a member of our social group. The easiest copout is to send such deranged infidels to counseling. Usually such only fills them with psychological theories of behavior modification and no real help at all unless they encounter a Christian counselor like me. Or better yet, Jesus the Counselor, Savior and Lord Who delivers one from evil

Since they obviously lie a lot, by adopting Christian values as their own, one major reason why the defense in court insists upon the exclusion of witnesses in any criminal persecution is because people like to act in 'group-think'. There are even 'groupies' who do not believe in a personal relationship with Christ like The Disciples of Christ. Liars like to have plenty of support for their false testimony. The first two issues discussed here; Rapture and The Second Coming both have to do with our group meeting with the Lord Jesus Christ when He comes again.

You may not be a 'groupie', but still be a believer. Such a case implies your individual ascent to the ethereal or the eternal life of personal resurrection. But before any personal glorified state is achieved you must die. 'IT IS APPOINTED UNTO MAN ONCE TO DIE', (Hebrews 9:27).

There are many things in this life that could result in your death or personal meeting with God:

Drowning as a child in your family's swimming pool.
Having a heavy article like a bookcase fall on you.
Having an unfortunate stroke.
Being drowned by a title wave.
Having a wild animal kill you.

Dying in a school bus accident as a student.
Drowning in a flood.
Being bullied to death at school.
Eating falsely labeled poison.
Over dosing on a street drug.
Falling off your bike and traffic running over you.
Being bit by a venomous snake.
Having a swarm of wasps, bees or hornets sting you to death.
Being killed in an auto accident.
Being shot by a 'drive by' in your own neighborhood.
Being killed as a teenager in a motorcycle accident.
Falling off the roof of your home.
Being electrocuted by a faulty appliance.
Being shot by policeman engaged in false arrest.
Burning to death in a forest fire.
Slipping and falling in the tub and busting your head.
Tripping over an extension cord in your home.
Catching a horrible plague like COVID 19.

Let's face it; when you die you go to meet God and then your judgment begins: 'IT IS APPOINTED UNTO MAN ONCE TO DIE AND AFTER THAT THE JUDGMENT', (Hebrews 9:27).

Everyone both saint and sinner will face both death and judgment. The grandeurs idea that pre-tribulation raptured Christians will be 'pigging out' at the marriage supper of the lamb while the rest of us are tribulating is as false as the tooth fairy. Most people need to realize that Jesus coming again will be like that of a dentist that they do not know with a drill called tribulation that hurts. That's why all the tribes on earth will mourn.

RAPTURE RIPPOFF II

The other day while I was trying to watch some daytime Christian TV the Spirit of God interrupted my desires by telling me that I had another prophetic book to write to be called Rapture Rip-off II, to warn the body of Christ to disregard the dispensational delusion of the pre-tribulation rapture in order to warn them about what was coming before any rapture occurs. **Because most Christian TV preachers being dispensationalist are going on to teach mistaken End Time truths from Revelation without ever repenting from having taught the false doctrine of the pre-tribulation rapture.** To most Christians this issue about the pre-tribulation rapture seems to be an immaterial matter of opinion, but to God, He does not like His truth circumvented by error. Especially error which discredits His word and says what He didn't say.

Moreover you must remember, that the book of Revelation pronounces a curse upon those who add to it, 'FOR I TESTIFY UNTO EVERYMAN WHO HEARETH THE WORDS OF THIS BOOK: IF ANYMAN SHALL ADD UNTO THESE THINGS GOD SHALL ADD UNTO HIM THE PLAGUES THAT ARE WRITTEN IN THIS BOOK'.(Revelation 22:18). Could that be why so many modern dispensational Christians are coming down with COVID 19 too, or should we expect another worse plague after this COVID 19 thanks to these deceived Christians. Then I remembered that God also said that: 'JUDGMENT BEGINS AT THE HOUSE OF GOD', (I Peter 4:17). Could that also include other 'acts of God' like the tornados in Kentucky, a Bible belt state? So I am starting this prophetic book with these judgments first coming to the Christian community.

There is not a single passage in the entire New Testament that clearly says that there is coming an immediate pre-tribulation rapture. In fact on page 69 of his book: NO FEAR OF THE STORM, DR. Tim LaHaye, a famous theologian and Bible professor says: **'one objection to the pre-tribulation rapture is that no one passage of scripture teaches the two aspects of his second coming separated by tribulation.'**

So, this truth is well known and is brought out in my chapter called Rapture Rip-off 1. Yes, the timing of the rapture has no scriptural support despite what many denominational Christians are taught. It is not my purpose in this book to only attack this false doctrine but to also show that the people of God are not going to be removed from participating in the end time harvest of last days revival that is coming because of rapture.

From my appendix of these prophetic books it also says that there is no such thing as liberal Christianity. Yes, there is but only in reference to the Sabbath day: ONE MAN ESTEEMS ONE DAY ABOVE ANOTHER, ANOTHER MAN ESTEEMS EVERYDAY THE SAME, LET EVERYMAN BE FULLY PERSUADED IN HIS OWN MIND', (Romans 14:5). Many other things constitute Fake News and I include a whole chapter on that including these current topics in this prophetic book, so that you get your money's worth.

But things like **climate change** (climate change has no biblical support), ('WHILE THE EARTH REMAINS, SEED TIME AND HARVEST AND COLD AND HEAT AND SUMMER AND WINTER AND DAY AND NIGHT SHALL NOT CEASE', (Genesis 8:22). 'THERE IS NO NEW THING UNDER THE SUN', (Ecclesiastes 1:9). **transgender**, ('FROM THE BEGINNING GOD MADE THEM MALE AND FEMALE', Matthew 19:4), **sex change**, (since 'EVERYTHING GOD DOES ENDURES, Ecclesiastes 3:14, don't try to supersede God's will with your own). **same sex marriage,** (FOR THIS REASON A MAN SHALL LEAVE HIS FATHER AND MOTHER AND CLEAVE UNTO HIS WIFE AND THEY SHALL BECOME ONE FLESH'. Genesis 2:4 and Matthew 19:5). **gay marriage**, (the Bible does not condone marriages of the same sex, as unions of the same sex cannot become one flesh)

Socialism, ('THE WHOLE GROUP OF BELIEVERS WAS ONE IN HEART AND SOUL. NO ONE CLAIMED THAT ANY OF HIS POSSESSIONS WAS HIS OWN, BUT THEY HELD ALL THINGS IN COMMON', Acts 4:32. These believers were full gospel saints, filled with the Holy Ghost. They did not include unbelievers, people who worshipped other God's, people with hostile political beliefs such as revolutionaries, now called progressives.

Progressives did not begin with today's Democrats. Upon taking office in March 1861, Lincoln the deceitful also implemented a whole series of unconstitutional acts, including the invasion of the South without even consulting Congress, blockading southern ports, and declaring Martial Law. Afterward, he suspended Habeas Corpus.

With that suspension of Habeas Corpus together with his Martial Law decree thousands of American citizens were imprisoned without trial after being arrested without charge.

Today's democratic progressives are also haters of the capitalist economy including bums, leeches and welfare scum. substance abusers, scam artists known as thieves, and women of ill repute).

Socialism was once considered ideal by the early Christian Pilgrims who believed at first in sharing with one another, but as the bum attitude spread throughout the colony, there resulted insufficient farm supplies or food to feed the saints let alone all the outsiders so socialism was abandoned, (my chapter on Saints, Sinners and Socialists should also bring this out) but the next year their capitalist agricultural program worked so well that they could afford to have their first thanksgiving with the Indians.

Socialism has never worked in any society since, neither Russia, China, Vietnam North Korea, Venezuela nor whoever else that tries to make it work.

When Russia (the former Soviet Union) encountered its Communist Revolution, some expected economic and social changes did not happen. I learned from Rick Renner, our missionaries to Russia that the old czarist ornate palaces were kept despite the communist revolution. One particular place; the ornate Russian Orthodoxic Cathedral of St. Peter and St. Paul where the royal Romanoff dynasty going back a thousand years is buried complete with personal bejeweled swords and dazzling crowns with golden scepters was untouched.

Although the communist preached confiscation from the privileged with benefit to the poor apparently their ideology did not govern every action they took. Likewise, these progressive democrats claim to share the wealth of the rich while their speaker Pelosi is becoming rich herself

A skin walker witch that we remember from horror films like the Twilight Zone represented themselves as 'healers' in public and today with the wearing of masks, the mandating of vaccinations and boosters and the closing of churches as non-essential without any biblical support whatsoever.

It's no longer on the internet but yesterday Google called 'the mandating of the wearing of masks and the taking of vaccinations to be unchristian'. If so, then Dr. Anthony Fauci is a modern skin walker witch too. And his deceit is brought out in my chapter about COVID 19 being the FIRST END TIME PLAGUE and in my chapter about COVID 19, VACCINE OR REPENTANCE in this prophetic book too.

And though any part of 'cafeteria Christianity' may sound good it is not a part of biblical Christianity. For biblical Christianity is a Person, The Lord Jesus Christ. As it is written: 'HE THAT HATH THE SON HATH LIFE AND HE THAT HATH NOT THE SON OF GOD HATH NOT LIFE', (1 John 5:12).

Many Christians however take this false doctrine of pretribulation rapture into current events like mask mandates and vaccination requirements which then become liberal requirements of the faith.

But Jesus Christ, the Lord of Christianity said: 'RENDER UNTO CEASAR THE THINGS THAT ARE CEASAR'S AND UNTO GOD THE THINGS THAT ARE GOD'S', (Mark 12:17). The human body does not belong to Caesar. So, the government has no right to tell you what to do with it, if contrary to God's word. Therefore, all these government mandates not mentioned in the word of God are also unscriptural and not worthy of obedience.

This is an important test case which none of today's TV ministers being undisclosed dispensational representatives of this pre-tribulation rapture false doctrine fails to recognize.

If they could accept that Christians would continue to be here on earth during the times of 'Sorrows' and 'Tribulation' then they could see the importance of instructing Christians to get out of the habit of obeying governmental orders like: 'OBEY EVERY ORDINANCE OF MAN', I Peter 2:13 lest they be conditioned to obey the orders of the Antichrist too when such could deny you your eternal life.

All Christians are still here for this first COVID 19 plague in which many Christians and non-Christians have died. (Many Christian leaders: dispensationalists, who believe in and teach the false doctrine of the pre-tribulation rapture have also now died as God believes it's more important for his body to become Holy and perfected than to absorb the oral masturbation of Americanized Christianity with its prosperity message.

The dispensationalists also believe in this American prosperity message and say that prosperity along with rapture must happen before any economic collapse. To certify their beliefs from the Bible.

They use the verses in Luke 17:26-30, 'JUST AS IT WAS IN THE DAYS OF NOAH, SO WILL IT BE IN THE DAYS OF THE SON OF MAN

THEY WERE EATING AND DRINKING AND MARRYING AND BEING GIVEN IN MARRIAGE, UNTIL THE DAY WHEN NOAH ENTERED THE ARK, AND THE FLOODS CAME AND DESTROYED THEM ALL'.

'LIKEWISE, JUST AS IT WAS IN THE DAYS OF LOT-THEY WERE EATING AND DRINKING, BUYING AND SELLING, PLANTING AND BUILDING. BUT ON THE DAY WHEN LOT WENT OUT OF SODOM, FIRE AND SULFUR RAINED DOWN FROM HEAVEN AND DESTROYED THEM ALL. SO WILL IT BE ON THE DAY WHEN THE SON OF MAN IS REVEALED'.

Quoting scripture should not make you believe someone's doctrine. Even the Jehovah's Witnesses, the Mormons and other cults do that. Remember the devil quoted scripture in the temptation of Jesus in Matthew chapter-four.

These my friends are the days of inflation. After the days of inflation the economists tell us from history must come economic collapse in order for the one world order of the antichrist to arise as spoken by the prophets. The exact progression of events composing the last day events before Jesus comes again are listed in Matthew chapter twenty-four.

How come so few Christians have realized that this COVID 19 plague is the first plague of 'The Times of Sorrows'? Doesn't this along with the fulfillment of many end time prophecies (like Israel being restored to its land in 1948 or winning Jerusalem in 1967) also show that we have now entered into a new age of sorrow, then tribulation and finally antichrist abuse, before the Lord Jesus comes again in power and great glory?

Of course, most Christians don't want to accept this as their fate. Most modern Christians are not even inclined to accept the cross or the idea that Jesus had to suffer and sacrifice Himself for our sins.

The evangelist Jimmy Swaggart has attempted to bring this Apostolic Truth out in his 'Message of the Cross' but it has not fully caught on yet, but it will. Let's face it, rather than bear their own cross or accept the suffering of the cross as their own, or be included in 'THE FELLOWSHIP OF HIS SUFFERINGS', Philippians 3:10 they'd much rather be in heaven 'pigging out' at the marriage supper of the Lamb than having to endure the persecution and trials of the tribulation.

'Pigging out' reminds me of the time when I had to observe an autopsy for my Emergency Medical Technician training as a young man. Our subject that day was a woman about 60 years old who had unexpectedly died. Our doctor proceeded to examine a blood vessel to her heart which was encased in fat. About halfway to the heart he took the scrapple and cut the blood vessel to find that it was occluded with more fat too. So he kept cutting the blood vessel ever nearer the heart until he came to where it was stopped up entirely with fat where blood should have been. Then someone mentioned that this woman had committed suicide by eating herself to death. So that was the real cause of death although the coroner wrote down 'natural causes. Just like those today who die from flu, pneumonia or old age are listed as dying from COVID 19.

This is somewhat like the natural fraud of 'pew warming Christians' who consider themselves too blessed to need to prepare water and food among other items for the last days (as seen on the Jim Bakker show).

Then this same kind of fraud carries over into the other areas of life as seen on Flash Point, Kenneth Copeland's news program on Victory TV.

The Lord Jesus said: 'WHOEVER WANTS TO BE MY DISCIPLE MUST DE NY THEMSELVES AND TAKE UP THEIR CROSS AND FOLLOW ME', (Luke 9:23). Therefore, I suppose that it is past time for most Pastors to teach their flock of Christians just what they are to believe and then **DO** as children of God.

There is an unforeseen psychological problem in being a Christian and believing in this pre-tribulation rapture and believing that God has raised up these various democratic governments to mandate vaccinations and masks along with how people are to act under these COVID 19 circumstances and rules too.

As Christians we are to accept that we are to believe God first. Then we are to obey God's rules. **The government is not upon Jesus shoulders yet, so it is unwise to obey any government that feels it is at liberty to have us or our children yield up our bodies as a sacrifice to them to do with as they will supposedly for our own good.**

'YOUR BODY IS THE TEMPLE OF THE HOLY GHOST', (I Cor. 3:16-17, 6:19-20). Failure to believe this leads to psychological deficits in the Christian life. These include depression with the failure to laugh and understand humor. Along with the inability to trust the truth and 'BRING FORTH FRUITS WORTHY OF REPENTANCE', (Matthew 3:8).

The idea of going to heaven to escape all this tribulation is the mistaken self-belief of psychological self-importance whereby one considers themselves just too godly already to need any more trails or testing. This delusion of self-judgment lets the Christian decide for themselves what judgment to receive. As if they had the right to determine what only God like the store clerk or casher has the right to weigh and charge like buying a fruit or vegetable in the grocery store. I hope that you are now beginning to see just how delusionary this pre-tribulation rapture really is.

There is another very important evangelical point that needs to be made here: that is if Christians and the Holy Ghost are removed by rapture before any sorrow or tribulation happens then they will not be here to help bring about the final Great Awakening. This brings up the question of just how much do you love souls? Do you love them enough to stay here until they get saved? Are you willing to endure all things like the members of the God head?

I know that some Christians have different doctrinal beliefs, but in the case of the two witnesses prophesying during the tribulation, who other than the Holy Ghost is anointing them to do such? Moreover speaking of those Jews who are evangelizing during the tribulation too, who is anointing them?

It appears to me that this time of tribulation is not only a period of awakening and anointing but also a time of contest and judgment. And I don't know of any time where our God avoids any contest with the devil. Even the Lord Jesus was tempted (abused) by the devil immediately after His baptism by John as recorded in Mathew 4:1 and then proceeded to have his personal contest with the devil. 'THEN JESUS WAS LED BY THE SPIRIT INTO THE WILDERNESS TO BE TEMPTED BY THE DEVIL. AND AFTER FASTING FORTY DAYS AND FORTY NIGHTS, HE WAS HUNGRY. AND THE TEMPTER CAME AND SAID TO HIM 'IF YOU ARE THE SON OF GOD, COMMAND THESE STONES TO BECOME LOAVES OF BREAD'. BUT JESUS ANSWERED: 'IT IS WRITTEN MAN SHALL NOT LIVE BY BREAD ALONE, BUT BY EVERY WORD THAT COMES FROM THE MOUTH OF GOD'. THEN THE DEVIL TOOK HIM TO THE HOLY CITY AND SET HIM ON THE PENTICLE OF THE TEMPLE AND SAID TO HIM; 'IF YOU ARE THE SON OF GOD, THROUGH YOURSELF DOWN, FOR IT IS WRITTEN; 'HE WILL COMMAND HIS ANGELS CONCERNING YOU AND ON THEIR HANDS THEY WILL BEAR YOU UP, LEST YOU STRIKE YOUR FOOT AGAINST A STONE'. AND JESUS ANSWERED HIM, 'AGAIN IT IS WRITTEN, YOU SHALL NOT PUT THE LORD YOUR GOD TO THE TEST'. AGAIN THE DEVIL TOOK HIM TO A VERY HIGH MOUNTAIN AND SHOWED HIM ALL THE KINGDOMS OF THE WORLD AND THEIR GLORY. AND SAID TO HIM; ALL THESE I WILL GIVE YOU IF YOU FALL DOWN AND WORSHIP ME', THEN JESUS SAID TO HIM; 'BE GONE SATAN, FOR IT IS WRITTEN; 'YOU SHALL WORSHIP THE LORD YOUR GOD AND HIM ONLY SHALL

YOU SERVE'. THEN THE DEVIL LEFT HIM AND BEHOLD ANGELS CAME AND MINISTERED UNTO HIM', (Matthew 4:1-4:12).

Of course all of this happened before Jesus began His earthly ministry. He had to be baptized by John first because 'THE HOLY GHOST IS GIVEN TO THOSE WHO OBEY HIM', (Acts 5:32). And He had to be anointed by the Holy Ghost first before He began to do the works of God as a man anointed by the Holy Ghost.

Now most dispensational Christians including most evangelicals and Pentecostals believe that the next great prophetic event will be the rapture of the church, but let's see what Jesus says in Matthew chapter twenty-four about that. (Here I also will include the various relevant chapters of my prophetic book: RAPTURE RIPOFF II which must occur before that rapture happens).

Back at Bethel Tabernacle we went on to read Matthew 24 and found our own few words of wisdom. At the start of the second chapter (**THE ORIGINAL JESUS MOVEMENT**) The Lord Jesus disciples said in Verse 3: 'TELL US WHEN SHALL THESE THINGS BE? AND WHAT WILL BE THE SIGN (The twenty fourth chapter: **APOCALYPTIC CATASTROPHIES**) OF YOUR COMING AND OF THE END OF THE AGE?' The Lord Jesus answered by saying: Matthew 24:5-30: Verse 5: 'FOR MANY SHALL COME IN MY NAME, SAYING, I AM CHRIST; AND SHALL DECIEVE MANY. (among these many will be the false gods of old like Lord Krishna and various avatars, Buddha, Maharishi Yogonanda, Odin, and other false and pagan gods of old plus the new artificial intelligence or technological ones like the False Prophet, the Beast and the Antichrist. Most of these will be able to do impersonal supernatural acts (like causing a statue to another false god to have life and to talk; Revelation 13:15, but none of these will be able to save anyone from the consequences of their sins like Jesus does and be reconciled to God thereby**,** (chapter 10, **RAPTURE RIP-OFF I**). Verse 6: AND YE SHALL HEAR OF WARS AND RUMORS OF WARS (The nineteenth chapter: **WARS AND RUMORS OF WARS**: SEE THAT YE BE NOT TROUBLED: FOR ALL THESE THINGS MUST COME TO PASS, BUT THE END IS NOT YET. Verse 7: FOR NATION SHALL RISE AGAINST NATION (The twentieth chapter: **THE AMERICAN CIVIL WAR**) AND KINGDOM AGAINST KINGDOM: AND THERE SHALL BE FAMINES, (in chapter 21**, FAMINES**) AND chapter 22 **PESTILENCES**, (like Corona Virus in chapter 11 and 12**, FIRST END TIME PLAGUE: COVID 19, COVID 19 VACCINE OR REPENTANCE**)

EARTHQUAKES (The twenty-third chapter, **EARTHQUAKES**) IN DIVERSE PLACES.

Verse 8: ALL THESE ARE THE BEGINNINGS OF SORROWS. (**BIDEN'S SORROWS 1**, chapter fourteen) (**BIDEN'S SORROWS II**, chapter 17) (**BIDEN'S SORROWS III,** chapter 18) Verse 9 (this contradicts the dispensational delusion): THEN SHALL THEY DELIVER YOU UP TO BE AFLICTED AND SHALL KILL YOU: AND YE SHALL BE HATED OF ALL NATIONS FOR MY NAME'S SAKE. Verse 10: AND THEN SHALL MANY BE OFFENDED, AND SHALL BETRAY ONE ANOTHER, AND SHALL HATE ONE ANOTHER. Verse 11: AND MANY FALSE PROPHETS SHALL RISE, AND SHALL DECIEVE MANY (real prophecy is a gift from God, see chapter 4, **MY PROPHECIES**) false prophecy comes from the false doctrines of denominational Bible schools and as such it is intentionally and deliberately taught with malice). Verse 12: AND BECAUSE INIQUITY SHALL ABOUND, THE LOVE OF MANY SHALL WAX COLD. Verse 13: BUT HE THAT SHALL ENDURE UNTO THE END, THE SAME SHALL BE SAVED. Verse 14: AND THIS GOSPEL OF THE KINGDOM SHALL BE PREACHED IN ALL THE WORLD FOR A WITNESS UNTO ALL NATIONS; AND THEN SHALL THE END COME. Verse 15: WHEN YE THEREFORE SHALL SEE (how can you see it if you're not here) THE ABOMINATION OF DESOLATION, SPOKEN OF BY DANIEL THE PROPHET, STAND IN THE HOLY PLACE (WHO SO READITH, LET HIM UNDERSTAND). Verse 16: THEN LET THEM WHICH BE IN JUDEA FLEE INTO THE MOUNTAINS. Verse 17: LET HIM WHICH IS ON THE HOUSETOP NOT COME DOWN TO TAKE ANYTHING OUT OF HIS HOUSE: Verse 18: NEITHER LET HIM WHICH IS IN THE FIELD RETURN BACK TO TAKE HIS CLOTHES. Verse 19: AND WOE UNTO THEM THAT ARE WITH CHILD, AND TO THEM THAT GIVE SUCK IN THOSE DAYS! Verse 20: BUT PRAY YE THAT YOU'RE FLIGHT BE NOT IN WINTER, NEITHER ON THE SABBATH DAY. Verse 21: FOR THEN SHALL BE GREAT TRIBULATION, SUCH AS WAS NOT SINCE THE BEGINNING OF THE WORLD TO THIS TIME, NO, NOR EVER SHALL BE. Verse 22: AND EXCEPT THOSE DAYS SHOULD BE SHORTENED THERE SHOULD NO FLESH BE SAVED: BUT FOR THE ELECT'S SAKE THOSE DAYS SHALL BE SHORTENED. Verse 23: THEN IF ANY MAN SHALL SAY UNTO YOU, LO, HERE IS CHRIST, OR THERE: BELIEVE IT NOT, (chapter 15:

FAKE NEWS), (chapter 8, **MUSLIM OBAMA'S MUSLIM DECEPTION**, chapter 9, **MUSLIM JESUS VS JESUS CHRIST,** chapter 17: **SAINTS, SINNERS, SCOUNDRELS, SODOMITES AND SOCIALISTS**). Matthew 24: verse 24: FOR THERE SHALL ARISE FALSE CHRISTS, AND FALSE PROPHETS, AND SHALL SHOW GREAT SIGNS AND WONDERS (the devil and his followers can do miracles too, but only God's miracles are confirmed with the message of salvation from sin and reconciliation to God as Jesus taught), INSOMUCH THAT, IF IT WERE POSSIBLE, THEY SHALL DECIEVE THE VERY ELECT. Verse 25: BEHOLD, I HAVE TOLD YOU BEFORE. Verse 26: WHEREFORE IF THEY SHALL SAY UNTO YOU, BEHOLD, HE IS IN THE DESERT; GO NOT FORTH: BEHOLD, HE IS IN THE SECRET CHAMBERS; BELIEVE IT NOT, (chapter fifteen **FAKE NEWS,** chapter 8 **MUSLIM OBAMA'S MUSLIM DECEPTION,** chapter 9 **MUSLIM JESUS VS. JESUS CHRIST**, chapter 16 **SAINTS. SINNERS. SCOUNDRELS, SODOMITES AND SOCIALISTS**) Matthew 24: verse 27: FOR AS THE LIGHTNING COMETH OUT OF THE EAST AND SHINETH EVEN UNTO THE WEST; SO SHALL ALSO THE COMING OF THE SON OF MAN BE. Verse 28: FOR WHERESOEVER THE CARCUSES IS, THERE WILL THE EAGLES BE GATHERED TOGETHER. Verse 29: IMMEDIATELY **AFTER** THE TRIBULATION OF THOSE DAYS SHALL THE SUN BE DARKENED, AND THE MOON SHALL NOT GIVE HER LIGHT, AND T1HE STARS SHALL FALL FROM HEAVEN, AND THE POWERS OF THE HEAVENS SHALL BE SHAKEN. Verse 30: AND THEN SHALL APPEAR THE SIGN OF THE SON OF MAN IN HEAVEN: AND THEN SHALL ALL THE TRIBES OF THE EARTH MORN, AND THEY SHALL SEE THE SON OF MAN COMING IN THE CLOUDS OF HEAVEN WITH POWER AND GREAT GLORY', (chapter 24, **APOCALYPTIC CATASTROPHIES**).

Please note that while the Lord Jesus runs down these unpleasant future events, He never once said to his disciples: Do not fear these things for while they are happening on earth, you'll be safe in heaven with Me. Or, you'll only see these things from afar, but they will not happen to you. Nor, 'Thousands shall fall on your right hand and tens of thousands on your left, but it shall not come nigh thee'.

Back when you were a child going to Sunday school they used to sing a song about the Bible that said: 'Every promise in the book is mine, every chapter, every verse, every line'. But today's theologians now say that Matthew is only for the Jews or Israel as all Christians will be gone from tribulation thanks to the pre-tribulation rapture. Just like over a hundred years ago they used to say that certain verses applied to the slaves, while others applied to Whites only. But the Bible says that: 'ALL SCRIPTURE (including Matthew) IS GIVEN BY THE INSPIRATION OF GOD AND IS PROFITABLE FOR DOCTRINE, FOR REPROOF, FOR CORRECTION, FOR INSTRUCTION IN RIGHTEOUSNESS', (II Timothy 3:16). Moreover: 'THERE IS NEITHER JEW NOR GREEK, BOND NOR FREE, MALE NOR FEMALE IN CHRIST JESUS', (Galatians 3:28).

And as far as tribulation is concerned, this is an unpleasant doctrine that most Christians do not like to face: 'SHALL WE RECEIVE GOOD FROM THE HAND OF THE LORD AND NOT EVIL ALSO?', (Job 2:10). This of course is a 'prophetic word of scripture'. While the word in Jeremiah 29:11, ('FOR I KNOW THE PLANS I HAVE FOR YOU DECLARES THE LORD, PLANS TO PROSPER YOU AND NOT TO HARM YOU, PLANS TO GIVE YOU A HOPE AND A FUTURE') are wisdom words of scripture. These words might seem contradictory but actually they depend upon and are relevant to the situation at hand. Tribulation is a bad time, so bad is to be expected. Living in modern life is supposedly a good time (the age of grace), so good is to be expected,

In another case, after Nathan had pronounced his prophecy against David for David's many sins against Bathsheba and Uriah: 'THE LORD CAUSED THE CHILD THAT URIAH'S WIFE (BATHSHEBA) HAD BORN TO DAVID TO BECOME VERY SICK (just like this COVID 19.end time plague) DAVID PRAYED TO GOD THAT THE CHILD WOULD GET WELL. HE REFUSED TO EAT ANYTHING, AND EVERY NIGHT HE WENT INTO HIS ROOM AND SPENT HIS NIGHT LYING ON THE FLOOR (when trouble hits Christians do spiritual exercises too in order to relieve the consequences for sin instead of worshipping God like David did). A WEEK LATER THE CHILD DIED. THEN DAVID GOT UP FROM THE FLOOR, TOOK A BATH, COMBED HIS HAIR, AND CHANGE HIS CLOTHES. THEN HE WENT AND WORSHIPED GOD IN THE HOUSE OF THE LORD. THEN HE RETURNED TO THE PALACE AND ATE SOME FOOD. THEN HIS SERVANT SAID: WE DON'T UNDERSTAND THIS. WHILE THE CHILD WAS ALIVE YOU WEPT FOR HIM AND WOULD NOT EAT: BUT AS SOON AS HE DIED YOU GOT UP AND ATE. YES, I DID DAVID ANSWERED. I DID FAST AND WEEP WHILE HE WAS STILL ALIVE. I THOUGHT THAT

THE LORD MIGHT BE MERCIFUL (tribulation is a time for judgment not mercy, remember this).TO ME AND NOT LET THE CHILD DIE. BUT NOW THAT HE IS DEAD WHY SHOULD I FAST? COULD I BRING THE CHILD BACK TO LIFE? I WILL SOME DAY GO TO WHERE HE IS BUT HE CAN NEVER COME BACK TO ME?

THEN DAVID COMFORTED HIS WIFE BATHSHEBA. AND HE HAD INTERCOURSE WITH HER AGAIN AND THEY PRODUCED SOLOMON,' (II Samuel 12:14-24).

THE AMERICAN CIVIL WAR

From the definition of Wars we already expect wars to be between Nations and Kingdoms. The Geneva Convention recognizes nations at war as those sovereign states that are recognized by or are members of the United Nations. Whereas back in Jesus day kingdoms were simple city states ruled over by a local king. The size of the nation or the kingdom may vary but war was an official conflict between them.

A nation may be limited or defined by common language, common religion or recognized political boundaries. Some nations may have different economies and different types of governments. But all are capable of war. And apparently that's what these few phrases in **Matthew 24: verse 7** indicated. In fact, war is a universal condition common to all political entities. And war comes to all just like changes in the weather.

Some wars are called civil wars when in reality they are an independent branch of the whole, fighting against the whole for differences in belief based on economy, theology or politics. The American Civil War is a good example.

In any war usually, those who win the war write the history of it that is approved to be taught in school. **But here through God's prophetic gifting we get to say some truthful things that need to be said.**

Those engaged in this war wanted to be gentlemen and show forth from their manners that they were raised well. As in the first battle of the American Civil War, which the Confederates won. Stonewall Jackson exercising gentlemanly civility and respect asked Jefferson Davis if it was alright for him to go on to take Washington. Jefferson Davis wanting to show civilian control of the military said no. Stonewall Jackson should have kept his mouth shut. Since **when you're winning you don't ask someone else how far you should go.** If Stonewall Jackson, the soldier, had moved against Washington he could have easily taken it, burned it to the ground and hung Lincoln in the front yard of the White House. **If this had happened, just think what a different country America would be today. There would not now be any American welfare state with trillions of dollars in debt to maintain social programs that our children must pay for instead of being able to live their own lives.**

Remember when you were a child and used to play games with other kids. If another kid was wrong about something and exhibited bad behavior toward you, like stealing your marbles or spitting on your cards, you gathered up your stuff and went home. Well, that's just what happened at the start of the Civil War. The pious North began playing hardball with the Southerners over the issue of extending slavery into the territories. So, the South said we're keeping our economic system and went home (withdrew from the union by succession). But after they left, the North refused to also leave and still kept Fort Sumter in Charleston harbor, South Carolina, Confederate States of America and refused to vacate so after some reasonable time, the South opened fire.

This same problem also exists today. America has been warned repeatedly to get out of Japan, Germany, Korea and now many Muslim lands but refuses to do so. Such invites tragedy and causes outlandish expense being passed on to our children in the form of deficit spending.

Expect: more government deficit spending even on wars on credit.

At the beginning of the Civil War many commissioned officers felt that this was just a dispute and not worthy of total war. So, President Lincoln went through many gentleman generals until he found a few savage rouges (drunks) in uniform that would do Lincoln's bidding.

One took Richmond, the other burned Atlanta to the ground. Their underlings also in uniform killed all the farm animals and every horse in order to keep the occupants of these Southern cities confined there to starve to death. This war crime was Lincoln's **'charity to all and malice toward none'.**

Blacks had much more under slavery than they wound up with thanks to these 'Northern liberators. For example; under slavery, Blacks had a job for life that they could not be fired from. Now they have unemployment and unemployment compensation thanks to your increased taxes.

Under slavery Blacks also lived in the country with clean air and water and freedom from crime. Now they live in filthy Black ghettos like Chicago where Black people are killed every night.

The Blacks were also promised by the North 40 acres and a mule to encourage a slave rebellion. Of course, the North never divided up any plantations in order to fulfill this promise but instead Northern armies pillaged slave cabins and stole from the civilian population both Black and White, which is another war crime.

Maybe there is still one truth about this war that made it into a few history books anyway. That is how Lincoln threatened and abused with military action the state legislature of Maryland in order to keep them from also voting for succession just like the rest of the South.

The Bible says that: 'THERE IS NOTHING NEW UNDER THE SUN', (Ecclesiastes 1:9). Many real patriots resent the Patriot ACT and the loss of liberty imposed recently on us by George Bush 43. Actually, Lincoln had a similar modus operandi plus Lincoln also had people held without trial and in many cases without charge. The conditions of the prisons that Lincoln used would also be considered a war crime today.

Lincoln was a very mean and ruthless man. Much of his anger was caused at the beginning of the war by the unfortunate shooting of his pet homosexual lover in Virginia when that young man went to take down the confederate flag flying in Virginia which Lincoln had to see every day. Yes, the high voiced Lincoln was also a known Sodomite. That's what they called gays back in those days.

The book: <u>THE INTIMATE WORLD of ABRAHAM LINCOLN</u> BY Professor and sex researcher of Alfred Kinsey fame Dr. C.A. Tripp reveals on page XVII of its introduction that there were at least five verifiable cases of President Abraham Lincoln's sexual activity with other men, although you never heard anything about them when we studied American History in school.

As you know the Bible has been taken out of school, but it still says in Numbers 32:23: 'BE SURE YOUR SIN WILL FIND YOU OUT'. And the Lord Jesus said in Luke 12:2: 'FOR THERE IS NOTHING COVERED THAT SHALL NOT BE REVEALED, NEITHER HID THAT SHALL NOT BE KNOWN'.

<u>Your Bible is your guidebook to keep you free from sin. Study it!</u>

In that light the last one, and certainly the most famous one was the relationship President Abraham Lincoln had with Captain David V. Derickson during The Civil War, of whom Lincoln said; 'The Captain and I are getting quit thick'.

The Captain, David V. Derickson, was a forty-four year old (grown man which makes him a consenting adult) Buck tail soldier from Pennsylvania.

He was five feet nine inches tall; with intense eyes, a strong nose and thick black hair from a socially prominent family in Meadville, Pennsylvania and was assigned to be Lincoln's bodyguard.

Of Derickson sleeping in the same bed with Lincoln, Virginia Woodbury Fox noted in her detailed diary, in an entry dated November 16, 1862, "there is a Buck tail soldier here devoted to the President, drives with him, and when Mrs. L. is not home sleeps with him. What stuff!"

Margaret Leech in her book entitled; Reveille in Washington, 1860-1865 mentions this man on page 303 in which she states: "Lincoln grew to like the Buck tails, especially company K, with whose Captain he became so friendly that he invited him to share his bed on autumn nights when Mrs. Lincoln was away from home".

Also, in a detailed history entitled; History Of The One Hundred And Fiftieth Regiment, Pennsylvania Volunteers, Second Regiment, Buck tail Brigade, Published in 1895 written by Lieutenant Colonel Chamberlain, the immediate commanding officer of Captain Derickson, states in chapter four of his book that; "the President was also not an infrequent visitor in the late afternoon, and had endeared himself to his guards by his genial, kind words. He was not long at placing officers in his two companies at their ease in his presence, and Captains Derickson and Crozier where shortly on a footing of such marked friendship with him that they were often summoned to dinner or breakfast at the Presidential board. Captain Derickson, in particular, advanced so far in the President's confidence and his esteem that in Mrs. Lincoln's absence he frequently spent the night at his cottage, sleeping in the same bed with him, and – it is said – making use of his Excellency's nightshirt! Thus began an intimacy which continued unbroken until the following spring, when Captain Derickson was appointed provost marshal of the Nineteenth Pennsylvania District with headquarters in Meadville".

Finally, in the book; Lincoln Day By Day: A Chronology 1809 to 1865. It is recorded that Mrs. Lincoln left the White House to shop and visit friends both in New York and Boston. She left on October 25th 1862. She returned on November 27th. The entry Virginia Fox made in her diary about the Buck tail soldier sleeping in the same bed with Lincoln falls during this time.

So, the fact that Abraham Lincoln had bed time partners or sexual partners other than his wife, who were even male, is now well documented and clear for all to see. **The Lincoln bed is still famous for lust even today. So much so that former President Bill Clinton used to rent it out.**

Lincoln's fraudulent sexual orientation has already been examined, but since this book is neither a sex research work nor a political attack something else lies behind Lincoln's devious sex life that is far more important for us to consider now, and that something is Sovereignty. Although Abraham Lincoln was elected with just forty percent of the popular vote, he still considered himself to be the elected Sovereign of the U. S. much like President Bush who only won by a few votes yet considers himself to have won a mandate complete with political capital to do as he pleases with your tax dollars and the lives of your children wasted in this stupid anti-Muslim Iraq war. While at the same time allowing Muslim 'interpreters' to settle in America to curse our land.

Being an elected Sovereign did not make Lincoln any less of a Sovereign, he can still rule just as constitutional monarchs do, and even without any constitutional restraints if at war, for then he had 'war-powers'. But starting a war, like the Civil War, without the consent of Congress in Vallandigham's opinion; "would have cost any English Sovereign his head at any time within the last two hundred years".

Common practice in that day for the various Sovereigns of Europe was to sleep with their bodyguards, especially if at war. Sovereigns could have any type of sex that they wanted at any time with anyone, 'Devine Right of Kings'. Usually their bedmates were also their sexual playmates. In America, the true image of a Sovereign is not fully grasped. A Sovereign usually has absolute power to do as they please. That includes being above the law, as The Indemnity Act of 1863 provided. That act insulated Lincoln, the Lincoln Administration and all federal government officials from being sued in any state court.

Sovereigns could also act as they please where sex was concerned. In the Middle Ages in Europe, Sovereigns had not only harems of women, but also those of young boys. In fact, Pope Innocent III had eight boys to bed down with. At that time, having sex was expected by those in high office and was usually lavished upon them. It was just another one of the entitlements that usually came with the job of high office especially under the spoils system where anything goes.

Contrary to public opinion, entitlements did not begin with the Democrats or Democratic President Franklin Roosevelt, or his 'New Deal', or with Social Security's cost of living**. Entitlements began with Sovereignty and with the Republican President Abraham Lincoln, 'The Magnificent'.** For a man like Lincoln, without Christian inhibitions, to be sexually starved at first just resulted in frustration. But as time went on, his frustration became fury, since as a Sovereign, having sex was his due.

Expect: someone else's entitlement may cause you to do without. So get your stuff NOW!

You might remember how that another Republican President, Richard Nixon, when denied having marital sex during the Vietnam War got hostile and secretly bombed Cambodia, which he denied in public. Likewise, Republican President Lincoln, also full of testosterone sent General Sheridan to waste the Shenandoah Valley and General Sherman to burn Atlanta.

General Sheridan was told by General Grant, whose portrait appears on your fifty-dollar bill, "to make another trip down the valley, pillaging, plundering and burning everything in sight. Carry off stock of all descriptions and Negroes, so as to prevent further planting". Thus, the Shenandoah Valley was to become so devastated that "crows flying over it would need to pack their own-lunches ". It was thus turned into a desert and its residents rendered homeless.

Lincoln thanked Sheridan's Army for doing this in this way since he believed that 'might makes right' and he could ignore the Constitution, the Geneva Convention and even common decency and morality as long as his military won. If Lincoln lost, he knew that he and his top generals would be hung as war criminals, because that's just what they were!

Expect: any war to be a total war that will either hurt or kill you.

His top Generals; Grant, Sheridan, and Sherman all followed his lead, and obeyed his orders as soldiers always do. Their objective was to totally destroy the Southern economy and starve out its civilian population as much as possible to end once and for all **states' rights Sovereignty**, not to free the slaves, which was merely a cover.

Many slaves who ended up in the hands of the Union army were not set free despite the Emancipation Proclamation, but were put to work doing the most unpleasant work in and around army encampments. In short, Lincoln's Emancipation Proclamation was only applied to rebel territory. Some States like Maryland, Kentucky, and West Virginia were specifically exempted.

Lincoln, one of the natio*n*'s preeminent lawyers, an obviously trained liar and master of deceit was careful to so craft his Emancipation Proclamation in such an arbitrary way as to please the abolitionist without really freeing a single slave. Thus 2 years later 'Juneteenth' freed the slaves.

Lincoln maintained that his Emancipation Proclamation was just 'a war power' that he had the power to declare since the U.S. was at war. <u>In reality, the President had no such power at that time to dictate such to any state.</u> Today of course presidents routinely dictate thousands of laws, regulations and executive orders that they also fail to fund to every state and local government. It was the Republican President Abraham Lincoln who started this. <u>Expect: unfunded executive orders that will cost you dearly.</u>

Most people of the North in 1863 were shocked and surprised by the Emancipation Proclamation for they had not been told by either the U. S. government or the Lincoln Administration that they were fighting and dying by the thousands for the wellbeing of slaves in faraway states most northerners had never been to and had never seen. **Hostile White immigrant mobs had assaulted Blacks in Northern cities for years, so in July 1863 there were race riots in New York City as Whites protested both the Emancipation Proclamation and Lincoln's new conscription law.**

<u>Expect: race riots so be sure you live in an area that is at least 90% your own race to avoid racial conflict, or to be safe move to a place that is.</u>

This conscription law applied only to Whites, but those with sufficient funds could buy their way out of this draft for three hundred dollars. Those without this money were outraged and the resulting rioting mob consisted of these defrauded people. Instead of even attempting to reason with these people, Lincoln immediately sent five regiments of battle-hardened troops from the recently concluded Battle of Gettysburg to New York City to quell the riots. These battle-hardened troops achieved their goal of quelling the riots by shooting and killing over three hundred protestors and using their bayonets to disperse the crowds of protestors.

At this time the mayhem in New York City was atrocious. The streetlights were out, many hangings and murders occurred as terror and anxiety was common. All the shops were closed and business was at a standstill. All carriages and buses had ceased running. Telegraph wires were cut, and even railroad tracks were torn up. No Black person dared to show themselves on that day. Colored people weren't even safe in their own homes.

<u>Expect: Mayhem so move to a safe place NOW!</u>

The very idea that the Civil War happened because the people in the North adopted abolitionist feelings and were morally constrained to free

the slaves is obviously fraudulent. For no abolitionist was ever elected to any major political office in any Northern state. The overwhelming majority of White Northerners cared little if at all about the welfare of slaves and treated Blacks that lived among them with contempt, ridicule, discrimination, and even violence.

The author Eugene Beranger described the condition of Blacks in the North at this time in his book: North of Slavery. He writes: **"In virtually every phase of existence (In the North), Negroes found themselves systematically separated from Whites. They were either excluded from railway cars, omnibuses, stage coaches, and steam boats or assigned to special 'Jim Crow' sections; they sat, when permitted, in secluded and removed corners of theaters and lecture halls; they could not enter most hotels, restaurants, and resorts, except as servants: they prayed in 'Negro pews' in the White churches, and if partaking of the Sacrament of the Lord's Supper, they waited until the Whites had been served the bread and wine first. Moreover, they were often educated in segregated schools, punished in segregated prisons, nursed in segregated hospitals and buried in segregated cemeteries".**

In addition to these riots, the Emancipation Proclamation also caused a desertion crisis in the U. S. Army. At least two hundred thousand federal soldiers deserted; another one hundred and twenty thousand avoided conscription by fleeing to Canada or hiding out in the mountains, just like during the Vietnam War, a hundred years later.

History also records that the Emancipation Proclamation then, just like the Iraq War now also caused an enlistment shortfall in the US Army. Many soldiers said that they felt betrayed as they were willing to risk their lives for the Union but not for Black freedom from slavery. Likewise, today Americans are willing to defend America, but not die for Iraq's democracy or that some Muslim girl can get an education.

Lincoln failed to take the common practice every other nation employed during this time where slavery was ended peacefully and even compensated for. Lincoln maintained that he was not particularly supportive of emancipation. He viewed it as only a tool to be used by him to deceive in order to achieve his real objective: **the consolidation of all state power in him, the elected Sovereign.**

By this time, Sherman's Army had become extremely adept at pillage and plunder. His Army was composed of both big city criminals and foreign convicts fresh from the jails of Europe. Somewhat like Fidel Castro's dumping on America of his 'low life scum' from his jails during the Muriel boat lift.

Additionally, history records that the federal soldiers routinely robbed everyone at gunpoint and in broad daylight during the mayhem of the Civil War.

Expect robbery by government official's not just gangs.

In those days, federal soldiers under Sherman sacked after plundering the finest Southern Plantations then **proceeded to do likewise to the lowest slave cabins.**

Mark Grimly records in his book: The Hard Hand of War: Union Military Policy toward Southern Civilians, 1861-1865 'with the utter disregard for Blacks that was the norm among Union Troops, that the soldiers ram shackled the slave cabins, taking whatever they liked'. Many accounts also record that Black woman (who were often gang raped by Union troops) suffered the most and that many Black men as a result hated the Union Armies. (The University of South Carolina has diaries, which record many rapes of Black woman right out in the public in broad daylight as if they had been caught like farm animals in heat ready to be exploited).

EXPECT Rape.

Emancipation was a farce, which the Blacks could see through. For they lost not only their jobs with whatever benefits they may have earned but also their homes. In those days, a slave usually got good health care along with free housing as owners 'property care'. Once Lincoln forced his will upon the South, the Blacks were free from any job, any place to stay or any care except Government care. This is where unemployment and government handouts like welfare came from.

Expect unemployment.

Sherman's Army also killed many thousands upon thousands of horses, cattle, hogs, dogs, and every domestic animal in sight so that the Southerners would starve.

The Geneva Convention of 1863 said that any naval blockade is an act of war upon a country's civilian population as well as its armed forces. The nations of the civilized world also agreed then that it was a war crime, punishable by either death or imprisonment for armies to: (1) Attack defenseless cities and towns, (2) Plunder and destroy civilian property, (3) Take from the civilian population more than what is necessary to feed any occupying army. They also have concluded that the only just war

was a defensive war. On this count alone Lincoln's invasion of the South made him a war criminal, not a hero worthy of a memorial in his honor. Moreover occupying soldiers who destroy private property, farms and houses are to be called 'Savage Barbarians' not national heroes.

Expect: Unconventional, uncivilized, non-Geneva Convention, barbaric war.

Lincoln wanted Southern civilians to suffer. This required him to abandon the Geneva Convention. Republican President Bush has now followed suit in order to make the 'terrorist Iraqi' suffer without any Geneva Convention rights. This abuse comes from the Civil War, known as Lincoln's 'total war'. And it was such waged against innocent, non-combatant civilians, mostly woman, children, and old men, and not a regular army. Now if these victims of 'total war' should survive enough to fight back they are called insurgences. Back then they were called gorillas. And innocent civilian had to pay with either their lives or their houses burnt along with their crops destroyed for whatever harm was inflicted by the Confederates upon the Union Forces.

Before reaching Atlanta, Sherman's army had already abused much of the South. Sherman described what his army had done as they passed through Meridian, Mississippi. He reported; "for five days, ten thousand, worked hard and with a will, in that work of destruction, with axes, sledges, crowbars, claw bars, and with fire, and I have no hesitation in pronouncing the work well done. Meridian . . . no longer exists".

The first major battle of the Civil War was fought in Manassas, Virginia, on July 16, 1861. The Union Army of General Erwin McDowell had amassed some thirty-three thousand troops to attack twenty-two thousand Confederate troops only thirty miles west of Washington. DC. There was great optimism especially in Washington that the Civil War would end that day. Many locals from Washington road out to Manassas Junction in their carriages with their packed lunches in hopes of watching the Confederates soon and certain surrender. But it didn't turn out that way, for the battle was a resounding Confederate victory. In fact, the battle ended with a wild scramble of mob force of defeated Union Troops and shocked civilians retreating back to Washington. This whole mob was several miles long and a few football field lengths wide composed of wild-eyed survivors running for their lives, hoping to find shelter in Washington.

It was here that General Jackson earned his nickname by furiously turning back and defeating decisively an overpowering Union Force. After the battle, he approached the Confederate President, Jefferson Davis, whom he saw on the battlefield and said to him; "give me ten thousand men and I will take Washington tomorrow". Davis being the gentleman, refused. He later said that he regretted that decision for the rest of his life and considered it to be **'one of the greatest mistakes of the war'**.

The Confederates made many other mistakes too, which cost them the war. They were too honorable, so they refused to assassinate Lincoln even though they knew that he traveled without an armed escort from Washington to the Presidential retreat in the Maryland Mountains. They could also have used landmines at their boarders to keep Lincoln's invaders out, but they failed to grasp that their disagreements with the Union had now degenerated into Lincoln's 'total war' which at first they failed to recognize, and did not desire to wage.

So gentlemanly conduct on the part of the South probably cost them the first Civil War. The fluoridation of municipal tap water across America may cost you Christians the next Civil War.

On a recent radio talk show Ty Bollinger was discussing his new book about his cancer research entitled: Cancer: Step Outside the Box. In his interview he mentioned how that many contaminants now in our society are causing an increase in cancer. One of these contaminants is fluoride.

Fluoride was first developed in the Nazi death camps during World War II to remove ones will to fight so that the unfortunate inmates would remain docile and apathetic until their eventual execution. Back then the Americans classified fluoride as a rat poison for civilian use not as a chemical weapon in war.

Today fluoride is used in almost all municipal tap water systems across America. Besides rendering the population docile, this chemical also has a very interesting side effect.

Apparently fluoride also increases the estrogen level and helps decrease the testosterone level of those who ingest it. In other words, this fluoridation of public drinking water is responsible for feminizing the population (increasing breast and other female cancers). This is also seen visibly in the increase of the gay population, with normal men becoming gay and indulging in Gay marriage. ***Thus, the gay lifestyle results from chemical poisoning more so than from just being born that way.***

After all General Sherman's War Crimes were reported to Lincoln, Lincoln said that this was exactly the type of war that he wanted waged against the South. Whereupon he promptly awarded General Sherman and told him to proceed to Georgia, and especially to Atlanta to 'steal his further reward'.

After likewise abusing the outskirts of Atlanta, Georgia, General Sherman entered the city, the city of Atlanta was then bombed night and day until barely a building survived. After destroying much of the city, General Sherman's army then looted and burned whatever remained. Even the cemeteries were looted, with graves being dug up and cadavers stripped of their jewelry and valuables especially including any gold, like gold pocket watches and gold teeth, just like the Nazi's did in another war complete with war crimes some eighty years later.

There were approximately four thousand homes in Atlanta before the bombardment started; afterward only four hundred were left standing. More than ninety percent of the city of Atlanta was totally destroyed and its churches were demolished too.

Once in Atlanta, Sherman decided to depopulate the city and he ordered everyone out with whatever belongings that they could carry. Those so ordered were the civilian inhabitants of the city, thousands of woman, children, and old men. Those who couldn't or wouldn't leave were first rendered homeless as their homes were burnt, and if they still refused to vacate, then they were shot. There was so much blood from the many bodies of Atlanta, Georgia that the name of the Chattahoochee River was recommended to be changed to the Crimson River.

One diary of Sherman's soldiers was found to document what happened when Sherman was still in Atlanta. It records: "never before have I witnessed so much wanton destruction as on this march. This was indeed an ogre of robbing, plundering, and then burning. The soldiers acted as if they had become drunken brut beasts on a rampage". Another Union soldier recorded that "he doubted that there was a single virgin in the whole army with all the homeless black woman needing to be rescued from the streets of Atlanta".

As Sherman's army left Atlanta burning, they trampled down the local farm fields so that no crops for food could reach those in Atlanta. The streets of Atlanta were filled with the rotting carcasses of horses, hogs and cattle that the invaders shot to keep those who survived the burning of Atlanta from eating. Since people will not eat from rotting carcasses it was believed that this practice would bring about the starvation of whomever in Atlanta survived the burning.

At this time, a Mrs. Walton wrote her description of this event to her daughter. She wrote, "The Yankees broke up and split up two of my bureau drawers, split up one of my secretary drawers, they broke up and opened one of your bundles I don't know what was in it, took things. They took all my meat, sugar, coffee, flour, the knives and forks, the spoons and all they could get into...They then broke up my caster, carried off the pepper box top, stomped the caster and broke it. Tell Mary that they took the Amber type she gave me of Joe's. They took all my corn, hogs, killed the goats, took chickens, broke open every trunk I had in the house...They took my home spun dress and one smarter one, Took all my shoes and stockings, my scarf and the silk that was left of my dress. They got my needles, thimble, scissors, and thread". But much of this and other plunder was usually abandoned at the Yankee campsite since it impeded the Union army in waging more destruction on their way through The South. It should also be noted that '**they did not steel out of any need, but simply out of greed and pure meanness'.**

Sherman's Army, after destroying Atlanta made a swath of destruction through the rest of Georgia all the way to the sea. From there they went into South Carolina, the birthplace of the Confederacy. Here they continued pillaging, plundering, and sacking every inhabited community as they had just done in Georgia. As they entered South Carolina, it seems that an intoxication of enraged fury overcame them. This intoxication intensified as the Union Army neared Columbia, the state capitol.

A Major Connolly in Sherman's Army wrote to his wife that: "the army burned everything it came near in the state of South Carolina". Another one of Sherman's officers said; "A majority of these cities, towns, villages, and country houses have been burnt to the ground".

It should be noted that, at this time, the slaves suffered too. Slaves were frequently ordered on pain of death to disclose where their master had hid his valuables. Once these valuables were found, they were destroyed right in front of the slaves and the plantation was looted and then destroyed and burned. As a result, hundreds of half-starved Blacks who were already psychologically damaged by 'shell shock' had to follow Sherman's army to eat whatever they could find that was still edible. **To get rid of these 'low life scavengers', whenever Sherman's army came to a river or stream that they had to cross, first after his army built a bridge of pontoons they would cross over them, then they dismantled the pontoons and removed them before the Blacks had a chance to follow. (Since Blacks could not swim and feared the water they had to stay in the South and starve and could not migrate North).**

Here is a personal testimony of the aftermath of Sherman's army of destruction as recorded in the diary of one Miss Andrews: "about three miles from Sparta we struck the burnt country, as it is well named by the natives, and then I could better understand the wrath and desperation of these poor people. There was hardly a fence left standing all the way from Sparta to Gordon. The fields were trampled down and the road was lined with the carcasses of horses, hogs, and cattle that the invaders either unable to consume or to carry away with them, had wantonly shot to starve out the people and prevent them from eating and making the crops. The stench in some places was unbearable. The dwellings that were standing all showed signs of pillage, and on every plantation we saw the charred remains of the cotton gin house and pat can screw, where here and there lone chimney stacks, 'Sherman's sentinels', told of homes laid in ashes". Was this not the typical terrorist assault of what was to become known as "Total War"?

Once Sherman's army did enter Columbia, South Carolina after burning every town on the way, the diary of one eighteen-year-old survivor named Emma LeConte described what happened. According to her; "Sherman's army was well equipped with matches, crow bars, and other tools of the arsonist and plunderer". She wrote, "as soon as the bulk of the army entered the work of pillage began". The city was literally destroyed right before her eyes. She went on to describe how the Union soldiers, men dressed in uniform, acted like criminal arsonists. "They would enter a house and in the presence of helpless woman and children pour turpentine on their beds and set them on fire. When the women and some old men tried to put out the fire with fire hoses, soldiers armed with bayonets would cut through the fire hoses to ensure that the fire burned all the way to the ground ".

She further wrote: "imagine a night turned into noonday, only with a blazing scorching glare that was horrible – a copper colored sky across which swept columns of black, rolling, smoke glittering with sparks and foam embers, while all around us were falling thickly showers of burning flakes. Everywhere the palpitating blaze walling the streets with solid masses of flames as far as the eye could reach, filling the air with its horrible roar. On every side the racking and devouring fire, while every instant came the crashing timbers of thunder of falling buildings. A quivering molten ocean seems to fill the air and sky. The Library building opposite us seemed framed by the gushing flames and smoke, while through the windows gleamed the liquid fire".

She further described those soldiers as being "infuriated, cursing, screaming, exalting in their work".

She concluded that she did not believe that any house had escaped pillage. She said of the houses throughout the city of Columbia, "those that the flames sparred were entered by brutal soldiery and everything wantonly destroyed".

After his march of destruction Sherman met with both Lincoln and Grant at City Point on the James River on March 27, 1865 where he described his exploits of evil. Sherman described all about his marches to both Lincoln and Grant. Sherman's personal memoirs also record that Lincoln particularly enjoyed hearing about the mayhem of the bummers as looters were called back then.

When I was in high school we studied American history. Of course back then in my youth, none of these truths were ever revealed, even though I went to school in a southern state. Some historians now claim that Lincoln had no knowledge of these events and did not order Sherman's destruction of the South. Those who make such claims fail to face the recorded facts of history and to acknowledge even the simple military chain of command. Sherman was not on his own to do his own thing as he pleased. But was a soldier under orders to abolish the Southern economic system in order to both starve out the secessionists and **to stamp out once and for all, states' rights Sovereignty.**

Even if somehow it came to light that Lincoln's exact orders did not bring about all this destruction, nevertheless Lincoln's recorded meeting with Sherman on March 27, 1865 documents for history both his approval and gratitude for what the terrorist Sherman had done to the South. British military historian B.H.L. Hart wrote that: 'Lincoln's policy was in many ways the prototype of modern total war, for it employed terrorism against innocent, non-combative, civilians and the destruction of civil life in the South. This policy broke the code of civilized warfare as it inflicted suffering on innocence not on armed soldiers in a conflict of war'.

As I have shown and as the historical facts confirm both generals Sheridan and Sherman were in effect terrorists of their day for they not only burnt civilians alive, both also slaughtered farm animals burnt barns and crops and looted and torched cities. They made their destructive abuses and war crimes against humanity into legitimate acts of war.

Expect: War Crimes to become legitimate acts of war.

Later on when the U.S. had trouble with the plains Indians, Sherman who had burned Atlanta said; 'We must act with vindictive earnestness against the Sioux, even to their extermination, men, women and children'. Sheridan having also learned 'total war' said, 'the only good Indians I ever saw were dead'. Sherman not wanting to be clipped called for the massacre of all American Indians as the 'final solution to the Indian problem'. As you know this same term; 'Final Solution' was also used by another terrorist government (Nazis) in another war some eighty years later.

Being fair here, the Nazis were not the only ones to employ terror. During the Second World War, in February, 1945 the alias fire bombed Dresden and killed hundreds of thousands of desperate civilian refugees fleeing the Soviet Army. The Washington Post wrote on its fiftieth anniversary that; "If any one person can be blamed for the tragedy of Dresden, it appears to have been Churchill'. Before leaving Yalta, Churchill had ordered Allied Air Power to 'de-house' German civilians to make them into refugees clogging the roads over which German soldiers had to move to fight off the Red Army's winter offensive".

This mission of terror involved 770 Lancaster bombers that dropped 650,000 incinerary bombs on Dresden with 1,474 tons of high explosives. Then five hundred American B17's also helped to bomb that city into the Stone Age. The fires thus ignited burned for seven days and melted the streets. Those attempting to flee got their shoes burned off and feet scorched. Thousands who sought refuge in their cellars, died there, as they were starved for the oxygen that the flames devoured, then their buildings collapsed upon them, thus they became entombed.

Once this terror begins in the Civil War it continued on to where General Curtis Le May's forces of B 29's bombed Tokyo. One describes it as; "On March 9, 1945, 179 American bombers, armed with incinerary bombs intended to torch the wood and paper Japanese Capitol appeared over Tokyo, a city with a population density of one hundred and thirty five thousand per square mile. All went according to plan. Tokyo was consumed by fire so ferocious that the heat boiled the water in the lakes and ponds, cooking those who fled to safety there like human lobsters".

Six months later Truman dropped the Atom bomb on both Hiroshima and Nagasaki blotting out the lives of hundreds of thousands of civilians instantly. "If war terror is the deliberate slaughter of noncombatants, to break the will of the enemy, were not Dresden, Tokyo, Hiroshima and Nagasaki war terror on a monumental scale?"

While we condemn terror, it succeeds and will be employed again and again to achieve goals worth dying for. Generals Sherman and Sheridan had the Union armies crush and destroy the South so as to set it back a hundred years.

Expect: Terrorism.

In modern times, the IRA, the Stern Gang, the FLN, the Mau Mau, the Irgun, the ANC, the Viet Minh all used terror to change history. The innocent blood shed in revolutions that succeeded was quickly washed away by victory.

Terrorism often succeeded in the twentieth century, and when it did, the ex-terrorist achieved political power, glory, and immortality, with streets, towns, and cities named for them. And today America recognizes every one of these regimes that came out of wars where terrorism was used. For example, today Saigon, once the capitol of South Vietnam is now called Ho Chi Minh City.

'One man's terrorist is another man's freedom fighter'. Nations, empires, ethnic groups, republics, monarchs, dictators, rebels, revolutionaries, and anarchists have all used terror to win their respective wars including consolidating their tyranny, expelling colonial powers and achieving the national independence of their cause.

So then Bush's "War on Terrorism" is just a propaganda fraud of getting the American people to pay his Iraq war debt for foolish political pork barrel projects, **like the rebuilding of Iraq so that the American people can no longer afford their domestic social programs that they now need big time.**

"Modernity often forgives the sins of terrorists because of the nobility of the cause they served". For example, today both Generals Sheridan and Sherman are forgiven because they supposedly freed the slaves. But today the Blacks are not yet free of poverty, police brutality or other miscarriages of justice. True, they are now free of their masters, his housing, and his 'property care'. In other words, now they have neither jobs nor a place to stay with food to eat and provided health care or other benefits. So just how much good did the terrorism known as The Civil War really accomplish for anybody's good?

Let me conclude this section on terrorism by quoting Pat Buchanan from his book: <u>Where The Right Went Wrong</u>. Behind almost every act of revolutionary terror lies some political purpose. '**How other countries govern themselves is NOT a vital interest of the United States. We Americans have no commission from God to police the world'.** There cannot be an American solution to every problem. Our unquestioned support for Israel is universally resented and costing us dearly. When Bush appeared in Bagdad, he united Islam against America. U.S. dominance of the Middle East. Is not the corrective of terror. It is the cause of terror. Were we not over there, the nine eleven terrorists would not have been over here. '**Terrorism is the price of empire. If we do not wish to pay the price, we must give up the empire'.**

<u>Expect: to have to provide for yourself so buy your own food stuff now.</u>

Moreover Bush's "War on terrorism" was designed politically to so deprive the American people of their basic human and democratic rights to the good life as to get them to foolishly accept Bush's dumb worldview, idiotic ideology and stupid foreign policy instead of getting their own needs met. Whereas **the Bible does not say that democracy is God's gift to man or that it is God's will for America to spread democracy to bring about world peace, especially Mideast peace.** In fact, the Bible does say, and Bush and now Obama had better heed this: **"IF ANY WILL NOT PROVIDE FOR HIS OWN, ESPECIALLY THOSE OF HIS OWN HOUSE HE HAS DENIED THE FAITH AND IS WORSE THAN AN INFIDEL', (I Timothy 5:8).**

The Bible also says in the twenty fourth psalm that: "THE EARTH IS THE LORD'S', so why don't we stop trying to control it and let God have it back to do with as He will!

Besides all this physical abuse during the Civil War, there were many atrocities. Just like in domestic violence there is not only the assault of a loved one, but also the psychological and mental torture of the victim. Lincoln not only waged a war of physical conflict and an invasion upon the South, but also a mental conflict between two opinions as to the type of federal government the constitution really envisioned for the American people.

Lincoln's "reeducation house" was Fort Lafayette in New York harbor known as the "American Bastille". It was a filthy old fort crowded with the stinking bodies of the many political prisoners of the Lincoln Administration. Its beds consisted of mattresses made of straw or moss and infested with body lice, fleas, cockroaches and other vermin. The food there was horrible, too. Some occupants recorded that their breakfast consisted of "some discolored beverage, dignified by the name of coffee, a piece of fried pork, sometimes raw and sometimes half cooked, and coarse bread cut in large thick slices." Some days the water that was served at meals "would contain a dozen tadpoles from a quarter to half an inch long". Of course, the guards were "insolent", and the warden or commandant, since it was a military prison "took no apparent interest in the comfort of prisoners." Among these political prisoners were newspaper editors from around the country who dared to question Lincoln's invasion of the South. You remember from American history; Seward of Seward's Folly fame, who at that time headed Lincoln's secret police which scoured the countryside to apprehend any editors of newspapers that did not support Lincoln's war policies to arrest and imprison them there.

This policy of Lincoln's suppression of the press began with the New York City newspapers including the New York Daily News and The Journal of Commerce. These two newspapers had to be shut down for they were the leaders of the opposition press and contained many articles opposed to Lincoln's war policy, which were then reprinted in many other papers.

For these newspaper articles to get reprinted by other local newspapers they had to first reach those other newspapers. This was just usually done by the U. S. mail. But in May of 1861, The Journal of Commerce published a list of over one hundred northern newspapers that had editorialized against going to war and adopting Lincoln's war policy. The infuriated Lincoln Administration promptly ordered their Postmaster General to deny these papers use of the U.S. mail. Since at that time all U.S. newspaper circulation was done by mail, this illegal order put these opposition newspapers out of business. **So much for 'freedom of the press'! Yes, many of Lincoln's war policies like this one were clearly unconstitutional which courts should have ruled against.**

Expect: The unconstitutional.

Among those newspapers so censored by Lincoln were the two New York newspapers already mentioned. Plus, The Daybook, Brooklyn Eagle, and Freeman's Journal also of New York. Along with The Chicago Times, The Dayton Empire, Louisville Courier, The Maryland News Sheet, Baltimore Gazette, Daily Loyalist, Wheeling Register, and Louisville True Presbyterian, Among other smaller newspapers too numerous to mention.

Dean Sprague in his book, Freedom under Lincoln has brought out that this policy whereby Lincoln actually suppressed the news and twisted it to fit his liking had the long-term impact of "laying the groundwork for such centralized coercive governmental power measures as military conscription and the federal income tax." He goes on to say; "at the outbreak of the war the federal government was not a real source of power. But when the arm of the Lincoln Administration reached into Cooperstown, New York and took away George Browne, when it slipped into Freedom, Maine and spirited away Robert Elliot, when it proved powerful enough to send three citizens of North Branch, Michigan to Fort Lafayette, and imprison, without any recourse of law, a man in Newborn, Iowa it was apparent that the federal executive had real power and that '**Father Abraham**' had been born to the American people."

As the fatalities from the Civil War multiplied, The Peace Movement in the North grew stronger and more vocal, and its repression by the Lincoln Administration became more severe. The editor of The Essex County Democrat of Haverhill, Massachusetts, was tarred and feathered by a mob of Unionists who also destroyed the papers printing equipment. Gradually the same thing happened to The Sentinel of Easton, Pennsylvania, The Jeffersonian of West Chester, Pennsylvania; The Democrat of Stark County Ohio; The Farmer of Fairfield, Connecticut and other newspapers too. **All of these newspapers were known as 'peace advocates' for they editorialized in favor of ending all the bloodshed of the Civil War in working out some kind of a peaceful solution which included compensated emancipation, that many nations of that time had already done peacefully. Lincoln would have none of it, so he sent both his military and his supporters to destroy newspaper after newspaper in the North to silence The Peace Movement there**. Thus The Northern Peace Movement was not only intimidated, but also physically assaulted and destroyed. Thus Fort Lafayette was filled with newspaper editors from all over the country who had dared to question the wisdom of Lincoln's military invasion of the South and his war of conquest against it. But newspaper editors were not the only political prisoners in Fort Lafayette.

A Maryland college professor; Thomas J. DE Lorenzo says in his book about: The Real Lincoln that "in May 1861 a special election was held to fill the ten empty seats of the Maryland House of Delegates". The men elected to fill those positions were all high-class important people, composed of leading industrialists, physicians, and judges, including lawyers from Baltimore. But because they were suspected of harboring secessionist sympathies by the Lincoln Administration, most of them were arrested without charge and sent to Fort Lafayette without trial. Some of them managed somehow to flee but Dean Sprague explains, "This was perhaps the only election in American History in which every man who was nominated and elected went to prison." Too bad corrupt politicians today go free while the innocent are sent to prison too.

By September of that same year the entire state of Maryland was under military occupation. Lincoln in Washington was taking no chances that Confederates could surround him. So, he would not let the Maryland Legislature convene to discuss or vote on whether or not Maryland was to remain neutral or join the Confederacy. Therefore, he sought to prohibit it from doing so by military force. One of his generals threatened to bombard Annapolis if the legislature met there, so they met in Frederic, Maryland instead. Lincoln gave another one of his generals the order to allow the Unionist members of the legislature to meet but not The Peace Party members. Lincoln's Secretary of War told his generals; "If necessary, all or any part of the members of the Maryland Legislature must be arrested." All of the members of the legislature from the Baltimore area were subsequently arrested, without any due process and including the mayor of Baltimore plus their U.S. Congressman, Henry May. All other Maryland Legislatures who were even suspected of having any secessionist sympathies were arrested too. Along with these victims of false arrest were several newspaper editors and owners from Baltimore. All these people after being arrested without cause were imprisoned without trial in Fort Lafayette. **(You might say that Fort Lafayette was the Guantanamo Bay prison of its day for Americans with constitutional rights).** From Republican Presidents Lincoln to Bush, history does repeat itself. Now doesn't it?

At the time when the Maryland Legislature went to Frederick, the entire town was sealed off by the military, under Lincoln's orders, and a house-to-house search was conducted for any Maryland Legislatures who were not friendly to the Lincoln Administration. The general in charge of this abuse, General Banks reported to Lincoln that every single advocate for peace in the Maryland Legislature had been both arrested and imprisoned.

That November other elections were scheduled to occur. These were suppressed in democratic America, the land of the free. General Banks was ordered to send troops to the voting places to protect Union voters so that their votes would count but to arrest and hold in confinement till after the election all Disunionists or peace advocates of the Peace Party. **Was this not officially sanctioned voter fraud somewhat like Bush's 'legitimate' Florida vote?**

Election judges there were instructed to forbid anyone voting against Lincoln's war. The ballots were made of different colors so that the soldiers could easily throw out any Peace Party vote and then arrest the voter. "Many who attempted to vote the Peace ticket in Baltimore Maryland were arrested for carrying a ballot of the wrong color. They were charged for 'polluting the ballot box.'" Thus, Lincoln's Republican candidates won every single election in Maryland. Sprague writes; **"The orgy of the suppression of civil liberties reached its apex in Maryland".** "Under the protection of 'Federal Bayonets', similar suppression of free elections occurred in most other Northern states." **Yes, America has a history of voter fraud long before the Presidential election of 2000 in Florida!**

<u>Expect: Your elections to get stolen too just like in 2020.</u>

Time has not healed this process of fraud, for in their book; <u>Vote Scam: The Stealing of America</u> two brothers who are investigative journalists from the Miami area, Jim and Ken Collier, document how that **for nearly twenty**

years former state attorney and attorney general, Janet Reno, of Waco Massacre fame, covered up the ramped voter cheating and outright fraud common in local Florida elections. That is, the voting machines of the butterfly ballot with chads were rigged in hundreds of precincts so that only pre-approved candidates could win. Thus with help of unscrupulous Cuban immigrants who had achieved political power in South Florida, Bush was enabled to easily steal the Florida vote of the 2000 presidential elections. **Apparently from Lincoln to Bush the Republicans are still up to stealing elections. But the Democrats also do this too.**

Republican President Abraham Lincoln suspended Habeas Corpus as part of his presidential war powers on April 27, 1861. Habeas Corpus was a right or weapon for the defense of the common man first signed into English common law by King John in about A.D. 1215 via the Magna Carter. This rule of English common law set down the legal procedure for a prisoner of the state to be released from prison. Among those rights now guaranteed jailed American citizens are: the constitutional right to a speedy public trial by an impartial jury of one's peers, to be informed of the nature and cause of the accusation against them, to be confronted with witnesses against them, to bring witnesses in their favor, and to have the assistance of legal counsel. Republican President Abraham Lincoln, or I should say; 'Lincoln the Magnificent', **Sovereign** of the U. S.A. suspended all these constitutional rights in 1861 and his suspension of them remained in effect for Lincoln's entire Administration, even after the Civil War ended. Does not this same condition exist with another former Republican President George W. Bush?

Upon taking office in March 1861, Lincoln the deceitful also implemented a whole series of unconstitutional acts, including the invasion of the South without even consulting Congress, blockading southern ports, and declaring Martial Law. Afterward, he suspended Habeas Corpus.

With that suspension of Habeas Corpus together with his Martial Law decree thousands of American citizens were imprisoned without trial after being arrested without charge.

Expect: Marshal Law and imprisonment without trial.

'Lincoln the Magnificent' Martial Law decree in the North enabled his military to arrest and imprison thousands of American citizens, sometimes on just mere rumors, which led to the false imprisonment of thousands of antiwar protestors in Fort Lafayette. By 1862, 'Lincoln the Magnificent' suspension of Habeas Corpus had been expanded to include those who 'discouraged voluntary enlistments' in Lincoln's war. His Martial Law enabled the military to bypass all civil liberty protections to arrest and imprison many thousands of citizens too. So American citizens of the North were subjected to this unconstitutional abuse for the duration of the Lincoln Administration. Prisoners were never told why, or for what reason they were being arrested, no investigations of any kind were ever made, and no trials were ever held. Doesn't this sound like the forerunner of George W. Bush's and Barack Obama's Guantanamo Bay for Americans?

'Lincoln the Magnificent' also censored all telegraphic communication, nationalized railroads, created several new states, ordered his troops to interfere with free elections in the North by intimidating Democratic voters there and deporting Congressman Clement L. Vallasdingham of Ohio, **and confiscated private property including firearms in violation of the Second Amendment.**

Expect: The confiscation of private property including firearms in violation of the Second Amendment.

This unconstitutional abuse of the civil liberties of American citizens went as far as the passage of the Indemnity Act of 1863, which placed President Lincoln his cabinet and his military above the law. **Today's Patriot Act of similar design also squashes the civil liberties of American citizens just like Lincoln's Indemnity Act of 1863 did. Obviously, times have not really changed that much, although President Obama promised real change. What was first instituted by President Lincoln and reintroduced by President Bush has now been reinforced by President Obama and made into official public policy. So, watch out and get prepared NOW as War is certainly coming. The Lord Jesus said so!**

MUSLIM OBAMA'S MUSLIM DECEPTION

During the Arab Spring when many dictatorships were falling across North Africa, the Liberals said that such was the long-awaited expansion of democracy. But in reality, it turned out to be the expansion of The Muslim Brotherhood instead with the support and help of the Obama Administration.

Jimmy Swaggart was one of the few Christian Ministers who said back then that Obama was a Muslim sympathizer. And Michael Savage called Obama 'the Islamic sympathizer in chief' on page 200 of his book: Trickle Down Tyranny. And Obama is really a nominal Muslim by birth and not a Christian at all. There is no Record that Obama was ever baptized Christian in any Christian Church. So Obama is an undocumented phony Christian just like all these illegal aliens are undocumented false Americans. (No baptism certificate – no Christian, no birth certificate – no American).

On page 40 of his book: The Amateur, when Edward Klein asked Dr. Jeremiah Wright, Obama's former racist pastor, if Obama was ever converted from Islam to Christianity. Dr. Wright said: 'That's hard to tell'. Look, if you' re saved, you know it, and so does everybody else that's close to you!

Obama's personal hypocrisy reminds me of an incident that happened when I was a child. We called a simple young girl that lived by us Reba residue. Since, one day she went home crying to her mother with her face smeared with dog residue. Her simple mother hollered; 'pew, due, residue!' Then she asked Reba what had happened. Reba said that she found what she thought was chocolate in a neighbor's front yard. Since she was friends with that neighbor's dog she thought that dog wouldn't mind if she ate what she saw that dog drop. But when she picked up what she thought was chocolate it had melted in the sun and ran down her arm and somehow got smeared on her face and then it changed from being chocolate to something that stunk.

Her upset Mother told her to come in right away and take a bath. Well, the child was hurting. So, she couldn't say I'm gonna wash your mouth out with soap.

This reminds me of exactly what Obama's election has produced. Here was a man that many Blacks believed was somehow good, sweet, educated, well spoken and chocolate just like them too. But in reality this man turned out to be just something a dog had dropped as his repugnant socialist policies now stunk to high heaven.

For example, when Obama first took office Black unemployment was over 15% but he still had the Congress waste a whole year on his socialist Obamacare. So that at the start of his second term Black unemployment was now up over 19%. In all this time he has taken over all healthcare, student loans, the auto industry and mortgages in an attempt to change capitalism into socialism by promoting his Obamacare at your expense and also vetoing the Keystone Pipeline to keep you from working and busting Social Security with disability for bums.

If Obamacare was so great then how come Democratic Senators and Congressman grant the reward of exemption to Obamacare for those businesses that make political contributions to the Democratic Party?

And all you Christian Denominations who provide social services including hospitals MUST provide sexual services including abortions to your employees under Obama Care while Muslims remain exempt to Obama Care.

Speaking again of Obama Care, there is one issue that has not yet been mentioned. That is Obama Care provides for extended life support services for deformed minority babies (particularly those of illegal aliens and Blacks) who will now grow up to become future socialist voters. That your taxes will support since they will never be able to work just like all those illegal alien children.

Social Work Counselors and Ministers who will become Hospital Chaplains are now being trained to council families to pull the plug on granny in order to save Social Security for these deformed minority babies. How stupid this racist policy is. Yes, Obamacare hurts the elderly and gives false hope to the deformed. The deformed can't amount to much in life unless they encounter Christian healing. So, it also seems dumb to have kicked prayer out of school when such will be necessary for these deformed students to succeed in life. **If these people have a right to a public education, than that education has a duty to expose them to whatever Christian gifts like healing that may be available to them in this life.**

The Muslim Obama has also stood by as millions of Americans; both White and Black were unfairly driven out of their homes and into homelessness. For those who somehow may still have homes, Obama has given seventy-five million of your tax dollars to help GE build smart electric meters that aid burglars in spying on who's home and what electric appliances you have as they 'case' your house.

Speaking of spying, it is now being done at your expense. Your tax dollars are paying for the Utah Data Center of the National Security Agency (NSA). This agency keeps a record of every phone call and internet transaction that you make. And you are not getting your tax money's worth for there is no evidence that their efforts have ever prevented any terrorist attack. For example, where were they when the Boston marathon bombing happened?

This spying is the main enterprise of the 'military, industrial complex' that former President Eisenhower resented. Back in history several of his advisors (those who also wanted him to appoint that liberal Earl Warren) wanted him to move away from relying upon Christian Prophecy to a more secular and industrial spying on the Soviet Union during the cold war. At that time he used to visit a Christian Prophet in Pasadena California each month to find out what was happening. This worked out well because **'The eyes of the Lord are in every place beholding the evil and the good' (Proverbs 15:3).**

But even so this prophetic spying was replaced with expensive 'military industrial' spying that your tax dollars now pay for. Think of all the billions wasted on spy satellites that you could have used. **A country cannot use Christian methods if it's no longer Christian. So it's time for revival.** It's far better to restore prayer and Bible reading to school and make America Christian again than to have to pay excessive taxes to fund expensive drug rehab with other welfare programs and social services that distribute 'free' condoms and birth control pills at your expense.

If real revival is to happen first this fatalistic notion of 'learned helplessness' that all things are supposed to get worse and worse and then the Antichrist will take over this country must be overcome. Several years ago the then President George H.W. Bush (Bush41) said that America was going to become part of the One World Order. About that same time the famous Bible teacher, Marilyn Hickey said on page 52 of her book: Armageddon that the future Antichrist's world empire would include 'only that part of the world that was once part of the Roman Empire'. So NOT America. So, then it's past time to retake America for the Christians!

This brings up the misconception that President Obama is secretly the Antichrist. President Obama might have the spirit of Antichrist but he is not that person. The two forerunners of the Antichrist, Napoleon and Hitler were both Europeans. The coming Antichrist will also be a European. But some prophetic scholars say that the Antichrist might be an American or Syrian or some other Muslim. The scriptures however do describe the Beast that will become the Antichrist as coming from out of the sea **(Revelation 13:1).** This proves that he does not come from America.

Revelation 13:2 says that he will have a mouth as a lion. Lion is the symbol for the United Kingdom (England). So, he will be able to speak English in great swelling words and blasphemies. Most Europeans can speak English and many European languages too. Islamic people however can speak mainly their native tongue. Example Arabs speak only Arabic.

In **Revelation 13:7** we see that war is coming as the Antichrist will be able to make war with the saints and to overcome them and power was given him over all kindreds, and tongues, and nations. Jimmy Swaggart's Expositors Study Bible says 'this doesn't include the entirety of the world, but rather the area over which he has control, which is basically the area of the old Roman empire'.

So, Marilyn Hickey and Jimmy Swaggart, both Spirit filled ministers see the same boundaries to the Antichrist's Empire.

If you remember how that Obama promised change from the Bush policies of Middle East War, Guantanamo terrorist imprisonment, using drones to kill civilians and torturing terrorists.

Here is what has really been happening despite Obama's polished rhetoric: The Middle East war in Afghanistan is continuing and now the one in Syria is due to expand. Guantanamo Bay which holds terrorists beyond the reach of America's constitutional law protections remains opened and still in service. The Obama Administration has used a drone to kill an American citizen. And the Obama Administration's ambassador to Libya and several other Americans were killed by Jihadist Muslims because of resentment over Libya being used as a liberated place to now torture terrorists.

It is now seen to be more advantageous to violate the constitutional, civil and human rights of American Citizens than to throw out the extreme liberal policy of an idealistic pluralistic society complete with Jihadist Muslims (enemies of the people) living among us as mandated by law. Which law is now supreme, the Constitution and freedom of association, or immigration rights with its liberal notion about pluralistic democracy that curses our land?

Moreover, the Muslim Obama is not really an Afro-American Christian as many Blacks believe but a Black African Muslim, descendant from those same Black African Muslims that got rich by selling their Black brothers into slavery.

So, the Muslim Obama comes from a Muslim family and was raised as a Muslim. When he went to school every day he had to pray to the false Muslim god, Allah. Most of his schooling during the formative years of childhood took place in the Muslim country of Indonesia.

Speaking of Indonesia, it should be noted that the government of that Muslim nation wanting to bless its own people with healing and deliverance among other miracles recently invited in a famous Christian miracle worker who also used to minister here in Florida. (This was done because as Muslims know their Allah is remote, distant and unconcerned about peoples everyday needs).

Indonesia's action may seem strange but such is typical of Muslim nations that really care for the welfare of their people. Those in authority over such nations know that prayers to Allah do not obtain personal blessings for their people. But Jesus whom they consider a mere prophet can both heal and deliver. Though Muslim theology is wrong, God (the God of Abraham) still blesses through Jesus.

In fact what constitutes most Christian prayer is for God to bless people physically, socially and financially. But Muslim prayer (like Obama learned) is for vengeance (Sheria Law), 'social justice' (reclaiming Iraq and Syria for Isis), armaments (like nuclear weapons for Iran) and empowerment to fight and behead the enemies of Islam and to accept martyrdom if need be.

Speaking of Muslim prayer, it is also obvious that the child Obama prayed against US forces in Vietnam just like other Muslim students right there in Indonesia. But these prayers didn't seem to work much then. So most Christians would say that this is because the Muslim god Allah is not real but false.

But prayers to a false god cause people to get worked up with the intention to make their prayers come to pass themselves (self fulfilling prophecy). Psychologists say that's what we have here with the Muslim Obama. **(Since Allah can't, Obama will!)** And now subconsciously Obama has cut back America's armaments to the smallest infantry since 1940 and the smallest navy since 1915. He has also removed all tanks from Europe and missile defense especially for Poland. (If you remember the invasion of Poland began World War II).

Plus he has emasculated America's armed forces by promoting the gay lifestyle and authorizing gay marriage.

But don't laugh at America, once the greatest nation on earth, for all that these deceived Muslim prayers of Muslim school children and Muslim immigrants from Palestine, Iraq, Syria, Somalia and other Muslim lands have given us is the disgrace of the Muslim Obama.

Soon and very soon those millions of Muslim immigrants in Western Europe will give to the world through their deceived prayers and votes the horror of the Antichrist, known to them as the twelfth Imam! WAKE UP and EXPECT WAR as it's on the way. The Lord Jesus in the Bible (Mathew 24) says that before He comes again WARS will come. So EXPECT WARS!

Obama's One World Order, Agenda 21, Political Correctness has allowed the enemies of the Gospel of Christ (Jihadist Muslims) to have freedom of religion to impose their evil practices (Shari Law) right here in America to curse our land.

Recently when the Muslims demonstrated for Sheri law in Australia, the Prime Minister of Australia told the Muslims there: 'If you don't like our laws, leave'! Hopefully after this reprobate Obama leaves office, this political correct mess and Jihadist Muslims will also get thrown out with the Obama trash too.

This is where the new prophetic book: The Harbinger by Rabbi Jonathon Chan comes in. This prophetic book (The Harbinger) discloses from scripture (Isaiah 9:10) in detail the nine harbingers coming America's way, now that it is under judgment and has been so since the 9/11 tragedy.

This judgment is due to turning away from God just like ancient Israel did. **So God's many blessings have now been replaced with judgment. America's failure to repent of its personal sins like abortion and of social sins like condoning the immigration of Jihadist Muslims has now increased that judgment just as the nine Harbingers indicated so expect more and more damaging tornadoes, more untimely snowstorms and blizzards, more flooding, more unexplained hurricane force winds, more and stronger hurricanes, more severe droughts and more plant diseases as God's judgment expands into plagues that will cause crops to rot in the field and deprive illegal aliens of farm work and Americans of food. This will be Obama's legacy.**

These next points are for the benefit of the low information Christian, American citizen and voter who have been too busy trying to earn a living to notice or even care that they have been deceived.

There is one more truth that I must share. This one signifies rebellion against God, the sin of witchcraft, akin to voodoo. In this last election 93% of all Blacks in America voted for Obama, the abortionist. **This means that many so-called Christian Church Members cared more for phony chocolate (Obama) than the truth of God's word.** When Christian people deliberately go against the Bible teachings of God heard in Churches across America to follow after phony chocolate instead, then their god has become their belly and every church has a duty to exercise church discipline and excommunicate them or put them out of the fellowship unless they repent.

Now that I have said what God wanted me to say about that, since this book is not a political commentary but a Christian guide on what to expect and since I would rather exonerate someone then to have to constantly expose them and since the more you expose Obama, the more he stinks. Let's just flush this Obama mess and get back to the Evangelist, Jimmy Swaggart.

Some may be disappointed as this evangelist supposedly fell into sin years ago and may feel that such disqualifies him from further Christian ministry now. But 'THE GIFTS AND CALLINGS OF GOD ARE WITHOUT REPENTANCE' (Romans 11:29). So this man still has the Spirit of Truth in him which we can all benefit from. Let him speak truth to us as the oracle of God that he is on all evangelical issues.

When it comes to prophecy however he does not interpret tongues given as prophetic words in his church services, so the dispensing of first-hand end time prophetic truth is not his specialty or ministerial calling. As an Assemblies of God minister, he just gives out the typical Assemblies of God theological view points on prophetic topics.

Nevertheless, he is one of the three apostolic ministers now broadcasting from America to the whole world today. He can be reached at www.JSM.org or phone 1-800-288-8350. One of the others is Pat Robertson of CBN, and the 700 Club who also heads Regent University in Virginia Beach, Virginia and also operates 'Operation Blessing' for the good of all mankind. His website is WWW.CBN.COM and his phone number is 1-800-759-0700.

The other apostolic leader, Jim Bakker used to head PTL. He served some time in prison for PTL's misdeeds. While there he received visions and wrote his 'prison epistles' about soon coming events and that he had been wrong about both the prosperity message and the pre-tribulation rapture. And he received additional visions after he was released from prison on parole. So thanks to his personal repentance he has now received a new mandate from God by which he has been commissioned to save much people alive by helping them prepare for the hard times of tribulation that's coming our way. He even has a new book out now called: TIME HAS COME. He can be reached at: The Jim Bakker Show. Com or by phoning him at 1-888-988-1588 to buy some of his food-stuff that we'll all soon need as Obama's stupid policies brings God's judgment upon America.

Over the Jim Bakker Show on April 17, 2013 the Christian Prophet John Paul Jackson said; 'The president that God really wanted America to have in 2012 had been aborted in 1972'. Then he said that: 'the man of God tells the truth even if it's inconvenient to tell the truth'.

From what I remember of John Paul Jackson he was typically more direct than the other prophets who had come to visit us at the Vineyard in Anaheim, California back at the end of the 1980's.

John Wimber the pastor of that main Vineyard in Anaheim had invited this prophetic team from Kansas City, Missouri to minister to us. From what I remember their prophetic team was made up of Paul Cain, Rick Joiner, John Paul Jackson and Bob Jones.

Bob Jones looked like a real prophet though (he had silver-grey hair) and he called the exact date of the San Francisco earthquake. Moreover, he also said how that it would be seen worldwide. Many thought that was extravagant but a football game was on TV worldwide at the time. So that prophecy rang true.

John Paul Jackson was much younger in those days with long black hair. Some in the congregation said that he was also too good looking to be a real prophet. In any case his clear, direct and outspoken nature was still the same over the Jim Bakker Show. Only this time he looked more like a real prophet with grey hair.

Back in those days I was one of the congregational prophets (those who prophesied to the congregation of the Anaheim Vineyard).

But this visiting team of professional prophets were all nationally recognized. Some of them had been on radio and TV. And a few of them had written books that had been published.

I liked John Paul Jackson the most because of the direct words he shared. He had obviously not been co-opted by having to be politically correct.

I liked the prophet Paul Cain the least because his main concern was about tithing. John Wimber had come out of the Quaker denomination which does not believe in nor practice tithing. Quakers shake; they do not pick anybody's pocket. So most of Paul Cain's message fell flat there in Anaheim as it was seen as unannointed Baptist propaganda.

By the way, before I move on to something else some may wonder how Jimmy Swaggart, an evangelist could possibly operate in an Apostolic ministry. God showed me something about this back in the 1980's after I had become wheelchair disabled and could no longer work and decided to further my education by going to Fuller Theological Seminary after I graduated college in Florida.

I wound up going to Fuller Seminary because the day I went to take my graduate record exam after graduating from college in Florida, early that morning someone had left their stereo on and it was playing an old surfer tune called: 'The little old lady from Pasadena,' and Fuller Seminary is in Pasadena, California. So, I went there as I took that song to be my clear word from God to go there.

While there this controversy over Jimmy Swaggart's sexual sin happened and some of my professors started to ridicule me too because they knew that I also was a Pentecostal person. I remember that I fought back though, which most Christians don't do, especially to those who are over you in the Lord. I told them that although I'm not an AG (Assemblies of God) person, nevertheless I'm not gonna let someone talk down one of my brothers for whom Christ had shed his blood on the cross for.

Then I hit them with a word of knowledge I had just gotten back then. I told them that Jimmy Swaggart is a southern gentleman who needed sexual release, not somebody with a sexual problem anyway. Rather than force sex on the mother of his children, he'd rather have anonymous sex with some mistress like other southern gentlemen have done. You men of God know full well from the scriptures that some of the heroes of the faith not only had multiple wives but also concubines. (Solomon the wisest man that ever lived had 700 wives and 300 concubines, I Kings 11:3). Since there is nothing new under the sun, (Ecclesiastes 1:9) a man's sexual needs back then are still the same today.

Anyway this whole issue comes down to ministerial jealousy. Another minister took pictures of Jimmy Swaggart at a brothel in New Orleans and circulated those pictures in an effort to destroy Jimmy Swaggart's ministry. It's dangerous to attack God's ministers even if your information is correct. So I left this issue there at that time and went on to do my studies.

Several years later God reminded me about this again and also said this to me: 'IN THIS WORLD AND AMONG HIS OWN PEOPLE, JIMMY SWAGGART WILL CONTINUE TO BE KNOWN AS AN EVANGELIST. BUT IN THE KINGDOM OF HEAVEN HE SHALL

BE PROMOTED AND GIVEN THE HIGH HONOR OF BEING RECOGNIZED AS THE APOSTLE OF THE CROSS SINCE HIS CONSTANT PREACHING ABOUT THE BLOOD SACRIFICE OF THE LORD JESUS ON THE CROSS GREATLY PLEASES ME.'

Some may want to discount this and say it cannot be a real 'word of knowledge'. To those who feel that way understand this: Jimmy Swaggart is a singer, right. Now singing is a gift, right. When one has this gift but steps back to let others exercise their gifting to sing instead of showing himself off isn't that what the scripture calls 'PREFERRING ONE ANOTHER' (Romans 12:10)? I think that God knows the man's heart full well. And whatever reward He wants to give to anyone, I say, thank you Jesus.

While I was at that school some years ago Pat Robertson was also young and ventured into prophecy by falsely stating that the Soviets would invade Israel and set off Armageddon. He declared this back in May 1982 and also said that by the fall of that year there would be judgment on the world. Although his attempt at prophecy did not materialize back then, nevertheless the man conveys much needed truth that the Spirit of God wants said today for the benefit of all. His 'words of knowledge' encourage many to reach out and receive from God. He can be reached by contacting him at WWW.CBN. COM or 1-800-759-0700.

We've got to get over this mindset of wanting to throw out the baby with the bathwater. We need to accept those Christian Ministers who may be failing people but God has sent them to help us get ready and prepared for the last days now upon us. And reject those reprobates like the Muslim Obama and his Czars that God has not given us but have been fostered up on us both by the seducing spirits of socialism and the evil spirits of deception which made many believe that Obama was 'good chocolate' when his socialist policies have revealed him to be just something a dog has dropped.

This last Obama czar of EBOLA is a political hack and a lawyer master of deceit. As you know lawyers are trained liars. Haven't we already had enough lies from the Obama administration about EBOLA?

Speaking of lies I now remember how that a liberal newspaper from up North published an article naming over 100 lies given by the Obama Administration to the American people just about Obama Care alone. You may even remember one of those lies which said that; <u>'if you like your doctor, you can keep him'.</u>

Now with EBOLA the official lie is: <u>'closing the borders will be counter-productive to peoples movement from the EBOLA zone necessary for both</u>

world trade to keep these nations solvent and from getting the medical treatment of necessity for EBOLA'. But the truth is most Black African dictators have closed their borders to any and all EBOLA zone travelers. Does the Muslim Obama a half breed Black man have more common sense in this matter than these Black African dictators just because he is an elected democrat?

It is very significant that this last EBOLA czar used to be the political mouthpiece of vice president Biden. Perhaps Obama is paving the way for Biden to take over. But Biden cannot take on Obama's job unless Obama dies in office.

As a nominal Muslim, Obama has absorbed into his subconscious the need for Muslim suicide. Thus he may consider suicide once he realizes that the new Republican Senate will stop this socialist agenda and already has more than enough evidence to impeach him.

In any case all should now see clearly that the Black man 'Duncan' who lied about not being exposed to EBOLA in order to get on the plane and come to America also died here as 'the wages of sin is death'. But he only told one lie. What judgment now awaits the Muslim Obama and his many czars for telling thousands of lies about 'everything under the sun' to the American people during his two terms of office.

1. I told you before about Muslim Obama's Muslim Deception that Obama is still a nominal Muslim. And there is no record that he was ever converted to Christianity. Complete with a baptism certificate issued by any Christian Church or Christian community of faith.

Muslims are allowed by their false doctrine to conceal, disguise or hide their personal beliefs, Ideas, feelings and opinions in order to achieve personal success for the Muslim cause. Like ruling over Christians or even hiring other Muslims like Valerie Jarrett as public employees to abuse Christians and promote Iran's nuclear arms as well.

Consequently, one leading newspaper (it may have been the Washington Post) recently reported over a hundred lies about Obama Care alone. You may even remember one of those lies yourself: 'If you like your doctor, you can keep him'.

Now in the Iran nuclear agreement the Muslim liar Obama is trying to deal with the Muslim liars of Iran. This agreement has to be bad as two lies do not make truth and two wrongs do not make a right!

To make my disclosure about Muslim lying clearer, it must be reiterated that as long as a Muslim is in a country where Islam is a

minority, then the Muslim (in this case, Obama) deceptiveness about anything is officially expected and sanctioned by the 'evil religion of Islam' (the Muslim faith).

2. Obama is really a nominal Muslim by birth and not a Christian at all. Since there is no Record that Obama was ever baptized Christian in any Christian Church. So Obama is an undocumented phony Christian just like all these illegal aliens are undocumented false Americans. (No baptism certificate – no Christian, no birth certificate – no American).

You Afro Americans probably find yourselves more disappointed in your unemployment today than when Obama first took office. Well Obama's priorities have just overshadowed your need for jobs. After all he was so busy doing evil like bailing out the banks, signing anti-American trade agreements, vetoing the Keystone Pipeline and supporting gay marriage that he just had no time to concern himself with 'Black Issues'. Like the real social justice of Black unemployment.

I remember and you probably do too that Dr. Martin Luther King Jr. had a dream where he was looking forward to the time when a man would be judged by the content of his character and not by the color of his skin. **But 93% of all Blacks voted for Obama because they thought that as a Black man, he would see things from a Black perspective.**

Unfortunately for all Americans, Obama is a Black African Muslim descendant from the same Black African Muslims who sold their Black brothers into slavery, since that's what Muslims do just as ISIS showed us. And not an Afro-American Christian at all. Muslim Obama's deception has now turned Dr. Martin Luther King Jr.'s dream into a Muslim socialist nightmare complete with demonic despotism masquerading as 'the beautiful (Muslim) religion'. Therefore now it's time for you to repent and for Muslim Obama to be impeached!

3. On page 40 of his book: The Amateur, when Edward Klein asked Dr. Jeremiah Wright, Obama's former racist pastor, if Obama was ever converted from Islam to Christianity. Dr. Wright said: 'That's hard to tell'. Look, if you're saved, you know it, and so does everybody else that's close to you!

So Muslim Obama was never converted from Islam to Christianity. The Bible also says that 'YOU JUDGE A TREE BY ITS FRUIT' (Matthew 12:33, Luke 6:44). In that case **America has had two bad presidents in a row. As you know, George W. Bush (Bush 43) lied America into the Iraq war. But he also bailed out the banks as if such was Republican. Look,**

Republicans believe in business. And according to them all legitimate businesses take necessary risks to succeed or not. If they should fail, that's on them, not on the taxpayers to bail them out. So Bush was wrong about this and Obama was also wrong for continuing this anti-American policy. Remember this when this economy fails again.

So now Hillary Clinton is also getting ready to do wrong to the American people too. Her husband, former President Bill Clinton launched his NAFTA trade agreement which turned America's factories into a wasteland called: 'The Rust Belt'. These policies are NOT Democratic. So, no Democrat should vote for the liar Hilary Clinton to become America's next President.

And no Republican should vote for Jeb Bush who would do the Iraq war again. Apparently Jeb Bush believes that the head of his brother, President George Bush 43 is worth far more than the innocent heads of Christian children that ISIS has beheaded now that Iraq is lawless thanks to his brother.

Obama's trade policies are also evil. The Bible even says so. It's wrong to bless strangers and curse your own people with unemployment (I Timothy 5:8) 'IF ANY MAN PROVIDE NOT FOR HIS OWN, ESPECIALLY FOR THOSE OF HIS OWN HOUSE, HE HAS DENIED THE FAITH AND IS WORSE THAN AN INFIDEL'.

4. Obama's personal hypocrisy reminds me of an incident that happened when I was a child. We called a simple young girl that lived by us Reba Residue. Since one day she went home crying to her mother with her face smeared with dog residue. Her simple mother hollered; 'pew, due, residue!'

Then she asked Reba what had happened. Reba said that she found what she thought was chocolate in a neighbor's front yard. Since she was friends with that neighbor's dog she thought that dog wouldn't mind if she ate what she saw that dog drop. But when she picked up what she thought was chocolate it had melted in the sun and ran down her arm and somehow got smeared on her face and then it changed from being chocolate to something that stunk.

Her upset Mother told her to come in right away and take a bath. Well, the child was hurting. So she couldn't say I'm gonna wash your mouth out with soap.

This reminds me of exactly what Obama's election has produced. Here was a man that many Blacks believed was somehow good, sweet, educated, well-spoken and chocolate just like them too. But in reality this man turned out to be just something a dog had dropped as his repugnant socialist policies from his deceptive Muslim nature now stunk to high heaven.

5. For example, when Obama first took office Black unemployment was over 15% but he still had the Congress waste a whole year on his socialist Obama care. So that at the start of his second term Black unemployment was now up over 19%. In all this time he has taken over all healthcare, student loans, the auto industry and mortgages in an attempt to change capitalism into Muslim socialism by promoting his Obama care at your expense and also vetoing the Keystone Pipeline to keep the American people from working and busting Social Security by awarding undeserved disability for bums (especially Black and minority bums).

6. If Obama care was so great then how come Democratic Senators and Congressman grant the reward of exemption to Obama care for those businesses that make political contributions to the Democratic Party?

Speaking again of Obama care, there is one issue that has not yet been mentioned. That is Obama care provides for extended life support services for deformed minority babies (particularly those of illegal aliens and Blacks) who will now grow up to become future socialist voters. That your taxes will support since they will never be able to work just like all those illegal alien children.

Social Work Counselors and Ministers who will become Hospital Chaplains are now being trained to council families to pull the plug on granny in order to save Social Security for these deformed minority babies.

How stupid this racist policy is. Yes Obama care hurts the elderly and gives false hope to the deformed. The deformed can't amount to much in life unless they encounter Christian healing. So it also seems dumb to have kicked prayer out of school when such will be necessary for these deformed students to succeed in life. **If these people have a right to a public education, then that education has a duty to expose them to whatever Christian gifts like healing that may be available to them in this life.**

7. The Muslim Obama by executive order has removed any display of Christianity (like Crosses and God's Ten Commandments) from American society (especially in the military as they might offend Muslims).

8. Muslim Obama, the Democrat let foreclosures and homelessness happen to sabotage the American economy and even paved the way for GE smart meters to spy on your home if you should still have one.

Obama has also stood by as millions of Americans; both White and Black were unfairly driven out of their homes and into homelessness. For those who somehow may still have homes, Obama has given seventy five million of your tax dollars to help GE build smart electric meters that aid burglars in spying on who's home and what electric appliances you have as they 'case' your house.

9. Not satisfied with that, the Muslim Obama was also behind the expansion of the National Security Agency to spy on you as a supposed intrical part of watching out for terrorism.

Speaking of spying, it is now being done at your expense. Your tax dollars are paying for the Utah Data Center of the National Security Agency (NSA). This agency keeps a record of every phone call and internet transaction that you make. And you are not getting your tax money's worth for there is no evidence that their efforts have ever prevented any terrorist attack. For example, where were they when the Boston marathon bombing happened?

This spying is the main enterprise of the 'military, industrial complex' that former President Eisenhower resented. Back in history several of his advisors (those who also wanted him to appoint that liberal Earl Warren) wanted him to move away from relying upon Christian Prophecy to a more secular and industrial spying on the Soviet Union during the cold war. At that time, he used to visit a Christian Prophet in Pasadena California each month to find out what was happening. This worked out well because 'THE EYES OF THE LORD ARE IN EVERY PLACE BEHOLDING THE EVIL AND THE GOOD' (Proverbs 15:3).

But even so this prophetic spying was replaced with expensive 'military industrial' spying that your tax dollars now pay for. Think of all the billions wasted on spy satellites that you could have used. **A country cannot use Christian methods if it's no longer Christian. So, it's time for revival.** It's far better to restore prayer and Bible reading to school and make America Christian again than to have to pay excessive taxes to fund expensive drug rehab with other welfare programs and social services that distribute 'free' condoms and birth control pills at your expense.

10. I think I said in number 2 above that Obama is a nominal Muslim. Actually,, the radical Muslims consider him to be backslidden. When Muslims backslide they usually fall back into some indigenous natural religion like sun worship. That's probably why all this stimulus money got wasted on solar enterprises like Solindra.

11. Another means of abusing a Christian nation popular with Muslims is subjugation. An old way to do this was by torture (burying a Christian in the sand up to his head and then letting the ants and scorpions bite and sting him). A modern way to do this is to use 'Common Core' to dumb down the children of the 'infidels' so that they can't compete with Muslims in the global economy. As the Muslim Obama has already been doing with your tax dollars.

Some years ago when this economy first failed the Muslim Obama took a large part of the stimulus money and gave it to the Department of Education to supposedly ensure the continued full employment of teachers. When it was really used for the enforcement of 'Common Core' upon the states. There are even several books about this skullduggery from both a Christian perspective *(1-800-288-8350) and a secular (Crimes of the Educators) perspective.*

12. If you remember how that Obama promised change from the Bush policies of Middle East War, Guantanamo terrorist imprisonment, using drones to kill civilians and torturing terrorists.

Here is what has really been happening despite Obama's polished rhetoric: The Middle East war in Afghanistan is continuing and now the one in Syria is due to expand. Guantanamo Bay which holds terrorists beyond the reach of America's constitutional law protections remains opened and still in service. The Obama Administration has used a drone to kill an American citizen. And the Obama Administration's ambassador to Libya and several other Americans were killed by Jihadist Muslims because of resentment over Libya being used as a liberated place to now torture terrorists.

The Muslim Obama now sees it to be more advantageous to violate the constitutional, civil and human rights of American Citizens than to throw out the extreme liberal policy of an idealistic pluralistic society complete with Jihadist Muslims (enemies of the people) living among us as mandated by law. Which law is now supreme, the Constitution and freedom of association, or immigration rights with its liberal notion about pluralistic democracy with having to accept Muslim immigrants that curse our land?

13. In fact what constitutes most Christian prayer is for God to bless people physically, socially and financially. But Muslim prayer (like Obama learned) is for vengeance (Sheri Law), 'social justice' (reclaiming Iraq and Syria for Isis), armaments (like nuclear weapons for Iran) and empowerment to fight and behead the enemies of Islam and to accept martyrdom if need be.

Speaking of Muslim prayer it is also obvious that the Muslim child Obama prayed against US forces in Vietnam just like other Muslim students right there in Indonesia where the Muslim Obama grew up. But these prayers didn't seem to work much then. So most Christians would say that this is because the Muslim god Allah is not real but false.

But prayers to a false god cause people like the Muslim Obama to get worked up with the intention to make their prayers come to pass themselves (self-fulfilling prophecy). Psychologists say that's what we have here with the Muslim Obama. **(Since Allah can't, Obama will!)** And now subconsciously Obama has cut back America's armaments to the smallest infantry since 1940 and the smallest navy since 1915. He has also removed all tanks from Europe and missile defense especially for Poland. (If you remember the invasion of Poland began World War II).

Plus he has emasculated America's armed forces by promoting the gay lifestyle and authorizing gay marriage.

His Muslim personality has made him an enemy of the American people, since as a Muslim he really hates gays and is just using his promotion of gays to hurt America.

14. Obama's One World Order, Agenda 21, Political Correctness has allowed the enemies of the Gospel of Christ (Jihadist Muslims) to have freedom of religion to impose their evil practices (Shari Law) right here in America to curse our land.

Recently when the Muslims demonstrated for Sheri law in Australia, the Prime Minister of Australia told the Muslims there: 'If you don't like our laws, leave'! Hopefully after this reprobate Obama leaves office, this politically correct mess and Jihadist Muslims will also get thrown out with the Obama trash too.

15. Muslim Obama's evil Obama Care so monopolized the US Senate for over a year thanks to Senator Harry Reid, that the Democratic policy of bringing justice to the unlawful use of the National Guard fighting in foolish foreign wars, like the wasteful misadventure in Iraq never got addressed.

Obviously the National Guard's job is to guard the nation of America and the domestic needs of our people here and not run off to foreign lands to fight foreign enemies. This evil practice can only be changed by enacted law that the Democratic Senate bombarded with all this Obama Care deception was not free to do.

16. The Muslim Obama although he is a Spade, does not like to call a Spade a Spade. So he has called Muslim terrorism workplace violence and plain terrorism. By being a Muslim himself he certainly does not want to give the Muslims a bad name.

Muslims are allowed by their false doctrine to conceal, disguise or hide their personal beliefs, Ideas, feelings and opinions in order to achieve personal success for the Muslim cause. Like ruling over Christians or even hiring other Muslims like Valerie Jarrett as public employees to abuse Christians and promote Iran's nuclear arms as well.

17. The Muslim Obama who represents Islam as 'a religion of peace' has used your tax dollars to arm with outlawed killer bullets most agencies of the Federal Government that have no police power or any right under the law to engage in armed conflict or to police the public and thus need Bush's continued policy of militarizing local police forces.

18. Muslims, like the Muslim Obama like to take over a nation of 'infidels' secretly. So the Muslim Obama has used your tax dollars to secretly supply underground bases to safeguard himself and other Muslims along with the 'useful idiots' of Washington's bureaucrats from whatever social unrest they may cause.

19. The Muslim Obama, resenting 'infidel' military leadership has fired most of America's experienced generals who know how to fight and win. And has replaced them with psychological misfits who lack enough testosterone to even swat a mosquito let alone win a war.

20. But don't laugh at America, once the greatest nation on earth, for all that these deceived Muslim prayers of Muslim school children and Muslim immigrants from Palestine, Iraq, Syria, Somalia and other Muslim lands along with deceived Blacks have given America is the disgrace of the Muslim Obama.

Soon and very soon those millions of Muslim immigrants from Syria in Western Europe will give to the world through their deceived prayers the horror of the Antichrist, known to them as the twelfth Imam! WAKE UP and EXPECT WAR as it's on the way. The Lord Jesus in the Bible (Mathew 24) says that before He comes again WARS will come. So EXPECT WARS!

MUSLIM JESUS VS. JESUS CHRIST

I had already written the first 2 pages of this chapter. While I was reviewing them. The Lord told me that they were both too soft and too pleasing to the people. He reminded me that He originally said that this book would not be 'politically correct'. Nor is it written 'to win friends and influence people'.

These issues must be confronted by 'THE SWORD OF THE SPIRIT WHICH IS THE WORD OF GOD' (Ephesians 6:17).

Then he told me exactly how to proceed: What the Muslims say is to be presented first. Then the Christian scriptural response is to be given Three-Fold. One verse is to be given from the King James Version of the Bible. Then one verse from the Amplified Bible and finally one verse from the King James Version of Jimmy Swaggart Expositor's study Bible. With commentary if it makes the verse clearer.

The first issue to be discussed is that Jesus is the Son of God. Muslims do not believe nor allow anyone to teach that Jesus is the Son of God. To them, their god; Allah doesn't need a son to do his work.

The Muslim Koran pronounces a curse on those who believe that Jesus is God's Son.

In fact, the Muslim Dome of the Rock in Jerusalem has the following words inscribed around the inside of its dome; **'Far be it from God that he should have a son'.** With this kind of anti-Christian propaganda this Mosque should have been destroyed in 1967 that the new Jewish Temple may have been built there as Jewish Temples are for Gods service not for the exhibiting of anti-Christian hate speech. All temples lift up, praise and glorify some god in some way. Even Temples to false gods do such. No real temple of any god instead of glorifying its own god condemns the real God we may all have to face someday.

Another point to bring this issue to your attention that Muslims apparently have written their main teachings from an attempt to discredit Christian doctrine is their disbelief in the Trinity to the extent that they go out of their way to specifically call such blasphemy in their 'Holy books'.

To Christians the Old Testament King James Bible asks about God's Son if we know who He is (Proverbs 30:4).

To Christians the New Testament Amplified Bible says in I John: 5:12 'HE WHO POSSESSES THE SON OF GOD HAS LIFE AND HE THAT DOES NOT POSSESS THE SON OF GOD DOES NOT HAVE THAT LIFE'. Isn't that truth plain and clear enough for you?

To Christians the New Testament, King James version of The Jimmy Swaggart Expositor's Study Bible says in Colossians 1:14, 'THAT HE (GOD) HAS TRANSLATED US INTO THE KINGDOM OF HIS DEAR SON'. And not into a Muslim caliphate. Could it be any clearer?

The second issue to be discussed is that Muslims do not believe that the Muslim Jesus died on the cross for our sins. Or that He is in anyway a savior.

But the Bible in the Old Testament King James version calls God: 'THE HOLY ONE OF ISRAEL OUR SAVIOR' in Isaiah 45:15. And to Christians of course Jesus is God. The King James Version of the Amplified Bible says in from Jimmy Swaggart's first John 2:2 'THAT HE (JESUS) IS THE ATONING SACRIFICE FOR OUR SINS AND NOT FOR OURS ONLY BUT ALSO FOR THE SINS OF THE WHOLE WORLD'. And Expositors Study Bible, King James version, Colossians 1:20: 'AND HAVING MADE PEACE (WITH GOD) THROUGH THE BLOOD OF HIS CROSS BY HIM (JESUS) ALL THINGS ARE RECONCILED TO GOD.

Our third issue to consider here is the outlandish Muslim claim that Jesus returns as a radical Muslim.

The very idea that Jesus, the Lord of Glory, the King of Kings should return not to rule and reign 'OVER EVERY NATION, KINGDOM TRIBE AND TONGUE' as recorded in Revelation 19:16 of any Bible. But to kill every non-Muslim like the radical Muslims ISIS is abhorible, revolting and false.

The prophet Isaiah speaking of this time in Isaiah 2:4 in the Old Testament of any Bible says that 'ALL SHALL BEAT THEIR SWORDS INTO PLOW SHARES AND THEIR SPEARS INTO PRUNING HOOKS. NATION SHALL NOT LIFT UP SWORD AGAINST NATION, NEITHER SHALL THEY LEARN WAR ANYMORE'. That does not sound like any radical Muslim killers will be around to kill by beheading all non-Muslims, now does it?

The very idea that the Lord Jesus should return as a radical Muslim like ISIS is not only repulsive but against the prophetic word of God.

In The Jimmy Swaggart Expositor's Study Bible, Muslims should realize that the Lord Jesus judges everyman for every sin and 'WHOMSOEVER IS NOT FOUND WRITTEN IN THE BOOK OF LIFE WILL BE CAST INTO THE LAKE OF FIRE', (Revelation 20:15).

The only way to get recorded in that book of life is to be saved from the consequences of your sins and to receive Jesus not just as savior but also as Lord. And if you obey Him in this life so that 'WHEN HE RETURNS (YOU) SHALL BE REWARDED AS HE SHALL GIVE TO EVERY MAN ACCORDING TO HIS WORKS', (Revelation 22:12), (the Amplified Bible).

But The Jimmy Swaggart Expositor's Study Bible gives more detail about Jesus coming on page 2100. It says that 'GOD WAS MANIFEST IN THE FLESH' (incarnated) 'JUSTIFIED IN THE SPIRIT' (vindicated, endorsed, proved, and pronounced by the Holy Spirit) 'SEEN OF ANGELS' (Angels witnessed his birth, life, passion, resurrection and ascension). 'PREACHED UNTO THE GENTILES' (preached unto the nations that his atonement was for all mankind) 'BELIEVED ON IN THE WORLD' (accepted by many) 'RECEIVED UP INTO GLORY'. (His mission was accomplished, finished and accepted in total by God', (I Timothy 3:16).

The fourth issue to be discussed here is the stupid Muslim claim that Jesus is inferior to or subservient to their Mahdi.

The Muslim Mahdi was first mentioned by a former President of Iran as the one who will change the world into a godly paradise. How can a false god do such by beheading Christians and Jews?

The prophet Joel mentions the coming of the Lord in chapter 2 of his Bible book. And he goes on to discuss in chapter 3 of his Bible book the judgments God will bestow on the enemies of his people. Perhaps it would be wise for Muslims to read these verses themselves before they become deceived into believing that their Mahdi or any man or spirit outranks the Lord Jesus Christ, 'GOD MANIFESTED IN THE FLESH', (I Timothy 3:16).

The New Testament of the Amplified Bible says: 'THAT MANY SHALL COME IN CHRIST'S NAME (propagating the name that belongs to him) AND SHALL DECEIVE MANY'. Is the Muslim Mahdi one of these impersonators?

But The Jimmy Swaggart Expositor's Study Bible gives more detail about Jesus coming on page 2100. It says that 'GOD WAS MANIFEST IN THE FLESH' (incarnated) 'JUSTIFIED IN THE SPIRIT' (vindicated, endorsed, proved, and pronounced by the Holy Spirit) 'SEEN OF ANGELS' (Angels witnessed his birth, life, passion, resurrection and ascension). 'PREACHED UNTO THE GENTILES' (preached unto the nations that his atonement was for all mankind) 'BELIEVED ON IN THE WORLD' (accepted by many) 'RECEIVED UP INTO GLORY'. (His mission was accomplished, finished and accepted in total by God as I Timothy 3:16 records).

The fifth issue to be discussed here is the stupid Muslim belief that Jesus comes again to enforce Shari Law all over the world.

This would require the Lord Jesus to be a celestial cop with a badge and police power to arrest with mace, a stun gun and a service revolver to then abuse with police brutality any non-Muslims. This obviously is an insult to the divine nature of God.

Law is the concrete of any society. Like for most Muslims, law = Shari Law. For the Romans, law = Roman law. And for English speaking nations, law = English common law. There is not now any one law for all.

But to arrest every non-Muslim for violating Sheri Law like the radical Muslims ISIS is abhorrible, revolting and false.

The very idea that the Lord Jesus should return as a radical Muslim like ISIS to enforce Muslim Shari Law is not only repulsive but against the prophetic word of God.

Most Muslims are Arabs used to living in Sandy places. But Jesus will not be building his house upon the sand for the wind to abuse but on a solid rock, as it is written in Matthew 7:26-27: 'AND EVERYONE THAT HEARTH THESE SAYINGS OF MINE, AND DOETH THEM NOT SHALL BE LIKE UNTO A FOOLISH MAN, WHICH BUILT HIS HOUSE UPON THE SAND. AND THE RAIN DESCENDED, AND THE FLOODS CAME, AND THE WINDS BLEW AND BEAT UPON THE HOUSE: AND IT FELL: AND GREAT WAS THE FALL OF IT'.

In those same verses in the Amplified Bible it says: 'AND EVERYONE WHO HEARS THESE WORDS OF MINE AND DOES NOT DO THEM WILL BE LIKE A STUPID (FOOLISH) MAN WHO BUILT HIS HOUSE UPON THE SAND. AND THE RAIN FELL AND THE FLOODS CAME AND THE WINDS BLEW AND BEAT AGAINST THAT HOUSE. AND IT FELL AND GREAT AND COMPLETE WAS ITS FALL'.

Jimmy Swaggart Expositor's Study Bible comments on these verses by saying in verse 26: (but for the foundation, this house looked the same as the house that was built upon the rock). And in verse 27: (while the sun shines, both houses look good; but when adversity comes and come it shall, *FAITH, WHICH IS ALONE IN CHRIST AND HIM CRUCIFIED WILL STAND (I Corinthians 1:18).*

Our sixth issue to discuss is the false Muslim prophecy that Jesus will return to declare himself a Muslim. And He will lead many Christians to convert and become Muslims too. Those who will not convert, he will judge. Muslims go on to say in their Koran that the people of scripture (Christians and Jews) on the day of resurrection He (Jesus) will be a witness against them (Sura 4:159).

This shows clearly that Muslims twisted the Christian Scriptures that already existed in order to make their perverted (antichrist) claims. What need would the King of Glory have to become a Muslim? If you are the King of a kingdom already it will be empty if you and your Christian people desert it for another. Now let's confront this false Muslim prophecy. After Jesus was crucified on the cross (for your sins) and rose from the dead and ascended into heaven, angels standing by Him said in Acts 1:11 'YE MEN OF GALILEE WHY STAND YE GAZING UP INTO HEAVEN THIS SAME JESUS. . . .'

The word 'same' indicates not just similarity but congruence. In other words, exactly now as before (no change in anyway). Consequently the idea that the King of Kings returns as a deceived Muslim to ensure Muslim evangelism to the Christian's own detriment is inconsistent with reality.

The Amplified Bible says that this verse means to them that Jesus will return in like manner as you have seen Him go. Apparently to them the word 'same' means the same method of transport.

But the same method of Jesus transport is already described in the sentence, So, the word 'same' modifies Jesus, not how He gets around. **This is why it's necessary to have the Jimmy Swaggart Expositor's Study Bible.**

The Jimmy Swaggart Expositor's Study Bible says that the word 'SAME' refers to the Person (Jesus) in this case and they go on to say that 'SAME' refers to Jesus having the SAME human body with the nail prints in his hands and feet.

This is very important because if Jesus were not a Muslim before his death, He could not be a Muslim evangelist after his crucifixion, resurrection, ascension and second coming in order to be the 'SAME' Jesus.

Our seventh issue to discuss examines that Muslims go beyond their previous false prophecy to say that Jesus also returns to abolish Christianity entirely.

And that He will break all crosses, kill all swine and other things. And will proceed to insult the Christian faith just like a hedonistic spoiled child. In fact that's what the Muslim who wrote this childish insult must be – just a spoiled brat wanting to play Jihad.

The Lord Jesus will not be coming back to abolish Christianity but to confirm it by rewarding it. In fact HE SAYS THAT HIS REWARD IS WITH HIM (Revelation 22:12).

A reward is something to cherish not something that gets abolished and thrown out in the trash. The Amplified Bible of Revelation 22:12 says: 'I SHALL BRING MY WAGES AND REWARDS WITH ME; TO REPAY AND RENDER TO EACH ONE JUST WHAT HIS OWN ACTIONS AND HIS OWN WORK MERIT'.

And Jimmy Swaggart Expositor's Study Bible says: **'**MY REWARD IS WITH ME (the word reward can either be positive or negative) to give every man according as his work shall be (our faith however placed will produce a certain type of works. *(Only faith in the cross is accepted*).

Our eighth issue to discuss is the false Muslim claim that the Muslim Jesus is a primary instigator of the final war. This does not sound like a proper vocation for the Prince of Peace, now does it? The scripture says in Romans 5:1: 'THEREFORE BEING JUSTIFIED BY FAITH, WE HAVE PEACE WITH GOD THROUGH OUR LORD JESUS CHRIST'.

That same verse, Romans 5:1: says in the Amplified Bible: 'THEREFORE BEING JUSTIFIED BY FAITH, WE HAVE PEACE WITH GOD, THROUGH OUR LORD JESUS CHRIST' (The Messiah, the anointed one).

And in Jimmy Swaggart Expositor's Study Bible (Romans 5:1) THEREFORE BEING JUSTIFIED BY FAITH LET US HAVE THE PEACE OF RECONCILIATION WITH GOD THROUGH OUR LORD JESUS CHRIST (this is the only way one can be justified refers to *faith in Christ and what he did at the cross).*

So far this chapter has only dealt with Muslim false doctrine. We will return to that in a moment. But first God wants me to deal with the evil Muslim cultural deception that discriminates against women.

The authorized King James Bible says in I Corinthians 11:10 that: 'A WOMAN OUGHT TO HAVE POWER OVER HER OWN HEAD

(Not some Muslim family nor some Muslim authority) BECAUSE OF THE ANGELS' (who are higher in authority than any imam).

Then it goes on to say in I Corinthians 11:15 that 'IF A WOMAN HAVE LONG HAIR IT IS A GLORY TO HER' (her natural God given covering). In order for her to be attractive her beautiful long hair must be exhibited openly and not hidden beneath an artificial man made covering like a Muslim Hijab, Niqab or Burka.

A normal man likes to show off his wife. In some cultures, the wife wears the family heirlooms, gold and diamond necklaces. And in primitive cultures rare sea shells of what her husband caught or even the trophies of animals that her husband killed in battle for food. No normal man hides his wife. To do so indicates a psychological problem.

Our tenth issue to discuss is the Muslim claim that the Muslim Jesus will return to earth at some Mosque in Damascus. He will arrive just in time to meet the Muslim Mahdi to prepare for the final war.

The Scriptures however state that 'JESUS FEET WILL STAND THAT DAY ON THE MOUNT OF OLIVES WHICH IS BEFORE JERUSALEM ON THE EAST', (Zachariah 14:4).

Jimmy Swaggart Expositor's Study Bible says that this will be His landing point at the second coming.

Speaking of Damascus, the prophet Isaiah says in Isaiah 17:1 that 'DAMASCUS SHALL BE TAKEN AWAY FROM BEING A CITY, AND IT SHALL BECOME A RUINOUS HEAP'.

Then the Amplified Bible wants us to cry a dirge over it FOR 'DAMASCUS WOULD CEASE TO BE A CITY AND WILL BECOME A HEAP OF RUINS' the Amplified Bible, Isaiah 17:1. Damascus will be the capitol of Syria when this happens. And that did not happen until 1946. So it must be destroyed sometime soon. *Then this false Muslim prophecy shall also find the ruin it deserves for twisting the word of God.*

Our eleventh issue to be discussed is the false Muslim belief that the Zionist Empire of Israel will fall and the religion of Islam will prevail since the Muslim Jesus never really liked the Jews anyway.

Jesus (the Prince of Peace) now supposedly Muslim will fight against Zionist Jews (His own people) according to the Muslims.

How stupid this Muslim false teaching is for anyone can see for themselves from any Bible that the New Testament begins in Matthew 1:1 with the genealogy of Jesus Christ clearly showing Christ's Jewish ancestry.

Contrary to what Muslims believe, Israel is due to expand to the original borders that God gave Abraham in Genesis 15:18.

Jimmy Swaggart Expositor's Study Bible says in Genesis 15:19 that 'ABRAHAM WILL BE GIVEN ALL THAT LAND FROM THE RIVER OF EGYPT (NILE) UNTO THE GREAT RIVER, THE RIVER EUPHRATES' (the actual area promised by God to Abraham goes all the way to the Nile river in Egypt which includes Sinai, the Arab Peninsula, then up to much of modern day Iraq, most of Syria and all of Lebanon and Jordan too).

Our twelfth issue to discuss is that the Muslim Jesus = the Biblical false prophet.

Muslims thus use Jesus as a lure to draw Christians in.

The Biblical false prophet can also perform miracles. So Muslims do not believe that their healing or any miracle evidences the Jesus of the Bible but the counterfeit Jesus of Muslim false doctrine. Consequently if I were a faith healer or Christian miracle worker I would not go to Muslim lands to minister to Muslims or to associate with and befriend them. In Ephesians 5:11 the Bible says: 'HAVE NO FELLOWSHIP WITH THE UNFRUITFUL WORKS OF DARKNESS BUT RATHER REPROVE THEM'. Muslims just corrupt your Christ; don't give them the ammunition to do so.

One famous Christian healer, Norvel Hayes performs mighty miracles and healings by the laying on of hands (a Christian Biblical doctrine).

The Muslim false prophet also performs miracles. So, does their Dajjal or Antichrist. In fact he heals the sick by wiping his hands in them just like Jesus did. Do you want to have any part in such a fraudulent 'beautiful religion'?

Since some of you have already fallen for this politically incorrect plural democracy propaganda about accepting Muslims into your communities and nations, I need to share this Bible verse with you: II Corinthians 5:14: 'BE NOT UNEQUALLY YOKED TOGETHER WITH UNBELIEVERS; FOR WHAT FELLOWSHIP HAS RIGHTEOUSNESS WITH UNRIGHTEOUSNESS; AND WHAT COMMUNION HAS LIGHT WITH DARKNESS'.

The Amplified Bible elaborates further by saying: 'DO NOT BE UNEQUALLY YOKED WITH UNBELIEVERS' (do not make missmated alliances with them or come under a different yoke with them inconsistent with your faith)! 'FOR WHAT FELLOWSHIP HAS RIGHTEOUSNESS WITH UNRIGHTEOUSNESS'; (and right standing with God with inequity and lawlessness)? 'OR HOW CAN LIGHT HAVE FELLOWSHIP WITH DARKNESS'.

Do you now understand what the Bible and me are saying? If so, let's now move on to discuss our next issue.

<u>Our thirteenth issue to discuss is will the Antichrist Empire be Muslim?</u> Muslim deceit and trickery more than any religion, philosophy, ideology or belief system exhibits the antichrist spirit complete with brimstone breathe. I mentioned somewhat about this in the chapter about the Byzantine Empire. As you probably remember Byzantine was the eastern part of the Roman Empire which fell to the Muslim Ottoman Turks in 1453.

For our purposes the Empires of man are those which control Jerusalem (the center of God's Earth). So first came Egypt then Assyria then Babylon then Medo-Persia then Greece then Rome then the Muslim Ottoman Turks.

There is scripture that says that the last Empire shall be revived to become the Antichrist Empire. Before this book, most theologians and church historians believed that the last empire to be revived would be Rome. But history shows that it will be the Muslim Turks instead.

All of the current western democracies that were once part of Rome, now have significant Muslim Turkish population. A historian from England now says that there are more Mosques in England than churches and that England will no doubt become Muslim shortly after his death.

If democracy is to prevail then the rule of the majority will give these Muslim Turks rule over you. So then expect Muslim rule along with the beheadings of Christians. It's coming for sure. The Bible says so (Revelations 20:4), 'I SAW THE SOULS OF THEM THAT WERE BEHEADED FOR THE WITNESS OF JESUS'.

<u>Our fourteenth issue to discuss is was Mohamed demonic?</u> Actually, Mohamed is in good company here since Jesus too was also accused of being demonically inspired for healing on the Sabbath day (**Luke 13:10-17**). Jesus was also accused by the Pharisees of casting out devils through the prince of the devils **(Matthew 9:34, Matthew 12:24, and Mark 3:22).**

Mohamed however never healed anyone. Neither did he cast out devils. Perhaps he couldn't cast devils out because he had one. What other reason is there for his attacks on Christianity?

But Jesus never killed anyone or exhorted his followers to kill. Plus Jesus never lied about anything to anyone. In fact Jesus kept the law of God blamelessly.

Mohamed claims that he was on his way to commit suicide when he heard a voice from heaven saying: 'O Mohamed! Thou art the Apostle of God and I am Gabrielle'. Gabrielle announces good news, like he foretold the birth of Jesus Christ (Luke 1:30-37). To negate that by calling Mohamed an Apostle makes Gabrielle a two faced, double talker **(an insane murderer is not an apostle).**

There is no Bible record of Gabrielle ever telling anyone what their ministerial spiritual gift will be. So, the idea of Gabrielle calling Mohamed an Apostle is false. Even the Mormons (an American false religious cult) had enough sense to call their angel giving them a different gospel a different name: (Moroni).

By using Biblical figures to confirm their false doctrine just shows that Islam is an antichrist religion. Plus, the idea that God would give theological information to someone instead of stopping them from committing suicide is against the nature of God (the life giver).

God usually speaks to people in a gentle way if by angels. In fact, most angels began their speaking by saying: 'FEAR NOT'. To have dark spiritual experiences like Mohamed had in the cave Hira is like the experience of a spiritualist or someone who channels spirits. Since I come from the county in Florida where Cassadaga (the main retirement community of spiritualists) is located, I know something about them. One obvious fact is that any experience from dark spiritual experiences that leads to anti biblical revelations and also eventually to killing (like the killing of every Jew, Christian and non-Muslim). **It is the devil and not Gabrielle who leads people to kill, rob and destroy (John 10:10).**

As I said before the taking of biblical characters to espouse and to confirm anti biblical false doctrine makes Islam, (the religion of Muslims) antichrist. This should now be plain for all to see, so let's move on to discuss our next issue.

<u>Our fifteenth issue to discuss is another coming Muslim Middle East war.</u>

Contrary to what former President George W. Bush (Bush 43) said Islam is certainly not a religion of peace. Their Holy books say that the Muslim Mahdi will return during troublesome times (no food, water, jobs, money or peace) to wage war against the Jews in Jerusalem, to reconquer it for Islam and to establish a Muslim Caliphate there to rule over the whole earth from Jerusalem. This will happen as his armies carrying black flags will come from Iran to the Dome of the Rock in Jerusalem where they will then erect their black flags as a sign of conquest.

But contrary to this false prophecy, the Bible says in Genesis 15:18 that Israel is due to expand its borders to the original borders that God showed to Abraham.

Jimmy Swaggart Expositor's Study Bible says in Genesis 15:19 that 'ABRAHAM WILL BE GIVEN ALL THAT LAND FROM THE RIVER OF EGYPT (NILE) UNTO THE GREAT RIVER, THE RIVER EUPHRATES' (the actual area promised by God to Abraham goes all the way to the Nile river in Egypt which includes Sinai, the Arab Peninsula, and from there on up to much of modern day Iraq, most of Syria and all of Lebanon and Jordan too).

We'll soon see which prophecy is true and which God is real. I hope that at that time Israel takes it upon itself to use its neutron bomb to eliminate once and for all the Palestinian problem by dropping it on Gaza, Damascus and wherever else it might be appropriate. The Bible says that 'THERE IS A TIME OF WAR AND A TIME OF PEACE' (Ecclesiastes 3:8). It's time to kill the killers!

Our sixteenth issue concerns the Muslim weapon of mass destruction called: killing (beheadings, homicide and suicide). Previously we discussed Mohamed's attempt at suicide. I could have used a whole page to condemn Mohamed but that's not my purpose right now. As I feel that if something is truly of God no one can fight against it and if not it will come to naught. When we discussed Mohamed some in our fourteenth issue and mentioned his attempt at suicide, some unexpected truth came before me.

As you know many former US soldiers are now returning from Iraq to commit suicide once home in America.

Former President George W. Bush (Bush 43) as I said before failed to have necessary biblical scholars with knowledge of Biblical prophecy to advise him about the Iraq war. Consequently (Bush 43) sent our young men to get even for 9 11 and to supposedly extend democracy to that demon infested land.

Even Mohamed was attacked by demons of suicide himself in Arabia, the dry and thirsty land that demons love.

But Iraq is far worse when it comes to demon possession since there are demons in Iraq under the Euphrates River who have been given the right to kill 1/3 of mankind (Revelation 9:14 &15). Knowing this fact no American soldiers should have been sent to that land for revenge, extension of democracy or any other reason, certainly not for a Muslim girl's right to get an education our next issue to discuss.

Our seventeenth issue is: is a Muslim girl's education worth your life?

Anyone with any sense would say that women already talk too much about things they don't even know things about. They certainly don't need to know more so that they can talk more.

Today in America and many other nations too, there are more women in college than men, learning more to talk more.

Women were given by God as a gift to man to be man's help meet (Genesis 2:18). Not to be his dictator or boss.

Just knowing these few facts I would not waste my life for any girls education (certainly not a Muslim girl). Thanks to all these unnecessary and stupid wars there are already far more women than men in every city and town in America. I definitely have no intentions of adding to that statistic.

Our eighteenth issue discloses why Obama is such a bad President: Because he is a Muslim and Muslims even Obama can and do lie!

I told you in my former chapter about Obama's Deception that Obama is still a nominal Muslim. And there is no record that he was ever converted to Christianity complete with a baptism certificate issued by any Christian Church or Christian community of faith.

Muslims are allowed by their false doctrine to conceal, disguise or hide their personal beliefs, Ideas, feelings opinions in order to achieve personal success for the Muslim cause. Like ruling over Christians or even hiring other Muslims like Valerie Jarrett as public employees to abuse Christians and promote Iran as well.

Consequently, one leading newspaper (it may have been the Washington Post) recently reported over a hundred lies about Obama Care. You may even remember one of those lies yourself: 'If you like your doctor, you can keep him'.

Now in the Iran nuclear agreement the Muslim liar Obama is trying to deal with the Muslim liars of Iran. This agreement has to be bad as two lies do not make truth and two wrongs do not make a right!

To make my disclosure about Muslim lying clearer, it must be reiterated that as long as a Muslim is in a country where Islam is a minority, then Muslim deceptiveness about anything is officially expected and sanctioned by the Muslim faith.

You Afro-Americans probably find yourselves more disappointed in your unemployment today than when Obama first took office. Well Obama's priorities have just overshadowed your need for jobs. After all he was so busy bailing out the banks, signing anti-American trade agreements, vetoing the Keystone Pipeline and supporting gay marriage that he just had no time to concern himself with 'Black Issues'.

I remember and you probably do too that Dr. Martin Luther King Jr. had a dream where he was looking forward to the time when a man would be judged by the content of his character and not by the color of his skin. But 93% of all Blacks voted for Obama because they thought that as a Black man, he would see things from a Black perspective.

Unfortunately, Obama is a Black African Muslim descendant from the same Black African Muslims who sold their Black brothers into slavery, since that's what Muslims do, just as ISIS showed us. And not an Afro-American Christian at all. Muslim Obama's deception has now turned Dr. Martin Luther King Jr.'s dream into a socialist nightmare. Therefore now it's time for you to repent and for the Muslim Obama to be impeached!

<u>Our nineteenth issue concerns the Muslim goal of World domination.</u>

All nations need to take note: Islam, the faith of Muslims, intends to destroy every government made by man, even you! The goal of this Muslim faith is to rule over the entire world and subject all mankind to its false doctrine.

To all democracies Muslims say that thanks to your democratic laws Muslims shall invade you, and thanks to Muslim religious (Shari) law Muslims shall rule over you!

Islam, the so called religion of peace is now responsible for the most fighting currently occurring in the world. This 'evil religion' motivates the vast majority of terrorists worldwide. Franklin Graham, the son of the famous evangelist Billy Graham called the Muslim faith 'an evil religion'. For that statement of truth he was excluded from Obama's prayer breakfast (since the Muslim Obama only prays to Allah, a false god anyway, 'it's no big deal'.

Many European nations had Muslim demonstrations some years ago in which the Muslims that lived there held signs which said: **'Islam our religion today, your religion tomorrow'**. This evil Muslim manifesto of conquest must be crushed by whatever means it takes.

Young Muslims are subsequently told in their holy books to expect warfare because it is ordained for them. And that Allah commands every Muslim to fight unbelievers. **According to them killing (Jihad) is an act of worship, 'One of the supreme forms of devotion to Allah, their false god**. This evil Muslim manifesto of conquest must be crushed by whatever means it takes.

One way they take over nations today is clearly evident by what they did to Lebanon. There the President must be a Muslim by Constitutional law, while the vice president must be a Christian. Actually then Muslim terrorists took over the country to use its army to fight Israel. And the Lebanese people do without government services. Now this same plan of conquest is getting ready to happen again in Nigeria which suffers from the same Constitutional legal abuse: Muslim President, Christian Vice- President.

Our twentieth issue asks which will it be: A Muslim revival or a Christian revival.

Islam, the religion of Muslims, is the fastest growing religion in the world.

9 11, the spirit of death, has triggered Muslim growth four fold.

Most American Muslims reside in our cities, most in New York City. In fact, ***by 2020 most American cities will be Muslim.***

Thanks to Obama, 85% of all American Muslims will be Black.

There is a higher birth rate among Black American Muslims than White Americans. (After all, Muslims enjoy four wives).

Islam, the religion of Muslims, hopes to be the main instrument of Satan to fulfill Bible prophecies in these last days.

Christianity in Latin America, Africa and Asia is now experiencing revival.

Many Muslims are now having Christian dreams about Jesus that overshadows their false Muslim doctrine about Jesus not being the Son of God.

Through 'the falling away' God is allowing lukewarm or nominal Christians to fall away from the Christian faith, to adopt Islam, the religion of Muslims on their way down to hell.

There is much false teaching today from the pacifists that now rule the Christian church that we should just accept this Muslim conquest as the will of God for Christian martyrs.

Although the Lord Jesus died for your sins, your blood and life can't save anyone. So why sacrifice yourself? The Lord Jesus did give us an example to follow in his steps, but neither in His passion nor crucifixion.

There is much misunderstanding among modern Christians about loving your enemies. The Bible does say to 'LOVE YOUR ENEMIES' (Matthew 5:44).

But the Bible does NOT say anywhere to love the enemies of God! 'WHEN THE LORD JESUS RETURNS, HE WILL FIGHT AGAINST HIS ENEMIES' (Zachariah 14:1).

The Lord Jesus also said that 'THE WORKS THAT I DO SHALL YOU DO ALSO AND GREATER THAN THESE SHALL YOU DO' (John 14:12).

The Bible goes on to say: 'AS HE IS (the king of glory with all enemies under his feet), SO ARE WE IN THIS WORLD' (1 John 4:17).

So God will make your enemies (these radical Muslims) your footstool.

As far as Christian revival is concerned remember: 'I CAN DO ALL THINGS (win wars against Muslim Jihadists, expose corruption, perform miracles, impart healings, feed multitudes, command storms to be still, make it rain, supply people with jobs and get people saved, sanctified, filled and ready to now serve God) THROUGH CHRIST WHO STRENGTHENS ME' (Philippians 4:13).

Then the Lord Jesus in the Bible says: 'RENDER UNTO CAESAR THE THINGS THAT ARE CAESARS AND UNTO GOD THE THINGS THAT ARE GODS', (Luke 20:25, Mark 12:17, Matthew 22:21). Don't get entangled in political controversies that no one can solve, but do the will of God by just obeying Him.

'I'M COMPLETE IN HIM, WHICH IS THE HEAD OF ALL PRINCIPALITY AND POWER,' (Colossians 2:10). So there is no power that I need to be scared of!

'EXCEPT THE TRUMPET GIVE A CERTAIN SOUND WHO SHALL PREPARE THEMSELVES FOR BATTLE,' (I Corinthians 14:8). ***Your trumpet call has already been given to you via my prophetic book. What will you now do about it?***

SAINTS, SINNERS, SCOUNDRELS, SODOMITES AND SOCIALISTS

After writing my other prophetic books: **'WHAT TO EXPECT', 'ANOTHER JESUS MOVEMENT', 'RAPTURE RIPOFF', 'REPARATIONS FOR SLAVERY', 'JESUS THE REAL STAR CHILD', 'COVID 19 TRUTHS REVEALED', 'COVID 19-VACCINE OR REPENTANCE' 'WEALTH TRANSFER','END TIME PLAGUES'**, and '**BIDEN'S SORROWS I,** I felt that I was due for a period of rest. But instead I saw a book at the library where we type my manuscripts plainly displaying in its contents part of the title of my next prophetic book. (That book was a political expose of socialists written by Glenn Beck and entitled: **ARGUING with SOCIALISTS**). Since I am a wheelchair disabled man and do not like to confront stupid political ideology I will nevertheless use my Bible knowledge to correct professional and denominational error in this case.

As a prophetic book, my prophetic manuscript must first mention the saints of God and how a sinner becomes a saint (CHRISTIANITY IS NOT JUST A TEACHING BUT A **PERSON, THE LORD JESUS CHRIST).** As it is written in I John 5:11 & 12: 'HE THAT HAS THE SON HAS LIFE AND HE THAT DOES NOT HAVE THE SON OF GOD DOES NOT HAVE LIFE'. There is another Bible verse which emphasizes this: 'IF THOU SHALT CONFESS WITH THY MOUTH THE LORD JESUS AND SHALL BELIEVE IN THY HEART THAT GOD HAS RAISED HIM FROM THE DEAD, THOU SHALT BE SAVED'. (Romans 10:9 & 10).

Please forgive me for not adding all the requirements of sacramental salvation, or the required details of works salvation, or all the religious junk that some say are Bible requirements for so called: 'salvation by faith'.

Salvation based on faith in Jesus alone and what He did at the cross for you and the fact that you believe that God raised Him from the dead saves. Faith in anyone or anything else like water baptism in the name of Jesus only does not save. I hope that my explanation is clear enough for you and your salvation. Remember the Bible is a book of love letters from God to man, it does not compose a marriage to God no more than love letters do to any engaged couple.

To get saved from the consequences of your sins please pray this:

'Heavenly Father; thank you that it is your good will that through the sacrifice of your Son, Jesus on the cross, and my repentance from my dead works (sins) and my belief that you raised your Son, Jesus from the dead for me results in my salvation according to your word'.

When the death angel swept over Egypt to execute the last plague of the death of the first born – today this song is sung about that:

'JUDGMENT IS COMING, ALL WILL BE THERE, EACH ONE RECEIVING JUSTLY THEIR DUE. FIND PEACE AND SHELTER UNDER THE BLOOD (and) I WILL PASS, I WILL PASS OVER YOU'. 'WHEN I SEE THE BLOOD, WHEN I SEE THE BLOOD, WHEN I SEE THE BLOOD, I WILL PASS, I WILL PASS OVER YOU').

Whatsoever or whosoever does not include these Bible sayings is a sinner. Most people consider being a sinner the doing of bad stuff like murder. As they see it it's alright to lie or to tell a little, white, lie. But the bible teaches: that WHATSOEVER IS NOT OF FAITH IS SIN, (Romans 14:23).

But then I will also question the erroneous interpretation of some current professional and denominational widely held theological beliefs about the pre-tribulation rapture and the so called expansive scriptural view point that 'GOD DOES NOTHING WITHOUT REVEALING HIS SECRET TO HIS SERVANTS: THE PROPHETS', (Amos 3:7), so all so-called prophets can now throw in their two cents about this mater too.

These prophets recognized here where the so-called secular prophets who have claimed that the truth that God sent, this COVID 19 plague is actually a work of the devil, that can be cured by vaccinations alone. These secular people see all things from the standpoint of solving all problems without God. According to them the shortages causing famine in the tribulation period will be solved by socialism, (share the poverty) and not by God at all.

When we all know that many so called prophetic ministers on TV have condemned this COVID 19 plague as if it were just another respiratory disease like the flu or a mischievous act of the devil that America did not deserve and could be cured of by vaccinations alone without any need for any repentance; certainly not any repentance from the abominable sins of abortion and same sex marriage which President Biden's democratic political policies of deceived and hatful Anti-Christ progressives support.

But when it comes to God's judgments, no one knows exactly how long each plague will last nor what type of curse they will become. Even the Lord Jesus in Matthew 24 spoke about what would come, but not in any specific order nor in type or severity. It should not be expected for prophecy to be exact since 'WE KNOW IN PART AND PROPHECY IN PART, (1 Cor. 13:9).

Although this prophetic book concerns Christian End Time Prophecy, it is not about an esoteric eschatology so much as the hidden issues of the day. This book discloses truths that God wants known. As an example, the ever increasing deficit comes about in part from the throwing out of free spying by Christian Prophets in favor of expensive secular 'military industrial' spying by spy satellites, wire-tapping of phones, computer hacking, tapping into the internet and cell phones, and drones complete with 'octopus' agencies like Homeland Security, FEMA, NASA, TSA, CIA, FBI, ATF and IRS keeping their eyes on your every move thanks to your taxes.

This came about during the cold war when former President Eisenhower used to visit a Christian Prophet in Pasadena, California about once each month to find out what God saw behind the 'iron curtain'. His advisors told him that his policy was relying too much on Christianity and the Christian Prophets. So, they encouraged him to acquire a more 'military industrial' means of spying like the new U2 spy plane. President Eisenhower adopted this idea but it blew up in his face as the new U2 spy plane was shot down over the Soviet Union and its pilot, Francis Gary Powers was held hostage.

Nevertheless, this policy grew right along with your taxes. Today the Soviet Union has fallen apart but now America not only spies on other nations with these technological instruments but on its own citizens as well and also lies about it all too. As you can now see all these things compose sin and the misdeeds of sinners.

Muslims like Obama (MY PARAMOUNT EXAMPLE OF A SCOUNDREL WHO MORE THAN JUST A SINNER IS ALSO UNPRINCIPLED AND DECEITFUL TOO) are allowed by their lies thanks to Muslim false doctrine to conceal, disguise and hide their personal beliefs, ideas, feelings and opinions about anything and everything in order to achieve personal success for the Muslim cause. Like ruling over Christians or even hiring other Muslim Scoundrels

like Valerie Jarrett as public employees to abuse Christians and promote Iran's nuclear arms too.

To make my disclosure about Muslim lying clearer, it must be reiterated that as long as any Muslim is in a country where Islam is a minority, then the Muslim (in this case, Obama's) deceptiveness about anything and everything is officially expected and sanctioned by the 'evil religion of Islam' (the Muslim faith). That's why we should throw all the Muslims out!

For those who feel that my feelings against the Muslims are too harsh consider this: here in Orlando Florida about 5 years ago a deranged and deceived Muslim (a Muslim domestic terrorist and obvious scoundrel) who considered all Christians to be infidels (worthy of death) just like other Muslim scoundrels was intent on killing gay Christians even though they were Black, so the mass killing of 49 people at the Pulse night club took place.

Over the years this shooting (OBVIOUS SIN) has been noted each year. But not one word was ever mentioned about the homosexual lifestyle and its costs nor the evil judgmental attack on the Pulse nightclub gays by one of these Muslims who don't even belong in this country.

What judgment now awaits this Obama scoundrel and his many deceived czars, rogues and rascals for telling thousands of lies about 'everything under the sun' to the American people in his two terms of office? With President Biden now serving out Obama's third term to do the same evil that former President Obama did resulting in the same entitlements for deserved plagues and **joining former President Obama to dump Christianity has bequeathed America and the entire world to deceptions, wars, delusions, deficits, disasters and many more plagues, Watch out!**

1. To make my disclosure about Muslim lying clearer, it must be reiterated that as long as a Muslim is in a country where Islam is a minority, then the Muslims a minority, (in this case, Obama) deceptiveness about anything is officially expected and sanctioned by the 'evil religion of Islam' (the Muslim faith).

2. Obama is really a nominal Muslim by birth and not a Christian at all. Since there is no Record that Obama was ever baptized Christian in any Christian Church. So Obama is an undocumented phony Christian just like all these illegal aliens are undocumented false Americans. (No baptism certificate – no Christian, no birth certificate – no American).

You Afro-Americans probably find yourselves more disappointed in your unemployment today than when Obama first took office. Well Obama's priorities have just overshadowed your need for jobs. After all he was so busy doing evil like bailing out the banks, signing anti-American trade agreements, vetoing the Keystone Pipeline and supporting gay marriage that he just had no time to concern himself with 'Black issues'. Like the real social justice of Black unemployment.

I remember and you probably do too that Dr. Martin Luther King Jr. had a dream where he was looking forward to the time when a man would be judged by the content of his character and not by the color of his skin. But 93% of all Blacks voted for Obama because they thought that as a Black man, he would see things from a Black perspective.

3. Unfortunately for all Americans, Obama is a Black African Muslim descendant from the same Black African Muslims who sold their Black brothers into slavery, since that's what Muslims do just as ISIS showed us.

And not an Afro-American Christian at all. Muslim Obama's deception has now turned 3. Unfortunately for all Americans, Obama is a Black African Muslim **Dr. Martin Luther King Jr.'s dream into a Muslim socialist nightmare complete with demonic despotism masquerading as 'the beautiful (Muslim) religion'. Therefore now it's time for you to repent and for Muslim Obama to be impeached!**

On page 40 of his book: The Amateur, when Edward Klein asked Dr. Jeremiah Wright, Obama's former racist pastor, if Obama was ever converted from Islam to Christianity. Dr. Wright said: 'That's hard to tell'. Look, if you're saved, you know it, and so does everybody else that's close to you!

D**So Muslim Obama was never converted from Islam to Christianity**. The Bible also says that 'YOU JUDGE A TREE BY ITS FRUIT', (Matthew 12:33, Luke 6:44). In that case **America has had two bad presidents in a row. As you know, George W. Bush (Bush 43) lied America into the Iraq war. But he also bailed out the banks as if such was Republican. Look, Republicans believe in business. And according to them all legitimate businesses take necessary risks to succeed or not. If they should fail, that's on them, not on the taxpayers to bail them out. So Bush was wrong about this and Obama was also wrong for continuing this anti-American policy. Remember this when this economy fails again.**

So now Hillary Clinton is also getting ready to do wrong to the American people too. Her husband, former President Bill Clinton launched his NAFTA trade agreement which turned America's factories into a wasteland called: 'The Rust Belt'. These policies are NOT Democratic. So no Democrat should vote for the liar Hilary Clinton to become America's next President. And no Democrat or Independent should vote for any Democrat.

And no Republican should vote for Jeb Bush who would do the Iraq war again. Apparently Jeb Bush believes that the head of his brother, President George Bush 43 is worth far more than the innocent heads of Christian children that ISIS has beheaded now that Iraq is lawless thanks to his brother.

Obama's trade policies are also evil. The Bible even says so. It's wrong to bless strangers and curse your own people with unemployment (I Timothy 5:8) 'IF ANY MAN PROVIDE NOT FOR HIS OWN, ESPECIALLY FOR THOSE OF HIS OWN HOUSE, HE HAS DENIED THE FAITH AND IS WORSE THAN AN INFIDEL'. This holds true for Ukraine too.

4. Obama's personal hypocrisy reminds me of an incident that happened when I was a child. We called a simple young girl that lived by us Reba Residue. Since one day she went home crying to her mother with her face smeared with dog residue. Her simple mother hollered; 'pew, due, residue!'

Then she asked Reba what had happened. Reba said that she found what she thought was chocolate in a neighbor's front yard. Since she was friends with that neighbor's dog she thought that dog wouldn't mind if she ate what she saw that dog drop. But when she picked up what she thought was chocolate it had melted in the sun and ran down her arm and somehow got smeared on her face and then it changed from being chocolate into something that stunk.

Her upset Mother told her to come in right away and take a bath. Well, the child was hurting. So, she couldn't say I'm gonna wash your mouth out with soap.

This reminds me of exactly what Obama's election has produced. Here was a man that many Blacks believed was somehow good, sweet, educated, well-spoken and chocolate just like them too. But in reality, this man turned out to be just something a dog had dropped as his repugnant socialist policies from his deceptive Muslim background now stunk to high heaven.

5. For example, when Obama first took office Black unemployment was over 15% but he still had the Congress waste a whole year on his socialist Obama care. So that at the start of his second term Black unemployment was now up over 19%. In all this time he has taken over all healthcare, student loans, the auto industry and mortgages in an attempt to change capitalism into Muslim socialism by promoting his Obama care at your

expense and also vetoing the Keystone Pipeline to keep the American people from working and busting Social Security by awarding undeserved disability for bums (especially Black and minority bums).

6. If Obama care was so great then how come Democratic Senators and Congressman grant the reward of exemption to Obama care for those businesses that make political contributions to the Democratic Party?

Speaking again of Obama care, there is one issue that has not yet been mentioned. That is Obama care provides for extended life support services for deformed minority babies (particularly those of illegal aliens and Blacks) who will now grow up to become future socialist voters. That your taxes will support since they will never be able to work just like all those illegal alien children.

Social Work Counselors and Ministers who will become Hospital Chaplains are now being trained to council families to pull the plug on granny in order to save Social Security for these deformed minority babies. How stupid this racist policy is. Yes, Obama care hurts the elderly and gives false hope to the deformed. **The deformed can't amount to much in life unless they encounter Christian healing. So, it also seems dumb to have kicked prayer out of school when such will be necessary for these deformed students to succeed in life. If these people have a right to a public education, than that education has a duty to expose them to whatever Christian gifts like healing that may be available to them in this life.**

7. The Muslim Obama by executive order has removed any display of Christianity (like Crosses and God's Ten Commandments) from American society (especially in the military as they might offend Muslims).

8. Muslim Obama, the Democrat let foreclosures and homelessness happen to sabotage the American economy and even paved the way for GE smart meters to spy on your home if you should still have one.

Obama has also stood by as millions of Americans; both White and Black were unfairly driven out of their homes and into homelessness. For those who somehow may still have homes, Obama has given seventy-five million of your tax dollars to help GE build smart electric meters that aid burglars in spying on who's home and what electric appliances you have as they 'case' your house.

9. Not satisfied with that, the Muslim Obama was also behind the expansion of the National Security Agency to spy on you as a supposed iatrical part of watching out for terrorism.

Speaking of spying, it is now being done at your expense. Your tax dollars are paying for the Utah Data Center of the National Security Agency (NSA). This agency keeps a record of every phone call and internet transaction that you make. And you are not getting your tax money's worth for there is no evidence that their efforts have ever prevented any terrorist attack. For example, where were they when the Boston marathon bombing happened?

This spying is the main enterprise of the 'military, industrial complex' that former president Eisenhower resented. Back in history several of his advisors (those who also wanted him to appoint that liberal Earl Warren) wanted him to move away from relying upon Christian Prophecy to a more secular and industrial spying on the Soviet Union during the cold war. At that time he used to visit a Christian Prophet in Pasadena California each month to find out what God saw happening behind the iron curtain. This worked out well because 'THE EYES OF THE LORD ARE IN EVERY PLACE BEHOLDING THE EVIL AND THE GOOD' (Proverbs 15:3).

But even so this prophetic spying was replaced with expensive 'military industrial' spying that your tax dollars now pay for. Think of all the billions wasted on spy satellites that you could have used. **A country cannot use Christian methods if it's no longer Christian. So it's time for revival.** It's far better to restore prayer and Bible reading to school and make America Christian again than to have to pay excessive taxes to fund expensive drug rehab with other welfare programs and social services that distribute 'free' condoms and birth control pills at your expense.

10. I think I said in number 2 above that Obama is a nominal Muslim. Actually the radical Muslims consider him to be backslidden. When Muslims backslide they usually fall back into some indigenous natural religion like sun worship. That's probably why all this stimulus money got wasted on solar enterprises like Solidary.

11. Another means of abusing a Christian nation popular with Muslims is subjugation. An old way to do this was by torture (burying a Christian in the sand up to his head and then letting the ants and scorpions bite and sting him). A modern way to do this is to use 'Common Core' to dumb down the children of the 'infidels' so that they can't compete with Muslims in the global economy. As the Muslim Obama has already been doing with your tax dollars.

Some years ago when this economy first failed the Muslim Obama took a large part of the stimulus money and gave it to the Department of Education to supposedly ensure the continued full employment of teachers. When it was really used for the enforcement of 'Common Core' upon the states. There are even several books about this skullduggery from both a Christian perspective *(1-800-288-8350) and a secular (Crimes of the Educators) perspective.*

12. If you remember how that Obama promised change from the Bush policies of Middle East War, Guantanamo terrorist imprisonment, using drones to kill civilians and torturing terrorists.

Here is what has really been happening despite Obama's polished rhetoric: the Middle East war in Afghanistan is continuing and now the one in Syria is due to expand. Guantanamo Bay which holds terrorists beyond the reach of America's constitutional law protections remains opened and still in service. The Obama Administration has used a drone to kill an American citizen. And the Obama Administration's ambassador to Libya and several other Americans were killed by Jihadist Muslims because of resentment over Libya being used as a liberated place to now torture terrorists.

The Muslim Obama now sees it to be more advantageous to violate the constitutional, civil and human rights of American Citizens than to throw out the extreme liberal policy of an idealistic pluralistic society complete with Jihadist Muslims (enemies of the people) living among us as mandated by law. Which law is now supreme, the Constitution and freedom of association, or immigration rights with its liberal notion about pluralistic democracy with having to accept Muslim immigrants that curse our land?

13. In fact what constitutes most Christian prayer is for God to bless people physically, socially and financially. But Muslim prayer (like Obama learned) is for vengeance (Sheri Law), 'social justice' (reclaiming Iraq and Syria for Isis), armaments (like nuclear weapons for Iran) and empowerment to fight and behead the enemies of Islam and to accept martyrdom if need be.

Speaking of Muslim prayer it is also obvious that the Muslim child Obama prayed against US forces in Vietnam just like other Muslim students right there in Indonesia where the Muslim Obama grew up. But these prayers didn't seem to work much then. So most Christians would say that this is because the Muslim god Allah is not real but false.

But prayers to a false god cause people like the Muslim Obama to get worked up with the intention to make their prayers come to pass themselves (self-fulfilling prophecy). Psychologists say that's what we have here with the Muslim Obama. **(Since Allah can't, Obama will!)** And now subconsciously Obama has cut back America's armaments to the smallest infantry since 1940 and the smallest navy since 1915. He has also removed all tanks from Europe and missile defense especially for Poland. (If you remember the invasion of Poland began World War II).

Plus he has emasculated America's armed forces by promoting the gay lifestyle and authorizing gay marriage.

His Muslim personality has made him an enemy of the American people, since as a Muslim he really hates gays and is just using his promotion of gays to hurt America.

14. Obama's One World Order, Agenda 21, Political Correctness has allowed the enemies of the Gospel of Christ (Jihadist Muslims) to have freedom of religion to impose their evil practices (Shari Law) right here in America to curse our land.

Recently when the Muslims demonstrated for Sheri law in Australia, the Prime Minister of Australia told the Muslims there: 'If you don't like our laws, leave'! Hopefully after this reprobate Obama leaves office, this political correct mess and Jihadist Muslims will also get thrown out with the Obama trash too.

15. Muslim Obama's evil Obama Care so monopolized the US Senate for over a year thanks to Senator Harry Reid, that the Democratic policy of bringing justice to the unlawful use of the National Guard fighting in foolish foreign wars, like the wasteful misadventure in Iraq never got addressed.

Obviously the National Guard's job is to guard the nation of America and the domestic needs of our people here and not run off to foreign lands to fight foreign enemies. This evil practice can only be changed by enacted law that the Democratic Senate bombarded with all this Obama Care deception was not free to do.

16. The Muslim Obama although he is a Spade, does not like to call a Spade a Spade. So he has called Muslim terrorism workplace violence and plain terrorism. By being a Muslim himself he certainly does not want to give the Muslims a bad name.

Muslims are allowed by their false doctrine to conceal, disguise or hide their personal beliefs, Ideas, feelings and opinions in order to achieve personal success for the Muslim cause. Like ruling over Christians or even hiring other Muslims like Valerie Jarrett as public employees to abuse Christians and promote Iran's nuclear arms as well.

17. The Muslim Obama who represents Islam as 'a religion of peace' has used your tax dollars to arm with outlawed killer bullets most agencies of the Federal Government that have no police power or any right under the law to engage in armed conflict or to police the public and thus need Bush's continued policy of militarizing local police forces.

18. Muslims, like the Muslim Obama like to take over a nation of 'infidels' secretly. So the Muslim Obama has used your tax dollars to secretly supply underground bases to safeguard himself and other Muslims along with the 'useful idiots' of Washington's bureaucrats from whatever social unrest they may cause. This holds true for President Biden now too.

19. The Muslim Obama, resenting 'infidel' military leadership has fired most of America's experienced generals who know how to fight and win. And has replaced them with psychological misfits who lack enough testosterone to even swat a mosquito let alone win a war.

20. But don't laugh at America, once the greatest nation on earth, for all that these deceived Muslim prayers of Muslim school children and Muslim immigrants from Palestine, Iraq, Syria, Somalia and other Muslim lands along with deceived Blacks have given America is the disgrace of the Muslim Obama and now the of President Biden, the infidel.

Soon and very soon those millions of Muslim immigrants from Syria in Western Europe will give to the world through their deceived prayers the horror of the Antichrist, known to them as the twelfth Imam! WAKE UP and EXPECT WAR as it's on the way. The Lord Jesus in the Bible (Mathew 24) says that before He comes again WARS will come. So EXPECT WARS!

BIDEN'S SORROWS I

After writing my other prophetic books: **'WHAT TO EXPECT', ANOTHER JESUS MOVEMENT', 'RAPTURE RIPOFF', 'REPARATIONS FOR SLAVERY', 'JESUS THE REAL STAR CHILD', 'COVID 19 TRUTHS REVEALED', 'WEALTH TRANSFER','END TIME PLAGUES'** and **'COVID 19-VACCINE OR REPENTANCE'** I felt that I was due for a period of rest. But instead suddenly the Spirit of God let me know via a prophetic dream around May 26, 2021 that I was not yet done writing and had more to write about President Biden, especially in regards to answering his question about where COVID 19 originally came from. This manuscript intends to tell the truth about and also to correct error concerning it.

This particular prophetic dream informed me that the current plagues sent to America and the world for the abominations of abortion and same sex marriage would mirror how God had dealt with national sins before, when He sent ten plagues upon Egypt in the days of Moses not only for the slavery of the Hebrew people but also for the failure of the pagan Egyptians to repent from worshipping their false gods while not allowing the worship of the one true Hebrew God,

As a prophetic book, my prophetic manuscript would also question the erroneous interpretation of some current professional and denominational widely held theological beliefs like the pre-tribulation rapture and the so called expansive scriptural view point that 'GOD DOES NOTHING WITHOUT REVEALING HIS SECRET TO HIS SERVANTS: THE PROPHETS', (Amos 3:7), so all so called prophets can now throw in their two cents too.

When we all know that many so called prophetic ministers on TV have condemned this COVID 19 plague as if it were just another respiratory disease like the flu or a mischievous act of the devil that America did not deserve and could be cured of by vaccinations alone without any need for any repentance; certainly not any repentance for the abominable sins of abortion and same sex marriage which President Biden's democratic political policies of deceived and hatful Anti-Christ progressives support.

The prophets recognized here where the so called secular prophets who have claimed that what God sent, this COVID 19 plague is actually a work of the devil, that can be cured by vaccinations alone.

But when it comes to God's judgments, no one knows exactly how long each plague will last nor what type of curse they will become. Even the Lord Jesus in Matthew 24 spoke about what would come, but not in any specific order as prophecy to be exact, since 'WE KNOW IN PART AND PROPHECY IN PART, (1 Corinthians. 13:9).

Although this prophetic book concerns Christian End Time Prophecy, it is not about an esoteric eschatology so much as the hidden issues of the day. This book discloses truths that God wants known. As an example, the ever increasing deficit comes about in part from the throwing out of free spying by Christian Prophets in favor of expensive secular 'military industrial' spying by spy satellites, wire-tapping of phones, computer hacking, tapping into the internet and cell phones, and drones complete with 'octopus' agencies like Homeland Security, FEMA, NASA, TSA, CIA, FBI, ATF and IRS keeping their eyes on your every move thanks to your taxes.

This came about during the cold war when former President Eisenhower used to visit a Christian Prophet in Pasadena, California about once each month to find out what God saw behind the 'iron curtain'. His advisors told him that his policy was relying too much on Christianity and the Christian Prophets. So they encouraged him to acquire a more 'military industrial' means of spying like the new U2 spy plane. President Eisenhower adopted this idea but it blew up in his face as the new U2 spy plane was shot down over the Soviet Union and its pilot, Francis Gary Powers was held hostage.

Nevertheless this policy grew right along with your taxes. Today the Soviet Union has fallen apart but now America not only spies on other nations with these technological instruments but on its own citizens as well and also lies about it all too.

Muslims like Obama are allowed by their lies thanks to Muslim false doctrine to conceal, disguise and hide their personal beliefs, ideas, feelings and opinions about anything and everything in order to achieve personal success for the Muslim cause. Like ruling over Christians or even hiring other Muslims like Valerie Jarrett as public employees to abuse Christians and promote Iran's nuclear arms too.

To make my disclosure about Muslim lying clearer, it must be reiterated that as long as any Muslim is in a country where Islam is a minority, then the Muslim (in this case, Obama's) deceptiveness about anything and everything is officially expected and sanctioned by the 'evil religion of Islam' (the Muslim faith). That's why we should throw all the Muslims out!

For those who feel that my feelings against the Muslims are too harsh consider this: here in Orlando Florida about 5 years ago a deranged and deceived Muslim (a Muslim domestic terrorist) who considered all Christians to be infidels (worthy of death) was intent on killing gay Christians even though they were Black, so the mass killing of 49 people at the Pulse night club in Orlando, Florida took place.

Over the years this shooting has been noted each year. But not one word was ever mentioned about the homosexual lifestyle and its costs nor the evil judgmental attack on the Pulse nightclub gays by one of the Muslims who don't even belong in this country.

What judgment now awaits Obama and his many czars for telling thousands of lies about 'everything under the sun' to the American people in his two terms of office? With President Biden now serving out Obama's third term to do the same evil that former President Obama did resulting in the same entitlements for deserved plagues and **joining former President Obama to dump Christianity has bequeathed America and the entire world to deceptions, wars, delusions, deficits, disasters and many more plagues, Watch Out!**

Just at that moment I turned on the TV to see a Christian TV program that God wanted me to see as it told me just what I needed to know in order to obey Him.

This Christian TV Program was entitled: ***Joni Table Talk*** in which the wife of a famous TV evangelist on a TV talk show interviewed various people who were notable in current events to give the people of God more information about the issues of the day,

Last year I remember how her topic was COVID 19 and she was discussing with her doctor guest a medicine to supposedly heal this plague. At that time hydroxychioroquine with zinc was brought up as a possible cure. And it did work to cure President Trump of his Corona Virus infection.

According to the Bible however a plague is NOT healed by any medicine but by repentance only. That Christian TV show failed to bring this out. But to me such was obvious as I remembered how that: 'ALL

SCRIPTURE IS GIVEN BY THE INSPIRATION OF GOD AND IS PROFITABLE FOR DOCTRINE, FOR REPROOF, FOR CORRECTION, FOR INSTRUCTION IN RIGHTEOUSNESS THAT THE MAN OF GOD MAY BE COMPLETE, THOROUGHLY EQUIPPED FOR EVERY GOOD WORK', (II Timothy 3:16, 17).

So here is what the scripture says about this plague topic: 'WHEN I SHUT UP HEAVEN AND THERE IS NO RAIN, OR COMMAND THE LOCUST TO DEVOUR THE LAND, OR SEND PESTILENCE (**plagues**) AMONG MY PEOPLE, **(yes, God does send plagues even on His own people)** IF MY PEOPLE WHO ARE CALLED BY MY NAME WILL HUMBLE THEMSELVES AND PRAY AND SEEK MY FACE, AND TURN FROM THEIR WICKED WAYS (**repent**), THEN WILL I HEAR FROM HEAVEN, AND WILL FORGIVE THEIR SIN AND HEAL THEIR LAND', (II Chronicles 7:13 & 14).

Back in those days, the last year of President Trump's term, many promises were made and apparently kept by President Trump about developing a vaccine for this CORONA VIRUS.

Thanks to the reprobate DR. Fauci (the masked robber of American free enterprise) such vaccines were to be developed even though it is illegal to use an experimental vaccine for a medical problem that already has a known and established medical cure like Ivermectin or hydroxychioroquine with zinc that is recognized worldwide. **If a delayed side effect like sterility shows up on your adult (sexually active) children you cannot sue the makers of an experimental drug. That's one legitimate legal reason to forgo these vaccines.** Perhaps DR. Fauci was more concerned about making some more money off his patents on various vaccines than the welfare of the American people.

Now that Vice President Harris has returned from Mexico hopefully she learned that the Mexican government has used Ivermectin to stop COVID 19 in Mexico City and not Dr. Fauci's expensive vaccines.

To DR Fauci's surprise and elation many Democratic progressives have now required that school children also be vaccinated against this COVID 19 (even though children have less than 1% susceptibility to this virus) before they return to school this fall as required by the NEW AGE Democratic teacher's union. Another requirement about needing a booster shot was also mentioned. And Dr. Fauci once said that this COVID 19 is not over yet and may even require a booster shot.

But in this electric age of increased technology I would like to submit to you (parents especially) this recommendation:

Recently I was watching the Jim Bakker Show on Christian TV where they discussed a new product called): the SIGNAL RELIEF PATCH. From what I understand this patch that you apply to your skin relieves pain. Since I don't have much pain, I ignored this product at first. But then the Lord started revealing more truth to me:

The electrical design of this patch apparently redirects nerve impulses to such an extent that they relieve one's pain. Taking this same concept into consideration it may also be possible to redirect nerve impulses in such a way as to modify unwanted and unholy behaviors like addiction and to even redirect or to force the organs of the body to make needed hormones to help form antibodies to attack this virus.

I understand that to the medical community this may sound far-fetched. But a patch is not that much different from a prayer clothe which has been used in the healing of the sick. In fact, one Bible verse says: 'GOD DID EXTRORDINARY MIRACLES THROUGH PAUL SO THAT WHEN HANKERCHEIFS OR APRONS THAT HAD TOUCHED HIS SKIN WHERE BROUGHT TO THE SICK THEIR DISEASES LEFT THEM AND EVIL SPIRITS CAME OUT OF THEM', (Acts 19:11 & 12). This my friends is absolutely wonderful it not only shows healing from disease but also deliverance from demon oppression. And it should be well known that **many Americans need deliverance. That is deliverance from headaches, depression, anxiety, lack of get up and go, lack of love, insufficient self-esteem, lack of memory, unreasonable fear, mixed up desires, lack of proper emotional response, deception, hostility, hot temper with increased anger, unreasonable hatred, delusions, hallucinations, fits, uncontrollable laughter, talking to self.**

There must also be deliverance from resentment over medicines and medications that don't work. Deliverance from animosity over plumbers and other repairman who don't fix your pipes right and over electricians that screw up your wires.

Christians who believe in Jesus still have bad habits like smoking and drinking booze, driving drunk, participating in extramarital affairs, having sex with animals and their own children, gay relationships and all manner of naughtiness including over-eating, gluttony and eating disorders and also need deliverance from all these 'grave clothes of death' that mask their new lives in Christ.

However professional medical doctors, like Dr. Fauci can't make more money off any of these new (experimental) vaccines unless he discounts any other medicine that may work to cure the invading virus.

In any case, a few months later Joni interviewed as her guest; Robert F. Kennedy Jr. who had been busy researching fraud dealing with this issue.

(I remember specifically that he had somewhat of a raspy voice somewhat like my own). Some of the fraud discovered back then was about the increased or added amount of sugar in most breakfast cereals and some of this fraud also had to do with various recommendations about certain diets that could supposedly cure this CORONA VIRUS. One of these was the gluten free diet. Which seems to be working in Taiwan and especially some in South India where they mainly eat rice as a gluten free staple. While this diet does reduce blood pressure and one's weight it is not a medicine and does not heal (which I already told you about in my previous prophetic book entitled: **COVID 19: VACCINE OR REPENTANCE).**

In that book I also stated that this CORONA VIRUS or COVID 19 is also a curse or plague sent by God for sin (and I named the sins: ABORTION and SAME SEX MARRIAGE). And not just another disease that vaccines or booster shots can cure like polio.

About this time, I also remember that when I graduated from the University of South Florida in 1982 I went to take the Graduate Record Exam to see what I had learned and what grad school I might be able to get into. That morning a student had left his stereo on and it was playing an old surfer tune: The Little Old Lady From Pasadena. Pasadena, California was the location of the seminary that God wanted me to attend. So, I took that song as my sign to go to Fuller Theological Seminary in Pasadena, CA

When I arrived there a young student receptionist told me that they would train me but I probably would never be able to get any church job, 'since wheelchairs do not inspire faith'. I ignored that negative confession since I wanted to become a college counselor anyway and not just another professional Christian minister.

I subsequently graduated from that Seminary in 1985 and went on to another grad school to take my psychology classes in education that I would need in order to earn my college counseling credential.

I remember while at that other grad school a learning psychologist who was visiting them from some Ivey League School told most of these future college teachers there and me that a behavioral psychologist had recently discovered that if you want someone to really learn and remember your information you need to be sure to repeat it so that it makes a deeper impression on their brain. So that's what I intend to do here even though some of my critics may call my repeat information redundant. Thus, this whole chapter is going to be repeated again later in this prophetic book.

There is one more cataclysmic point he had to make (this will anger most authors of books). He said that if you have an important point to make, make it right away. Then repeat it later in your lesson or manuscript. Do not beat around the bush like most writers of mysteries or researchers into discoveries do. Teach your main point up front and then repeat it later in your lesson or manuscript if you want your students to remember it.

When God gave Moses the Ten Commandments and Moses gave them to the people of Israel, he also told the children of Israel what blessings would come their way if they would obey them.

But if they disobeyed God's commandments and statutes Moses began to list in Deuteronomy 28:15 the curses for the children of Israel to expect from God: 'BUT IT SHALL COME TO PASS, IF YOU DO NOT OBEY THE VOICE OF THE LORD YOUR GOD, TO OBSERVE **CAREFULLY** (this word is far more important in the spiritual dimension than the slang words of everyday unconcerned speech) ALL HIS COMMANDMENTS AND HIS STATUTES WHICH I COMMAND YOU TODAY THAT ALL THESE CURSES WILL OVER TAKE YOU': (Curses have power behind them, the power of God and curses are the exact counterpart of blessings so they are also very dangerous).

In any case these curses are listed in my other prophetic book about: **'COVID 19: VACCINE OR REPENTANCE'.**

I also remember that as a volunteer minister I had the experience of counseling in large churches where the pastor could give himself to his own personal anointing to preach whatever truths he felt that God had given him. Therefore, he had counselors to do the work of the ministry other than preaching. These counselors included behavior counselors who handled the homeless, ex-criminals, aliens and domestic abusers. And other benevolence counselors who handled ministers to the poor, including the giving away of free food to the poor. Then love counselors who handled pre-marriage and marriage counseling, personal loss due to death of loved ones, loss of family members via divorce and the loss of new family members via abortion or the abortion of a female child.

President Biden has lost his son, Hunter to brain cancer. And as a normal parent he grieved over this loss. Such makes sense. But to remain indifferent to another's loss via abortion makes no sense. In fact this brings up an emotional deficit. If this were an intellectual or mental issue this would be considered a type of insanity. But in Biden's case this is seen as dementia. Psychologists however call this indifference to or unconcern for abortion to be: 'flat effect', as my earned psychology degree states.

Now I want to take this opportunity to answer President Biden's question about where this COVID 19 came from. **God sent it and I already told you that abortion and same sex marriage caused it.** Of course, God uses people to do what he wants done (even the Chinese communists). Years ago in the administration of George H W Bush the pacifists Democrats wanted the Neutron bomb removed from America's arsenal because it was seen as a weapon of genocide. Just think how that weapon could be helping Ukrain now, Taiwan later on and ultimately Israel. Of course, with President George H W Bush's approval the Deep State handled this. They got rid of that Neutron bomb but sought to secretly develop another such weapon to replace it **(oops, that's another secret that you were not supposed to know, as prophecy has no governors on it it's easy to say too much that people just don't need to know).**

That brings up how this COVID 19 came about. Let's first consider The Deep State. The Deep State is NOT just made up of Democrats and Republicans but also some very bad people like professional wire tappers, computer hackers, spies, thieves and other such conmen and especially deceitful speech writers. These workers of iniquity also include some medical masters of deceit like Dr. Anthony Fauci and even some like Hitler's Final Solution Doctors of World War II. That's why former President Trump wanted to drain this Washington swamp of government thugs. **(Oops there I go again bringing to light truth that the never Trumpers and progressives wanted to stay hidden).**

By this time it should be well known that the mischievous Dr. Anthony Fauci lied America into funding this Wuhan lab in Communist China (with your taxpayer money) for the express purpose of turning this virus into a biological weapon **(oops that was secret that you weren't supposed to know**) since such could no longer be done in America since the days of President George H W BUSH despite the eleven labs that America has that do this sort of thing.

The main reason this was done in Communist China is the same reason that terrorists are imprisoned in Guantanamo, Cuba; to keep them beyond the constitutional limits of US Courts where constitutional provisions like defense attorneys at public expense can not be provided.

By 'gain of function' research this virus was subsequently altered with American taxpayer money in such a way as to increase its pathology and transmission. This making of the corona virus into a biological weapon now called COVID 19 is the direct opposite of making it into a vaccine supposedly. **But these so-called (experimental)vaccines which are made from this biological weapon (that's right these vaccines are made from a manmade biological weapon and are at least questionable now and may even prove to be very dangerous in the future when young people grow up and want to start families of their own. As I already proved elsewhere that the biological makeup of these vaccines produce antibodies which can attack the human placenta (just like the biological weapon COVID 19 does). So that those who have wanted abortion will be given spontaneous abortions, thereby having the same death result as other sin like the neutron bomb. How's that for God's justice.**

Before I move on I should say that the neutron bomb's purpose was to kill all the people, but leave the buildings intact. This biological weapon COVID 19 also kills the people and leaves the cities vacant.

Another prophet Mark Blitz has written a book about how that the Shemaiah year indicates when the tribulation will start. His prophetic viewpoint based on years of research indicates that the seven-year tribulation period must begin on the first year of the Shemaiah cycle.

And the next Shemaiah cycle begins next year. This is very upsetting. For it means a Biden less America. Which may come about in one of two different ways: 1. President Biden may die in office and be replaced by the progressive leftists of the tribulation period before the tribulation even begins. This will lead to or result in Civil War which is exactly what the military minded will want to destroy those who are 'hell bent' on destroying America. I also brought this out in my chapter about **Wars and Rumors of Wars.** Now most one sided and stupid progressive and cultural race theories claim that as victims' non-whites have a right to defend themselves. When actually they are engaged in destroying America by force of arms and not just defending themselves at all.

Most Black AME churches preach race as if it were the stigma affecting every Afro-American. I submit to you that every so-called church that preaches things like race, American economices and such, sex, extra marital sex, homosexuality, carnal activities or anything else except Christ and Him crucified should be closed as a non-Christian entity preaching 'hate speech' against Christ and Christian values.

Or President TRUMP regains office by court order as it is seen publically that these progressive reprobates really did steal the election with the paid help of foreign subversives. Of course all this will just result in more judgment which can come in several different ways: Civil War (in this prophetic book is also a chapter about **The American Civil War**), war with other nations, destruction through natural or manmade disasters, another terrorist attack, economic or financial collapse, famine, military defeat, decline, disorder, division, disintegration, delusionment or lack of diversity complete with hatred and even weather problems like strong hurricanes, more tornados and more severe droughts and floods.

The severity of these events will be determined by the degree of forgiveness which the Trump Team will exercise. There is scripture that says both to love your enemies and to forgive them. **But no scripture anywhere tells the Christian to love and forgive the enemies of God.**

In any case President Biden is only awarded 'The Times of Sorrows'. I would not wish the tribulation period on any man. In fact, according to the Bible the Antichrist is to lead the tribulation period, not any man. Before we examine all that again in this prophetic book, let's take another look at that lab in Wuhan, China responsible for this COVID 19.

This particular lab was used by the communist government of China to turn this corona virus into a biological weapon per America's work orders. No FACEBOOK, CNN, MSNBC and other 'fake news' outlets of this was not the '**conspiracy theory**' of the escape of that virus from the lab but the manufacturer of that biological weapon by the lab in the lab.

It should be noted here that the communist government of Red China honor its contracts to produce weapons, especially weapons of mass destruction. So, the idea that this virus escaped the lab and went airborne by some diseased bat makes absolutely no real sense.

This reminds me of what I heard over the Christian radio when Dr. Gean Scott was the Pastor of the Assemblies of God Church in Glendale California. Instead of calling stupid government ideas a profane word, he called such 'bull spit' and that's what we have here with this lab escape.

This COVID 19 was then tested per normal chemical work orders, as it had to be tested to ensure that America was getting what it had paid for.

The first test was done on the Chinese people in Wuhan province. These contaminated Chinese people were then forbidden to travel to other parts of

China as any further testing on Chinese people was seen as unnecessary. But these contaminated Chinese people from the Wuhan province were allowed to travel elsewhere in the world to test this biological weapon on other people groups composing people of other ethnicities, races and cultures. So, then this was all part of a normal testing process needed to validate that this corona virus had been made into a biological weapon.

Because America's borders were opened thanks to the dementia of President Biden, this COVID 19 weapon also got tested on the American people as well. **(Oops, now you know how dangerous Biden really is).**

All these side benefits of closing down capitalist economies was a significant surprise which the communist party intends to take note of. Nevertheless, such was never planned by the communist party. After all now they are into making money just like other nations. In fact, it was the God of heaven who sent this virus to discipline His people for the sins He mentioned: abortion and same sex marriage, since obviously the communist party is not concerned about any sin at all.

One unpleasant way this may have all come about was when the opening prayer of dedication in the US Congress for 2021 was dedicated to **Brahma, the four faced false Hindu god.** This angered and forced the God of Israel (Who is very egotistical which I may cover in my next prophetic book) to remove his blessing from America and turn that blessing into a curse of which COVID 19 is only the first named instalment. **(Oops forgive me for saying this but I must speak as God's watchman.**

There will be other curses including earthquakes, volcanic eruptions and tsunamis. So, it seems foolish to attempt any repair of or plan of payment for any repair of infrastructure right away,

Before these tragedies happen. Biden's progressives have stolen the election, do not let them now steal from the US Treasury Our tax dollars to fund stupid stuff like Global Warming, Black Reparations and Anti-Christian evil acts and laws too.

BIDEN'S SORROWS II

It began like this: The kid and I were going to the grocery store through a Black neighborhood and we saw a young Black man very upset and angry over some 'nigger' who had just stolen part of his stereo and he kept calling that thief a 'nigger' as it was apparently a Black on Black crime. I had not heard the 'N' word in a long time back then but paid no attention to it because a Black man was saying it apparently with justification.

That very night the Lord spoke to me in a prophetic dream saying:

> ***'REMEMBER HOW THAT BLACK MAN USED THE 'N' WORD TO DESCRIBE THAT THIEF THAT STOLE FROM HIM? THIS NEW PRESIDENT BIDEN WHO JUST WON BY HIS LEFTIST DEMOCRATS STEALING THE ELECTION WILL ALSO HAVE HIS POLICIES NOW MANIFEST THAT 'N' WORD TOO IN ORDER TO REMAKE AMERICA THE BEAUTIFUL INTO A SOCIALIST NATION'.***

This same 'N' word showed up again as I completed this chapter. In that case that word was used to describe Haitian migrants, as the Biden administration calls them. But Blacks usually are not known as migrant workers that come in to help Americlan farmers harvest the crops.

So these people were just being brought into the country as welfare recipients at our taxpayers expense. For show only a few single Black men were deported back to Haiti for public relations. The rest of these parasites, over 12,000 of them were sent to other 'ports of entry' to escape public scrutiny of their immigration or sanctuary cities.

It's well known that we have enough poor Blacks of or own without inviting in the worlds Blacks to be dependent on our taxpayers. From his political propaganda of 2015 it was pointed out that Joe Biden wanted to make America the beautiful into a 'Niger Nation' with as many dark-skinned immigrants as possible. He even called it 'a continuous flow of them'.

Before America's Blacks get upset from me using the 'N' word. Consider this such only applies to illegal immigrants and NOT to American Black citizens. Biden is bringing in these illegal immigrants to steal your jobs and make America into a socialist One World Order out of the poverty stricken.

But back then I only realized that Biden's leftist Democrats had stolen the election. Now after a few months of Biden's naughty policies I'm beginning to grasp the last part of that DIVINE WORD especially in the area of the wasteful and reprehensible ending of that Afghanistan war in order to initiate and then fund the Green New Deal at our expense.

That's right, **the new 'N' policy of Biden's anti-American leftist Democrats is to ignore the $2 trillion that they and their parents wasted on trying to make a Muslim country adopt American democracy to now waste over $3 trillion on a policy of wasteful spending on social programs for illegal aliens, criminals, dopers, drunks and other welfare recipients dependent on us for the rest of their lives.**

God is the creator of all life, so abortion offends Him. In His word He says: I HAVE COME THAT YOU MIGHT HAVE LIFE AND HAVE IT MORE ABUNDANTELY, (John 10:10). **So Biden's anti-life policy results in death.**

You saw on TV where Biden is still trying to confront COVID 19 with masks and vaccinations as if it were a disease that DR. Fauci could cure. As I revealed in my former prophetic books COVID 19 is a plague caused by sin, the sins of abortion and same sex marriage. **Nothing will end this plague until these sins are abandoned and repented of.**

Heretofore nothing has been said about the Vice President, Kamala Harris who is part Vietnamese and part Black that Biden hoped to win the Black vote with. In personality this woman is too Asian for most Blacks. She is too quiet and uninvolved. Plus, she laughs a lot like some insane person that escaped from a mental institution. She is the type who would be happy riding a bicycle instead of a nice car to work in a socialist country of 'hot dogs' (all the same size, color and weight, all boiling at the same temperature). So, she is not an adequate representation for diversity.

Most young Black men that I know like to drive fancy expensive cars.

One of my Black friends drives his new red Mercedes sportscar. You can't have that in a socialist country. Even in Cuba, a communist country like Vietnam, the people drive old cars not bikes. You must be able to earn money in a capitalist economy in order to afford a new prestigious car.

This anti-Christian and anti-American wasteful desire was so strong in Afghanistan that President Biden's passivist military who instead of fighting now teach cultural race theory, transgender ideology, the possibility that sex and sexual orientation can be changed by indoctrination or surgery and that males can give birth instead of learning military tactics gave up over $2 billion in sophisticated, ultra-modern arms to the Taliban and left many Americans and their helpers and allies behind causing another war crime.

Some spiritual and circumspect Christians, there are still a few of us left, are aware that the Devil really governs Afghanistan, the Taliban are just his ruthless figure heads. Thanks to the leftist Democrats the Devil wants to govern America by this same means too and use leftist Democrats, Muslim and Latino and non-Mexican immigrants with back-sliden and lukewarm Christians in order to do so.

The recent earthquake in Mexico and the floods in Germany and elsewhere in Europe are all **the results of sin, the sins of abortion and same sex marriage exported by the United States and not because of the leftist propaganda of climate change. Therefore we real Christians can rise up and take America back. With faith in the Lord Jesus Christ (the God of all justice) let's do so and turn over to Satan for the destruction of the flash these racist, sodomite and socialist Democrats with all those other reprobates who oppose us!**

Chile has about 100 dormant volcanos. But it is protected because it has the strictest anti-abortion law on earth, whereas Mexico had its earthquake the day before last as its supreme court ruled in favor of abortion. El Salvador also has the strictest abortion law, maybe that's why all their Latino reprobates are illegally coming here.

The most important way to evaluate any vaccination is to look at it historically. By that I mean real medical history not that culturally race theory nor 1619 anti-slavery propaganda as if race determines the value of all things including vaccinations.

In my personal history I was vaccinated against polio in the early 1950's from what I remember. Back in those days we lived on a suburban mini-farm right outside Kingsport, Tennessee. My family had a black and white TV like everyone else and they saw on it how that polio was becoming a very dangerous disease with children incarcerated in 'iron lungs'. Of course this scared them, so they took me to school to get my Salk vaccine Dr. Jonas Salk was the inventor of the polio vaccine (in a socialist society there are no inventors nor medical doctors for everyone is an equal bum).

Unlike todays COVID 19 vaccine this polio vaccine acted perfectly like all vaccinations should. With this polio vaccine there were no 'breakthrough' problems either. That is where after getting the polio vaccination you still were susceptible to catching this polio disease. Neither did you take the polio vaccination by faith, hoping for the best. This polio vaccine had a 100% success rate as seen on black and white TV with Douglas Edwards (remember him).

We had black and white TV back in those days not only because of technology but because we lived in a black and white culture back then. You might remember how there were no shades of grey back then with double meanings (like those of Dr. Fauci and the leftist Democrats that could cost you your life by taking a vaccination without historical backup).

In this present depressing age many have not been able to pay their back rent and have had to move back in with their parents and grandparents. Some thankfully have been able to recall these successful polio vaccinations and have communicated to their children their own very suspicious attitudes about this COVID 19 vaccine that doesn't seem to work as well despite DR. Fauci's outlandish and President Biden's stupid claims.

Not being satisfied with the low death count of his 'scrambled egg' Afghanistan catastrophe, **last night President Biden went on TV to further threaten and demand that more Americans partake of Dr. Anthony Fauci's 'Frankenstein' vaccination that's killing people. (There is talk that this COVID 19 vaccination is from former President TRUMP but really DR. ANTHONY FAUCCI added into it his HIV vaccination to make (more money by making this COVID 19 vaccination into a Frankenstein vaccination that's killing people). This vaccination also acts as a PORTAL to 'breakthroughs' of COVID 19 as is now seen in Israel. And death attracts the Death Angel to kill even more by bureaucratic mandates both here and in Israel.**

I said before that these Democrats were motivated by the spirit of death in killing the unborn (abortion) and now by killing children after birth via mandated COVID 19 vacinations to reduce the population of America so that it qualifies for being part of the One World Order.

In my next prophetic dream: ***A YOUNG PROPHET WAS DISCLOSING THE RECENT MEETING BETWEEN JOE BIDEN AND SOME CHINESE COMMUNIST OFFICIALS IN WHICH THEY (THE COMMUNIST CHINESE) PROMISED JOE BIDEN THE 2020 ELECTION (THEY FELT COMFORTABLE DOING SO AS THEY COULD HACT INTO AND CONTROL VOTING MACHINES) IF HE WOULD GIVE THEM AFGHANISTAN. KNOWING THAT THEY HAD INCRIMINATING EVIDENCE ON BIDEN'S FAMILY DEALINGS IN CHINA JOE BIDEN, THE DEMOCRATIC PRESIDENTIAL CANDIDATE GOT UP FROM THE TABLE AND WENT OUTSIDE WITH HIS ADVISORS TO DISCUSS THE MATTER.***

(It now also comes to light that the Biden administration has ordered its prosecutors to drop all espionage charges against Red China).

In older people sometimes, their memory is erratic. That means that they can remember their childhood well but not what just happened yesterday. Biden remembered from his childhood his Catholic catechism days that the devil owned all the kingdoms of the world and could give them to whomever he would ('THE DEVIL TOOK JESUS UP INTO AN EXCEEDING HIGH MOUNTAIN AND SHOWED HIM ALL THE KINGDOMS OF THE WORLD AND THE GLORY OF THEM. AND HE SAID UNTO JESUS ALL THESE THINGS WILL I GIVE YOU, IF YOU FALL DOWN AND WORSHIP ME', Matthew 4:8, 9).

Of course, all that was before Christ died on the cross, as through the Lord Jesus' victory over Satan by his death on the cross now gives the Lord Jesus dominion over all things which is true but such was not part of that Catholic Catechism back then.

So although Joe Biden did not think the communist Chinese could do what they claimed, he knew full well that as instruments of Satan they could probably fulfill their promise and might even help him become President too. (But real Christians don't let the devil do things for them).

Speaking of the Catholic Catechism again; it should be noted that the Roman Catholic Church teaches against abortion just like the Bible does. And usually Catholic politicians in favor of abortion are not served communion as the Roman Catholic Church also believes in sacramental salvation. Those who cannot partake of communion under this belief system are not saved and do not obey the Gospel to confess their sins either.

When one has not confessed his sins for a long time, he becomes hardened in his sins. Therefore, I recommend that President Biden goes to confession and confesses his many sins of encouraging others including other nations to get abortions at American tax payers' expense and receive communion after doing penance. For Catholics and most protestant Christians this is the word of the Lord. THANKS BE TO GOD.

In another prophetic dream which I had about the same time: one of Joe Biden's advisors told joe biden sometime before the election, about the same time as the first prophetic dream: ***THAT LITHIUM, THAT RARE EARTH ELEMENT NEEDED FOR LITHIUM BATTERIES FOR BIDEN'S GREEN NEW DEAL HAD JUST BEEN DISCOVERED IN A MAJOR GEOLOGIC DEPOSIT IN NEVADA. SO BIDEN NO LONGER NEEDED TO OCCUPY AFGHANISTAN AND PARTICIPATE IN ITS CIVIL WAR AGAINST THE TALIBAN. HE WAS NOW FREE TO ABANDON IT AS SOON AS POSSIBLE. THE SOONER, THE BETTER FOR CHINA'S SAKE***

Oh no. I hear somebody saying that President Biden gave up Afghanistan to the Taliban not the communist Chinese. Look the Taliban are just Satan's figure heads in Afghanistan. The Taliban believed in Muslim Socialism which is really anti-god communism. Which the communist Chinese already practice. **The fact that the communist Chinese are really Satan's servants in Afghanistan is the real hidden truth.**

Some people have difficulty seeing this so let me put it this way. The flag of the Taliban is white, somewhat like a surrender flag. But the flag of Red China is red – the dominant masculine color of bloodshed in war. Now is the image of this political relationship clearer and more understandable?

Upon hearing this President Biden agreed with the communist Chinese and kept his word to them to do this after his first six months in office.

To show his good faith to them President Biden not only gave them Afghanistan with all its mineral wealth but also Bagram military base with all its weapon systems and expensive military hardware. So that the communists could inspect and learn military secrets from them too. Most normal people call this sort of reprobate and evil behavior ***TREASON.*** What does it sound like to you? And what are you willing to do about it? And what is it called when one does this sort of thing behind the back of their allies?

As you probably remember, former President TRUMP used to call this COVID 19, the Chinese virus as he named it back then from where it came from. After much research it appears that former President Trump was right and that this Chinese virus which American tax payers paid for with Dr. Fauci's evil 'blessing' was deliberately sent by communist China to all the capitalist nations of the world to reduce their populations per 'the one world order' (notice it did not seem wise to the Communist Chinese to reduce China's population too, because it was felt that one communist is worth at least two capitalists),

There is a very prevalent false teaching in the Christian churches that overemphasizes that God is love. So most Christians believe that God is love alone and has no other psychological traits or values. But when the Lord Jesus Christ came to earth he proved that God has other instincts and reactions other than love alone. You might even remember when Jesus, God in the flesh in anger whipped (beat) the money changers out of the Temple, God's house of prayer for all nations, as recorded in (John 2:13-17).

'AND THE JEWS' PASSOVER WAS AT HAND, AND JESUS WENT UP TO JERUSALEM. AND FOUND IN THE TEMPLE THOSE THAT SOLD OXEN AND SHEEP AND DOVES AND THE CHANGERS OF MONEY SITTING: AND WHEN HE HAD MADE A SCOURGE OF SMALL CORDS, HE DROVE THEM OUT OF THE TEMPLE, AND THE SHEEP, AND THE OXEN; AND POURED OUT THE CHANGERS OF MONEY, AND OVER TURNED THE TABLES. AND SAID UNTO THEM THAT SOLD DOVES. TAKE THESE THINGS HENCE, MAKE NOT MY FATHER'S HOUSE AN HOUSE OF MERCHANDISE. AND HIS DISCIPLES REMEMBERED THAT IT WAS WRITTEN (of Him): 'THE ZEAL OF THINE HOUSE HATH EATEN ME UP'. (Yes, they apparently had some Torah Scripture with them to check as they traveled with Jesus). (Back in those days most Jews could read the scriptures in their native tongue and had to do so to be bar-mitzvahed).

Most Americans know something about baseball and its rules too. Please keep that in mind as we consider my next prophetic word.

USUALLY IN BASEBALL THE RULES SAY THREE STRIKES AND YOU'RE OUT. THAT'S WHAT WE MAY HAVE HERE WITH THESE VACCINATIONS FOR COVID 19. MANY AMERICANS HAVE ALREADY HAD TWO VACCINATION SHOTS. THE THIRD BOOSTER VACCINATION MAY PROVE TO BE VERY HAZARDOUS TO ONE'S HEALTH AS IT PREFERS MEDICAL VACCINATION FOR THIS COVID 19 PLAGUE INSTEAD OF REPENTANCE. FAILURE TO REPENT OF ABORTION AND SAME SEX MARRIAGE MAY INFURIATE GOD THE CREATOR OF LIFE. IT IS A FEARFUL THING TO OFFEND AND THEN FALL INTO THE HANDS OF THE LIVING GOD. AT THIS PARTICULAR TIME I CERTAINLY WOULD NOT PROVOKE GOD TO VENGENCE.

The problem of vaccination mandates for school children has now come up. (It should be remembered that the Lord Jesus said: 'IT WERE BETTER FOR HIM THAT A MILLSTONE BE HANGED ABOUT HIS NECK, AND HE CAST INTO THE SEA, THEN THAT HE SHOULD OFFEND ONE OF THESE LITTLE ONES, Luke 17:2). Actually, this is divergent from the sins of the sinners. School children obviously are innocent of sexual sins and it is naughty to focus on children as if this COVID 19 Plague were part of their lifestyle too.

Most school children have high personal or individual immunity. They may need to take a children's vitamin. And especially during the fall of the year and approaching winter they probably will need a vitamin D 3. But **under no circumstances should they take a manmade vaccination for a manmade biological weapon such as COVID 19.**

The discriminatory idea that normal school children need to do such in order to protect other school children in special education is not a constitutional requirement. If it were we would be a nation of the degenerate, disabled and diseased but God has better plans for us if we have faith enough to reach for Him instead of depending on vaccinations.

When I mention vaccinations, I DO NOT mean normal vaccinations for diseases like measles, mumps, diphtheria, scarlet fever, pneumonia and tetanus, or the diseases we used to have in this country like yellow fever, small pox and polio. I mean synthetic vaccinations against biological weapons like this COVID 19.

When a young person with high natural immunity catches the corona virus they should take vitamin D 3, vitamin C, ZINC and an over the counter anti-histamine or nasal decongestion like Claritin right away. Since winter is coming you might want to get these products ASAP- As soon as possible. Your pharmacist has other approved drugs too. But if not please contact: America's Frontline Doctors.org for their kit for COVID 19.

Always remember that Bill Gates, Dr. Fauci, President Biden, all the Democrats, all abortionists, all socialists and all anti-God liberals believe in population reduction for a 'successful one world order'. Don't let their population reduction include your children via an unnecessary COVID 19 vaccination.

If this vaccination were so mandatory for your children then how come the Congress has voted itself exempt from this COVID 19 vaccination just like the former Obama administration voted itself exempt from Obama Care.

I perceive that the same type of deception is being used on the American people right now as was used in the Obama administration where Joe Biden was then Vice President. You might even remember one of their famous scams or lies for Obama care: 'IF YOU LIKE YOUR DOCTOR YOU CAN KEEP HIM.' Thus deceit breeds deceit.

Upon realizing this it also has come to light that former President Barak Obama could be behind the scenes pulling the strings to operate the puppet Biden. For they both seem to be putting forth the same socialist agenda disguised as Obama care and now vaccinations and masks for COVID 19 which are free for us, but someone somewhere is making a lot of money.

Speaking of these mandatory vaccinations again before you Succumb to considering this, please consider this: Not long ago CHANNEL 7 in the Chicago area, Obama's home town, conducted a survey backed by the leftist democrats trying to prove that unvaccinated people were spreading COVID 19 when actually **the survey backfired as it appears that that TV station received over 140,000 phone calls complaining about how vaccinated people were not only spreading COVID 19 but actually killing some people in their own neighborhoods thanks to the side effects of these vaccinations.**

I suspected that there was the love of money behind all this mandating for vaccinations for COVID 19 especially for school children. (Now it's beginning to come to light that Dr. Faucci has earned over 12 million dollars from his previous patent on an HIV drug. Which is now being incorporated into this COVID 19 vaccine so that Dr. Faucci still makes more money, while your children may eventually get hurt. So it might be necessary to obtain a lawyer to prevent this foolishness. But such may be too expensive, but as an indigent you can proceed in your civil suit with no charge. It should be noted that school boards without a licensed medical doctor lack the necessary medical expertise to insist on COVID 19 vaccinations with masks for your school children, so sue 'em.

Besides this unnecessary vaccination issue there is another form of population control which no one has yet even imagined. Yes I'm speaking about both climate change and global warming. As my psychologist friends see it both of these are just phobias of the bad liberals I mentioned before in the preceding paragraph.

As non-Christians these bad liberals do not believe in hell fire in the afterlife. So in order to stay mentally balanced they do believe in fire here and that that fire will increase environmental heat right here right now.

The California forest fires and the dreaded drought out there are only the beginnings of sorrows in the Bible but they call it climate change or global warming resulting from man's carbon pollutions from his over industrialization. But the way to avoid these 'sorrows' is not to move up North. But to **move away from these sins that offend God**. As I said before, these sins that offend God are abortion and same sex marriage. They are not stealing cookies from your cookie jar or saying 'dirty' words. So children are innocent of these sins and have no need to work on their repentance or take an unnecessary vaccination for such. That's why when your family goes to church, the children go to children's church. It is not seen as wise for them to sit in an adult doctrinal class of end time truths. Whereas here with the COVID 19 plague this society is trying to make children take vaccinations and wear masks like adults who are sexually active. As you know, children are not sexually active yet, so why should they be vaccinated against this manufactured biological weapon?

There is something psychologically wrong with this process. Because just a few months ago when there was no vaccine for children nor open school for them to attend, they seemed to not have this COVID 19 problem.

Going to school now however can be dangerous to one's health especially if you must be vaccinated and still wear a mask in order to learn socialist among anti-God concepts and cultural race theory with anti capitalistic economic theories to students who will need to do some type of work in order to earn money for their personal needs by participating in America's capitalist economy. The socialist economy is for bums who don't want to work to be able to afford any prestigious items, like designer jeans or imported 'swank' shoes or even a prestigious imported sports car.

If you want to be a 'zombie' with no ambitions in life then dead-beat socialism could become your life goal. Such would begin right after school when you lack enough courage to ask the woman of your dreams out for a date, but settle for some dead-beat plain jane, transvestite or sexually confused person instead.

Here with these liberal public schools so called 'Sex education' and its Ultra-leftist and pro-deviant theories of these leftist democratic teachers come together to indoctrinate your children to a low-life of error.

And now school children below the age of puberty are being taught to masturbate by so called enlightened Democratic union educators. Some school children are also being taught to take sexual hormones to change whatever sex they were born with to whatever feels more comfortable to them now. As if sex should be changed according to one's comfort or sexual orientation right now. **It should be noted that nurses not teachers are legally authorized to give out pills or shots to do this.**

Then other more unpleasant problem having to do with sex come up concerning young married couples which these children may grow into someday. One of these issues concerns psychological and emotional fulfillment in having sex with one's married partner. This problem most often arises because it was ignored in sex class in school. In this sexual issue the question asked most often was about the size of the male organ of sexual intercourse.

From American history it seems that many of the diversity mindset tried to hide the main sexual reason why native Americans or 'Indians' were removed to reservations was because their males lacked 'normal' secondary sexual characteristics; no beard ect. Plus their males also had a 'Vienna sausage' size penis.

Of course these issues are not brought out today as many illegal immigrants are really Central and South American Indians with these same physical characteristics. So then the real issue here is not with school children and whether or not they are vaccinated and wear masks but with the unvaccinated and diseased illegal immigrants that the Biden administration calls migrants as if they had any desire to work in America.

Behind most of this is a major problem school children have to deal with. That issue is death. Many school children have had their grandparents, uncles and aunts die from this COVID 19. I recently heard on the TV nightly news that more people have died from this COVID 19 than died from the 1918 Spanish flu.

Unfortunately, this fact brings up fear. Fear is a profound psychological problem. Its only opposition is faith that is usually only taught in a Christian school. Therefore, if you can afford to send your children to a Christian school and one is nearby please send your children to a good Spirit filled Christian school. If not, please do this: Contact a Christian Spirit filled prosperity preacher, evangelist or missionary and ask them if they have any spiritual projects that have to do with the saving of souls that God has showed them to do. Then join them by giving them some seed money to accomplish their spiritual project and expect God to meet your needs too. Do this in front of your children so they may see you exercise faith that works. And expect God to tell the devil to give you back what he stole from you and your family including a Christian education for your children.

BIDEN'S SORROWS III

After writing my other prophetic books: **'WHAT TO EXPECT', 'ANOTHER JESUS MOVEMENT', 'WEALTH TRANSFER','END TIME PLAGUES','RAPTURE RIPOFF', 'REPARATIONS FOR SLAVERY', 'JESUS THE REAL STAR CHILD', 'COVID 19 TRUTHS REVEALED', 'FAKE NEWS', COVID 19-VACCINE OR REPENTANCE' 'BIDEN'S SORROWS I,' 'SAINTS, SINNERS, SCOUNDRELS, SODOMITES AND SOCIALISTS' and 'BIDEN'S SORROWS II** I felt that I was due for a period of rest. But instead the Spirit of God revealed to me openly at high noon the other day (October 15, 2021) part of what He wanted me to write down in a new prophetic book which I am calling: **BIDEN'S SORROWS III.**

Since I am a wheelchair disabled Prophet and do not like to confront stupid political ideology I will nevertheless use my Bible knowledge to correct professional and denominational political error in this case.

But first I must disclose 'the fake news' God corrected clearly by 'open revelation' on October 15, 2021. This corrects the idea that these vaccinations are safe for children. Actually, these vaccines are a 'portal' for COVID 19 as evidence of the thousands of people that have died as a result of them. This cataclysmic revelation went on to say that: 'BY THE YEAR 2025 THE DEATHS FROM THESE VACCINES TO SUPPOSEDLY PREVENT DEATH WILL NO LONGER BE MEASURED JUST IN THE THOUSANDS BUT IN THE MILLIONS AS THESE VACCINES BEGIN TO INTERACT WITH THE SEXUAL HORMONES OF THESE VACCINATED CHILDREN WHO HAVE NOW BECOME TEENAGERS EXPERIENCING THE ONSET OF DANGEROUS SEXUAL HORMONES IN PUBERTY'.

Before this date (October 18, 2021) few people believed that these vaccinations actually helped cause one's death from COVID 19. ***all the medical propoganda by the oral masterbater Dr. Fauci of the deep state Center for Disease Control and the demented President Biden has been saying falsely that unvaccinated people are spreading COVID 19. when actually the vaccinated are causing this too and to an even greater extent according to Isreali statistics. (Israel has vaccinated 85% of its people that are still coming down with COVID 19 and spreading this plague to others anyway).***

But today (October 18, 2021) the news media revealed that a famous man, Colin Powell had died from complications of COVID 19. **Although it was revealed by mistake that he had been fully vaccinated. This truth was not supposed to be known by the American people and obviously hurts Biden's vaccination mandates 'bull spit'.** Too bad, some 'born losers' can't seem to win even at their best laid plans. (Biden the deceitful wants to use COVID 19 to replace America's white population with these illegal aliens who will vote Democratic as the overrunning of the border demonstrates).

President Biden still refuses to repent of abortion and same sex marriage. So to make this revelation clear let me repeat it for you. 'BY THE YEAR 2025 THESE COVID 19 VACCINATIONS FOR CHILDREN WILL BECOME THEIR DEATH SENTENCES'. This is a pure prophecy which no one has ever said before and at this time has no confirming medical basis in reality. Although in its time it will become real. That's how God works especially with His judgment that has been ignored by those responsible Democrats.

In the Old Testament it is also seen how that 'JUDGMENT FOR SIN IS VISITED UPON THE CHILDREN TO THE THIRD AND FOURTH GENERATION OF THEM THAT HATE ME', (Exodus 20:5).

Last night I was watching a TV show on Christian TV where they interviewed an emergency room doctor. He said that when patients present themselves for healing from this COVID 19 plague he counsels them about various treatments to relieve their COVID 19 infection other than just vaccinations (which you cannot take anyway once you become infected).

I remember that he recommended a drug called Budesonide. This particular drug even has a website: Budesonide works.com. It is inhaled by a nebulizer. According to this emergency room doctor this prescribed treatment can work right away, before one winds up in the hospital.

Another treatment also was recently revealed to President Biden's horror: Regeneron's monoclonal antibodies.

Both of these methods of treatment must be combined with vitamin C, D, and ZINC.

However, during this pandemic many will unfortunately die. Some super spiritual Christians however believe that they will not die as they will be rescued by the pre-tribulation rapture and will not be here to experience any tribulation. (I have written a whole chapter in this prophetic book called **'RAPTURE RIPPOFF'** to expose this false claim of many dead denominational, extinct ecclesiastical and lukewarm liturgical churches).

As I see it, we have now entered into a time of death and sorrow called 'BIDEN'S SORROWS'. Many are hoping to get over these bad times and get back to normal (of course normal means as it was before this pandemic happened). This viewpoint maybe somewhat over optimistic as **after the time of sorrows comes tribulation according to the Bible**. (Please see that the book of Revelation says so in your Bible).

It therefore will not be strange then that teenagers are dying since this tribulation will be a time of death. You know: 'THERE IS A TIME FOR EVERY PURPOSE UNDER THE SUN, A TIME TO BE BORN AND A TIME TO DIE', (Ecclesiastes 1:1&2). At this time 'ONE THIRD OF THE CREATURES WHICH ARE IN THE SEA AND HAVE LIFE WILL DIE', (Revelation 8:9), 'ALL THE GREEN GRASS', (Revelation 8:8) 'and ONE THIRD OF ALL THE TREES'. (Remember the recent California forest fires that were blamed on 'climate change' by the deceived Biden administration).

Just as President Biden was made by Satan an instrument of evil to destroy America, God could raise up President Trump to be His instrument of vengeance instead of the restorer of great times again for America. God could use TRUMP for vengeance against those reprobate Democrats who do abortions and sanction same sex marriage. TRUMP could have his revenge against these deceived Democrats who tried to insinuate that his presidency was the result of Russian interference and wasted millions of your tax dollars to get the special prosecutor: Muller to prove such stupidity. By this TRUMP would be getting his revenge while really God will be getting His vengeance through TRUMP. And God could still bless America anyway.

God is a Spirit and spirits usually use people to do what they want done. No one since Sampson in the Old Testament has ever been used by God in this manner. Although Sampson was a sinner like everyone else, he was also anointed by the Nazarite vow to fight for and bless Israel in miraculous ways (You can read about him in your Bible book of Judges).

My next unpleasant revelation comes to you from Isaiah 57:1 Amplified: *'THE RIGHTEOUS PERSON (your innocent children) WILL BE TAKEN AWAY IN DEATH TO SPARE THEM FROM THE DISASTERS AND EVIL (of the tribulation that are coming').* I hope that this better explains the consequences of these vaccination mandates for school kids.

But you could vote for TRUMP again as before to delay this prophecy for four more years as with God Who 'INHABITS ETERNITY' four years is just like four seconds. Plus by your repentance God could visit with judgment another generation more evil than ourselves. So **'DO YOUR PART, VOTE BIDEN OUT'** and when you vote TRUMP back in let's see what happens, (Received by prophetic dream October 26, 2021).

Unfortunately, you can't turn the receiving of prophecies off as fits into your manuscript. So, I've received another prophecy around Thanksgiving which I need to share. It came about this way: first I heard on the radio news that President Biden had received a colonoscopy which removed one pallet. Then as I remembered this same exact event happened in 2008, the hectic year of former President Obama's and V.P. Biden's election.

Like most Presidents former President Obama was somewhat egotistical, flamboyant and fastidious. From what I remember he insisted that his food be organic. He also insisted that any male he was going to have anal intercourse sex with must also have a colonoscopy, so President Joe Biden's recent colonoscopy maybe very good news as it may mean that President Biden is now leaving the evil influence of the leftist, socialist, Democratic bitches and returning to former President Obama.

Of course, as a Christian I could not say that sex with another man is OK. But in this case, since most Democrats believe in this sexual deviance a good saying that applies is 'Que Sera, Sera' 'whatever will be, will be'.

Moreover, when former President Obama began his first term, Black unemployment was at 15%. By his second term, Black unemployment had reached 19%, so he was not into improving social infrastructure at all. Now if President Biden reduces his outlandish socialist 'Green New Deal' desires to Obama's reality then his re-election may become more plausible.

But a new variant of this COVID 19 has just appeared in South Africa and this may destroy President Biden's aspirations for another term. If you remember I said before that as God said: 'WITHOUT REPENTANCE FROM THE ABOMINATIONS OF ABORTION AND

SAME SEX MARRIAGE EITHER COVID 19 WOULD GET WORSE OR GOD WOULD SEND A NEW WORSE PLAGUE'. This variant probably will have a greater impact on Afro-Americans than anybody else. So President Biden may not be able to get enough Black votes to ensure his second term.

Biden's first term has been so bad by his own doing that even the few Afro-Americans still left alive may not feel Democratic enough to vote for him**. So please vote for TRUMP not only to restore prosperity to America but to better ensure the Great Evangelical Awakening that America as a result of President Biden's abuse now needs.**

www.ingramcontent.com/pod-product-compliance
Lightning Source LLC
LaVergne TN
LVHW041743060526
838201LV00046B/900

* 9 7 9 8 8 8 6 4 0 2 4 1 4 *